Pakistan in an
Age of Turbulence

Pakistan in an
Age of Turbulence

Masuma Hasan

PEN & SWORD
HISTORY

First published in Great Britain in 2022 by
Pen & Sword History
An imprint of
Pen & Sword Books Ltd
Yorkshire – Philadelphia

ISBN 978 1 52678 860 3

Printed and bound in the UK by CPI Group (UK) Ltd,
Croydon, CR0 4YY.

Pen & Sword Books Limited incorporates the imprints of Atlas,
Archaeology, Aviation, Discovery, Family History, Fiction, History,
Maritime, Military, Military Classics, Politics, Select, Transport,
True Crime, Air World, Frontline Publishing, Leo Cooper, Remember
When, Seaforth Publishing, The Praetorian Press, Wharncliffe
Local History, Wharncliffe Transport, Wharncliffe True Crime
and White Owl.

For a complete list of Pen & Sword titles please contact

PEN & SWORD BOOKS LIMITED
47 Church Street, Barnsley, South Yorkshire, S70 2AS, England
E-mail: enquiries@pen-and-sword.co.uk
Website: www.pen-and-sword.co.uk

Or

PEN AND SWORD BOOKS
1950 Lawrence Rd, Havertown, PA 19083, USA
E-mail: Uspen-and-sword@casematepublishers.com
Website: www.penandswordbooks.com

For my sons

Hasan Ali Khan

and

Asad Ali Khan

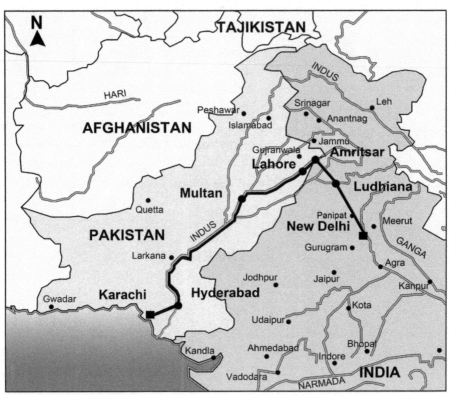

My journey from New Delhi to Karachi in August 1947. (*Courtesy Arif Hasan*)

Contents

Preface

When I retired from public service, I started researching for a book on the personal aspects of the life of Mohammad Ali Jinnah, the founder of Pakistan. Jinnah was a stern but beloved figure in the lives of the Partition generation and much revered by my father, Sarwar Hasan, who knew him personally and regarded him as a saviour and a hero. In the supportive environment of the National Archives of Pakistan in Islamabad, I read extensively through all Jinnah's papers and the record of the first few years of Pakistan's life.

On 26 September 2010, my husband and lifelong friend, Fatehyab Ali Khan, passed away and I shelved the Jinnah project for another time and, perhaps, for another author. The contribution of Fatehyab and his generation, which I consider the 'middle generation', to the political evolution and social culture of Pakistan had always remained in my thoughts. The city of Karachi, which had given my family shelter and a home after Partition, was the hub of this generation's politics of dissent and I had lived with its effects throughout my working life.

Most of the dissenting youth, like Fatehyab, came from across the border in the great migration or rather, the great expulsion, after 1947. They came from settled regions in India, both urban and rural, where their communities and clans had followed well-established traditions and ways of life. Many of their elders had participated in the political movements which swept across the subcontinent in the twentieth century. In the refugee camps, shanty towns and developing settlements in Karachi and other parts of the province of Sindh, they bonded together and discovered not only a common cause but also a way to come to terms with their personal distress. Most of them were poor or had become impoverished, but they found the vigour to organise and group together. Over the years, they were joined by the youth from other parts of the country, including East Pakistan, which had its own vibrant culture of dissent.

Few people are alive today who remember the mayhem and chaos of the early years of my country's existence and also the never-fading and almost quaint feeling of hope. I am one of those few. When Fatehyab passed away, I decided to write about his struggle in the wider perspective of Pakistan's political history. I did not know where to start. I was daunted by his vast collection of papers: statements, speeches, interviews, articles, correspondence, legal cases, the record of his own political activities and those of the members of other political parties. I decided, therefore, to begin with the known history of my family, spanning seven centuries, their ultimate journey to Pakistan, my own knowledge of various political movements and whatever success I may have achieved in my career.

I was fortunate that I had access to a large family archive. Conscious that he would never return to his home in India after he decided to move to Karachi in August 1947, my father had carried with him all his papers and also those of my grandfather, Anwar Hasan. For the account of the traumatic migration from Panipat to Lahore, I was lucky that I could interview a few surviving relatives. In the interviews of refugees, conducted by the Pakistan government even during those desperate and desolate times, surprisingly I found the statement of my maternal grandfather, Akhtar Hasan, which to date is the most telling story of the forceful eviction of my family from Panipat.

As the title of this book suggests, Pakistan has had a turbulent history. I have looked at political movements in Pakistan through the lens of Fatehyab's involvement in them. They introduced me to towering personalities like Nusrat Bhutto, Benazir Bhutto, Nawabzada Nasrullah Khan and Mir Ghaus Bakhsh Bizenjo. But they also brought me in contact with many other politicians who fought for democracy and fundamental freedoms. Above all, they gave me the opportunity to watch the struggle and suffering of grassroots activists, the foot soldiers in these movements of dissent.

This memoir traces the upbringing, education and career of a woman from a privileged and liberal background who, despite all odds and patriarchal values in governance, rose to become the cabinet secretary and head of the civil service in Pakistan. The road to success was beset with many hurdles. In those unusually pressing times, I had to balance my hectic private life with my public responsibilities, which were always under scrutiny. But I was eventually rewarded by the opportunity of working as ambassador in Vienna and making the acquaintance of outstanding statesmen and diplomats. And my meeting with Saddam Hussein will always remain a unique event in my memory. I have acknowledged the recognition accorded to me by those who held the reins of power and made positive decisions about my career. I have also paid a tribute to all those who, including the members of my family, stood by me in the difficult moments of my life.

In the last chapter, I have dwelt on the events of violence which my country has witnessed, which is not so different from the hostility and rage that has spread, in one form or another, in many other parts of the world. The people of Pakistan have shown remarkable resilience in the face of an unfriendly regional environment and their territory has been host for many decades to millions of refugees from across their borders. Although they are one of the largest populations hit by terror, they are also one of the largest contributors to maintaining peace in different countries of the world by sending their troops as peacekeepers under international arrangements.

Social change in Pakistan has created space for an assertive and vibrant civil society, transformed existing power relationships, and given rise to new styles of leadership among the youth. In fact, comprising more than two-thirds of the population, the youth will influence the direction and dynamics of further change as a new synthesis emerges between traditional and modern values. They have already made their mark on many aspects of our national life, not only in politics but also as community leaders, pioneers of social change, human rights activists, achievers in the arts and culture, literature and music. I have summed up and brought together some significant strands of change and progress in Pakistan, as I see them, such as advancements in the urban sector and the achievements of the women of the country.

In writing this memoir, I drew upon the vivid recollections of my sons, Hasan and Asad. They shared the turmoil of their parents' lives in their childhood and youth, and I dedicate this book to them with all my love.

Masuma Hasan
10 October 2020

Chapter 1

Panipat and My Family

My father, Sarwar Hasan, was 45 years old when he turned his back on his ancestral hearth and home and boarded the train to Pakistan in August 1947. His decision was deliberate and conscious and my immediate family was not pushed out ruthlessly in the deluge of refugees who crossed the border in the wake of Partition. Although my father was able to take his personal effects with him, we were also refugees, headed towards a region which we considered our own but which we did not really know. As I look at the details of his possessions, it is obvious that for him the break was permanent. Why else would he carry all his personal correspondence, his degrees, diaries, lecture notes, speeches in the Cambridge Union, his father's archive, old photographs and papers relating to his extensive properties? If he thought that he could retain his ancestral home and also build a life in Pakistan, he would not have clung to these mementoes and precious bundles of paper. Nor was he an adventurer, who would run back if his luck failed. His understanding of the turbulent politics of the subcontinent had convinced him that he would never return to live in the land which his ancestors had inhabited for nearly 700 years. There would be no turning back.

My forefathers had lived in the *pargana* of Panipat since the reign of Ghiyasuddin Balban (1200–87), an enlightened ruler who invited men of learning and wisdom to his court. Balban was the seventh and greatest sultan of the Slave dynasty in India. He wielded immense power, first in positions of influence under his predecessors, including Razia Sultana and Nasiruddin Mahmud, and then as a sovereign in his own right. He ruled with an iron hand and his greatest achievements were to suppress anarchy and fortify his kingdom against the barbaric attacks of the Mongol hordes who had ransacked Lahore several times and destroyed Lahore Fort under his predecessor. He restored the fort at Lahore and built a series of other fortifications along his northern and western frontiers to keep the Mongols out. In one of the encounters with the Mongols, Balban lost his favourite son, Muhammad, for whom he remained grief-stricken for the rest of his life. It is said that he tried not to venture far away from Delhi for fear that Halaku Khan would destroy his capital as mercilessly as he had sacked Baghdad in 1258.

Balban was austere and aloof by nature, but he ruled with a difference and his court had a grandeur all its own. His subjects travelled long distances to watch the splendour of his dazzling royal processions.[1] He insisted on enforcing strict justice, but on matters of governance he did not seek the advice of the *ulema* nor did he encourage his sons to do so. However, there were few periods in Indian history in which scholarship reached the heights it attained under Balban or which were so imbued with soul and spirituality. In the wake of the destruction caused by Halaku Khan, many men of learning had fled into Balban's realm from across his northern and western frontiers, in search of safety and protection. Balban welcomed them and facilitated their stay and the pursuit of their scholarly interests in their own *khanqahs*.

During Balban's reign, Delhi was teeming with scholars[2] but more important for the spiritual history of the subcontinent was the presence in his realm of many leaders of Sufi thought who were contemporaries, such as Bahauddin Zakariya of Multan, Fariduddin Ganjshakar of Pakpattan, Jalaluddin Surkh Bukhari of Uch and Nizamuddin Auliya of Delhi, and the two great *qalandars*, Bu Ali Shah of Panipat and Lal Shabaz of Sehwan. The teachings of these men, who were philosophers, writers and poets and who were in mutual contact and respected one another, their relationship with their followers as *murshid* and disciple, the miracles attributed to them and their own individual scholarship created a rare atmosphere of tolerance for different expressions of thought.

My ancestor, Khwaja Malak Ali, came to Panipat from Herat in 1286 on Balban's invitation when he had been on the throne of Delhi for twenty years. He was accompanied by his devoted *parwanas,* each outstanding in scholarship: Wajihuddin Payali, Muizuddin Daulatabadi, Najibuddin Samarqandi and Qutubuddin Makki. Malak Ali was descended from the tenth Shia imam, Ali Naqi, and the great scholar and Sufi master, Shaykh Abu Ismail Khwaja Abdullah Pir of Herat whose own forefathers had migrated to Herat from Medina in the time of the third caliph, Usman Ghani.[3] It is recorded that, 'The Panipat Ansaris or helpers of the Prophet, are descended from Khwaja Abdullah Pir of Hirat, one of whose descendants, called Khwaja Malk [*sic*] Ali, was summoned from Hirat by Sultan Ghias-ul-din Balban on account of his repute for learning... Many celebrated men have sprung from this family.'[4]

Abdullah Ansari traced his ancestry to Abu Ayyub Ansari (died 674) who was the Prophet's first host when he entered Medina. His was the first house before which the Prophet's camel had stopped. Abu Ayyub Ansari was one of the closest and most trusted companions of the Prophet and the *Hadith* attributed to him are held in high esteem in both Sunni and Shia tradition. He was an ardent warrior and took part in all the Prophet's battles and those waged by his followers. Imam Ali ibn Abi Talib had also appointed him as the governor of Medina. His last war, at the age of more than 80 years, was with the Arab army which took on the Byzantine empire and laid siege to Constantinople from 674 to 678. Abu Ayyub died of illness during the siege, which was unsuccessful and had to be abandoned. On his own request, he was buried beneath the walls of Constantinople. After the 'probably legendary'[5] discovery of his grave nearly 800 years later when the Ottomans finally captured Constantinople in 1453, he acquired the status of the patron saint of the city. His tomb, built on the Golden Horn in Istanbul, and the beautiful mosque adjoining it, became the site of pilgrimage and prayer.

Abdullah Ansari (1006–88), ninth in the line from Abu Ayyub Ansari, was one of the greatest mystics of all times. He was born in the Old Citadel of Herat and learnt at the feet of many Sufi teachers, but the decisive influence in his life was that of Shaykh Abul Hasan Kharaqani whom he met when he was 27 years old and who has been described as 'an unlettered villager filled with mystical fervor'.[6] The Abbasid caliphs bestowed on Abdullah Ansari the highest religious titles, such as Shaykh-al Islam, Shaykh-al Shuyukh, Zain-al Ulema and Nasir-al Sunnah and sent him robes of honour. However, due to his strict adherence to the Hanbalite *fiqh*, he suffered immensely at the hands of rulers and denunciations by rival theologians. He was prohibited from teaching and banished from Herat on a number of occasions, even in his twilight years, and was once imprisoned in chains. But he was fearless in the face of persecution, bided time with patience and always returned in triumph to continue teaching in the Grand Mosque in Herat and in his own Sufi khanqah.

A prolific author of mystical literature in Arabic and Persian, it is said that Abdullah Ansari knew 100,000 Persian verses by heart and composed 6,000 verses in Arabic.[7] His biographer, Beaurecueil, refers to his rich personality, exceptional gifts, surprising memory, great sensitivity, poetical and oratorical talents, ardent character, tenacious will, powerful sense of mission and responsibilities and his 'virulent Hanbalism'.[8] Maybodi, the author of *Kashf al-Asrar* often refers to him as Pir-i-Tariqat.[9] 'How many fountains and streams have I passed,' he wrote, 'so that one day I might discover the Ocean.' At the age of 74, he became blind but dictated the famous Sufi Arabic manual, *Manazil al-Sa'irin* (The Stations of the Wayfarers) to his disciples, having earlier dictated *Sad Maydan* (The Hundred Grounds), a Sufi manual in Dari. He was also the author of *Qalandar Namah*, a manual on mystical thought and practice, which he wrote after his sojourn with a wandering qalandar. However, his most popular work remains *Munajat* (Intimate Invocations). He opposed the rationalist views of his contemporaries, but regarded 'Sufism as an integral part of Islam'[10] and his own religious attitudes were imbued with the tolerance and syncretism which are the essentials of mysticism. Having always shunned worldly possessions, he died in poverty. He was buried in Gazargah, near his khanqah. A mausoleum was commissioned around his tomb by the Timurid ruler, Shah Rukh, between 1425 and 1427, which has developed over the centuries into a vast shrine complex.

Malak Ali belonged to the fifteenth generation of the family of Abdullah Pir of Herat. According to most traditions, the Pir had no male child. The narrative in our family tree states that he gave his daughter in marriage to his sister's son, Muhammad, whose father was the grandson of Imam Ali Naqi. He virtually adopted his nephew as his own son and personally attended to his education, putting him through all the stages of *dervishi* and bestowing his *khilafat* upon him. He also gave him the title of *khwaja*.[11] So highly revered was the Pir as a scholar and mystic that his daughter's family started carrying this title of khwaja or master which was traditionally used for descendants of the Prophet's companions who lived in Persian-speaking lands. This was also done to protect his son-in-law from persecution against the members of the Prophet's close family which was rife at that time. Therefore, our family have always been considered as both Syeds and Ansars.[12] As descendants of the Pir we were regarded as Ansars, but as descendants of Imam Ali Naqi we were described as Syeds in all the official records of the house of Timur in Delhi.[13]

When Malak Ali arrived in Panipat, it was already famous for its *mashaikh* and *auliya*. It was the spiritual turf of Shamsul Auliya Khwaja Shamsuddin Tark (died 1315)[14] who made Panipat the centre of the Chisti Sabiri *silsila*. Shamsuddin Tark had come from Turkistan to become a disciple of Fariduddin Ganjshakar but was sent by him instead to learn at the feet of his brother-in-law, Alauddin Ali Ahmad Sabir Kalyari. His scholarship and spirituality were so remarkable that Sabir Kalyari soon appointed his young follower as his successor and described him as the *shams* among his starry disciples, stating that this one sun was enough to illuminate the entire world.[15] Another inspirational figure, Jalaluddin Kabirul Auliya (died 1363) was Shamsuddin Tark's disciple. He was born in Panipat in a distinguished and wealthy family and was buried there in *Mohalla* Pirzadgan. He was a great figure in *tariqat* and was known for his love of *sam'a*.

Perhaps no mystical figure belonging to Panipat deserves more space in any narrative than Sharfuddin Bu Ali Shah Qalandar (1208–1324) whose spirituality has touched the lives of millions of people over the centuries. His parents had migrated from Iraq to India between 1193 and 1203 and had started living in Panipat. His father, Shaykh Fakhruddin, was a well-known scholar, a Sufi of sorts, who became a disciple of Bahauddin Zakariya of Multan. His first wife was the daughter of Bahauddin Zakariya and after she passed away, Shaykh Fakhruddin went to Hamadan where he married Syeda Hafiza Jamal, the sister of Syed Naimatullah Hamadani. Her tomb is located near Bu Ali's. Sharfuddin was born four years after the couple moved to Panipat.[16]

On reaching Panipat, Malak Ali was faced with a moral dilemma. The elite of the city had joined hands to draw up a written charge sheet or *fatwa* against Bu Ali for rejecting the traditional observance of religion and *Shariat*, such as offering ritual prayers, and for going about in a state of total nakedness. They demanded that he should be declared eligible for punishment. They requested Malak Ali to also sign and put his seal on these charges but he tore up the paper and threw it away, saying that one who is drunk with *marifat* and is in a state of total spiritual intoxication or *sakar*, is exempted from the observance of Shariat.[17]

After this event, Bu Ali visited Malak Ali and expressed a desire to conclude his twelve-year fast at his residence. This he duly did and prayed for the prosperity and well-being of Malak Ali's family and directed him to continue to reside in Panipat. He affectionately addressed Malak Ali's sons, Khwaja Masud as *maqsud-i-mun* and Khwaja Naseeruddin as *mansur-i-mun*. It is recorded that he arranged the marriage of Malak Ali's sons with the daughters of Jalaluddin Kabirul Auliya.[18] Other traditions also confirm that Bu Ali blessed Malak Ali's family, predicting that they would remain in Panipat until the Day of Judgment and attain great fame.[19] To his blessings, perhaps, we owe our survival and the respect we command as a family today, although contrary to his prediction, we had to eventually leave the land in which we had lived.

When Malak Ali presented himself before Sultan Balban in Delhi, the latter received him with great deference and bestowed upon him villages and vast estates around Panipat and urban property inside the city. It is said that he gave Malak Ali almost the whole of Panipat pargana as a *jagir*. These properties were exempted from the payment of taxes and remained exempted even under British rule. In recognition of Malak Ali's scholarship and respecting his sense of justice, Balban also appointed him as the *qazi* of Panipat, controller of prices and keeper of the sacred graves, and entrusted him with the responsibility of delivering the *khutba* on both Eids.[20] He died in 1319 at the age of 90 years and was buried in Payal.[21]

When my brother Arif and I were children, my grandmother often related the heroics of Malak Ali's journey to India through treacherous terrain, his encounters with the Mongols, wild tribes and equally wild animals –stories which had been passed down in our family from generation to generation, but to which we paid little heed. After Malak Ali's arrival, the members of our family journeyed to far-flung areas of India in search of learning and livelihood but Panipat remained their base, no matter how far they ventured.

Although many men of learning and public figures can be counted among Malak Ali's progeny, two of them deserve to be mentioned, Khanwala Shan Khan Khwaja Fazle Ali Khan and Malak Ali the second. Fazle Ali Khan (1720–1805) held the post of commander-in-chief of the army in the Deccan under Bahadur Shah I, following in the footsteps of his father and grandfather, both of whom served the Mughals in high offices in the Deccan. He was a poet, sporting the pen name 'Zabita' and wrote *Tarikh-i-Fazli* in Hyderabad in 1769 and a book on Persian poetry, *Bustan-i-Bekhizan*, in Aurangabad the same year. He also wrote our family history in 1770. He repaired and expanded the Jama Masjid in Panipat and laid the garden, Bagh Fazle Ali Khan, on land he purchased at one *ashrafi* per yard, after which our neighbourhood was later called *Baghcha*. His grave, made of marble, is still intact in Panipat.[22]

His grandson, the second Malak Ali, was educated in Lucknow, where he gained employment as a commissioner. The pen name he used for his Persian poetry was 'Malak' and he also compiled *Qawaid-i-Daulat-i-Inglishia*. Towards the end of his life, in 1837, he completed his masterpiece, *Tajalli-i-Nur*, a Persian *masnavi* interspersed with Arabic, the first volume of which is spread over 500 pages, on the life and achievements of Ali, the first Shia imam.[23] He constructed the Imambara Kalan or the big *imambara* in Mohalla Ansar. He died in 1838 and was buried in his family graveyard in Panipat.[24]

Panipat, situated 90 kilometres north of Delhi, off Sher Shah Suri's *Sarak-i-Azam* as it was then known, or the Grand Trunk Road (now Sher Shah Suri Marg) was one of the most ancient and historic places in India. Today it is a thriving industrial centre, famous for its textiles, fabrics and weaving, but in my father's youth it had hardly started becoming a city of weavers. Its earliest name was Panduprashtha. Legend has it, as my grandmother would tell us, that Panipat was one of the five cities founded during the time of the *Mahabharata* by the five Pandava brothers, Yudhishthira, Bhima, Arjuna, Nakula and Sahadeva. All of them were married to the beautiful and tragic Draupadi although each brother also had other wives. 'Pat' became a corruption of 'prashthra'. The other four cities were Inderpat, the magnificent legendary capital of the Pandavas; Sonipat or the golden city; Baghpat on the banks of the Jumna, also known as the land of tigers; and Tilpat. These five cities were demanded back by the Pandavas from their adversaries, the Kauravas, in return for peace and the kingdom of Hastinapur.

The great plain, Kurukshetra, in which Panipat was located, had been the battlefield of India since the time of the Mahabharata. It was also sacred ground. During the war between the Pandavas and Kauravas, a discourse took place between one of the Pandava brothers, the doubting Arjuna, and Lord Krishna who accompanied him as his charioteer. Krishna explained to Arjuna the duties of a warrior and their philosophical conversation was later sanctified as the *Bhagavad Gita* and became a part of the epic, Mahabharata. Therefore, it is to Panipat that the first verse of the Bhagavad Gita probably refers as 'Dharmakshetra'.

Almost every military adventurer who cast his eyes eastwards had passed through the great plain of Kurukshetra. When Timur invaded India in 1398, his army encamped by the river at Panipat and when he took control of the town, he lodged himself in the fort. The city was abandoned on the orders of the Sultan at Delhi, but he found thousands of *maunds* of wheat, testifying to the affluence of Panipat, which he seized. Marching towards Delhi in January 1739, Nadir Shah, another conqueror, crossed the river at the village called Taraori, a short distance from Panipat.[25] When he plundered the city, Nadir Shah struck down with his own sword a gold ornament from Bu Ali's shrine saying, *ain tuvangar ast ke qalandar ast*.[26]

Panipat was looted and evacuated throughout history. As Karnal and Panipat were on the high road to Delhi, 'from the time of Taimur to that of Akbar, or for 150 years, armies were constantly passing through the tract, and battles, more or less important, being fought in it.'[27] Chinese pilgrims moving in peace had traversed this plain, Fa Hian in 400 and Huen Tsang in 635.[28] Panipat was also the site of the three famous battles of 1526, 1556 and 1761 which had sealed the destiny of India. My father explained to me how it formed a natural battleground, situated as it was in the fold of the Jumna. This area was called *parao ki zamin* where the British army used to camp on its way from Delhi to their cantonment in Ambala. Their sojourn always aroused a lot of interest and the young men of the city would walk over to take a curious peek at the *goras*.

Before it changed course, the Jumna flowed around the walls of Panipat. According to local tradition, the river left the walls around 1300 in the time of Bu Ali Shah. In the centre of the town and towards Sarak-i-Azam stood the old fort, now dilapidated, on a high mound 'composed of the debris of centuries'.[29] The fort was probably built during Balban's reign and had the capacity to accommodate 100 horses and 2,000 infantry.[30] In days gone by, when Panipat was a walled city, its fifteen gates all faced towards the fort, the most prominent being Salarganj to the north, Shahwilayat to the south and Madhoganj to the east.[31] An old gun made of iron bars and hoops bearing the inscription *ganj shikan* (fort breaker) was housed in the fort but was thrown over the parapet after the uprising of 1857.[32] Today, the famous Salarganj

Gate with its crenellated arch, stands in the middle of the city, backed by the Salarganj mosque.

Panipat was famous for its monuments, Ibrahim Lodhi's tomb and the mosque, situated a little outside the city, which Babur had built to commemorate his victory over Ibrahim Lodhi in the first battle of Panipat in 1526. The mosque is located in Kabuli Bagh and was presumably named after Kabuli Begum, Babur's wife.

The handsome French botanist and geologist, Victor Jacquemont, who travelled and died in India, encamped in Panipat several times, describing it as 'one of the most celebrated fields of battle in India'.[33] Many renowned personalities and *shuhada* were buried there, some of whose graves have been lost to time and pillage, such as Khwaja Shamsuddin Tark and Jalaluddin Kabirul Auliya (already mentioned); Maulana Ghaus Ali Shah Qalandar (born 1804) who was famous for his miracles, and his devoted disciple Gul Hasan Sarwari; Amir Maudood Dulari Qadri; Shaikh Aman Chishti; Ali Akbar Shah; and Pir Ahmad Kairanvi.[34]

The spiritual hub of the city was the shrine of Sharfuddin Bu Ali Shah Qalandar. The people of northern India, including our family, considered Bu Ali as the greatest of all qalandars. That is before we discovered the spiritual eminence and mystique of Shahbaz Qalandar of Sehwan which was part of our acculturation in Sindh. Bu Ali was an exquisite poet and a great lover of song and music. His *Diwan* and *Masnavi* have been read, recited and sung for centuries, but in popular culture he is most famous for his verses in honour of Imam Ali: *haidaryam qalandaram mastam, banda-i-Murtuza Ali hastam*.[35] Towards the end of his *Diwan*, in a few pages described as *Hukmnama*, Bu Ali dwells on the journey of his life.

Bu Ali did not pledge allegiance to any master and drew his spiritual powers directly from Imam Ali. One legend has it that, since Bu Ali prayed constantly, he stood for seven years in the Jumna which then flowed around Panipat, so that he would not have to wash himself for prayer each time. He stood in meditation and devotion for so long that the fish ate away at his calves. Then he heard a voice asking him what he wanted. All he wanted was the love of his Maker. When he refused to move out of the water himself, in a trance he felt that a saint had lifted him to the bank of the river. It is said that this saint was Imam Ali who personally inducted him into the fold. Thus he was awarded the title of Bu Ali (fragrance of Ali), by which he has since been known.

Abul Fazl writes on the authority of Bu Ali himself that he was 40 years old when he left Panipat and went to Delhi where he met Khwaja Qutubuddin Bakhtiar Kaki and studied at the feet of many famous scholars, including the four companions who had travelled with Malak Ali from Herat to Delhi.[36] He taught for twenty years in Masjid-i-Quwwatul Islam, located in the Qutub Minar area, and was allowed to issue fatwas. For part of that time, he also served as a judge. His sermons and lectures were so popular that they were packed beyond capacity. But the political anarchy and moral decline which overtook the country after the death of Balban depressed Bu Ali just as they demoralised his contemporaries. In a fit of abandonment, he threw all his books into the Jumna. He embarked on extensive travels, journeying as far as Rum, during which he claimed to have met Shams Tabrizi and Jalaluddin Rumi, both of whom bestowed robes and turbans of honour upon him. They also gave him many scholarly books which he flung into the river in their presence. By the time he returned to Panipat, the urge for renunciation had overtaken him totally and he lived the rest of his life as a *majzub*.[37]

Bu Ali lived through the reigns of fifteen rulers of the Slave, Khilji and Tughlaq dynasties, some of whom travelled to Panipat to pay homage to him. Towards the end of his life, when he was completely overtaken by sakar and hardly in control of his senses, he left Panipat and started living in extreme poverty in the jungles around Budha Khera, about 45 kilometres from Panipat. According to one tradition, when Bu Ali died at the age of 122 years in the month of Ramadan in 1324, he was alone in the jungle and none knew for three days that he had passed away. Some woodcutters found him and sent word of his death to Karnal, where his body was shifted for the last burial rites. After his death, there appears to have been a tussle between the people of Panipat and Karnal about where he should be buried. Since he had chosen the site of his own grave in Panipat, this argument carried weight, and the saint was buried there. Shrines, with tombs, dedicated to Bu Ali also exist in Karnal, Budha Khera and Sonipat. The shrine at Karnal is particularly attractive, with a marble grave and carved figurines. An adjoining mosque and a tank with fountains were constructed by the Mughal ruler, Alamgir.

The *gaddi* of Bu Ali's shrine, located at Qalandar Chowk in the heart of Panipat, had passed through marriage to the Pirzadas, although it was originally considered to be the right and responsibility of our family.[38] Many Sufi orders have tried to claim Bu Ali as one of their own, the Chishti silsila being foremost in this campaign, but he was too unique to have belonged to any of them. It can be said of him only that he was a follower of the Qalandariyya Sufi order. The legends and miracles associated with his life were common in conversations at that time, as also frequent references to his *mastanas,* who wandered around naked, and his own totally unconventional and uninhibited way of life.[39]

Bu Ali's shrine is beautifully proportioned. It is probable that, as claimed, the earlier structure of the shrine was raised by Khizi Khan and Shadi Khan, sons of the Ghurid ruler, Alauddin Ghori.[40] But according to our archives it was built by Nawab Muqarrab Khan, an affluent and influential nobleman during the reign of the Mughal emperor, Jahangir, who was descended from our family from his mother's side.[41] The Nawab's own tomb, where his father is also buried, is adjacent to that of Bu Ali. However, beside Bu Ali's grave lies that of Mubarak Khan, a prince who had pledged allegiance to him and whom he loved above all others. Mubarak Khan passed away during Bu Ali's lifetime and the qalandar decided that his beloved would be buried at the site which he had chosen for his own grave.

The shrine is remarkable in that its outer pillars are built of touchstone, of which large slabs of unusual size had been procured by Muqarrab Khan from an island off the southern coast of India. Over the main archway at the entrance of the shrine is the *naqqarkhana* where huge drums were placed and played day and night during the *urs* and sam'a. Within the compound of the shrine is buried the most eminent son of Panipat, Khwaja Altaf Hussain Hali (1837–1914), poet, biographer, literary critic and great Muslim revivalist. Every year, Bu Ali's urs was celebrated for one week in the month of Rabiul Awwal. The urs was a very big occasion in the life of the city and was attended by people from far and wide and from all religions and faiths. When Pir Abdul Rashid, who was the keeper of the shrine, arrived at the urs, the people, especially women, went wild in the effort to touch any piece of clothing with his *palki*. My mother told me that so inspiring and mesmerising was the *qawwali* that was sung during the urs, that women devotees flung all their jewellery into the qalandar's lap.

The region in which Panipat was located witnessed periods of severe anarchy in the wake of the conquests of Timur, Nadir Shah, Ahmad Shah Abdali's eight invasions of India, the Maratha campaigns to extend and consolidate their confederacy, and the marauding Sikhs who swept into power vacuums during the decline of the Mughal empire. The city was the scene of bloodshed and plunder and even the flamboyant and notorious Begum Samru commanded her troops against the Sikhs from Panipat.[42] But under the greater Mughals there was more than 200 years of peace. The Western Jumna Canal was constructed, the Grand Trunk Road was repaired, *sarais* were erected at regular stages and *minars* and wells were built at equal distances for the use of travellers.[43] The Mughal emperors were partial to Panipat because of the victories in battle of Babar in 1526 and Akbar in 1556 and always rested there en route to Lahore and Kashmir. In Akbar's reign, Panipat was included in the Delhi province.

In 1803, Gerard Lake defeated the Marathas in the battle of Delhi, and Daulat Rao Scindia ceded all his northern territories to the British. And thus ended, it is said, the terrible period of *Singashahi ka Ram Raula*, the 'Sikh hurley-burley' or the 'Marhatta anarchy' which had laid the countryside waste and compelled villagers to abandon the homes where their forefathers had lived for centuries.[44] The British were generous in rewarding the rajas, chieftains and tribes who had supported them during the Anglo-Maratha wars or had repented and pledged allegiance later. Some of their collaborators received pensions for life and the land beyond the Jumna was parcelled out as jagirs and fiefdoms among other favourites. Administratively, Panipat became part of the Delhi territory.

The members of my family lived in Panipat through all these upheavals, apart from journeys to Lucknow and other parts of Oudh in search of jobs which were few and far between to find in those desolate times. In the years to come, when they became affluent, their homes were full of foodgrains, but for some decades before and after the British conquest, the land was ravaged by recurring food shortages, droughts and famines. Arrogant and insensitive, the British drove the people to the edge of survival. The populace was afflicted by the vexatious, cruel and oppressive land revenue collection system enforced by the British; it impoverished the farmers and compelled them to abandon cultivation and evacuate whole villages to avoid punishment and imprisonment.[45] They lived in a state of semi-starvation and the price of grain was unaffordable. In 1833, there was the 'most terrible famine... forming the epoch from which old men fix the dates of events'. A few years later, in 1837, the people had to move out physically to find food elsewhere 'and the demand for grain thus created drove up prices in Panipat to famine rates'.[46]

The destiny of Panipat had always been politically and culturally bound with that of Delhi. In fact, it was said that Panipat was a mohalla or neighbourhood of Delhi. The decline of the Mughals, from whose patronage my family benefited, and the ease with which the Marathas and Abdali sacked and depopulated Delhi, completely wrecked their lives. The Mughal court had become a 'pageant', the emperor was reduced to the status of the King of Delhi, and coins were struck in the name of the East India Company. The ultimate devastation came with the mutiny in 1857, or the first war of independence, as it is now known.[47] When the uprising happened, Macwhirter, who was the magistrate of Panipat, was killed in Delhi. A brave junior officer, Richardes, took control and stayed at his post even though 'burning and pillage reached to his very doors'.[48] Although all other Europeans had fled, he managed to collect seven *lakhs* of revenue for the British army. However, anarchy prevailed all over the region, which was overrun not only by freedom fighters but also by extortionists, freebooters and the plundering European soldiery.[49] There was no security worth the name.

During the uprising, the British found 'excellent allies' in the region among the rulers of the Sikh states, the Maharaja of Patiala, the Raja of Jind who turned his forces on Panipat, and the chiefs of Nabha and Faridpur. Even the Nawab of Malerkotla felt compelled to collaborate.[50] Above all, there was Nawab Ahmad Ali Khan of Karnal who placed all his resources, his sword, purse and followers at the disposal of the British. According to Kaye, 'Happily for us, in this juncture, the Nawab of Karnal, a Muhammadan nobleman and land-owner of large influence in that part of the country, threw the weight of his personal power into the scales on our side.'[51] Later, one Qalandar Ali Khan of Panipat, also turned traitor. After the uprising was quelled, they were all richly rewarded for their support. But the people of Panipat, who were famous for their 'turbulent character', took easily to this rebellion. In the city, and especially at the shrine of Bu Ali, 'open sedition was preached' and an attack on the Collector's camp was prevented only by the swift action of the Jind troops. The British seized the hostages, hanged the mutineers and reduced the pension of Bu Ali's shrine by half.[52] In 1858, Panipat was included in the territory ceded to the Punjab and administratively the link with Delhi was severed.

My ancestors were proud of the martial and spiritual heritage of Panipat, although they were not warriors or mystics but men of letters, with strong links to the literary circles of Delhi. The celebrated poet Ghalib extolled the literary style of Mir Mehdi Husain Majruh, residing in Mohalla Ansar in Panipat, and Ghalib's seal is affixed to some of our family documents.[53] They were also professionals, practitioners of *hikmat*, with links to the famous *dawakhanas* of Delhi, especially the *bara* dawakhana established by Dada Sibtain. The uprising of 1857 and the merciless British revenge which swept away every vestige of stability, dealt a terrible blow to my family.

Threatened as they were, they nevertheless gave refuge to the *ashraf*, women, children and other fugitives on the run from Bahadur Shah Zafar's court. So dispossessed were they themselves, however, that Muhammad Mehdi had to start working as a domestic in the establishment of an officer called Hodson. It is not known whether this was the impulsive and notorious Major William Hodson of Hodson's Horse who delighted in killing Indians and was famous for taking the law into his own hands. Whoever he was, this officer threw a fit one evening because some items of food were missing on his dining table. He sent poor Mehdi to purchase them in the pouring winter rain as a result of which he developed pneumonia and died.

Apparently, in the early days of the uprising, when British soldiers and their families were being hounded and killed, Panipat and Karnal were safe destinations. Later, when the tide turned in favour of the British and a bloody purge took place in Delhi, the people fled and sought safety in nearby towns. Zaheer Dehlavi, who was one of Bahadur Shah Zafar's courtiers, escaped the carnage in Delhi and hid in Panipat with his family and other refugees. He started a small business and, after four or five months of prosperity, thought that the worst was over. But the British, relentless in pursuing the Delhi aristocracy, sent spies to Panipat, surrounded the city and conducted a search from house to house. According to Dehlavi, although hell had broken loose, the people of Panipat did not give up the refugees. They hid them in their *zenanas*, protecting them with their own lives and providing them with food, money and clothing. 'History,' he wrote, 'can hardly show such examples of loyalty and courage.'[54] However, Dehlavi had to flee again, leaving his wife and relatives in the custody of the people of Panipat.

One family from Delhi which had sought refuge in a nearby village was that of the head pharmacist at Bahadur Shah Zafar's court, Syed Mohammad Baqar Abidi. My great-grandfather, Haider Hasan (1834–99), had studied medicine for three years in Lucknow under Hakim Nabi Ahmad Banna. He was a well-known *hakim* in Panipat and he married Zehra Sultan Begum, the pharmacist's 13-year-old daughter. And thus entered into our genes the strain of independent, strong-willed women, for Zehra Begum matured as a matriarch into a formidable force to be reckoned with.

From their decline after 1857, my forefathers learnt many lessons. Like other Muslims at that time, they retained respect and nostalgia for the Mughal dynasty and were probably shattered by the razing of large parts of the Red Fort and traditional Delhi neighbourhoods by the British. But they realised that knowledge only of Arabic and Persian, which was their proud heritage, would find them no place in the new India that was evolving under British rule. Persian had ceased to be the language of the courts in 1836. Therefore, they decided that their sons would study in English institutions and, as far as possible, acquire professional qualifications. Hali writes in his autobiographical sketch that English education was never even discussed in Panipat and, in spite of his passion for learning, he never dared to consider enrolling in Delhi College.[55] Zehra Begum, living in purdah in Panipat, understood the imperatives of this new era. Rocking my father, who was her favourite grandchild, in her arms, she would say, *mera beta tho BA karega* (my son will earn a BA degree).

Because of my great-grandparents' farsightedness and resilience, their fortune started to turn. Modern education for their sons was achieved at the cost of great financial hardship for which they had to scrimp and save. Of their five sons (they had only one daughter), the first three were professionals. The eldest son, Sharif Hasan, qualified from the medical school in Amritsar, and the second son, Latif Hasan, earned a diploma from the Thomason College of Civil Engineering at Roorke. But it was their third son, my grandfather Anwar Hasan, who was the star of the family. He graduated from Mission College in Delhi and got a degree in civil engineering from the Thomason College of Civil Engineering at Roorke. Tall, imposing and aloof in bearing, he stood above all others in good looks and sartorial elegance. As was the custom of the time, he had little say in the choice of a bride. He was married off to my grandmother, Amatul Uzra Begum, who was several years older than him. She was not a patch on him in good looks, but she made up for it by her accomplishments. She knew the Quran and was educated in Persian and Urdu. She was familiar with the poetry of the Persian masters Hafiz and Saadi, fluent in the *marsiyas* of Meer Anees and Mirza Dabeer and quoted from the verses of Bhagat Kabir, the fifteenth-century mystic poet. Later, when he took up employment in Hyderabad Deccan, my grandfather engaged an Englishwoman to teach my grandmother English. How much she managed to learn of that language is not known, but the generous dower she brought to her marriage certainly eased the early financial straits of her husband.

Panipat was rich in history, culture and tradition to which so many great Sufis and scholars, some of them contemporaries, had contributed. The city was divided into four *tarafs* or quarters inhabited by the Ansars, Makhdumzadas, Rajputs and Afghans. The neighbourhood in which our family houses were clustered was called Mohalla Ansar and it is to the credit of the Indian people today that the name still survives. My great-grandfather lived in Haider Manzil, named after him, but when my grandfather Anwar Hasan made his fortune, he built a house of his own. The side street on to which this house opened was paved and cemented. I remember the *devrhi* on the other side, the main entrance where my father's car was parked and where *moras* were placed for guests or casual visitors. It opened on to a largish compound in which there was a well and on one side of which the house was located. In comparison with the much smaller spaces in which our relatives lived, it was spacious, built in small red brick and sandstone, with lovely pink arches. It had a large hall furnished with carpets, on the walls of which hung photographs of persons I cannot recall and there were rooms on either side. In the large hall, my father held dinners with guests seated on carpets on the floor around low tables. The house was famous for its *chauburji* and the entrance from the side street was colonised by bats. After Partition, the house was used as a school and has since been demolished.

The family elders were strict disciplinarians and proper codes of conduct were imposed on all the children. They lived frugally. Although most houses had wells to fall back upon in times of war, water was brought in by *saqqas* in *mashqs*. The women and girls observed purdah. Since many houses were connected to one another, it was possible for them to step out to visit without being veiled. But when the destination was far, the *kahars* or *doli* bearers placed the doli inside the entrance and turned their faces away so that the women and girls could lift the curtains without being seen and sit inside the doli. I remember only one doli ride with my mother and was fascinated by the rhythm of the kahars' movement and the fast receding ground beneath.

Religion, prayers and fasting were observed. At Partition, it is said there were 364 mosques in Panipat. In many of these mosques, the Quran was taught and memorised. Panipat was a centre of Islamic studies and was renowned for its *qir'at*. All seven styles of qir'at were taught there and apart from many renowned *qaris*, there were also many accomplished women qarias.[56] Students came from far and wide, including Mecca and Medina, to learn qir'at and take part in competitions. Two outstanding teachers of qir'at, Mohiul Islam and Abdul Qayyum not only taught their young wards but also provided them with accommodation, food and protection in their own homes. Equally renowned were the unique styles of *soz* and *naukha khwani* practised in Panipat of which the two brothers, Hamid Husain and Sharif Husain, were the leading experts.

The family followed the Shia faith and the town had six imambaras (the word imambargah was not in use then).[57] Both the Imambara Kalan and the *Chhota* Imambara were located in Mohalla Ansar. But there was also Bansonwala imambara in the lane in which Hali lived, one in Mohalla Khair, and another in Mohalla Rajputan. One imambara belonged to Nawab Syed Aman Ali Sonipati. There were also eight *dargahs* or imambaras owned and managed by prominent women which had developed their own customs and rituals of mourning. The first ten days of Muharram were very much a Panipat affair. However, famous speakers from Lucknow, through the courtesy of Syed Kalbe Hussain and Ali Naqi Sahib Naqqan were invited to speak on other occasions during the months of Muharram and Safar. Prominent among them was Mufti Jafar Husain, whose bearing, dress and speech did not betray his Punjabi origin. Translator of *Nahajul Balagha* into Urdu, so imbued was he with the culture and style of Lucknow that none could have guessed that he hailed from Gujranwala in the Punjab.

Elaborate preparations were made for the Muharram processions, including the printing of posters and names of speakers. Two big Muharram processions were taken out in the city. The procession on 7 Muharram started at 8 p.m. and lasted until midnight. Its organisers, two brothers, were considered the lesser beings of Panipat. They belonged to the *Dom* or singers' community. The beautiful *alam* belonging to Ghulam Hussain *sarangi nawaz* Nawab Talpur was made of pure gold and that of his brother, Doomi the tabla player, was made of pure silver. The two brothers carried these standards in procession until the end of their street and then handed them over to the *mian log* or gentry. Accompanied by Sharif Husain's nauha khwani, the procession continued until the edge of Mohalla Khair. Here it was joined by the singing girls of Panipat who brought forward on their heads the *mehndi* of Qasim, the Prophet's grandson, made of pure mica, and delivered it to the procession. The mehndi proceeded through the bazaar which belonged to the Hindus, who also walked along with the procession, until it reached the big imambara in Mohalla Ansar by midnight.

The Ashura procession on 10 Muharram emerged from the residence of Syed Ismail Hussain and proceeded towards the small imambara in Mohalla Ansar. There, from the platform of the Nasirya Ansar primary school, Ghulam Hasnain would make a speech. And from *uncha chabutra* was the speech made by Ghulam Saiyidain[58] which was spellbinding and renowned for the beauty of its language. Here, Hamid Husain recited the famous dirge: *duniya mein sab fana hai kisi ko baqa nahin, auron ka zikr kya hai Nabi tak raha nahin* (everything in the world is transient, even the Prophet passed away). The procession then moved towards the big imambara where my father addressed the mourners. It arrived at Amir Dulari Sahib's graveyard around 12 noon where Latif Hasan served tea to the procession. Proceeding to Mohalla Rajputan, it was joined by the procession of the *julaha* (weavers) community and reached the big imambara in time for *faqa shikni*.

On the other side of the city, a high multi-level *tazia* made by saqqas, so massive that it had to be placed on a cart which was pulled by a bull, was taken out in procession around 3 p.m. This procession was joined by tazias belonging to the Ahle Sunnat Wal Jamaat who, it is claimed, were not a factious community. In the Ashura gathering all would participate, even the Hindu community showed respect for the alam procession, but there were occasional incidents of sectarian friction which were said to be fanned by some Wahabi speakers. No matter where they were, the members of the family always returned to Panipat for Muharram.

My family became conscious, very early, of the need to educate their womenfolk. Latif Hasan, who had risen in the Indian Engineering Service, was a kind of godfather to the family and had made female education the mission of his life. He was a handsome man, with an air of immense dignity, known for his austerity, modesty, and simple living, and was widely respected for his great sense of public service. He started a girls' school in his house, which was gradually extended to a couple of other houses. He hired a Christian woman as the principal and three women teachers whose salary he paid himself. Apparently, he opened the school in his own house because he feared that Muslim families would not send their daughters to schools located in other neighbourhoods, especially Hindu, and they would remain uneducated. He also set up an industrial school for women and girls whose entire financial expenses he bore himself. Maimoona, whose father Mohammad Sadiq was the doctor in charge of the hospital in Panipat, told me recently how he sat every day at the entrance to the street leading to the school, watching his young wards protectively, and how each girl greeted him as she walked by.

Hali Muslim High School (now Arya Senior Secondary School), a landmark institution housed in a beautiful building, was founded in Panipat by Altaf Hussain Hali in 1906, for which he acquired funds from Muslim philanthropists and his affluent admirers all over India. The school was located in Mohalla Rajputan and had three primary branches in different parts of the city. It became the first educational destination for the boys, followed by Aligarh Muslim University. Later, some girls of the family were also educated at Aligarh. My mother, on the other hand, who was raised by her uncle Latif Hasan and lived in his house after her father married a second time, was sent by him to study at Queen Mary College in Lahore. This was a liberating experience for her, away from the restricted life in Panipat and also gave her the opportunity to meet girls from well-to-do Punjabi families, some of whom became her close friends. The ultimate break with tradition came, however, when my father sent his younger sister, Durrah Begum, to study at Bedford College in London in 1930. She had led a very protected life, veiled in her father's homes in Hyderabad and Panipat, but she travelled unaccompanied across those treacherous seas and lived by herself in London for two years, only to return to teach in the school in Panipat.

A kind of hauteur seems to have developed in the family elders on account of what they regarded as their distinguished lineage and the clout they apparently wielded. Because my great-grandfather was a hakim, our family was collectively referred to as *hakimwalas*. Zehra Begum had given birth to good-looking children. They were an assertive and quarrelsome lot and everyone's business was common concern. Their journeys in search of education and employment had given them a worldview which the less-educated and less-travelled people of the city did not have. They adapted to the demands of modernity gradually but willingly, as was evident from the way they educated their womenfolk, encouraged them to travel to other cities to study, and made arrangements for them to play western games like badminton and table tennis. Unlike other parts of India, the Muslim women of Panipat were not denied inheritance rights and many of them were not only owners but also managers of considerable properties. However, the cultural truce had its limits. My mother threw off the veil after marriage, but prudently wore her *burqa* a couple of miles before reaching Panipat from Delhi.

The lives of the young people were governed by the collective wisdom of their seniors and joint family pressures. The professions the boys adopted were influenced by the choice of the elders although they lived on their own in institutions of higher learning in other cities. Cousins married one another and in marriage there were not many choices. The members of the family travelled occasionally in summer to spend the 'season' in Simla, Srinagar, or other hill stations. And they ventured even further. Travelling abroad was not unknown in British India in the early twentieth century, but it was rare to go overseas with women and many small children. My mother used to describe her journey to Iraq as a child and the primitive sanitary conditions she encountered when the family went to pay homage at the shrines of Najaf and Karbala.

Compared to the stupor of lost glory into which most Muslims had sunk, the members of my close family could certainly be considered as modern in the times in which they lived. They represented a quaint synthesis of tradition, modernity and austerity. There was a simplicity in their lives which comes from having struggled hard to keep afloat. No written record is available of how they viewed British rule, how much their national pride was hurt by foreign occupation, or how much they admired or hated the white sahibs and the series of British deputy commissioners posted in their district. My mother used to relate with relish, however, how her maternal grandfather had thoroughly thrashed a British officer who had tried to bully him and my father often repeated how a poor old man was mercilessly kicked to the ground by an Englishman in his presence, although he kept pleading for mercy with folded hands.

Panipat city had a Muslim majority. The Muslims were land and urban property owners, but business and trade were in the hands of the Hindus, so there was a natural economic link between them which seems to have been strengthened by the governance institutions established by the British. Hindu men participated in Muslim festivities and Muharram ceremonies and worked on the lands of Muslim landowners; they operated in the market and were moneylenders. The men of the family had Hindu friends but as far as women were concerned, the communal lines were clearly defined. My mother did not remember ever having visited a Hindu household. Almost certainly, my elders had no love lost for the Hindu religion and the elaborate Hindu rites and rituals, which were later assimilated into Muslim festivals, found little place in their daily lives.

Although the history of the land in which they lived could be traced back to the Mahabharata and they knew the names of the Pandava brothers, they glorified Muslim rule and were fiercely possessive of their distinctive culture. The wave of Muslim educational and cultural revival, led by Syed Ahmad Khan from Aligarh and by Hali from the very soil of Panipat, had touched their lives. It would be true to say that the older generation were followers of Syed Ahmad Khan's philosophy and were not as opposed to British rule as the younger generation later became under nationalist influence. But they recognised the call of the times. Latif Hasan, who was awarded the title of Khan Sahib by the British, returned the honour when the people turned against British rule. The *Musaddas* of Hali, who sprang from the same soil and the same ancestor, Khwaja Malak Ali, had taken the Muslims of India by storm. His stirring and anguished verses, despairing at the demise of Muslim power and the decline of their religious and cultural values, may be said to have reflected their own despair also.

My ancestors left their footprint in stone in different parts of India. Jamia Millia Islamia, established in 1920 in Aligarh as an alternative and more nationalist institution for Muslim students than Aligarh Muslim University, had shifted to a site in Karol Bagh in Delhi in 1925. Subsequently, in 1935, it acquired land for constructing a new campus in Okhla, outside Delhi. The buildings on this campus were designed by the temperamental Czech architect, Carl Heinz, who did not charge a fee. The services of an engineer were urgently needed to supervise the construction and the Jamia was critically short of funds. Its biographer writes that the poor Jamia could not afford to pay in thousands as supervision fee. However, Khwaja Latif Hasan Panipati came to their rescue and offered his services free of charge. In spite of advancing age, he walked around the site for hours on end, overseeing every detail. He also used to walk on foot from Okhla railway station to the building site to save the Jamia from having to pay his fare.[59]

Latif Hasan was adviser to Aligarh Muslim University for its construction projects, but he never accepted any payments for his services, nor for his fare to and from Delhi and Aligarh. He had served in several districts in the Punjab and his name is linked to many public buildings in that province. He is mentioned on plaques as the supervising engineer of the Victor Albert Wing of Mayo Hospital and Queen Mary College in Lahore. He oversaw the construction of the famous clock tower in Lyallpur (now Faisalabad) and the agricultural college and district council hall in that city. He was also entrusted with repairs to the Jama Masjid in Delhi. It is said that he travelled to Delhi and returned on horseback every day. My grandfather, Anwar Hasan, designed and supervised the construction of the imposing Mahbubiya Town Hall in Hyderabad Deccan which now houses the legislative assembly of Andhra Pradesh.

Chapter 2

Hyderabad Interlude

Aged 22 years and armed with his degree in civil engineering in 1899, my grandfather Anwar Hasan (1877–1928) looked around for a job. He had an obligation to the elders who had financed his education, encouraged him and placed so much faith in his ability. Now he also had to care for the wife he had recently taken, even though she had considerable property of her own. His career took him to distant parts of India and he emerged as a sound and capable engineer. All his seniors were British professionals who praised his performance in glowing terms. C.W. Olding, who was Chief Engineer to the Government of North-Western Provinces and Oudh Public Works Department (PWD), based at Allahabad, described him as 'a capable and industrious youngman' [sic] who should obtain 'a post on construction work'.[1] In the same department, W.G. Wood, Under Secretary, wrote: 'He is intelligent, very hardworking and anxious to please, quiet and methodical, and I can confidently recommend him to any Engineer requiring a reliable man, with more experience he will be most useful. I am very sorry to lose him.'[2]

From Allahabad, Anwar Hasan moved to work on the Ludhiana-Dhuri-Jakhal Railway, where F.D. Fowler, engineer-in-chief wrote about him: 'It was his first construction and he picked up the work very quickly ... He is zealous and energetic, has good theoretical knowledge and with more experience of outdoor work, will prove a very valuable assistant.'[3] Anwar Hasan had held charge of a section of the railway from beginning to end and also charge of a subdivision. W.C. Rodgers, executive engineer of the project commended his performance in the following words:

During sixteen or seventeen months that he has been working under me, I have had every reason to be thoroughly satisfied with the manner in which he has carried out all work entrusted to him. He is energetic, careful and accurate and takes great interest in his profession: I am particularly well pleased with the good work done by him in the construction of the Maler Kotla Station building, an edifice, requiring great skill and patience to bring it to a satisfactory completion ... I am very sorry to part with him, but he leaves the Railway on its being opened for traffic. I can confidently recommend him to anyone wanting the services of a good young Engineer and shall always be glad to have him with me again.[4]

Anwar Hasan's career then took him to the Mysore and West Coast Railway Surveys with its headquarters in Bangalore. He carried out location surveys on the Arksikere-Mangalore line and the Mysore-Tellicherry line, the final survey near Mangalore and on the Mangarabad Ghat Section and also investigation of the Natravti flood levels. H. Groves, chief engineer, found his service throughout 'most exemplary and satisfactory in all respects...In office he was very quick, sure and diligent, not only completing project work of his own field section, but also much left by other officers in an incomplete state.'[5]

So impressed was Groves that he took Anwar Hasan with him to work in the Irrigation Circle in Burma. He was employed on irrigation works in connection with the Mandalay Canal and the Mons Canals where H.W.V. Colebrook, chief engineer, Burma PWD found him 'a thoroughly sound practical Engineer with ability to push work and command labour' and described his services throughout as 'satisfactory in every respect'.[6] His immediate superior, F.W. Vyall, superintending engineer, described him as 'a thoroughly hardworking and reliable Sub Divisional Officer' who had given him 'the greatest satisfaction in the manner in which you carried out your duties whether in connection with project work, construction of distributaries and water courses or maintenance and repairs'.[7]

Anwar Hasan served in Burma for five years, between 1902 and 1907, and his pay shot up to Rs 600/- per month plus the Burma allowances. But in 1907 he resigned, to the regret and disappointment of his superiors, for personal reasons and in order to find suitable employment in the Punjab.[8] While still in Burma, he had sought permission from his superiors to apply for a job in the Punjab where large irrigation works had been sanctioned for construction, in view of his 'circumstances' and in order to be close to 'his people', a hidden reference perhaps to his wife and three little children. However, to his disappointment, he was told that his services were essential in Burma. His isolation on faraway sites in Burma and the long separation from the family waiting impatiently for him in Panipat may have been more than the young engineer could live with. He did not wait for the headworks to be opened and towards the end of 1907, he left 'this land of pagodas for good'.[9]

On returning to Panipat, Anwar Hasan sent applications for employment in all directions, to public works departments and railways in Baluchistan, Lahore, North-West Frontier Province, Bombay, Madras, Eastern Bengal and Assam but drew a blank in each case. There were no openings available for 'native' officers. Finally, he was accepted in the Nizam's public works department in Hyderabad which was an eldorado for many Muslims in the subcontinent. His career in Hyderabad was a watershed which changed his fortune and the worldview of his children.

Muhammad Quli Qutub Shah, the fifth Sultan of the Golconda kingdom had founded Hyderabad along the banks of the Musi in 1591 when Golconda Fort, in which his capital was located, became overcrowded. The founding of the city has been romanticised by Muhammad Quli's passion for a Hindu girl, Bhagmati, whom he spotted at a temple, fell in love with, courted and married. He gave her the title of Hyder Mahal. She died at the relatively young age of 40 years. Hyderabad was named after Imam Ali, who also carries the appellation of Hyder. The name was said to be a reflection of the Qutub Shahi family's Shia faith. During the reign of the Qutub Shahi ruler, Abdullah, the royal palaces were draped in black during the month of Muharram and the ruler led the Ashura procession himself from his palace to Mecca mosque.[10]

The region in which Hyderabad was located had the world's earliest known diamond mines and Golconda city developed into the market for and centre of the diamond trade. The existence of these mines was reported as early as 1292 by Marco Polo (1254–1324) when he visited Warangal, and there are many first-hand accounts of the mines in Persian manuscripts.[11] Because of the diamond trade, Golconda became a destination for western buyers and merchants, and later of smugglers and thieves. The Qutub Shahis used to send diamonds as tribute to the Mughal court. Some of the world's most famous diamonds were yielded by these mines such as the Koh-i-Noor and Darya-i-Noor diamonds which were forcibly taken away by Nadir Shah from the Mughal emperor, Muhammad Shah, as spoils of war along with Shah Jahan's Peacock Throne, when he ransacked Delhi in 1739. The mysterious and accursed Hope diamond was also traced to these mines.[12]

Hyderabad became the capital of successive dynasties, the Qutub Shahis from 1500 to the 1680s, the Mughals from 1680 to the 1720s and the Asaf Jahi Nizams from the 1720s to the 1950s. The Musi, a tributary of the Krishna, divided the historic old city from the new city which was built later. The four bridges fording the Musi must have attracted Anwar Hasan's interest because he specialised in the construction of bridges: Purana Pul built as early as 1598, Naya Pul, James Oliphant Bridge or Chanderghat and Musallam Jang Ka Pul which was completed in 1901. At the centre of the city was the celebrated Charminar, its first public monument, which was constructed in 1591. Charminar divided the city into four quadrants and became its emblem and principal landmark. Each quadrant was inhabited according to function or social class. The palaces and state offices were located in the north-western quadrant, the houses of the nobility in the north-eastern. A sixteenth-century artificial lake, the 2-mile wide Husain Sagar, separated Hyderabad from the British cantonment at Secunderabad.

In its earlier life, Hyderabad sprawled over open swathes of land but Asaf Jah I built a wall around its historic centre to ward off attacks, primarily from the Marathas. The city wall had fourteen gates of great historic and aesthetic significance of which only two survive today, the Purana Pul Darwaza and the Darbaripura Darwaza. Unfortunately, most of the other gates were demolished in the 1950s, after Hyderabad was integrated with India. They were considered impediments to the smooth flow of traffic by the local administration.

Anwar Hasan took up employment in Hyderabad when Mahboob Ali Khan (1866–1911) was the Nizam. He had worked in different areas of India, as far-flung as Burma, so the distance from home would not have mattered much to him. He was merely walking in the footsteps of his forefathers. Did not his distinguished ancestor, Khwaja Abdul Wahab, ride in pride beside Aurangzeb when the latter marched into the south? Had not Khwaja Fazle Ali Khan excelled in Aurangabad in the service of the Mughals? And much closer in time, his contemporary Hali, who lived near his neighbourhood in Panipat, had gone to Hyderabad in 1891 in the company of Syed Ahmad Khan where, in a public meeting in Bashir Bagh, he recited his Urdu poetry and Shibli Naumani read out his Persian verse.[13] Hali had also attended the celebration of Mahboob Ali Khan's reign on his fortieth birthday in 1905, although he was in poor health. He benefited from the Nizam's largesse and stayed in Hyderabad for six months.[14]

Alluring as Hyderabad was now to the Muslims of India, a soothing balm on their hurt dignity and pride, its independence was really 'fictitious'. After the Mughal empire passed away, Hyderabad became a symbol of Muslim power and culture in India, its last outpost, as it were, for Delhi and Lucknow had both been ravaged after the uprising of 1857. It became a land of opportunity for employment seekers, professionals, scholars and men of letters and the Nizams of Hyderabad were generous in their patronage. However, since the days of Nizamul Mulk, the governor of the Mughals in the Deccan who had pitched for independence in 1724 to start his own Asaf Jahi dynasty, they had never considered themselves kings in their own right or ceased to show allegiance to the Mughal court in Delhi. In his last will and testament, Nizamul Mulk Asaf Jah had advised his successors to be loyal to the Mughal emperor who had granted them their office and rank.[15] Hyderabad's Nizams were always installed through a royal *firman* from the Mughal court. The khutba during Friday prayers was read in the name of the Mughal emperor and not of the Nizam. Nadir Shah had offered Nizamul Mulk the throne of Delhi but he did not fall for the bait or yield to temptation, saying he was not a *namak haram*.[16] Neither did the Nizams mint coins in their own names. The British stopped the practice of minting coins in the name of the Mughal emperors in Delhi in

1858, because currency could not honour a dynasty which had simply ceased to exist.

The Deccan had always been threatened by the marauding Marathas and it became the turf on which the French and British competed to establish control in southern India. In order to protect their land from Maratha incursions with the help of European troops, as also during their own fratricidal struggles, the Nizams played first into the hands of the French, and later of the British. To establish their influence, both these powers backed different members of Nizamul Mulk's progeny for succession as Nizam and, in the process, strengthened their hold not only on their courts but also on vast territories. In this game, both powers would successfully exploit the antagonisms between the nawabs, rajas, chiefs and fief-holders of the Deccan. In return for military support and protection provided by the French and British through their well-drilled, well-heeled forces and superior weaponry, the Nizams bestowed upon them not only jewels and elephants, but also large grants of land. As Zubrzycki has written, 'As the geopolitical situation in the Deccan became more complex, the Nizams would pawn off more and more swathes of territory until they found themselves mere surrogates of empire-builders in Paris and then in London.'[17]

Ultimately the British gained the upper hand in this struggle for supremacy, initially through the brilliance of Robert Clive of the East India Company. Nizam Ali Khan, the second Asaf Jahi ruler who had come to power with the assistance of the British, did try to assert his independence and even to ally himself with his traditional foes, the Marathas, through a 'grand alliance' to throw out the British altogether. But he was quickly cut to size. The British exploited his shifting loyalties and alliances to force him to sign six treaties. By the end of 1800, he had 'played into their hands so completely that the East India Company was the strongest power in southern India and the leading trading conglomerate in the world'. Hyderabad became the premier princely state in India but 'its independence would be nominal'.[18]

The Marathas considered themselves the natural rulers of India and had always been nostalgic about the kingdom which Shivaji had founded. For them, the Muslims were a non-Indian invading race, just as the British and the French were outsiders, although they used French troops to prop up their rule and armies. To regain the glory of their lost kingdom and redeem their defeat at Panipat in 1761 by Ahmad Shah Abdali, was a passion in which they did not hesitate to ally themselves on occasion with or against the Nizam. But they were easily bought off in battle both by Haider Ali of Mysore and by the British themselves at various times.

The Marathas have been described essentially as 'predators' and as 'indefatigable and destructive'.[19] According to Edward Thompson, they were 'total strangers to charity' and possessed 'an insensibility of heart with which other nations are unacquainted'.[20] However, the second Nizam's determined effort to throw them out once for all in 1794, met with dismal failure. The Marathas routed him completely and forced him to cede more than half his territories and pay an indemnity of 30 million rupees.[21]

Eventually, the British managed to get rid of the Nizam's French contingents in Hyderabad and defeated Tipu Sultan with the help of the Nizam's forces in 1789, thus successfully removing all opposition to their presence. Through the Treaty of Perpetual and General Defensive Alliance of 1800, they gained complete external control over the Nizam's dominions and made him pay for the Subsidiary Force of 8,000 infantry, 1,000 cavalry and guns by giving up all the territories he had acquired for helping the British to win the war against Tipu Sultan. The treaty guaranteed protection to the Nizam's territories but forbade him to negotiate with any external power without the consent of the East India Company. The only issue with which the Company could not interfere under the Treaty of 1800 (Article 15) was 'with the Nizam's children, subjects, servants or concerns'. Also 'by signing the treaty, the Nizam signed away his status as an independent ruler for the next 150 years'.[22]

If any other Nizam dared to raise his head, he was immediately chastised and warned, sometimes in the crudest language, such as Lord Dalhousie's reprimand to the fourth Nizam, Nasir ud-Daula in 1851, urging him to clear his debts or make over territory instead and reminding him that the Government of India's powers 'can make you dust under foot, and leave you neither a name nor a trace'.[23] The British gradually gained control, through their residents, of all administrative and political affairs in Hyderabad. Any signs of independence were quickly suppressed, just the threat of consequences worked wonders. They may have turned a blind eye towards the affairs of the royal harem, the pomp and splendour and acquisition of personal wealth and jewels, but they watched over the selection of the Nizams and the education of their heirs apparent.

A strange contradiction, an uneasy peace existed in the governance of the realm; rulers who indulged in whims, fancies and addictions and a resident power which coveted their territory, fleeced them as much as it could, but was also guide and mentor in all matters relating to the state. Osman Ali Khan, the seventh Nizam, was able to rule somewhat directly for a few years, only because the British were engaged in the First World War and needed his support in an India which was largely critical of their involvement in the war.

The British residents in Hyderabad were a power in their own right and made sure that the Nizams' *dewans* or prime ministers were men who supported British interests. Under the second, third and fourth Nizams, Hyderabad was a plundered and lawless state and its administration was corrupt to the core. In the thirty-four years (1809–1843) in which he was de facto dewan, the notorious *peshkar*, Chandu Lal, a Hindu moneylender, made a huge fortune, as did some residents like Henry Russell, who resigned for fear of being sacked for corruption in 1820, but only after he had amassed enormous wealth. The peasants, on the other hand, were oppressed by cruel *zamindars* and those who were unable to pay their dues were imprisoned and starved to death.[24] Violence and restlessness ruled throughout the Nizams' dominions.

Hyderabad teetered on the brink of bankruptcy more than once, largely because of unceasing British demands to pay not only for the Subsidiary Force, but also for various contingents which the East India Company chose to raise and station in the state. The Nizams had to dish out money for these troops, which they did not really need as there was no external threat to Hyderabad after the defeat of Tipu Sultan in 1789 and the humbling of the Marathas in the last Anglo-Maratha war in 1818. Some Nizams tried to pawn their diamonds and collection of jewels and drew millions of rupees from their personal treasury to pay their debt to the British, while they had no funds for their own bedraggled soldiers whose salaries were in arrears for months on end. The message was clear: pay or give up territory. Failure to do so led to the forced ceding of Berar in 1853 under British military threat by Nizam Afzal ud-Daula. Berar was the dynasty's most prized territory. As Zubrzycki writes: 'As long as it did not plunge into anarchy, it suited British interests to see Hyderabad slide further into debt, and therefore greater dependency.'[25]

Not that all the Nizams were men of great intellectual substance or moral integrity. Chosen by the British, they were, nonetheless, bitter that their kingdom was held hostage by a foreign power. They presided over an opulent court in which sycophancy and intrigue prevailed and they maintained large harems in a style more extravagant than that of the impoverished Mughal emperors, with wives, concubines, eunuchs, dancing girls and female bodyguards. They took their favourite wives and the women of the zenana with them into battle and they lived in constant fear of being poisoned. Some of them were brave in battle. The third and fourth Nizams, Sikandar Jah and Nasir ud-Daula were uneducated, but they tried in their own ineffective ways to keep the British residents at bay.

The reign of Mahboob Ali Khan, the sixth Nizam, under whom Anwar Hasan took up employment, has been eulogised as the golden era of Hyderabad. He was the ultimate romantic figure in the Asaf Jahi dynasty. On British insistence, he was the first Nizam to 'receive a sound liberal education under the guidance of an English tutor'[26] along with traditional learning in religion, Persian and Urdu, and to be groomed as a 'Victorian' gentleman. Sensitive to the poverty of his people, charismatic, dashing and temperamental, he was addicted to drinking, opium and the pleasures of the zenana, which held hundreds of women. His wives and concubines 'ranged from singing girls upward and included Muslims, Hindus and an Anglo-Indian'.[27] He was elegant in dress and demeanour, flamboyant in generosity, a perfect rider and a perfect shot. He earned the reputation of having a cure for snakebites and his doors were always open to snakebite victims although there is no reckoning of how many really survived. When the great flood in the Musi washed away half of Hyderabad in 1908, he opened the doors of his palaces to the people who had lost their homes, fed them and clothed them. Far removed from communal prejudice, he tied the sacred thread and prayed to the Hindu river goddess, Bhavani, that the waters should recede; his trusted dewan was Maharaja Kishen Pershad, a Hindu nobleman. So popular was he among his people that they tended to regard his eccentricities as virtues.[28] Although he resented British control over his dominions and, like other Nizams, tried to counter their influence, he was weak or inebriated enough to lease the coveted territory of Berar in perpetuity to the British, under duress from Lord Curzon in 1902. Berar yielded the finest crops of cotton which were needed to run the cotton mills in Lancashire.

Mahboob Ali Khan was a moderniser. The first railway line was laid during his reign and he was the first to import a motor car into Hyderabad, but his court remained that of an 'oriental ruler and his *darbar* retained all the trappings of a Mughal court'.[29] Well did Sarojin Naidu recall 'the sumptuous fables of Baghdad' and the 'torches of a Thousand Nights' when she praised Mahboob Ali Khan in verse.[30] He was interested in classical Persian and Urdu poetry, was a poet himself, with the pen name of Asaf, and his mentor was the celebrated Urdu poet, Dagh Dehlavi (d.1905) whom he appointed as poet laureate at his court on a handsome salary.[31] He also had an eccentric preoccupation with devotion and prayed for hours at a time in penitential positions[32] and although he was a Sunni, he rode in the Muharram processions.[33]

Mahboob Ali Khan died in 1911 and Anwar Hasan's employment in Hyderabad continued under the seventh Nizam, Mir Osman Ali Khan (1886–1967). He was tutored in English, Urdu, Persian and Arabic but in the early years of his rule, Osman Ali Khan was very much a western gentleman, fond of shooting, tent pegging, drinking, cricket and ballroom dancing. Much as he resented their interference in the affairs of his kingdom, he was prudently faithful to the British. Just as his ancestor, Afzal ud-Daula, had refused to join the uprising of 1857, he stood by the British during the First World War, generously contributing both men and money to the war effort. He must have realised that his kingdom could, in any case, be wiped out physically by the

British. He wrote to the Viceroy Lord Hardinge, on 4 November 1914 that, 'true to the traditions of my house, as a faithful ally of the British Government, I regard it not only as a duty but as a privilege to place all the influence at my command towards assisting the British Government' and he appealed to the Indian Muslims to remain 'staunch in their fidelity to British rule'.[34]

His support for the British, when the major centre of Muslim power at Constantinople allied itself with Germany, raised the importance not only of Osman Ali Khan as a ruler but also of Hyderabad as the leading princely state in India. The British bestowed on him the titles of 'Our Faithful Ally' and 'Exalted Highness' but did not acquiesce to his desire to be called 'king'. After all, there could be only one king and one majesty – the British emperor of India.

The passing of the Mughal dynasty gave a great boost to Asaf Jahi power. For the first time, coins were struck and the khutba read in their name. However, Osman Ali Khan could not overlook his responsibility to the 'Mohammaden Nation' after Ataturk unceremoniously sacked and exiled Caliph Abdul Mejid from Turkey, and he saved him from penury by bestowing upon him a pension of £300 per annum.

During the war years, 1914–1919, Osman Ali Khan rose to the height of his power, administering the state directly without a dewan. Earlier in his rule he had banned the institution of *devdasis*, the practice of supplying dancing girls to officials on tour, and the practice of *begar*.[35] He now introduced many political and administrative reforms and a new constitution or Qanuncha Mubarak in 1919. But the power he wielded had bred an arbitrary streak in his temperament and he was reprimanded by the British for his 'increasingly wayward behaviour'.[36] He was issued warnings when his decisions became too independent and was threatened with removal from power if he did not mend his ways.[37]

Osman Ali Khan's personal wealth was legendary and he earned the reputation of being the richest man in the world. He was a collector of gold, silver, emeralds, rubies, pearls, beautiful artefacts and exquisite jewellery. Irritating for the British, his nobles and all those who, on some occasion or the other, had to bow in homage before him, was his money grabbing and the practice of accepting *nazrs*. The British regarded this as extortion and so, indeed, must have his nobles and other subjects. When British officers were imposed in all key positions in Hyderabad in 1926 against his will, restrictions were also placed on the practice of accepting nazrs which he nevertheless continued to receive in some form or the other.

Greedy, parsimonious and acquisitive Osman Ali Khan may have been, but he followed the Mughal tradition of patronising the arts. During his rule,

Hyderabad became the centre of Urdu literature and learning. Especially after Urdu replaced Persian as the language of the court, a stream of luminaries made their way to Hyderabad where they found patronage, employment and shelter. He was no mean poet himself, writing *ghazals*, *hamds*, *naats*, *manqabats* and *salaams* in Urdu and Persian. His greatest gift to his people was the establishment of Osmania University in 1918, the academic laboratory in which Urdu was used as the medium of instruction in all disciplines. He was a great builder and some of the finest public buildings were constructed in his time, to design which he engaged leading architects such as Vincent Esch (1876–1950) and Ernest Jaspar (1876–1940), the Belgian architect of Osmania University.

In spite of creeping modernisation, an administrative service, railways, telegraph lines, banking, motor cars, and some education, there was a strong social hierarchy and the culture of the court was based on flattery and sycophancy. Osman Ali Khan did not tolerate any criticism of his person and banished those who fell from grace or banned the entry of those who displeased him, as Jinnah had done in 1911. His nobles could not leave Hyderabad without his permission.[38] His harem was not as well-peopled as that of his father but in the final count in 1955, apart from four official wives, he had forty-two begums and forty-four *khanazads*. His favourite was a Hindu woman, Leila Begum, whose grateful family had sent her readily to his harem when he asked for her. She was an exquisite beauty and he cared for her long enough to sire five sons and two daughters. The Paigah nobles had their own courts and harems. Even Maharaja Kishen Pershad had many women - three Hindu and four Muslim wives.[39]

One redeeming feature of Osman Ali Khan's life was his devotion to his mother, Amat-uz-Zehra, whom he visited almost every day during her lifetime and at whose grave he prayed alone every evening after she died. From her he drew his Shia faith and he built an imambara – *ashurkhana* in Hyderabad – in her memory, called Azakhana-i-Zehra. His faith sustained him. Every Friday, he prayed in the small mosque in Bagh-i-Aam and every year he walked up the 495 steps of the Maula Ali shrine. He kept faith with his Christian subjects and attended the Christmas Eve service at All Saints Church. To placate his Hindu subjects, he banned the slaughter of cows and made offerings at their shrines.[40] Muharram was officially observed at the state level and all offices and institutions were completely closed for the first twelve days of that month.[41] Every Asaf Jahi ruler, at least once during his rule, offered *fateha* at Aurangzeb's grave. True to the advice of Nizamul Mulk, when Osman Ali Khan visited the grave along with his nobles in an elaborate ceremony, he paid homage not as the Nizam of Hyderabad but as the *subedar* of the Deccan.[42]

My grandfather's papers give an interesting account of his own career in Hyderabad state. His first posting was in Raichur which he commenced in March 1908. Raichur district (now in Karnataka), was situated in the extreme south-west between the Krishna and Tungabhadra rivers and was called the Doab of the Deccan. It was known for its difficult climate, hot summers and long droughts. The historic Raichur city was famous for its fort, which was constructed as early as 1294 and contained stone inscriptions in Arabic and Persian and other inscriptions in Sanskrit, Prakrit and Kannada. The district also boasted three rock edicts of the Mauryan king, Asoka. Anwar Hasan's offices were located in one corner of the district. Therefore, supervising works across the whole region was not easy and called upon all his engineering skills and ingenuity.

Anwar Hasan was one of the builders of the infrastructure of Raichur district. The list of works he undertook and supervised included *tehsil* and *taluqdar* offices; schools and customs buildings; post offices; police posts; numerous travellers' bungalows; tanks; extension and repairs to Raichur jail; building and maintenance of roads; construction of bridges and wells along roads; and maintenance of civil buildings.[43] His work won praise from his superiors. The inspection notes on Raichur district gave him credit for the 'signs of improvement everywhere', and stated further that 'The good result achieved therefore stands proof of care, vigilance & skill of the Executive Engineer Mr Khwaja Anwar Hasan which he maintains throughout.'[44]

Very quickly Anwar Hasan realised, however, that in the administrative culture of Hyderabad, 'claims on government' and peddling influence were as important, if not more, than competence and seniority. He had to struggle to retain his seniority as he was not blessed with the patronage of any nobleman or influential person. He reminded his superior, Karamatullah Khan, that he had accepted employment on a salary somewhat lower than what he was drawing under the British government in the hope that he would be able to get something better in due course. However, in spite of his 'honest hard work… under unusual difficulties' and 'large experience' he found that there were few chances of promotion and advancement. He was 'a stranger in Hyderabad and can expect no consideration from any one excepting you and Mr Fazil Mooraj,' he wrote. So unless the principle was observed that the few chances of advancement were given to 'deserving men', it would be of no advantage to him to continue serving in Hyderabad; perhaps it would be better to go back to British service where he had the opportunity of obtaining employment on a large work, presumably on the large irrigation works being started in the Punjab.[45] In a subsequent letter, he reminded Karamatullah Khan that he had entered the department 'through merit and not influence'.[46]

In spite of pondering over the option of moving to the Punjab, Anwar Hasan continued to stay in Hyderabad and apparently came to terms with its culture of patronage and pelf. He kept fighting to maintain his seniority and was posted in Hyderabad city in 1911. His private papers describe him as assistant superintending engineer from 1911 to 1921 and as superintending engineer from 1922 onwards. When he settled in the city, he brought his wife and children to live with him. He had moved to a much larger city than Panipat; it was more urban but had not yet attained its ultimate grandeur. There was only one major road connecting Bagh-i-Aam to Abid Road and, as in all medieval towns, the other streets and lanes were narrow and cluttered. The streets were lit by gas lamps spaced at small intervals as electricity had just been introduced and was available only to a few people.[47]

Anwar Hasan had studied in Delhi and was familiar with its majestic Mughal monuments and his family had long-standing cultural and professional links with the Mughal capital. No doubt he was gratified when the Prince of Wales declared in the Durbar of 1911 that the capital of British India would be shifted from Calcutta to Delhi. But Hyderabad was also studded with magnificent architectural gems which had not been ravaged – as Delhi was – after the uprising of 1857. I can imagine him now, looking at those beautiful buildings with the discerning eyes of an architect and engineer. It was a veritable feast.

Foremost, he must have turned his eyes towards the sprawling Golconda Fort, which pre-dated Qutub Shahi times. It was built by the Hindu Kakatiya dynasty which ruled over the region and is said to date back to the twelfth century. Originally made of mud, it became the capital of the Qutub Shahis around 1507 and they converted it into a massive structure made of granite. Aurangzeb had entered it in triumph through the Fateh Darwaza (Victory Gate) in 1687 when Golconda fell to him after a nine-month siege. It was expanded and embellished by four successive Qutub Shahi rulers until the capital was shifted to Hyderabad. Surely, Anwar Hasan must have marvelled, as the wonder still continues, at its amazing dome, superb acoustics and ventilation system. The echo of a clap at the base of the main portal can be heard at its highest point in Bala Hisar about one kilometre away and every part of the fort receives a cool breeze.

The Qutub Shahi royal tombs were spread out over a large expanse of green, north-west of Golconda Fort. They are 'majestic structures' described as a 'fascinating collection of Islamic funerary architecture'. Each tomb has 'an onion dome atop a cube surrounded by an arcade with rich ornamental details'.[48] All the Qutub Shahis, except one, were buried there. Also compelling to view were the tombs of the Paigah chiefs who were the leading nobility of Hyderabad. Another family cemetery was that of the Bilgramis. Syed Husain

Bilgrami (1824–1926) was a leading political and literary figure, whom Anwar Hasan came to know. In this cemetery lies buried Ali Yavar Jung (born Mirza Ali Yar Khan) the scion of the Bilgrami clan, who became a close friend of my father.[49]

Hailing from Panipat, the city of mosques and shrines, Anwar Hasan must have marvelled also at the prayer centres which dotted Hyderabad and its environs. I can see him entering Mecca Masjid, a famous landmark, begun by Muhammad Qutub Shah in 1617 and completed eight decades later by Aurangzeb in 1693. But there were other mosques, pre-dating the Mughals, built in the sixteenth and seventeenth centuries in the Qutub Shahi style with top heavy domes and minarets, some of which were named after the women of the nobility. There were also numerous ashurkhanas in Hyderabad which pre-dated the mosques, such as the Badshahi Ashurkhana built as early as 1593–5, which were testaments to the Shia faith of the Qutub Shahi rulers.

Hyderabad was famous for the splendour of its palaces and residential architecture some of which went back to the 1600s. Above all, there was a string of palaces belonging to the Nizams, either commissioned by them or extorted by them from their nobles. The earliest description of Chowmahalla Palace and Shahi Khilwat, comprising four palaces and nine havelis, dates from the 1750s. Falak Numa was commissioned by the Paigah nobleman, Viqar ul-Umra (1840–1903), in 1884 and was designed by the British architect, William Ward Marrett. It was gifted by him as nazr to Mahboob Ali Khan because he was deeply in debt. The Nizam accepted only a portion of the palace as a gift and paid him off generously for the rest. Lavishly built in a mixture of classical and neoclassical styles, it had Victorian and French baroque interiors. King Kothi was a complex of three palaces, spread over 21 acres, where the last Nizam, Osman Ali Khan, moved in 1914. Purani Haveli was one of the Asaf Jahi palaces built in the 1800s, enclosed by high walls, one mile in circumference, in which many Nizams had lived. Saifabad Palace, built in 1885 in European style, was the residence of Mahboob Ali Khan as was Suroornagar Palace commissioned by him in 1882 in the Indo-Islamic style. He considered Suroornagar inauspicious because he fell ill with typhoid there, so donated it to an orphanage. Hyderabad also boasted Sufi dargahs, Hindu and Parsi temples, cathedrals and churches.

The palaces of the Paigah nobles vied in splendour with those of the rulers of Hyderabad. There was the fabulous Diwan Deori, the residence of Mir Alam and his descendants who had served the Nizams faithfully as dewans for several generations. The deori was a cascade of terraces, cisterns, fountains, flower gardens, a 'melange of courtyards and quadrangles' housing paintings, statues, portraits and other works of art.[50] Salar Jang and his descendants lived in the deori until 1949.

Hyderabad's architecture reflected the multi-cultural composition of its aristocracy, many of whose members experimented with European styles to build their houses. The British Residency, constructed between 1803 and 1806 on the banks of the Musi, was the leading example of European architecture. Nizam Ali Khan, the second ruler, was bullied by the British into footing the entire bill for the construction and embellishment of the Residency, which was palatial in every respect. Indeed, the resident at that time, James Kirkpatrick, went overboard in his ambition to father a building which would become the symbol of British power and influence in Hyderabad. These European forms may have been new to Anwar Hasan who had worked mainly in traditional styles.[51]

During his career in Hyderabad, Anwar Hasan came into contact with the work of the remarkable architect, Vincent Esch, who, as mentioned previously, designed monumental buildings for Osman Ali Khan in the style which he had himself described as 'Mogul-Saracenic'. Esch was a qualified architect, with a fellowship from the Royal Institute of British Architects, but he may be regarded as a professional soldier of fortune. He became known when the Victoria Memorial, planned by Lord Curzon to honour Queen Victoria after her death in 1901, was conceived in Calcutta. Like William Emerson, who designed the Memorial, he came to India at the beginning of his career. He was appointed assistant engineer in the Bengal Nagpur Railway in 1899 and subsequently became the superintending engineer of the Memorial. By the time work started on the Memorial – Curzon's successors had less enthusiasm for the project – Esch had expanded his practice, designed landmark buildings and become Calcutta's leading architect.

Esch's association with Hyderabad started in 1914, when he was employed by Osman Ali Khan in an extensive project to reconstruct Hyderabad, and it lasted until 1921. In 1908, the Musi had broken its banks, flooding and destroying much of Hyderabad and causing thousands of deaths. A City Improvement Board was set up in 1912 to reconstruct roads and build housing colonies and public buildings. Esch was one of the European architects employed by the Nizam for these projects. Apart from lesser construction, Esch designed four monumental structures. The Hyderabad High Court, the first public monument along the Musi, was built with pink granite and red sandstone. The other buildings were the Kacheguda railway station, the City College and the majestic Osmania Hospital. Esch was also the architect of Jagirdar College.

Mahbubiya Town Hall, now the Andhra Pradesh Legislative Assembly, was built to commemorate the silver jubilee of Mahboob Ali Khan's reign. According to Omar Khalidi, Nawab Ali Yavar Jung has recorded that my grandfather, Khwaja Anwar Hasan, a state public works department engineer, designed it and the construction was handled by the public works department. It has 'a profusion of cusped arches and balustraded columns and many jharokas and chhatris grouped in dense but regular rhythms'.[52] Esch himself wrote that 'there is an atmosphere of extreme lightness and coolness in the grace and elegance of this design'. To what extent my grandfather was influenced by the work of Esch and other British architects is not known, but the town hall, which was completed in 1922, 'exudes the Indo-Saracenic design preference of British architects'.[53] There is a record of my grandfather's work in Raichur, but a personal record of other buildings he may have designed in Hyderabad has not survived in his papers.

In this mixture of dual cultures, medieval and modern, oriental and western, Muslim and Hindu, Anwar Hasan tried to create a place for himself and his young family. It was a world entirely different from the austerity of Panipat, a world full of diversity, pomp and splendour. It is my conjecture that, when he moved to the city, he lived first on Station Road in Nampally in a house which he probably did not own. But in 1917, he built his own house in Khairatabad,[54] a neighbourhood near Husain Sagar which was inhabited mainly by the Bilgrami family. According to Abdullah, the infant he took in and raised when his Dravidian parents abandoned him during a famine, Anwar Hasan lived in style, engaging many servants, as was the custom of the time, according to his status.[55] There were cooks and cleaners, sewing women, bearers, *ayahs* to care for his daughters, syces, stable hands, gardeners and chauffeurs. In the world outside his home, he was a modern man, with his impeccable English, western dress and oriental manners. He maintained a regular correspondence with his bankers, invested in shares, securities and life insurance and spent many evenings at Nizam Club, established in 1884 for 'gentlemen' in Hyderabad, where he played a neat hand at bridge. But his family and servants held him in awe and a hush fell in the house when he returned from work. He enforced strict discipline on the inmates of his household, particularly on his only son, Sarwar Hasan, my father.

Purdah was strictly observed by his wife and daughters and, as was customary among quasi-conservative families, a sheet was held along their path as they walked into a carriage or motor car to hide them from the view of men servants and strangers. But he could be tender to his daughters, listening to their chatter and calling them his *bulbuls* and *mynas*. He sent them to study at Mahbubiya Girls' School, an English medium institution set up for the education of girls from well-to-do families. Thus it was that his daughters, like his son, became English speakers even within their home.

Anwar Hasan was no aristocrat. He was a public servant, a professional engineer, a specialist in the design and construction of bridges. He made many social contacts and held his own in the society in Hyderabad. No doubt he would have had occasion to appear before both Nizams and offer nazr. Given his background and strict upbringing, he could have had scant respect for the ways of the court or the harems of the Nizams and their nobles. As his work as civil engineer progressed, so his income rose and the money he saved and sent back to Panipat funded the family fortune. He was generous with his earnings, sharing them with his extended family, and paying for the entire education abroad of his nephew, Habib Hasan, who later married his beautiful daughter, Butul.

My father, Sarwar Hasan, was just a young lad when he rebelled against the attitude of his uncle for whom my grandfather had arranged a small job in Hyderabad. Through the understanding and affection of his older uncle, Latif Hasan, he moved to study at B.D. High School, Ambala, from where he took his matriculation examination. His uncle came to visit him every week to check on his work. He was lodged in the home of a school teacher whose wife was a thrifty woman and often nagged him to switch off the lights when he studied late at night.

Back in Hyderabad, he enrolled in Nizam College (established in 1887) which was affiliated to Madras University to take his intermediate examinations. It was an elitist institution for the sons of rich men in the state and where he developed respect and admiration for his teachers, Ali Haider Tabatabai and Hosain Ali Khan, but aversion to the college itself. His disenchantment with the obsequious culture in Hyderabad and the comforts of his own life are reflected in his letter to Ghulam Saiyidain, his friend from Panipat:

> The question that you have asked, where from your disgust for the Nizam College springs has for its answer something interesting: A nice bungalow to live in, carriages and a horse to ride, plenty of nice things to eat, association with the best society, a very respectable position – son of a responsible official – tennis courts, riding schools (very decent clothes, a loving father and mother, fond sisters, a couple or so of dear friends) the attraction of a large city – cinemas, races, military sports and a hundred other *tamashas* and a very large library – all for me – are overshadowed and made invisible, detestable, abominable by the one outstanding fact that (the college had) a squalid, stifling uncultured unstudious atmosphere... with 3 students out of 18 taking their degree every year.[56]

He was the only son of his father and if he did not 'shine forth … all his hopes must dash to the ground'. But he had deceived his father. When he should have been reading history and logic, 'reading for his life', he was 'buried by my very quenchless passion for English poetry into the pages of Wordsworth'. He longed to move away from Nizam College. In letter after letter, Saiyidain pleaded with him to come to Aligarh where he was studying himself. However, his father, 'actuated by the dogmatic arguments of my uncle Munawwar Hasan who like our pedagogue "e'en though anguished could argue still"' had decided against it. And he had bowed to his father's decision.[57] It appears that wiser counsel prevailed and he was sent to study at MAO College Aligarh for his Bachelor's degree. He may have taken Saiyidain's advice:

> Sarwar, now please make a last effort for my sake, try to urge upon your uncle – I understand from your letter that your father has no hand in preventing you from coming to Aligarh – flatter, persuade, point out the advantages – allure, get a little angry and so on and let me know the result.[58]

Saiyidain's utterly affectionate correspondence with my father makes delightful reading and gives a glimpse of the concerns of the youth at that time.[59] He writes about the way the Khilafat movement hit Aligarh, the visits of the Ali Brothers, Abul Kalam Azad, Hakim Ajmal Khan, Dr Ansari and Gandhi, tears from the audience of thousands and resolutions calling upon the trustees of MAO College to reject the government's grant and disaffiliate the college from Allahabad University, failing which the students would take over the university. All the title holders among the staff were asked to resign their titles and honorary offices and the students to renounce their scholarships. Saiyidain also renounced his scholarship.[60]

The two friends discussed how religion was being used by Gandhi and the Khilafat activists and Saiyidain reported that the Muslim National University, completely independent in all respects (later Jamia Millia Islamia) would be founded in Aligarh in October 1920. He writes that 'The Maulvis are persistently pouring in our ears that it is a contest between *kufr* and Islam … between Government slavery and the Glory of Islam, between liberal mindedness and timidity.' He signs himself 'broken in mind and spirits, worried to death, extremely uneasy in mind'.[61] Never, he argues, has such a complex situation been created as it was in present-day India: 'A country peopled by *two nations* (emphasis added) entirely different in a hundred respects, headed by religion and race, are fighting against an all powerful foe for freedom and liberty.' The only 'organ at which a leader can play is the religion of the people...'[62] The significant decrease in the number of students in MAO College during the Khilafat movement, Saiyidain points out, would easily win a seat for his dear Sarwar.

Anwar Hasan had tried to adjust to the twin cultures of Hyderabad. His family had its own tradition of learning and scholarship, but more than any of them, he was far-sighted, recognised the call of the times and seized the opportunities which came his way. Well before he came to Hyderabad, 'the anglicisation of the Nizam and his court was almost complete. The attitudes, household furniture, the dress, the cuisine, in all matters it was a mark of distinction to be westernised.'[63] The affluent classes in Hyderabad had become somewhat cosmopolitan in outlook, saw their future in league with British rule and sent their sons to study at Oxford and Cambridge, and he decided to do the same. So it was that my father, Sarwar Hasan, left the shores of India for the first time in his young life.

Anwar Hasan made elaborate plans to send his son abroad to seek admission in a great English university. In his own hand, he wrote a detailed list of instructions for his son. Stern as he was, the last instruction was touching: 'you can always return home'. Sarwar Hasan set sail from Bombay in 1922 and as the shores of India receded, from the deck of the ship he wrote sentimentally about his country. He was leaving his loved ones for four long years but, above all, he was leaving his beloved India which held for him a 'thrilling meaning', a 'sensation'. The hills of Bombay harbour stood like 'quaint sentries' guarding the gateway of India. 'Goodbye India,' he wrote emotionally. But the India he loved was beset by race and resentment against the British and even on board the ship in the dining saloon the 'whites' and 'coloureds' were seated on separate tables. The majority of passengers were 'Musalmans' who were happy to be left to themselves. 'For my part I thought it rather lucky,' he wrote, 'that we had no Englishmen at our tables to be laughed at…by the no means dexterous use of knife and fork. Surely some of them (the Musalmans) recorded a practical protest against the uncouth western fashion of eating.'[64]

Once in England, Sarwar Hasan struggled with Latin but got admission in Peterhouse, the oldest college in the University of Cambridge, and he always looked back with longing at the time he spent there from 1923–5. He read for the law tripos. He was far away from home but he was not lonely in England. His friend, Mushtaq Ahmad Khan from Hyderabad was also admitted to Peterhouse and Ali Yavar Jung was studying at Queen's at Oxford.[65] They frequently shared rooms in London. He became friendly with A.R. Cornelius, a friendship which lasted a lifetime,[66] and there were other arrivals from Aligarh like Hashim Mohommed Ali who sailed to England on the *Kaiser-i-Hind*.[67] Saiyidain, who could not get admission in either Cambridge or Oxford, went instead to Leeds. From Cambridge, Sarwar Hasan continued to write for the Aligarh magazine and the Aligarh bond among this group of friends is reflected in his article, 'Aligarh in England' written in May 1923 under the pen name of 'Open Eye'.

His passion both for Aligarh and freedom for India is reflected in the toast he was asked to propose, although an undergraduate at Cambridge, at the annual reunion of the Aligarh University Association in London. The Aga Khan, Lord Olivier, the chancellor, pro-vice chancellor and registrar of Aligarh University, and Sir Ali Imam and Abdullah Yusuf Ali, members of its court, were present on the occasion. He said:

> To Aligarh men in England this annual reunion affords an invaluable opportunity of reviving old memories and strengthening old comradeships...Aligarh is a standing refutation of the charge levied against us that Indians are incapable of wielding responsibility, devoid of constructive imaginations and constitutionally unfit for positive work ...

He further stated that 'Aligarh must keep pace with time', it must exist for the Muslim community of India. No sophistry of argument could conceal the fact that the angle of vision of the Indian Muslims had undergone a distinct change. They had:

> lived in Aligarh in stirring times...the great movement for freedom began to sweep the country, shattering the barriers between communities and castes. And a new and nobler consciousness began to beat within our breasts. We want that our alma mater while remaining above party politics should make a more whole hearted response to that consciousness.[68]

Ali Maqsood Hameedi[69] once told me that when my father went to study at Aligarh, he 'took the Union by storm'. And at Cambridge too, he was a frequent speaker at both his college debating society and the University Union, defending all causes Indian. After all, Saiyidain had described him as a 'Swadeshi Indian'. *The Granta* declared that his debating style was 'trenchant'.[70] Speaking on the motion 'That this House supports the claim of India to immediate self-government within the Empire,' he said:

> India has no more right to be governed by England than England has to be governed by China. He stood for the absolute principle of self-determination. In Hyderabad there is nothing in the State that is not carried out by Indians – this can be repeated throughout India. The present lack of education is the supreme indictment of the British raj. It has emasculated the people of India. England went to India for trade, and it is for trade that she has stayed there. India to-day is the spiritual

pivot of the world –and if self-government is not given independence will be taken.

According to *The Granta*, 'it was one of the finest speeches we have heard for a very long time.'[71]

Sarwar Hasan and his group of friends seem to have enjoyed their stay in England, travelling frequently to the Continent. He became a great admirer of French culture, made many visits to Paris and studied French at Grenoble. He was absolutely fluent in French and spent some of his vacations in the chateaux of France. But true to his partiality to Wordsworth, he also admired the English countryside and spent some summer spells in the homes of local farmers. At Peterhouse, he was greatly influenced by Carey Francis who testified to his 'character – one prompted by high ideals and full of quiet kindness – of industry and of absolute honesty and straight forwardness'.[72] Subsequently, he was called to the Bar at the Middle Temple.

Being abroad exposed these young men to political opinion beyond the insular Aligarh idiom. Thus Saiyidain writes about his astonishment at meeting Indians who believed that all Muslim rulers since the Caliphs were tyrants and the present Indian government was a great boon which should be cherished and guarded at all costs. He was also irked by 'the hidden mentality of Hindus' towards Muslims and the 'inter-communal question'. The issues he addresses in 1924, almost a century ago, ring true even today and have made the Muslims 'the other' in Hindu consciousness[73] – the Hindu nationalist assertion that the Muslims had fewer stakes in India than the Hindus. Saiyidain deplores 'the naïve insinuation that they form an altogether unassimilated and eradicable portion of Indian population' because they came much later as conquerors which was an 'outrage on common sense'. If we came as foreign settlers, he argues, how did the Aryans come? The difference was in point of time. The grave defects of their community was 'lack of education, wealth and numbers'. While the joint Indian goal was the attainment of Swaraj, after dwelling on the 'salient points of difference between the Hindu Muslim [*sic*] mentality', he had come to the conclusion that India should be divided between Hindu and Muslim India, the northern portions being assigned to the latter, the rest to the former.[74] Thus, in this personal correspondence, Saiyidain emerges as a very early exponent of the two-nation theory. His friend's reaction to this suggestion is not available, but he must surely have pondered over it.

In 1927, Sarwar Hasan returned to India and set up a legal practice in Aligarh with which he soon became disillusioned, largely because he could not bring himself to prevaricate. His father must have been proud of the son who had become the first person from Panipat to earn a degree from Oxbridge.

However, he did not live long enough to see his son's success in life. In 1928, with a group of family members including his wife, Anwar Hasan went on a pilgrimage to the sacred places in 'Mesopotamia'. An engineer and architect, his love of historic monuments and fascination with ancient civilisations took him also on the distant journey to Egypt. He died there of renal failure, hopefully after he had seen the pyramids and the Sphinx. Before he passed away, he turned to his wife whom he was leaving to the care of relatives who had never taken to her kindly and said, 'I wish I could take you along with me.' Hers indeed was the ultimate tragedy in those early days of widowhood, far away from the comforting presence of her children and brother, as she travelled back on the difficult and never-ending journey to Panipat. Anwar Hasan was buried in the family graveyard of Mirza Mishky Bey in the great necropolis of Cairo. The relatives who accompanied him on this journey built a beautiful tombstone over his grave which was still intact when I touched it in the summer of 1964.

Chapter 3

Life in Intelligence School

My parents lived in Civil Lines in Delhi, close to the University of Delhi where my father taught law for fourteen years. My father's first residence after he settled in Delhi was on Church Road; when he married my mother, he took her as a bride to live in a house on 10 Imperial Avenue. Subsequently, they shifted to 4 Cavalry Lines. This house, which I remember, was huge – or so it seemed to my childish eyes – with high roofs and spacious verandahs. A vast expanse of unoccupied land ran along one side of the house, the surface of which was covered with mica. The driveway opened on a rather wide road which led to the university. As was customary, the kitchen was built at a distance from the main house and there was a kitchen garden beside it. The servants' living quarters were tucked away somewhere out of sight in the background. In front of the house was the garden which was my mother's pride. In the garden there was an alcove made of arching trees which we called the *jhonpri*, where my cousins and I hid when we were playing.

We seem to have been a fairly happy family. During the Second World War, my father left his job at the university and joined the war publicity office. Later, he became the director of the Indian Institute of International Affairs. He also travelled to London during the blitz as a member of the Institute's delegation to the third unofficial Commonwealth relations conference. In the summer, we slept in the open under the stars, watching glow-worms flitting across the sky. In the starlight, my mother asked me to raise my hands and pray for my father's safe return home from the blitz. Snakes abounded in the estate and one of my earliest memories is that of my father trying to entice a snake from a crevice in a wall by shooting at it with his shotgun. Also, when I was an infant, my mother found me playing with a snake. She was terrified but our Hindu gardener reassured her. He placed a bowl of milk on the floor and bowed before the snake which, after witnessing this act of worship, quietly slithered away. To break the summer heat, panels of *khus* were stacked behind open doors and windows and watered with a hosepipe to cool the air passing through the panels. And poor little Babu Lal sat under the sun behind the ventilator on the roof and pulled the rope to which a large fan made of fabric was attached. During summer, the ground around the house was sprinkled with water to keep down the heat and after the rains it was overrun by spotted red ladybirds with which I used to play.

My father was also a municipal commissioner, a city father. He cherished Delhi and its neighbourhoods as his forefathers had done before him. For him Delhi represented the quintessence of Muslim culture in India. He knew all the gates and neighbourhoods of old Delhi where his elders had lived: Kashmiri Gate, Ajmeri Gate, Delhi Gate, Turkman Gate, and especially Kabuli Gate or Khooni Darwaza where William Hodson had stripped and shot three Mughal princes in cold blood on 22 September 1857 after arresting them from Humayun's tomb, and later presented their heads to the emperor, Bahadur Shah Zafar. Father spoke fondly about the mohallas of Darya Ganj, Lal Kuan, Ballimaran and Feroz Shah Kotla. He revered the Jama Masjid as his elders had done and took us for picnics to Qutub Minar and the Lodhi tombs where my mother served sandwiches on a lovely green velvet rug. He regarded the Red Fort as the symbol of Muslim power and eminence in India.

However, my father was also a member of the modern society in Delhi. He may have enjoyed the hustle and bustle of Chandni Chowk, but he bought furniture from Pandit's in Connaught Circus and shopped for jewellery at Jagat Narain and Sons. He entertained at home in the westernised drawing room which was called the *gol kamra* and at his exquisite dining table. I remember peeping into the dining room in trepidation as I watched a seated dinner for Suraiya Jafri, my mother's friend, who had recently got married. I can still recall her beauty and the affectionate manner in which she embraced me. In summer, we took to the hills to escape from the heat where my brother Arif and I were allowed to ride on horseback. The world lay at our feet in the choice of hill stations: Simla, Dalhousie, Kasauli, Nainital, Darjeeling.

I was enrolled in New Delhi Church School. Apart from the chapel and a couple of buildings, all classes were held under pitched tents. My mother led me crying to the school bus every morning. I dreaded going to school and hated the teachers, who were white women, stern and forbidding. The older girls were rude and ticked me off occasionally and the boys in the school bus teased me and reduced me to tears. One burly Englishman – probably a senior teacher – used to toss the boys and girls in the air during the break, to give them a thrill. I waited eagerly near him for my turn, hoping to be tossed up also, but he always ignored me. Although I was merely 5 years old, I noticed that he picked up only the white children. That was my first encounter with racial discrimination. Frequently, I went home hungry from school because the sandwich my mother gave me was almost always snatched from my hands by swooping eagles.

Delhi was the seat of British power in India, but it was also a cosmopolitan city in which people from all walks of life and all parts of India lived and interacted. In spite of my parents' loyalty to their Muslim heritage, there was little social distance between them and their Hindu friends. Many of my father's close friends were Hindus, including Sham Nath, who later became deputy minister in Nehru's government. The dearest of all my parents' friends, however, was Tara Bai, director of Lady Irwin College for Women. I have often wondered if she was named after the legendary Maratha queen, Rani Tarabai, who took on and harassed the Mughal emperor, Aurangzeb. She was a beautiful person, loyal, affectionate and caring, who looked after me and Arif when my parents went out to dinner or to the cinema, also called the 'bioscope'. A pure Brahmin by descent, she hailed from Mangalore and was widowed at a very young age. She suffered terribly on account of the cruel treatment meted out to widows in Hindu families. After her husband's death, her hair was shaved off and she was compelled to wear coarse clothes. But she overcame the social stigma associated with widowhood and made a career for herself.

My father was precluded from joining any political party by the rules of his employment, but there was no doubt that his loyalty lay with the Muslim League. He had already turned down a political career with the Unionists in the Punjab under the patronage of Sikander Hayat Khan. In the 1937 general elections, he contested as an independent candidate from an urban constituency in Karnal district for the Punjab legislative assembly and lost. Like other young Muslims of his generation, he was moved by the call for a separate homeland for Indian Muslims. For him, the primary concerns were cultural and economic and not religious. Iqbal's inspiring poetry had prepared the Muslims for the mental and emotional adjustment to accept a new political architecture for India. How much he discussed this likely transition with his Hindu friends is not known. The India he had idealised as his ship sailed out of Bombay harbour in 1922 had changed beyond recognition. He had, after all, watched one setback after another for the Muslims in the tripartite negotiations between the British, the Congress Party and the Muslim League.

Jinnah, for whom my father's admiration was unbounded, was his polestar. He was a leader after his own heart who, somehow, combined secular and liberal values with the determination to defend the distinct economic and cultural rights of Indian Muslims. Too many irreconcilable differences had emerged between the Muslims and Hindus during political negotiations over the last two decades which had created doubts in my father's mind about the motives of the Congress Party. He became convinced that the Muslims would never get a fair deal from the Hindu-dominated Congress and, if proof was needed of the lack of faith between the two communities, the rivers of blood and communal violence – which had always existed in some form or the other – was proof enough. How could he and his children live with dignity in a land where there would be scant respect, both in the street and in governance, for the traditions, culture and values of the community to which he belonged?

Between 1942 and 1944, my father was in charge of the Delhi Province War Publicity Scheme. Subsequently, when he joined the Indian Institute of International Affairs,[1] he was associated with many eminent people, such as Zafrulla Khan and Sultan Ahmed Khan who was chairman of the Institute, as well as prominent Englishmen. He was a Muslim nationalist, was well known in Delhi and was friendly with important figures in Muslim League circles. In his own words, he was present at the Muslim League session in Lahore on 22–24 March 1940 where the Pakistan Resolution, as it was later called, was adopted. He watched the surge of support for Jinnah and the confident and vibrant mood of the Muslim public, but was unsure of when Pakistan would actually come into being. However, after the failure of the Cabinet Mission Plan and the massacre of Muslims in Bihar, he became convinced that there was 'no alternative to Pakistan'.[2]

My father's conviction that there was no alternative to Pakistan was strengthened by his disappointment at the attitude of Hindu leaders of the Indian community in East Africa where he went as a member of the Indian government's delegation in 1946 to enquire into the problems of Indian settlers. By then he had made up his mind that, when Pakistan came into existence, it would need an institute of international affairs and the Indian Institute of International Affairs should be shifted to Pakistan. This clearly means that he had taken the first mental step towards moving to Pakistan, if it ever became a reality. His view was placed before Liaquat Ali Khan, who was finance member in the Indian government, by his friend Ishtiaq Hussain Qureshi.[3] Liaquat sent for my father and enquired about the functions of the Institute and its 'likely utility' for Pakistan as well as its assets and liabilities. On being satisfied, he gave his approval to shifting the Institute to Karachi. As a first step, my father arranged for Qureshi to be elected as honorary treasurer of the Institute.

In the third week of May 1947, the decision was taken but not yet made public, to divide the subcontinent. One hot afternoon in May, in my father's words, his old friend, Mumtaz Hasan, came into his office accompanied by Chaudhry Mohammad Ali, whom my father had never met. They both belonged to the Indian audit and accounts service[4] and said they wanted to borrow some books which dealt with problems arising from the partition of countries. My father knew at once 'that Pakistan was coming'. The next day, they came again and asked him to write two papers for them on 'Problems Arising Out of Partition' and 'Principles of Boundary Making'. Since my father's stenographer was a Hindu, Mumtaz Hasan sent his stenographer everyday – to whom my father dictated for two hours from notes he had prepared the previous evening.

After the 3 June Plan was announced, Chaudhry Mohammad Ali and Mumtaz Hasan came to visit my father frequently for discussion and the preparation of maps for the Muslim League's case before the Punjab Boundary Commission. These large-scale maps were prepared in the back room of a house on Rajpar Road in Civil Lines which was occupied by a Muslim income tax officer. My father was also consulted on a number of points of constitutional law and prepared a paper on the organisation of the future foreign office of the Pakistan government. On 28 July 1947, he had an interview with Jinnah, which was devoted largely to the discussion of boundary problems.

How could a non-official institution, incorporated in Delhi, be moved to the capital of another country? My father marked the date 15 August on his desk calendar. He wrote:

> The due date was 15 August. I reasoned to myself and to the satisfaction of Dr Qureshi, before that date, Karachi would still be in India and the Institute could legitimately be shifted there, as under its constitution, its headquarters could be located at any place decided by its members in a general meeting.

Together with his friends, Ishtiaq Qureshi and Altaf Hussain, editor of *Dawn*, and with the support of Sultan Ahmed Khan who was an Indian nationalist but seems to have harboured a soft corner for Pakistan, my father worked on a plan to enrol many new Muslim members in the Institute. Strict secrecy was observed. A meeting of the general body was then called in the first week of August, in which Altaf Hussain, to the consternation of the Hindu members, moved a resolution that the Institute should be shifted to Karachi. Since most of the voting members present were Muslims, the resolution was carried.

The more difficult task was shifting the assets of the Institute to Karachi. Only a few days were left until 15 August. Immediately after the general body meeting, my father met Liaquat Ali Khan and Chaudhry Mohammad Ali, who was coordinating the transfer of Pakistan's share of moveable assets and records to Karachi. Liaquat directed that travel facilities should be provided to my father and his family and railway wagons to shift the library and furniture of the Institute. In very strict secrecy, and within a few days, all the books of the Institute's library and its furniture and records were packed with the help of his clerk, Lakshman Prasad Jain, who may be regarded as the black sheep among Hindus in this case. In pouring rain, the precious cargo was loaded at Delhi's main railway station on the wagons bound for Karachi. So dangerous had conditions become in outlying parts of Delhi by this time, that few people may have noticed this movement in and out of the Institute's offices in Connaught Place. We left Delhi on the morning of 13 August 1947 on the last passenger train to reach Karachi safely. Thus we abandoned forever the land where our ancestors had lived for almost seven centuries. When Tara Bai, anxious because of increasing violence in Delhi, came to the house to check on our safety, she found that the birds had flown.

I have no memory of how our personal effects were packed, crated and moved. But I can still feel the tension surrounding my mother's conversation with another woman, probably a neighbour, in the dimly lit street outside our house, as they discussed the impending doom in Delhi. I do not recall when my father went to Panipat to collect his personal possessions and papers and bid farewell to his houses, gardens, other properties and friends. He later related his conversation with his close friend Mushtaq Chuchakwas in Panipat, who asked him tearfully to whose mercy he was abandoning his community in his city. What thoughts or doubts raged through his mind as he followed the destiny he had chosen? How much did he consult my mother who adored him, or his own mother who would never have lived apart from him, but was really too old to be torn away from the life she had known? These will always remain question marks in my narrative.

We must have reached Delhi railway station while it was still dark on the morning of 13 August for I remember the first dim rays of the sun rising behind us as we sat on the platform, huddled around a few pieces of luggage. The train pulled in and my father, determined but apprehensive, located the small two-berth coupe reserved for us. In spite of the chaos in the street, there was still some order in the running of the railways. My father said goodbye to somebody as the train moved out and handed him some cash, probably to the collaborator, Lakshman Prasad Jain. And so our journey began with five of us – my parents, grandmother, my brother Arif and I – in the coupe. Cramped for space in the tiny coupe, we were far better off than the terrified passengers packed like sardines in other carriages. The first stop was Panipat, where some of our relatives came to meet us. My father pleaded with his uncle to join us on our journey to Pakistan, but he was confident that none could dislodge them from the ancestral homes where they had lived for centuries. And, after all, there was still some hope, for Panipat city had a Muslim majority and the award of the Punjab Boundary Commission was yet to be announced.

Our journey lasted three days and two nights and was full of fire and brimstone. The train stopped for long periods of time near the towns where pitched battles were being fought between Muslims and Hindus. I can still hear the shrieks of the victims, see the raging fires and the desperate attempts of fleeing people to board the train or get a foothold on the roof of a carriage. One man came running towards us – was it at Amritsar – saying they could fight no longer as all their ammunition had finished. I was too small a child to understand the significance of those events, but they sank into my subconscious and have haunted me all my life.

When the train crossed the future Pakistan boundary, the scene changed dramatically. We heaved a sigh of relief when we reached Lahore, although it was still not certain whether Lahore would come to Pakistan. Its Hindu and Sikh citizens had staked everything to ensure that Lahore, their cultural and economic heartland, would remain in India. On the platform where the trains stopped en route to Karachi, groups of people walked up and down, reciting and singing the verses of Hali and Iqbal, and food and water were served to the weary but lucky travellers who had escaped alive from their ordeal. These stations, so different from the ones we had left behind in India had a festive look and the platforms were strung with buntings and Muslim League flags. The engine of our train, called *Fakhr-i-Pakistan*, was decorated profusely as it pulled into Karachi Cantonment station on the evening of 15 August 1947. We had missed the Independence Day celebrations in Karachi.

As a resting post for passengers coming into Karachi Cantonment station, tents had been pitched in all the area around it. We sat on the ground in a tent while my father disappeared to find 'the house' he had been promised. It seemed like a lifetime before he returned in a car which drove us, with our few bags, through distant, dark and unknown streets. He understood our weariness and fear and consoled us all along the way. Finally, after much searching, we ended up before a stone house, stark and grim. There was not a scratch of furniture anywhere and my mother lighted one of the candles she had prudently brought with her. We sank on the floor and slept, bone tired. In the morning, my mother, forever resilient, held my hand and walked with me beyond the wall in front of the house and over the sand dunes to the edge of Chinna Creek. It was my first view of the sea which was to become such a powerful influence in our lives. And so began our stay in Intelligence School.

I have never discovered why it was called Intelligence School, perhaps because it was built to provide training and housing facilities to military personnel engaged in intelligence work during the two world wars. It consisted of a series of hierarchical stone and cement structures which the government had acquired to accommodate its personnel who were moving to Karachi from Delhi and other places in India. My father was not in government service, so we had to give up the first house for a 'senior' government officer and shift to a plain barrack across the road. This barrack had five rooms in a row, with verandahs on both sides lined with stone pillars, and a sloping roof in red tiles. The floors were cemented and every room had four racks, presumably for the personal belongings of the four men who had inhabited each room. Behind the barrack were three small rooms, one of which served as a kitchen and the other two as bathrooms. There were many such barracks in orderly rows, but superior structures were located within a 'compound' in which more important people lived. Water came through taps for a couple of hours a day and we had to rush to collect it in buckets and other containers. The electricity was dim and equally erratic. There were no fans.

The less privileged among us lived in long structures with concave tin roofs and uneven floors. And the even more unfortunate were cramped, whole families, in tiny rooms in straight lines behind our row of barracks. They had, poor wretches, few toilet facilities, the lack of which was a nightmare for the women of their families. Perhaps their plight was just a shade better than that of the refugees who were crowded in thousands of shacks which sprang up in Sultanabad near Lovers' Bridge, intensely filthy, without water, sanitation or any civic facility. Thousands of families also lived on the pavements. It was not just the squalour of their lives. Their helplessness is reflected in one incident which has disturbed me throughout my life. A little boy wept pathetically as he pushed a small cart in the dimly lit street outside our house. He was the sole breadwinner of his widowed mother and small siblings. In the morning they had borrowed money from a neighbour to buy small items of food which the boy set out bravely from Sultanabad to sell, so that the starving family could eat in the evening. However, one of his customers stole all his pitiful earnings in the darkness. The boy was devastated, too frightened to return to his shack and face his mother and the angry creditor. But return he did, pushing the cart with his little might and weeping profusely. Never have I been able to push out his sobs and tearful face from my memory.

In the words of Thomas Hobbes, life in Intelligence School, particularly for the poor, was nasty, brutish and short. The trauma of being uprooted and the peril of the journey to Karachi which many had made on foot, was augmented by the search for livelihood. In this engulfing misery, most of the victims were women and children. There were many orphans. I could hear the orphans imploring for mercy when they were punished by their guardians and relatives, but was too frightened and young to intervene. There was poor little 'Kalva'– who could remember his real name, he was known by the colour of his skin – whose mother had poured a liquid into his eyes to punish him which had left long scars on his cheeks. And Khalil, whose mother sent him to vend kebabs to earn a few rupees and thrashed him if a single kebab went missing. And Mehmood *dhobi* who beat his fat wife daily to vent his frustration and made her bear a child every year. Above all, there was the elderly and seemingly dignified Shaikh Sahib, the watchmaker, who tortured his young wife, Shafiya. He soaked a shoe in water to harden it overnight so that he could hurt her more when he hit her. Shafiya lived in dread of his cruelty. After one particularly brutal beating, she ran to my mother, beside herself with pain and humiliation. My mother was a feminist of sorts and stood up for the rights of the women in the 'quarters'. She encouraged Shafiya to dump Shaikh Sahib for good and seek refuge with a rickshaw driver.

My parents set about sinking their roots in this new soil and creating a home in the barrack where we lived for the next thirteen years. Our lives were enlivened by the arrival of my brother Kazim in 1951 and he became the darling of the whole family. My mother was homemaker not only to her own husband, children and mother-in-law, but also to my elder aunt's family of five who had migrated from Hyderabad Deccan and lived with us for several years. She planted a beautiful garden full of roses and seasonal flowers, working the soil with her own hands. In this garden she built a round pond beside which she and my father used to sit in the moonlight. We lived well and her table was excellent, but there were many mouths to feed. There were no refrigerators in those days and food was stored in *chhinkas*, hung outside from a height in the roof so that cats could not attack it. And inside the house was the *naimat khana*, a small cupboard to store food with netting on its doors to let in the fresh air.

By the evening, everything in the house was coated with a layer of sand, blown across the dunes from Chinna Creek. We had no toys, so my mother spread the friendly green velvet rug in the verandah, filled my father's empty cigarette cans of State Express 555 – he was a chain smoker – with pebbles and asked us to play with them. Later, we were able to buy some toys and Arif was provided with a cricket bat, balls and wickets. In the compound of the house, my cousins and I played hopscotch, *chirki billa* and *pithu*, games which have been lost to time. On Eid we were given new clothes and new pairs of shoes. We outdid the neighbours in celebrating *Shab-i-Barat* and our house was brightly lit by fireworks, *anars*, *hawaiis*, *phuljharis* and *patakhas*. Some of the practices of small towns still prevailed and the barber came to the house to attend to my father's haircut. In fact, most services were available at our doorstep.

My mother, Sughra Begum, was a beautiful, dignified and graceful woman. She had been emotionally hurt because of a motherless childhood - her mother had died when she was 5 years old - and the death by drowning of her younger 18-year-old brother in Panipat. But these tragedies did not cloud the warmth of her relationships with others. When she was angry with the servants, however, she threatened to send them to *kala pani*. She was an ace badminton player and an excellent seamstress and taught me how to embroider and sew. She was also a marvellous story teller. In the summer afternoons, we listened as she spun the tales and rhymes she had heard in her own childhood, improvising as she went along.

She gave me a rational view of religion in which there was no place for superstition and *piri muridi* which are part of our culture. But there was always a moral edge to her narrative. She told me about the oneness of God, the great sacrifice at Karbala but also about the horrors of hell, full of fire and poisonous creatures if I lied or sinned otherwise. She taught me how to pray and fast and observe the rituals of Ashura. She was an 'emancipated' and modern woman, singularly devoid of irrational beliefs and prejudices, although she was not highly educated like my aunts and English was not the language in which she conversed. She was also known for her courage. Because of the poverty around us, thieves often visited us and my mother took them on and drove them away. As my father settled into the social circuit in Karachi, she accompanied him, graceful and resplendent in her silk saris and *ghararas*. My father bought a few lovely pieces of jewellery for her, but she always avoided wearing jewellery. Her beauty was enough.

Arif and I attended St Joseph's Convent High School located beside the stately St Patrick's Cathedral in Saddar, the heart of the city. Previously a church, the cathedral was designed by Father Karl Wagner and was opened in 1881. In front of the cathedral, the Carrera marble monument of Christ the King was constructed in 1931. The simple interior of the cathedral is offset by its radiant stained glass windows. The school took in boys at the primary level, after which Arif shifted to St Patrick's High School. Before that, we were coached daily by an Anglo-Indian woman, Mrs Roberts, who lived in an old stone house close to Lovers' Bridge. I have heard that it was called Lovers' Bridge because a love-struck couple, an Indian man and a white woman could not continue to cope with social ostracism, and had jumped from the bridge to commit suicide together. Mrs Roberts was an excellent teacher and actually laid the foundation of our education.

Established in 1862, St Joseph's School was housed in a historic stone building which had many significant architectural features. It was run by nuns belonging to the Order of the Daughters of the Cross, founded in Liege, Belgium in 1833. Today, the Order is a rich charity in the United Kingdom. The first five pioneer nuns arrived in Karachi in 1862 via Bombay and set up the school with ten pupils in the same year, dedicating themselves to the 'salvation of souls'. At that time, Karachi had a population of only 60,000, of which 5,000 were Catholics. The famous hall, in which the morning assembly was held and where we played during the break, stood on the site of a chapel for the military which had been erected when no other building existed in the vicinity. It carried a plaque saying that it was the first house of God in 'pagan Scinde'.

St Joseph's School was an 'English medium' institution. It had two sections, a Matric section and a Cambridge section, considered elitist, in which I studied. There was great emphasis on punctuality, good behaviour and 'character building' and from the nuns I learnt the values of discipline and humility. The entire idiom of my school education, however, was western, English nursery rhymes and short stories, the poetry of Byron, Keats, Shelley, Wordsworth and Tennyson, the plays of William Shakespeare. I grew up reading the novels of Dickens and Thackeray. Except for the Urdu syllabus – I was one of the few students who took advanced Urdu – there was no reference in our education to the heroes, culture and literature of Muslim India, not even to the versatile and brilliant Ameer Khusrau. It was a far cry to expect any reference to the local culture of Sindh. The history curriculum was a neutral and chronological narrative but unlike the curriculum taught today, it gave a complete picture of all phases of Indian history. The uprising of 1857 against the British was still the 'mutiny'; it had not become the 'war of independence'. The composition of the student community reflected the pattern of migration to the city and the bureaucrats, professionals and nouveau riche whose daughters studied with me clung to this western system of education, partly because the government itself clung to the English language. Although my father was fluent in French, he wanted me to learn Persian as a second language, but the vote in my class was entirely in favour of French.

Schools always upset me and there were many bullies around. But I was a diligent student, won the praise of my teachers and was given a double promotion. Eventually, in my last year, I was made head girl of the school. The announcement was made in the morning assembly by the principal, Sister Mary Longina, and I can still recall the burst of clapping and cheering which followed and my own sense of utter amazement at my popularity and the honour for which I was selected. In my final examinations I got a first and taught the senior classes in the school while I waited to enrol in college.

I always marvelled at the robes worn by the nuns, the layers of cloth and tight headgear. Eventually, they were allowed to wear lighter robes which must have made the summers more tolerable for them. The garden and parlour in the school were out of bounds for the students, nor could we climb the stairs to the mysterious upper storey where the nuns lived, but if we stayed long enough we could hear them moving around and singing those captivating hymns. Most of my teachers were either Goans or Anglo-Indians, except

Miss Wasker, that most inspiring of all teachers who taught mathematics and geography, who was a Jew. During the morning assembly, all the students joined in the Catholic prayer and hymns; hence I am completely at home in any Catholic congregation even today. That was before the government got wise to the matter and the Muslim girls were exempted from participating in these prayers.

For two years, between 1958 and 1960, I studied for a Bachelor's degree in St Joseph's College for Women. The college was founded in 1948 by Sister Mary Alban of the Order of the Daughters of the Cross and was initially housed in a few rooms in the school. The present building, a very solid structure with large verandahs, adjacent to the school, to which the college shifted in 1951 was designed by Brother Hilary Lardenoye. I had always been fascinated by the stars, planets and constellations and wanted to become an astrophysicist or a cosmologist. I had fantasised about peering at those heavenly bodies through large telescopes and discovering new galaxies. Therefore, I enrolled for science subjects in the college but my father would hear none of it. He had set his heart on sending me to Cambridge and thought, for some reason I could not fathom, that I would not make it with a science degree. Crestfallen, I climbed the stairs nervously to the office of the principal, Sister Mary Bernadette, to request her to change my admission to the social sciences. She agreed reluctantly with the sarcastic remark, 'why doesn't your father open a college of his own?' I went home and wept my heart out. Years later, when the incident was well behind us, my father apologised to me for this imposition.

The college population was drawn from a wider social spectrum than that of the school and I spent two happy years there, partly because as older students, we were allowed greater freedom to move around. Many of my friends travelled by public bus from Empress Market and I often walked with them to Saddar, stopping in Bohri Bazaar to shop and eat *chaat*. More interesting, however, were our walking trips in groups, once a week, to the apartment of Maulana Shafiqur Rahman above Memon Masjid, to study Islamiat, which was a compulsory part of our curriculum. We had to venture out of the college for Islamiat classes, either because the Maulana was unwilling to enter a girls' college or because the college did not want Islamiat taught on its premises. I have a hunch that the latter consideration prevailed because the Maulana would have loved to spread the true divine message in the college. As it was, he was absolutely charming. We climbed the creaking wooden staircase leading to his apartment in Saddar and sat on the carpet on the floor of his *baithak* while he spoke to us softly on the differences between institutions of the state. The more precocious among us tried to tease him, but he never took offence and responded with utmost patience and good humour.

For my father, Urdu was somehow synonymous with everything that was sophisticated and civilised in Muslim culture in the subcontinent. He wanted his children to be modern but also to be imbued with his community's culture and family's literary heritage. These were not to be washed away in the sea change after Partition. Both my parents tried to create a balance in my upbringing between the East and the West. Every day I practised writing the Urdu script on a *takhti* with a reed pen dipped in *roshnai*, and to prepare the takhti for the next day by washing and coating it with sticky Multani mud and leaving it to dry overnight. From my mother I learnt the native idiom and metaphor; from my father the poetry of Hali, Iqbal, and Ghalib. My mother had read the liberating message of Rashidul Khairi's novels which focused on the injustices suffered by Muslim women under patriarchy in India, and she had subscribed to *Ismat* magazine. However, she held definite views of her own far beyond Khairi's rather patronising message on issues such as polygamy, freedom of choice and women's right to inheritance. She arranged for me to receive and read *Phool Akhbar* which was published for children by Hamid Ali Sahib from Lahore.

On the other hand, my father wanted me to be also 'accomplished' in the western sense and learn how to play the piano, which I resisted. Such were our cultural paradoxes that he never suggested that I should learn how to sing or play a 'native' musical instrument. However, I went along with his wishes and took to horse riding. An Irish woman, married to a Pakistani, had a stable in our neighbourhood. She taught me how to ride on the lonely expanse of land on either side of the present Clifton settlement and across the sand dunes leading to Chinna Creek. We were exposed to popular culture through Indian films and songs. We watched English films but were not encouraged to watch Indian films, perhaps because of their emotional intensity and morbidity. The first Indian film I watched was in Jubilee cinema and it left a lasting impression on me. However, my cousins and I were hooked on the lyrics and songs played on Radio Ceylon and Binaka Geet Mala. These songs taught me something about music and also introduced me to contemporary romantic Urdu verse.

Our dining table was the university where I listened to Iqbal's stirring verses, evening after evening, which my father read with emotion and which I learnt by heart. Hali's *Musaddas* evoked nostalgia for his lost Panipat, memorising which had been essential in Hali Muslim High School and, indeed, in many other schools. My grandmother and elder aunt also taught me how to read from the marsiyas of Anees and Dabeer, and my cousins and I recited the nauhas for which Panipat had been famous. Most of my school friends were strangers to these aspects of our culture. Since Panipat had been famous for its qir'at, my father wanted to honour that tradition. He found a good qari and my brother Arif was put under his tutelage. I can still remember the anguish in my father's eyes when Qari Sahib starting reciting the qir'at, the resonance of his voice filling our house in pin-drop silence.

Slowly, we got to know the city where we had settled. In spite of the sprawling refugee slums, the Karachi of my childhood and youth was a charming place. Saddar, with one striking colonial building after another, Elphinstone Street, now Zaibunnisa Street, named after Monstuart Elphinstone who was the Governor of Bombay and Victoria Road, now Abdullah Haroon Road, where many migrants from Delhi and other parts of India had started business so quickly after Partition, were delightful.

We discovered historic Bohri Bazaar, with its narrow lanes and shops run by this quaint community, the Bohris, whose men had identical beards and for whom *boni* or the first sale of the morning was so important. Every Sunday, I accompanied my mother to Empress Market where she shopped for provisions for the following week. Empress Market was built by the British during the 1880s on the site where freedom fighters were blown up by canon after the uprising of 1857. It was designed by James Strachan who was the architect of many other famous buildings in the city. Legend has it that after the freedom fighters were blown to smithereens, the site was regularly found strewn with flowers and nothing the British did could stop this anonymous homage to the martyrs. Therefore, they decided to do away with these reminders of martyrdom once and for all and build a market there to commemorate the reign of Queen Victoria as empress of India.

The Saddar area was mainly inhabited by the Goans who sat outside their homes in the evenings. A Catholic community, they had migrated to Karachi from Bombay in the middle of the nineteenth century and made a great contribution to education and culture in the city. Many roads in the city were named after prominent Goans as well as Cincinnatus Town (Garden East) which was developed by Cincinnatus D'Abreo. They served in almost every profession but distinguished themselves in the fields of music – Goan bands, classical music, jazz – theatre and dancing, as well as in all sports. Prominent businesses were owned by them in Saddar such as the bakers Pereira and Sons and Misquita, the famous photography outlet of I Sequiera, and the chemists Bliss and Company. And walking from the school towards the centre of the city, one could not fail to notice the shop of the tombstone makers, Anthony Coutinho and Company, with lovely carved tombstones displayed on the pavement. Unfortunately, the Goans could not come to terms with the new order in Pakistan and one by one my Goan friends and teachers migrated to what they considered the more tolerant countries of the West.

We often frequented the bookshops Greenwich and Kitab Mahal on Elphinstone Street and watched movies in Paradise, Capitol, Rex and Rio cinemas which later became victims of commercial greed and were replaced by ugly buildings not meant to last. Most painful of all was the demolition of the grand and stately Palace Hotel which used to be a political and cultural hub, where Movenpick now stands. On the site of present-day Mehboob Market stood Firdaus Cafeteria which was famous for its kebabs. My parents always patronised shopkeepers who had moved from Delhi, including the famous sweetmeat vendors Abdul Khaliq and Sons. My own familiarity with the buildings of old Karachi came through my journeys in the school bus which drove down the entire length of Bunder Road (now M.A. Jinnah Road), alongside the Muhammadi Tramway Company's tram lines, and through Queens Road, now Tamizuddin Khan Road, to Intelligence School which was almost the last stop.

My parents made sure that we explored the city. They drove us to Clifton beach, unspoiled and uncluttered as it then was, across the unsettled scrub and sand dunes beyond Clifton Bridge. We waded in the water and ran up and down Jehangir Kothari Parade. Sometimes, our car sank in the sand - there were no proper roads - and had to be pushed out by the fisherfolk who sold fish and seashells on the beach. Abdullah Shah Ghazi's grave at Clifton was unfrequented and had not acquired its present pilgrimage status. In fact, we discovered its significance much later when many forsaken graves in the city turned into commercially thriving and wealthy shrines. Old Clifton, hardly frequented now, was another favourite spot.

With his usual nonchalance, my father drove across Hub River, completely unconcerned that the car was floating perilously in the water, and we picnicked on the white sandy beaches of Hawkes Bay and Sandspit. We also stopped at Beach Luxury Hotel by the sea after driving past Native Jetty, affectionately called Netty Jetty, where the large Arab dhows from the Gulf used to anchor, and over Napier Mole Bridge. The bridge was a joyful place for the poor people of the city who brought their children there to view the sea and it was a favourite spot for anglers. Now the poor are shut out and it has been taken over by an expensive entertainment project. Whenever the city was lit up for any occasion, my father piled all the children into his car and drove them around to show them the 'lights'.

We lived in a sedate, safe, and quaintly liberal environment. There was a telephone exchange where one had to make a request to place a call, before we got our own telephone connection and a red telephone set. There was a one-room dispensary, run by the government, which catered to everybody's illness free of cost. Opposite the barrack in which we lived was a squash court where the budding Khan champions occasionally came to practise. The boys of the neighbourhood also played in the court but, being too poor to afford squash racquets, used the palms of their hands as racquets. And there were the special sounds I still associate with Intelligence School. The haunting heave-ho of dockworkers in the silence of dark nights as they pushed cargo wagons in the railway yard on Queens Road, the early morning sound of the band playing in the nearby naval base, Dilawar, the call of the *har mal wala* as he pushed his primitive cart to sell small items which poor women could afford to buy, the rhythmic sound of cotton being spun in the verandah to fill our coverlets, the vicious onslaught of swarms of locusts as they hit our house and, above all, the loud invocation of *Allahus Samad* by that friendless and sick old woman devotee from the shrine of Khwaja Gharib Nawaz at Ajmer, which resounded through the neighbourhood.

The first studio of Radio Pakistan was opened in a barrack near ours and Arif and I waited to catch a glimpse of Liaquat Ali Khan when he came to record a speech. How simple was his entourage; in fact, there was no entourage, just his limousine, followed perhaps by another car. There were no outriders, no sirens blowing, no police mobiles. His political role has come under critical scrutiny over the years but in my childhood he was universally popular. His public speeches were usually made in Jahangir Park in Saddar which was also the venue of the Muharram gatherings before they were shifted to Patel Park, now Nishtar Park. Liaquat Ali Khan was an orator of the old style, speaking in chaste Urdu to an enthralled audience, with just a hint of the Karnal accent, often challenging the enemy with defiance. His words strengthened the confidence and resolve to survive of those uprooted and miserably poor people of the country. His speeches were broadcast over the radio and we hung on every word he uttered. Just before he was shot dead in Company Bagh in Rawalpindi on 16 October 1951, our radio was tuned in and we were waiting impatiently to listen to him. We heard the only words he spoke and after a few moments, a recitation from the Quran started. When the worst was known, I started crying. My father consoled me. 'Liaquat was my friend,' he said, and left the house.

A social hierarchy existed, especially among the higher bureaucrats for whom Intelligence School was a transitional abode as many of them soon moved to better neighbourhoods or to their own houses when the Pakistan employees' cooperative housing society was established. But many senior government officials, including federal secretaries like Edward Snelson, lived there and others, such as members of the armed forces in search of temporary accommodation, found a room or two in the Mess, before they also moved on. In general, however, the families visited one another and some of the boys of more and less affluent families played with one another and formed lifelong friendships. Many well-known literati lived in strained conditions in the neighbourhood, including Hafeez Jalandhari, the author of Pakistan's national anthem, and the poet Ali Hasnain Zeba who always announced his arrival with the words, *Zeba adab baja lata hai.*

Our daily exposure to poverty and the struggle for survival of our less-fortunate neighbours filled our young minds with the understanding and compassion which shaped our future thoughts and careers. My father was kind to children of all backgrounds, drawing them out about their problems and plans for the future. He was always moved by deprivation and encouraged the youngsters who had no electricity in their crowded homes and studied on the ground under very dim street lights, citing examples of great statesmen who hailed from poor backgrounds but rose to utmost heights of fame. When we had all gone our different ways, some of them still recalled how his affectionate words had given them hope.

My father was the central figure in the universe of our lives. We were scared of his temper, but he was blessed with extraordinary joie de vivre and zest for life. He organised events in the drawing room in which all the children of the family participated. Sometimes he was a one-person audience as my cousins and I emerged from behind the curtain, curtsied and said our lines one by one. With great gusto, he sang aloud with us all the songs we had learnt at school and would turn himself into a locomotive with us holding each others' shirts, pretending to be railway carriages. The neighbours often watched our antics with amusement. Above all, he took an interest in the daily events of our lives. Very often, he held serious counsel with us about weighty national issues such as the performance of Pakistan's cricket team in England, asking us to devise a collective strategy to win. When he was not at work or entertaining us, I always found him reading, not only scholarly works but also detective novels. He was a great fan of Agatha Christie's mystery stories and also of the Perry Mason series. Above all, he read along with me, from touching works like *Little Lord Fauntleroy* to the hilarious *Flowers for Mrs Harris* over which we both laughed together. In the words of Mrs Harris, after each reading he would invariably ask, 'how about a little bubbly' and produce a soda drink which we split between us. He loved travelling and longed for the day when he could sit in a spaceship and explore the universe. He was also fond of automobiles and bought two Chevrolets during his trips to the United States.

In his professional life, as the moving spirit behind The Pakistan Institute of International Affairs, he was highly respected and his opinion was widely sought on all matters relating to foreign policy and international affairs. In its early days, Pakistan's foreign office relied heavily on the library of the Institute for books and documents. He laid the foundation of research at the Institute and taught and encouraged numerous young people whose work and careers he facilitated. Also, he started and edited *Pakistan Horizon*, the quarterly journal of the Institute, which has an unbroken record of publication from 1948 to this day. Later, in 2005, Pakistan Post issued a commemorative stamp in his memory in their Men of Letters series.

My father frequently travelled abroad, sometimes for three months at a stretch, as when he was adviser on Hyderabad's case at the United Nations and a delegate to the Security Council and General Assembly. He wrote extensively and was an expert on the Kashmir problem. The first authentic and analytic study of the issue is contained in his book, *Pakistan and the United Nations.*[5] Seeing him off at the charming old airport in Karachi, with its circular hall (now the Hajj terminal) and receiving him back when he returned became a regular feature of our lives. On the way to the airport, we always looked out for the city's imposing landmark, eventually dismantled and sold, the huge black hangar or *kala chhapra* which had been built for the ill-fated flight R101. After his departure, we waited for the usual telegram – 'arrived safe' – for there were no international telephone links in those days. He always brought back gifts for all the children. When he returned from his travels, we sat around him as an admiring group while he related his work at the conferences he had attended, his conversations with the people he had met and descriptions of the sites and monuments he had visited. From accounts of his journeys abroad, Arif and I learnt about distant places and faraway lands and people.

In 1955, he was selected as a member of the administrative body entrusted with organising the Afro-Asian Conference in Indonesia, also known as the Bandung Conference, and he gave his heart and soul to the work. As reflected in his writings, he was a great advocate of a non-partisan foreign policy for Pakistan and the independence in global politics of the people of Asia and Africa. The conference was studded with the giants of the Third World and, when he returned home, he told us about his meetings with legendary figures such as Zhou Enlai, Sukarno, Nehru and Tito and both the serious and amusing aspects of the sessions. His vivid descriptions made us feel that we had met these great statesmen ourselves.

In spite of our passionate patriotism, our lives were somehow coloured with the past we had left behind. The cities of northern India, all the magnificent symbols of Muslim power and culture in the subcontinent seemed to mean more to us than to the people whose land we had come to share. There was always a sense of nostalgia, so typical among migrant populations. A strange system of parallel social existence had developed. My father knew the Sindhi elite of the city – Jamshed Nusserwanji, Hashim Gazdar, Ayub Khuhro – but

I do not remember having entered a Sindhi home in my childhood or a Sindhi family having visited us. Nobody ever suggested in my childhood that I should learn the Sindhi language. Apart from the hang-up about English and western mannerisms, we were surrounded by the culture of Delhi and Lucknow with a smattering of the culture of Hyderabad Deccan. The Hyderabad element was reflected in our lives by my family's former association with that princely state and my father's close friendship with Mushtaq Ahmad Khan, who was the last Nizam's representative in Pakistan and lived in a grand house in Clifton. So strong was the influence of this combined culture, its language, literary traditions and social norms – in short, its *tehzeeb*– that the people whose land we now shared also admired and tried to adopt it. Was it not after all, it was argued, the culture of all educated and civilised Muslims across the entire subcontinent? Only after I met Fatehyab and encountered his extrovert worldview and social compassion was I able to step out of this cocoon.

There was this passionate patriotism but our immediate soil was the soil of Sindh which I learnt to love by listening to the music of Sindh. The names of the singers, musicians and musical instruments and the verses of Sindh's great poets and philosophers were unfamiliar to me. But the enchanting music touched my heart and I waited to catch the occasional lyric and melody on the radio. In a more pragmatic way, in accordance with official policy, my parents tried to sink their roots in the soil by claiming property in lieu of the assets they had left behind in India. My father was partial to Lahore, its monuments, Mughal aura and colonial charm. However, he decided to settle in Karachi which was the capital of the country, and also because he wanted to avoid his relatives who had moved to Lahore and other parts of the Punjab. Partition had inflicted great suffering, but it was also a great liberator from archaic customs and stifling traditions and relationships.

The acquisition of property under evacuee property laws benefited many undeserving people while it impoverished many who were formerly rich. It was based on a rough and ready understanding that the assets left behind by migrating Hindus and Sikhs would be allotted, on the basis of records and valuation, to the Muslims who had moved to Pakistan. A monumental administrative and judicial exercise was involved as the revenue records had to be moved both ways and verified. There was less verification with respect to urban assets and a system of witnesses was used. It was not uncommon for witnesses to be dishonest or for the same person to stand witness for the same property for different claimants. Those who were honest fell by the wayside, while the dishonest claimants reaped windfalls. My father owned the largest properties in Panipat – houses, shops, markets, agricultural lands, gardens – but for all his honesty, he came out poorer than some poor relatives in the evacuee property exercise. Others passed off their primitive dwellings as mansions, their mud-plastered houses as brick and concrete structures, their earthen floors as marble floors, their cramped spaces as large rooms and their basic facilities as modern amenities. Partition was a blessing for them and made them rich and large owners of property overnight, which they could never have dreamt of owning in Panipat. My father was unable to claim even a single house. Apparently one had to first occupy and then claim the houses abandoned by Hindus and Sikhs. My father was horrified when this was suggested to him and clung even closer to the barrack in Intelligence School.

While he was unsuccessful in getting a house allotted, my father scoured the agricultural lands around Karachi for months, accompanied by Taqi Ahsan, his dearest friend who hailed from Samana in Patiala State,[6] to file a claim for rural property. Malir, Gharo, Dhabeji, Mirpur Sakro, Sujawal, Thatta, new names, new places. And a whole new world was revealed as we came, for the first time, face to face with rural Sindh. After scores of visits along dust-strewn and unpaved roads and much deliberation, my father settled for evacuee property in Thatta, and he had to throw away some of his pride in dealing with arrogant bureaucrats and local officials. The land, our first tangible link with the soil of Sindh, came in three lots around Thatta town, unconnected with one another. Some of it was occupied by *haris*– a new word for us – who may have rejoiced at the departure of Hindu *waderas*–another new word – but could hardly have celebrated our arrival. They had rightly hoped that freedom would liberate them from generations of denial and miraculously make them owners of the land they cultivated, but it was not to be.

The haris lived in utter poverty and were a handsome lot. Some of the men, like the elderly Khuda Bakhsh, were impressive with their full turbans, draped *ajraks* and upbeat moustache, wearing caps the likes of which we had never seen before. The women wore colourful clothes and worked in the fields but were not visible to strangers. The children were scantily dressed and wore no shoes – my father had told me that the first visible sign of poverty was barefoot children. Some haris were a little better off than others, but their houses were generally made of mud and straw. They shared the land with snakes, including black cobras, and death by snakebite was common. Although they resented our presence, they gradually became accustomed to our frequent visits, just as we got used to their wiles and ways. In their dealings with us, they never abandoned their expression of civility, but beneath their smooth talk and obsequiousness they were smart and steely negotiators.

It was my mother, not my father, who took possession of the land after it was allotted to us. The haris regarded her as the actual landowner and she always conducted the conversation with them. They had dealt with cruel landlords throughout their lives and we soon realised that we, an uprooted urbanised lot, were no match for them and the shrewd local network in which they thrived. My parents had no friends or acquaintances in Thatta and had to start learning about local tribes, customs and linkages. They tried to get the land cultivated and even brought over tillers from the Punjab, but it was a losing game and they had little control over cultivation or revenue from the crops. Although they took a humane view of the haris' poverty and tried to help them as much as possible, they had to get on with their own fractured lives. After my father passed away, my brother Arif, moved by the same compassion, sold some of the land to the haris for a song.

My father probably chose Thatta rather than any other place because of its antiquity and some semblance, however small, to the splendour of the cities he knew in India. In days gone by, Thatta was the seat of learning under flourishing dynasties, including that of the Soomros and between 1593 and 1739, it was part of the Mughal empire. Its economy depended on its vicinity to the Indus; when the river changed course and the delta started silting up, it lost its affluence. It was a rather basic town, with a small market and few facilities. There was a strong Hindu presence and a beautiful temple across the road from the great necropolis at Makli. In the market place there were many Hindu shopkeepers and moneylenders. The inner city was attractive, with charming buildings, but these old structures and alleyways were neglected and many families moved to Karachi in search of livelihood. Arif and I wandered around the monuments dotting the necropolis and under the arches and domes of Shah Jahan's mosque, with its splendid but decaying glazed tiles. The mosque is unique in that it has no minaret. Its 101 domes have been designed in such a way that the call to prayer can be heard from every corner.

Nothing, it seemed, could remove the trauma and suffering of Partition from our lives. The agony was perennial. It was usual in those days, when families got together, to discuss how they were uprooted and pushed out, houses looted, refugee convoys attacked and decimated, women raped and abducted, children slain mercilessly. My parents tried to keep in touch even with distant relatives and brought them over to stay with us for a few days. The conversation always turned towards the details of the gruesome bloodshed of Partition. Somehow these sufferers sought comfort in sharing their loss and distress and their anguish entered the souls of their children.

Chapter 4

Farewell to Panipat

A disturbing dilemma confronted the members of my family, indeed countless families in India, when Partition became a reality. My grandfather (mother's father) Akhtar Hasan (1887–1960) became the head of the family after his elder brother, Latif Hasan, passed away in 1946. He had spent his career in the revenue department and served in many parts of the Punjab such as Kaithal, Hissar, Thanesar, Gurgaon, Ferozepur Jhirka, Riwari, Dabwali – all east of Delhi. After retirement, he settled in Panipat and opened a library in his house which subscribed to newspapers for the benefit of the reading public. He had supported the creation of Pakistan but, unlike my father, he was not willing to abandon the 'graves of his ancestors', as the saying goes in Urdu. He saw no reason to do so because, like many of his generation, he saw no conflict between Pakistan and retaining his roots of hundreds of years. How much he sensed the gathering storm, is not known.

Panipat had not escaped the pressure of the Muslim League's movement for Pakistan. The moving spirit behind the Pakistan movement in Panipat was Iftikhar Ahmad Khan Ansari, who was secretary of the local Muslim League. The president of the League was Maulvi Abdur Rahim. In the days following the announcement of the 3 June Plan to divide India, there were daily processions in the streets of Panipat. The processionists raised the official slogan of the Muslim League: *Quaid-i-Azam ka farman, le kar rahain ge Pakistan.*[1]

How did the Muslims of Panipat view their future in this divided land if, indeed, they gave any thought to the future? Continuing to stay in Panipat was natural because very few foresaw the bloodshed that followed. They may have drawn solace from the fact that their city had a Muslim majority and could, perhaps, be awarded to Pakistan. But this was not a realistic assumption because Panipat tehsil, in which the city was located, had a non-Muslim majority. There is no record of their reasoning or whether, in the fury which then gripped India, they rationally weighed or discussed their options. According to one account, when they marched in processions and chanted pro-Pakistan slogans, they gave no thought at all to their future. Nor were they aware whether their leaders had seriously considered this dilemma.[2] Some people wanted to go to Pakistan for a short spell and return to Panipat.

Others may have reposed faith in the rather ridiculous claim for a corridor between the two wings of Pakistan, hoping that Panipat would find a niche in the corridor. Apart from a passion for Pakistan, the only reason for moving would be economic, for jobs, employment and business, if it was seen as a land of opportunity, as indeed it became for many who were later forced to migrate.

There was also the question of whether Pakistan would survive as an independent state or collapse and be reunited with India. As we now know, this was the winning argument in the acceptance of Partition by the Congress leaders. Long before Mountbatten arrived on the scene, Hindu opinion, including opinion in the Congress, had started coming to terms with the idea of division. After they accepted the 3 June Plan, all the prominent Congress leaders predicted that Partition would be short-lived. A historian can understand their pain. Sardar Patel, the Congress strongman, was among the first to see the logic of this compromise. 'I felt,' he stated, 'that if we did not accept partition, India would be split into many bits and be completely ruined.' He strongly believed 'that those who had seceded today would be disillusioned soon and their union with the rest of India was assured'. The partition, he hoped, 'would remove the poison from the body politic of India'. This, he was sure, 'would result in the seceding areas desiring to reunite with the rest of India', which was one and indivisible.[3] Gandhi, whose words carried the greatest weight with the Indian people, prophesied: 'The Muslim League will ask to come back into Hindustan. They will ask Jawaharlal to come back, and he will take them back.'[4] Years later, Nehru admitted: 'We expected that partition would be temporary, that Pakistan was bound to come back to us.'[5] The people of Panipat read their newspapers and must surely have understood the message in the public doubts expressed by the Congress leaders.

The carnage and bloodshed in the Punjab in the summer of 1947 was the result of the frustration of the Sikh community which found itself divided on both sides of the notional boundary before the award of the Punjab Boundary Commission was announced on 17 August 1947. The Sikhs were the strongest protagonists of the division of the Punjab but were not in an absolute majority in any division or district of the province except in the tehsils of Tarn Taran and Moga. Mountbatten had regretted that, since he was not a 'miracle maker', he had been unable to keep the community together.[6] Immediately after the Lahore Resolution of 1940 was adopted, Jinnah had urged the Sikhs to realise that they would be reduced to 'a drop in the ocean in India' and would be much better off as an influential and honoured community 'in the Muslim homelands'.[7] During the Simla Conference in 1945, he had formally asked them to join hands with the Muslim League but they refused. He told Ispahani, 'The Sikhs are not in their senses. By their unwise attitude they are applying the axe to their own shins.'[8] In the months leading to Partition, the Sikhs started a social and economic boycott of the Muslims. They made arrangements for an exchange of population between the Muslim and non-Muslim majority areas in the province to preserve their community and prepared for a civil war.[9]

Jinnah had offered the Sikh leaders an autonomous Sikh state within Pakistan if the Sikh princely states also acceded to it. This was a fair condition because these princely states were scattered within the boundaries of British Punjab. Many years later, Tara Singh conceded: 'The Quaid-e-Azam had made a categorical offer to him for a Sikh state within Pakistan on the eve of partition. The difference arose when the Sikhs insisted on keeping the right of opting out of Pakistan whenever they wanted to. The Quaid-e-Azam did not accept the condition.'[10]

Jinnah also held discussions with the Maharaja of Patiala, which began in the presence of Mountbatten and lasted well past midnight. He offered, first, a Rajasthan or federation of Sikh princes and second, a separate Sikh state. He was so keen to accommodate the Sikhs that he was willing to let them have their own army. Patiala later wrote:

> Talks started and offers were made by Mr Jinnah for practically everything under the sun, if I would agree to his plan. There were two aspects: one was based on the idea of a Rajasthan, the other one for a separate Sikh State – Punjab minus one or two districts in the south... I was to be head of the Sikh State same as in Patiala. The Sikhs would have their army and so on...

But the influential Sikh leaders, Tara Singh and Giani Kartar Singh, with whom Patiala discussed the proposal, turned it down. Although he found the offer 'attractive', Patiala did not view it as practical 'and neither could I, in the mood that I was in, change my convictions'.[11] Two days later, Jinnah invited Patiala to tea for further discussion at his residence, where they were joined by Liaquat Ali Khan, but they parted without Patiala's agreement to the offer. Apart from the proverbial hatred of the Sikhs for the Muslims, the absence of a single accredited Sikh leader made it difficult to negotiate with them. They also distrusted the Muslims because of riots in north-western Punjab in March 1947 and were anxious not to lose the support of the Congress.

As early as 10 July 1947, Jinnah had warned that the Sikh leaders were reported to be inciting their followers to offer active resistance to unfavourable decisions, preparations for resistance were being made, and oaths to resist were being taken. Mountbatten had replied that no responsible government would tolerate such resistance and the government's superior armed forces, aeroplanes, tanks and artillery, would inflict severe losses upon those who would be armed only with rifles and out of date weapons.[12] The Governor of the Punjab, Evan Jenkins, had conveyed Giani Kartar Singh's ultimatum to Mountbatten that the Sikhs would not accept the notional boundaries and would go for 'guerrilla warfare' after 15 August.[13] And all this, before Cyril Radcliffe, chairman of the boundary commissions had even arrived in India.

That the Sikhs would create trouble was obvious to all discerning people. According to one intelligence report, dated 28 July 1947:

> Sikh leaders have made no secret of their designs to annex by force the areas that the Boundary Commission would deny them. Master Tara Singh, Giani Kartar Singh, S. Swaran Singh and S. Ujjal Singh have made a number of speeches one after the other as well as simultaneously declaring that Sikhs will not rest content till their solidarity is assured, their sacred shrines and share of colonial areas restored to them. They have by these speeches tried to place premium on their demand to fix the River Chenab as the demarcation line and thus affect the decision of the Boundary Commission … the Sikh leadership is giving out to the Sikh masses a huge estimate of the military support which the party is expecting to receive from Sikh Princes in the event of turmoil to safeguard the Panth. And among the safeguards unluckily are included invasions, annexations, and exercise of retaliation and finally a Sikh homeland without regard to even the rest of India.[14]

On 5 August, a CID officer from the Punjab revealed to Jinnah, Mountbatten, Liaquat Ali Khan and Sardar Patel, the involvement of Tara Singh with bomb makers and the plan to blow up a Pakistan Special train with remote control, set it on fire and shoot the occupants. Completely set on taking revenge on the Muslims, he had started collecting arms through Sikh army officers and dumping them in the Sikh states, and the Raja of Faridkot had actually helped with transport.[15] Tara Singh had also said that Jinnah should be killed in the ceremonies at Karachi on 15 August. Although Jinnah urged that the more extreme Sikh leaders should be arrested at once, Mountbatten and Jenkins were unable to arrive at a suitable time to ever make these arrests. Jinnah, however, judged his opponents well, stating that Sardar Patel would welcome trouble from the Sikhs in Central Punjab.[16]

The Sikhs' distrust of the Muslims later emerged in full force as they pleaded and planned for a boundary along the Chenab. Their arguments before the Punjab Boundary Commission meshed references to the glory of Ranjit Singh's rule in the Punjab with their ancient feud with the Muslims and the humiliation and torture suffered by their gurus at the hands of the

Mughal emperors.[17] The Congress leaders argued, on the other hand, that the death and destruction which descended on the Punjab had its roots in the attacks on Sikhs and Hindus in March 1947 which had led to their exodus from Multan, Rawalpindi and Attock districts. But that the Sikh revenge was carefully planned and was supported and encouraged by the rulers of the Sikh states of Patiala, Nabha, Faridkot and Kapurthala has been well documented in all historical records.[18]

We can trace the blood-soaked events of that time through intelligence reports, recollections, and the papers of the commander of the Punjab Boundary Force, Major General Thomas Wynford Rees. The work of the Force, which was given an impossible task, has not received due recognition. It was set up on 1 August 1947 and disbanded, following criticism by all parties, on midnight between 1 and 2 September 1947. Rees had joined the Indian army in 1916 and seen active service during the First World War in Mesopotamia, Egypt, Palestine and Syria. He was much decorated and in later service in India and Burma, he was described by his superiors as an excellent soldier and exceptional officer. He was fluent in Hindustani and was 'admirable' and 'outstanding' with the troops. Rees was commanding officer of the famous Kajuri Force which blockaded and punished the Afridi tribesmen in October 1939 in Waziristan, during his tour of duty in the Frontier Province. During the Second World War, he fell out with his superiors in the Middle East and was sent back to India, but saw active service against the Japanese in Burma.[19] Throughout, he retained the respect and trust of Field Marshal Claude Auchinleck, commander-in-chief of the Indian army, who became the supreme commander of all forces in India and Pakistan after Partition until November 1947.

The Punjab Boundary Force was established in aid of civil power, as a neutral force, to maintain law and order in the 'disputed area' of the Punjab, consisting of twelve districts and its units comprised Muslims and non-Muslims drawn from troops about to be allotted to India and Pakistan. All British troops were moved out. It covered an area of 37,500 square miles, larger than Ireland, and a population of 14½ million 'tough pugnacious Punjabis, given to a high rate of crime in ordinary times' in the districts of Lahore, Amritsar, Gurdaspur, Sialkot, Sheikhupura, Ferozepur, Hoshiarpur, Jullundur, Montgomery, Lyallpur, Ludhiana and Gujranwala.[20] It operated along the borders of the Sikh states but not within their territory. Panipat did not fall within the disputed area but, as we shall see, it was ravaged by the spillover of bloodshed in that area.

Rees recalled the 'waves of recurring and increasing violence' and arson in May, June and July, centring around the cities of Lahore and Amritsar, where the communal trouble actually began, and in the rural areas of Amritsar district, where mass violence by Sikh *jathas* against Muslim villagers started, until 'in August the turbulence and lawlessness increased in full measure'. The police had become completely partisan, and before 15 August all the Muslim police in East Punjab had been disarmed, which Rees considered one of the worst calamities. (70–80 per cent of the Punjab police were Muslim.) It was impossible to stop the violence 'in the narrow lanes of an Indian city' and soon attacks on gurdwaras, shrines and temples started. The Sikh jathas 'were well organised and led' and 'their considerable number of horsemen were also very skilfully organised'. They were 'skilled in the use of modern lethal weapons'. In the early stages, the Muslims never reached this scale of organisation. As the slaughter by the Sikhs spread from their stronghold in the Manjha to the Amritsar, Lahore, Gurdaspur, Hoshiarpur, Jullundur and Ludhiana districts, Rees noted that: 'Throughout the killing was pre-medieval in its ferocity – neither age nor sex was spared, mothers with their babies in their arms were cut down, speared or shot, and the Sikhs cried "Rawapindi" as they struck home. Both sides were equally merciless.' The 'magic date' of 15 August was a 'shocking day' in Lahore and Amritsar on which 'the gloves were off with a vengeance'. The publication of the boundary award on 17 August 1947 'added fuel to the flames'. Large gangs were aboard which could swell up to thousands, and then melt away. And in Amritsar city, 'the nights were a nightmare of panic, with uncontrolled firing of weapons, much of it by the Police.'

In the last week of his command, Rees found 'no real abatement' though later there were, ironically, signs of 'satiety' and 'fatigue'. The trouble had mounted in West Punjab, especially in Sheikhupura, which was almost completely gutted, and in Montgomery and Sialkot districts. There was continued 'terror, abductions and attacks throughout the rural districts…slaughter, abductions and arson were rampant' as were forcible conversions.[21] The Sikh leaders had started raising new suicide forces, Shahidi Dals, and in their campaign, the Sikhs undoubtedly had the support of the Rashtriya Swayamsevak Sangh, 'the private army of the Hindu community'.[22]

Rees has left a detailed record of the tactics and armaments used by the 'law breakers'. From furtive attacks in city lanes to planned attacks on villages, trains and convoys; weapons ranging from primitive axe, spear and club to most modern Tommy gun, light machine gun and grenades were used. In Lahore and Amritsar, there was nothing to choose between the two sides. In the rural areas of East Punjab, the Sikh jathas were the first to take the field and as opposed to their enemies 'were thoroughly organised and had prepared for such events as took place; indeed, they have since admitted this'. They were fed by villagers and could swell from 5,000 to 6,000 in number, attack villages, convoys and trains and then disperse to their homes. They had recognised leaders and messengers travelling on foot, horseback, motor transport and trains who issued orders to the gangs, and members of the former Indian National Army were present both as leaders and among the rank and file. The Sikhs also used shields, armour, fire arrows and suitcase bombs and had the added advantage of carrying *kirpans* by law. Apart from organised attacks on villages, their favoured method of attack was ambushing trains and marching columns of refugees, leading to stampedes and sheer panic.[23]

Rees' account is corroborated by the report of Brigadier Ayub Khan, his liaison officer.[24] 'To put it mildly,' he wrote, 'the Muslims were caught napping.' Large Shahidi jathas of Sikhs 'attacked isolated Muslim villages and Muslim pockets throughout these areas'. The procedure was:

> for a Jatha to make demonstration with bombs and fire-arms from one side of a village to drive the people on to another party waiting on the other side of the village armed with spears and swords. They then saw to it that every man, woman and child was massacred. The dead bodies were then collected and piled in heaps of 50 to 100 and then set on fire or covered over with earth so as to obliterate any trace of evidence... Having finished with the butchery, the Jathas would then loot the place and set it on fire. These Jathas and their targets were very carefully controlled by a central organisation run by the Sikh personnel of the I.N.A.[25]

E. de V. Moss, Pakistan's Commissioner for Refugees and Evacuees wrote in the same vein that the jathas,

> first of all drive out or kill all the inhabitants. They then put pickets round the village and send in a small specially trained party to collect the valuable loot. This looted property is then loaded into one or more motor lorries which are attached to the Jatha. Then the rank and file are told to enter the village and take what is left over. After that the village is burnt.[26]

Ambush, murder, arson, loot and rape went together. It was a package deal.

Rees described the carnage as a 'civil war of very great ferocity', planned and organised by the Sikhs, the 'terror and savagery' of which was 'really pre-medieval'. Flying over his 'area' and approaching Amritsar in an aircraft, Rees wrote in despair as early as 7 August about the Sikh dilemma: 'The Sikhs, in fact, are in a hole; and they realize their leaders have let them down and not been far-sighted enough.' Earlier, they had the chance of opting for a united Punjab in Pakistan. With their 5 million,

> united, of the same religion, and of considerable business and artisan skill compared with the Punjabi Mohammedan, they would have been a

power in the land in a united Punjab. But, No! They have been very noisy and truculent; and, by competent judges, are considered to have provoked the Punjabi Mohommedans into the savage massacre of Sikhs... in the northern and western Punjab in March, April, May of this year...The Sikhs realize they have backed the wrong horse and are bound to be split wherever the Boundary is to run...their leaders did not have the prescience to foresee such a situation...[27]

At an early stage during the negotiations for the transfer of power, Jinnah had raised the issue of a transfer of population, but it was not seriously considered by the other leaders. With forced evictions and hundreds of thousands on the march, the safeguarding and transporting of refugees and the protection of refugee camps became the responsibility of the Punjab Boundary Force. Neither government wanted this transfer of population or felt that it could deal with the scale of the movement. But what was considered administratively impossible stared them in the face. A meeting of leaders was held at Ambala on 17 August 1947, which was attended by Liaquat Ali Khan, Nehru and Baldev Singh. Earlier that day, the boundary awards had been shown by Mountbatten to the leaders. All present emphasised the need for a quick and orderly transfer of refugees. Nehru ingenuously enquired whether 50 to 100 lorries could not complete the present task within a few days. Rees, apprehensive about the dreadful carnage, which would continue into September and beyond, estimated equally naively that ten days would be required to deal with the immediate problem.[28]

A few days later, at a conference held in Jullundur on 22 August 1947, Chandulal Trivedi, governor of East Punjab, argued that the population could not be transferred and the aim should be to restore law and order and 'we do want our Muslims to stay'. Mumtaz Daultana, the premier of West Punjab, on the other hand inquired that if the policy was, as it seemed, to force out the other community, could it not be done peacefully? The conference adopted a policy to discourage migration and set up a few big refugee camps, not penny pockets which the military could not protect.[29] The Chief Liaison Officer, West Punjab wrote, however, that the East Punjab government was unwilling to declare concentrations of Muslims as refugees because they did not want to feed them, protect them, or provide medical care. His detailed report is full of references to death by starvation, lack of food, and particularly lack of water.[30]

E. de V. Moss had given a list of twelve concentrations of Muslims, numbering about 600,000 souls who were:

desperately anxious to leave for Pakistan by any means possible but are prevented from doing so by the Sikhs who are systematically destroying them. This is in great contrast to the Sikh jathas on our side which are well armed and are able to move with comparative freedom. The Muslims on the other hand are practically unarmed and are at the mercy of the Sikhs.[31]

In the end, it was the realisation that continued attacks on Muslims in East Punjab would lead to the massacre of non-Muslims in West Punjab that compelled the Sikh leaders to call off violence. Rees wrote to Auchinleck on 21 August 1947 that, 'unless the killings in the South & East Punjab are stopped, there is the very real danger, of which you are aware, of Mohommaden retaliation on Sikhs and Hindus in Western Punjab...In conclusion, the real necessity is for the East Punjab massacres to be stopped.' On Rees' insistence, Tara Singh embarked on a mission of peace to Jullundur, Ferozepur, Ludhiana and Ambala, and Giani Kartar Singh undertook to do his best to explain this to the Sikhs in the east.[32] He noted that the country from Montgomery to Sialkot was simmering, and if the Sikh killings of Muslims in East Punjab did not stop, his troops in West Punjab may not be able to stop the massacre of Sikhs and Hindus. Nor could he even attempt to maintain his troops as a neutral force.[33]

The refugees were moved and evacuated in trains, foot convoys, motor transport and by air. Also, the Pakistan Specials had to transport 16,000 personnel and 16,000 tons of goods of the Pakistan government. Trains were the most vulnerable targets as revealed by situation reports. 'Few trains, if any, have been lucky to reach Pakistan unscathed,' wrote the Chief Liaison Officer of West Punjab.[34] Derailments were common and each train could be stopped several times and the wounded and killed left by the roadside. The movement was conducted until the end of 1947. Between the end of August and the first week of November, it was estimated that 673 refugee trains carried over 2.3 million people across the border on both sides.[35] Movement by trains was the most risky, especially those which ran through the territory of the Sikh states. They were usually stopped and ambushed near Doraha in Patiala.

Foot convoys were the most 'profitable' ways of moving the refugees. Each convoy could consist of more than 100,000 people and could be several miles long. The Muslim and non-Muslim foot convoys had to be kept at a safe distance from one another and separate routes were designated for them, but it was difficult to prevent clashes because of the small number of bridges over waterways. One report even mentions *tonga* convoys. However, hundreds of thousands were still stranded and by 22 September there were 60,000 Muslims in Karnal district alone which, presumably, included the Panipat Muslims.[36]

Abul Kalam Azad has written that it would not be unfair to say that Sardar Patel was the 'founder of Indian partition' and was convinced that Pakistan was not viable and could not last.[37] But one must turn to Nehru, whose inflexible and patronising attitude has also been held by many to have contributed to the division of India, for the philosophic angle to this tragedy. History (in India), he said, has been one of assimilation and 'the tragedy which is happening today is that it seems to go against the whole trend of Indian history. We are not quite sure that this is a permanent change-over. We cannot easily think in terms of their wanting to come back...' Even if the exchange of population had been organised and regulated, it would have been a 'terrific problem'. He referred to the exchange of population which took place between Turkey and Greece under the League of Nations which 'took a lot of organisation and time'.[38]

Rees estimated that about 6 million refugees were involved in the movement and evacuating them became the most difficult of all tasks. He has spelt out clearly the magnitude of the responsibility with which he was entrusted. With a touch of humour, he wrote:

Collection, feeding, sanitation, sick and wounded, maternity, care of lost and orphaned children, widowed women, movement of sick and young and aged. Movement by rail, MT [Motor Transport] and march route. The numbers involved were so vast that rail and MT at best could only nibble at the task, and huge marching caravans or foot convoys were the only solution for big numbers with chickens, horses, cattle, bullock carts, camels with grandmothers perched on top in traditional fashion.[39]

Judging from official and private accounts, one would think that the entire male Sikh community was mobilised and on the rampage in the Punjab in the summer of 1947. The Sikh states and the areas of the Punjab bordering on these states suffered the full fury of the Sikh revenge. There is no doubt that murder, arson, loot, abductions and rape were committed with the encouragement of the Sikh rulers of these states, led by Patiala. This is borne out not only by intelligence reports but also by accounts of ordinary people, influential citizens and Muslim officials who had served in these states as deputy commissioners, judges, engineers, and police officers. Their narratives of sheer terror and search for safety make gruesome reading. Particularly vulnerable were the trains passing through Patiala in which all the young women could be abducted and every remaining passenger slain. There are painful references in almost every account, as also in those from East Punjab, of public rapes and processions and parading of thousands of naked women and girls who were abducted or taken away.[40] My intention is not to deny the ferocity of the backlash in West Punjab which has been well recorded.[41]

Looking back now, after seventy-three years, the lack of wisdom shown by the rulers of the Sikh states which so dispossessed and distressed their community, does not fail to surprise. Yadavindra Singh of Patiala, GBE, the most important Sikh ruler, later rose to the rank of lieutenant general and became a leading Indian diplomat. But he forgot in 1947 that Patiala State was co-founded by a Muslim, Lakhna Kasana, from whose family hailed a series of renowned military commanders. Patiala's ancestors had actually fought against Ranjit Singh during the first Anglo-Sikh War of 1845–6 and the title of maharaja was bestowed upon them by Ahmad Shah Abdali, alongside whom they had also fought against the other Sikhs. The rulers of Nabha and Jind had a common ancestry with Patiala, and all these states, including Kapurthala and Faridkot, had remained loyal to the British during the uprising of 1857. In fact, Faridkot had a Muslim majority and a strong spiritual and cultural link with the Muslim faith because Faridkot city was named after Baba Fariduddin Ganjshakar of Pakpattan (1173–1266), who is considered the first Punjabi poet and whose verses form part of their sacred Guru Granth Sahib. With such a past in history and war, it was ironic that they should have wanted to revive the glory of the kingdom of Ranjit Singh whom they had betrayed. It was not only Jinnah who believed that Sardar Patel would welcome trouble in Central Punjab. Unknown to Jinnah, Khan Bahadur Abdul Aziz, chief judge of Jind State wrote: 'It cannot be denied for a moment that there was a manifest conspiracy between the Akali leaders, the rulers of Patiala, Nabha and Faridkot States supported by Mr Patel, the Deputy Prime Minister of the Indian Union.'[42]

In that pitiful movement of humanity, numbers and figures had lost all meaning. The summer heat was sizzling even in the shade, floods and rains washed away bridges and embankments. Railway tracks were threatened and sank and stations were closed as the staff were killed or deserted their posts. There was a shortage of motor transport, petrol, food and water. Cholera broke out in many camps. Wells were poisoned and were stuffed with the bodies of women who had jumped into them to avoid capture. Canals were flooded to cut off refugees and were afloat with corpses. Some refugees set fire to their homes and possessions before they moved, some killed their wives and children. Forced conversions did not save those who were left behind. The rape, abduction and horrific mutilation of women and girls for its sheer perversion and brutality as a weapon of communal war, beggars description. War, violence and fate go together. As Timur wrote after he destroyed Delhi in 1398: 'The pen of fate had written down this destiny for the people of this city.'[43]

After the Punjab Boundary Force was disbanded from 1–2 September, the Pakistan and India governments took over full military responsibility for law and order. They decided to take drastic action against those disrupting law and order, capturing and putting armed gangs in concentration camps and shooting criminals on sight. Both governments agreed to take urgent steps 'to look after the unfortunate refugees...to feed the refugees and to provide the necessities of life'. Their camps would be protected by military guards belonging to their own community. Illegal seizures of property would not be recognised and the property of the refugees would be restored to their 'rightful owners'. Both governments were determined to rid the Punjab of the nightmare of 'horror and destruction' in which men had 'become worse than beasts' and murdered 'with savage brutality'.[44]

*   *   *

What was the impact of these events on the Muslims of Panipat who did not want to migrate but were compelled to abandon the 'land of their ancestors'? Their story can be best told in the words of my grandfather, Akhtar Hasan. His narrative stretches from the beginning of September to November 1947, when he actually left Panipat.[45] During most of this time, a curfew was imposed in the city which, according to him, was enforced only on the Muslims; non-Muslims 'enjoyed complete freedom of movement at all hours'. My grandfather and other leading citizens made consistent efforts to convince the administration of their desire to maintain peace and their loyalty to the Indian government. Peace parleys were held, which he described as a 'smoke-screen' because the 'real policy carefully chalked out before-hand and followed according to plan was the expulsion of the Muslim populace'. He was told on two occasions to be ready to go to Thanesar for consultation on the Panipat situation with K.C. Neogi, India's minister for relief and rehabilitation, and Gopalaswami Ayyangar, a cabinet member, but these visits did not materialise.

The military had been sent to Panipat as a result of Hindu representations to the deputy commissioner at Karnal. In the first week of September, all the Muslims without exception had to surrender their arms to the police on the orders of the deputy commissioner. However, not a single Hindu was required to give up his arms. This was the universal pattern in all the cities of East Punjab: disarming the police, collecting all licensed arms from the Muslim population and imposition of curfews during which non-Muslims could move around freely and indulge in loot and plunder.[46]

Violence hit Panipat in the first week of September when Muslim railway passengers were killed and thrown out of trains and three or four dead bodies of Muslims were found daily along the railway track in the vicinity of the city. Muslims pushed out from neighbouring villages, in this case from the Syed villages of Barsat and Faridpur, started coming to Panipat for refuge in large numbers, much as Muslims had done during the uprising of 1857. Many were murdered, almost all were looted by the police and 'shamefully treated'. Initially a curfew was clamped down to prevent their entry: 'The way their women-folk were treated was so inhuman and shameful' said my grandfather, 'that on no account could I describe it.' Their relatives in Panipat were not allowed to take them home and to the beat of the drum – *jo rahega Sarkar ka chor hoga aur jute se pitega* (whoever stays back will be considered a thief by the government and will be beaten with shoes) –they were lodged in the compound of Hali Muslim High School, the institution which was the pride of the Panipat Muslims. A Hindu sub-judge was given charge of the camp with the powers of a first-class magistrate. Their relatives and friends started sending them food, but this was denied to them and the September floods drowned the camp in water, making it difficult to visit them. The 'crowning misery' according to my grandfather, was the way young women were treated by 'the military men who let slip no opportunity to ravish them. One young woman sent out an appeal for poison to put an end to her miserable existence.'

Earlier, according to one report, on account of murder, arson and loot by Hindu Jats which was organised by Sub Inspector Baij Nath of Panipat city in the countryside, the Muslims had fled in thousands to Panipat. The men were butchered while the 'women were made to march to Panipat, stripped naked to the skin and goaded with rifle butts by the accompanying Hindu and Sikh constables'. They were lodged in Hali Muslim High School along with the refugees from Barsat and Faridpur. In the first week of September, when my grandfather's story begins, they were evicted by the military and forced to march to Karnal on foot, many dying on the wayside. Their belongings in the camp were looted by Baij Nath and the Hindu policemen.[47] It should be noted here that traditionally, under British rule, the head of the police in Panipat city had always been a Muslim. Baij Nath was the first non-Muslim station house officer. He hailed from Jhelum and it was said that his family had been murdered in West Punjab. According to Lieutenant Colonel Isaacs, who commanded a unit at Panipat, Baij Nath 'passed on to the jathas any information of value to them'.[48]

On 7 September, surgeon Mohammad Sadiq shifted for safety to one of our houses in Baghcha. Cholera struck the camp in October. By then, all the doctors had left Panipat; the only one who stayed behind was Sughra Begum (not my mother). She also took refuge in Baghcha but had no access to medical supplies or cholera vaccine. The death toll mounted and the dead were thrown away or buried without any shroud or ritual. One day, my grandfather saw four burqa-clad women bringing a dead body to the imambara. Burying the dead became a colossal problem. No grave diggers were available. Because the commander of the military garrison refused to let the refugees shift to another site, they infiltrated the city, bringing cholera along with them. But no medical help or relief was provided by the municipality.

Gradually, the economic noose began to tighten around the Muslim community. Their cotton rations were stopped and Muslim depot holders of food grains had to close down business because of lack of fresh supplies. Except in rare cases, Hindu depot holders refused to sell to the Muslims and black marketing became rife. Food was bought by the Muslims 'at fabulous prices from Hindu dealers' and regularly obtained 'through chamars and sweepers'. By the second week of October, the Muslims started selling their belongings in the bazaar, although they fetched only one-fifth of their value. But an official decree was issued forbidding the sale or purchase of articles and the police nabbed both seller and purchaser, releasing the goods to the buyer and pocketing the sale price themselves. The free sale of firewood was forbidden and permits were issued for firewood only to the Hindus, compelling the Muslims to burn their household furniture for fuel. No fodder was available in the city. The tehsildar had started leasing the land owned and cultivated by the Muslims to Hindu and Sikh refugees. A great number of Muslims in the rural areas around Panipat had been put to death or had converted to Hinduism. My grandfather saw the Muslims who had converted to Hinduism being brought to the tehsil to declare their new religion, asking to be allowed to retain possession of their land. But even after becoming converts, 'these unfortunate and God-forsaken erstwhile Muslims were not spared.' As far as he knew, there were no Muslims left in the rural areas except in the neighbouring villages of Noorwala and Bichpari in the suburbs of Panipat.

My grandfather stated that there was a general slaughter of the Muslims in November. The first week of November saw three days of deafening firing and intense and free looting. It started when the police themselves plundered the belongings of evacuees leaving Panipat in a motor convoy. This was 'a signal for a general loot in the city' and mohallas Kotla Sher Afgan Khan, Naya Bans, Chaund, Dabgaran, Sarwar and Shahwilayat were looted under police and military cover and totally cleared of Muslims. The dead and wounded just lay where they fell and there was no food for the living. On 5 November, firing started again and Baij Nath, who was the organising villain so far as the Muslims were concerned, informed my grandfather that except for mohallas Makhdumzadgan and Afghanan, the Muslims were to be evacuated from the entire city and they should get ready to leave. My grandfather mounted the roof of his house and shouted in all four directions that the residents of Mohalla Ansar should prepare to move out. Terror-stricken, 'they sallied forth with the little they could carry on their persons, leaving their ancestral homes and their life-long accumulations.' He mentions my father's house, among others, overflowing with valuable furniture and household effects. The Sikh deputy superintendent of police took the keys of the houses. My grandfather lamented that the most prized possessions of his family members were their libraries which contained in boxfuls valuable manuscripts and royal decrees which could not be had at any price. In fact, thousands of books and manuscripts were either carried away, burnt by the mob or used as wrapping paper by the shops in the bazaars. Some manuscripts were said to have found their way to Aligarh.

My grandfather's statement, unfortunately, ends here and we are deprived of what he encountered after he and his relatives and friends were moved to a camp. Nor do we know anything about their suffering during the journey to Pakistan. It is reported that, on 5 November, all the Muslims of Panipat were ordered to move to mohallas Makhdumzadgan and Afghanan and the rest of the city was evacuated. Actually, they were first moved to a temporary camp outside the historic Salarganj Gate. As he left his home, my grandfather carried only two boxes full of documents on his head. His Hindu neighbours called out to him, enquiring when he would come back. To some of them he replied more in anguish than in jest that very soon he would return, like Mahmud Ghaznavi, sword in hand.[49] He reached Lahore in the last week of November 1947. Earlier, he had sent some of his children to Lahore, believing that they could return after conditions improved in Panipat. The convoy in which they travelled passed through Ambala, Ludhiana and Jullundur and was escorted by one Captain Bukhari. The trucks in the convoy drove along the edges of the fields, leaving the roads free for use by the foot convoys.

According to one estimate, two-thirds of the Muslim population of Karnal district had been murdered.[50] But the Muslims of Panipat were unwilling to leave the land they had nurtured with their sweat and blood and tried desperately to keep their homes and save their lives. Telegraphic messages of loyalty and appeals for help to Nehru, East Punjab minister Lehri Singh and Abul Kalam Azad had evoked no response. The situation in Panipat came into focus when Liaquat Ali Khan's message was broadcast in the news on 12 October 1947, demanding an inquiry into the order of the deputy commissioner, Karnal, for the evacuation of all Muslims from Panipat within forty-eight hours. Panipat came into the limelight also when Gandhi visited the city.

Rajmohan Gandhi writes in his grandfather's biography that Gandhi first visited Panipat on 10 November 1947 and failed 'in a bid to persuade Muslims in Panipat, sixty miles north of Delhi, not to migrate to Pakistan'.[51] While not doubting the nobility of Gandhi's gesture, how could the Muslims have possibly been persuaded to stay? Where could they have lived? They had been evicted from their homes on 5 November, which were now occupied by others, and their possessions and valuables had been looted. They were lodged in a camp and had they opted to remain, they feared they would be massacred by the angry non-Muslim refugees in the city, with the connivance and help of the local administration.

Gandhi held a big meeting near Bu Ali Shah's shrine. He urged the Muslims not to leave Panipat, which he wanted to make into a model of reconciliation. By then, the Muslims had lost everything and my grandfather and other leading citizens said it was too late. If Gandhi really wanted to help them, could he arrange safe passage for them to Pakistan? However, Rajmohan Gandhi writes that some Muslims told Gandhi they would stay if they were assured protection, although the agreement to transfer minorities between India and Pakistan had already been made. On 22 November, Gandhi wanted to shift to Panipat to encourage the Muslims to stay. But Nehru advised against this move.[52]

Gandhi came to Panipat again on 2 December. By then, arrangements had been made for the departure of the Muslims. He told them:

> If...you want to go of your own will, no one can stop you. But you will never hear Gandhi utter the words that you should leave India. Gandhi can only tell you that you should stay, for India is your home. And if your brethren should kill you, you should bravely meet death.[53]

Unfortunately for Gandhi, nobody wanted to get killed or meet death bravely.

Here we can continue the story in the words of Khwaja Rafat Ali.[54] His father, Khwaja Nemat Ali, 70 years old, who was my father's maternal uncle, was arrested along with other leading citizens under the Public Safety Ordinance and lodged in prison in Karnal on 7 September 1947. This was done at the instance of Lala Khem Chand, the president of the local Congress Party. My father received a telegram from Panipat about his uncle's arrest – and was it not bizarre that, in spite of so much disorder and distress, the telegraph system was still working? Like others in Panipat, Rafat Ali attributed much of the harassment of the Muslims to Baij Nath who became notorious for corruption and for maintaining a 'torture centre' in the local cinema. Rafat Ali was also hauled up by the police. He used to visit his father in the prison in Karnal every week, the meeting time being Thursdays, at 11 a.m. He sat on the Grand Trunk Road on Tuesday evenings and waited for a Muslim convoy from Delhi to pass by, so that he could join it and reach Karnal in time to meet his father.

Rafat Ali recalled that the people of Panipat were disturbed by rumours that the city would be attacked and sought a way to escape, but they had nowhere to go. Some of them persuaded young Rafat Ali to go to Delhi to meet Ghulam Saiyidain and request him to ask Gandhi to intervene and save the Panipat Muslims. Saiyidain and his family members were ardent Congress followers and he was considered close to Nehru. He had safely evacuated his entire family from Panipat. Rafat Ali was in a quandary. How would he ever manage to reach Delhi safely? Since taking the local bus was tantamount to inviting death, he decided to leave on his horse.

At 2 a.m. one day, he rode on his horse towards the Jumna and reached its banks before dawn. He was afraid of drowning but feared that if he delayed his journey, he would be spotted as a Muslim and get killed. So he strapped his weapon to his back, put his arms around the neck of the horse and plunged into the river. The horse walked in the water for some time and started wading when the river became deep. On reaching the other bank, he looked for a landing site because the embankments were ten feet high. After he reached the top, he dried his horse and rode to a relative's house in Kairana. Leaving his horse behind, he took a tonga to Shamli railway station from where he boarded the train to Delhi. When he arrived at Saiyidain's house in Delhi, he narrated the plight of the Panipat Muslims. Saiyidain called Nehru and it was decided that Gandhi would visit Panipat two days later. Rafat Ali returned to Panipat the same night, plunging his horse into the now familiar Jumna, to whose life-giving waters he would soon bid farewell forever.

After they were compelled to abandon their homes, lodged first near Salarganj Gate and later in Mohalla Makhdumzadgan which was declared a camp, the Muslim families started looking for ways to go to Pakistan, but how and by what means? The convoys transporting Muslims from Panipat to Pakistan were spoken for and carried lists of family members and other individuals who could travel in them. However, sometimes they took along a few other passengers. Rafat Ali's father, still in prison in Karnal, advised him to leave for Pakistan. The deputy commissioner and station house officer had assured him that he would be transferred to Ambala prison from where it would be easier for him to reach Pakistan. Rafat Ali finally found a place in a convoy on the roof of a bus, with the permission of the other passengers. Before the bus moved, Lala Jagannath and his sons who were Rafat's friends, pleaded with him not to leave, promising to look after him and protect him. But Rafat Ali sadly replied: 'Lalaji, let me go, I have nothing left to hold me here.'

There were six to seven buses in the convoy belonging to a company which plied between Lahore and Vehari. Rafat Ali remembered the number of the bus in which he rode. The buses gathered at the old fort in Panipat from where the convoy started. The women and children sat inside the buses, the men on the roofs. They travelled on the Grand Trunk Road and were escorted by Muslim soldiers in two trucks, one at the head of the convoy, the other at the back. Each truck held about ten soldiers, including officers. The buses did not ply at night. On the way, Rafat Ali saw many dead bodies, with animals feeding upon them but, as he said, the convoy just moved on. Because some wells on the way were poisoned, the soldiers provided water to the passengers, which ran out at Jullundur. They were able to find milk for the children by stopping milk sellers cycling around the streets of Jullunder. The journey took four days. Rafat Ali's father was sent from Karnal to Ambala prison and then to Lahore when prisoners were exchanged in November 1947.

We can continue the story further through the recollections of my cousin, Wasiq Hasan, who served in the Royal Indian Navy from 1942–6.[55] He hated the British and their occupation of India and had scant respect for his British officers. He joined the naval mutiny of 1946 which he considered clearly as a nationalist revolt. The mutineers – if they can be so described, instead of freedom fighters – did not find many friends among the Indian leaders. After the mutineers were rebuffed by Patel, some Muslim officers decided to call on Jinnah at his residence in Bombay. Jinnah came out to meet them as soon as they arrived. Addressing them he said crisply: 'India wants to achieve freedom by constitutional means, not by killings. Go back to your ships.' When Wasiq Hasan heard that his arrest had been ordered, he fled to Panipat. His release order from the navy came three months later. By then, he had started a private business of his own in the city.

In July–August 1947, trouble started in Panipat. Ghulam Saiyidain had sent a truck to carry his family members to Delhi and Wasiq found a place in this truck. In old Delhi, he stayed in the Bara Dawakhana which had been established decades earlier by Dada Sibtain. One evening, along with his relative Tasawwur Ali, he went to New Delhi to meet Nehru. That evening the queue was very long and, in spite of waiting the whole night, they could not meet Nehru. He would come out of his house at 7 a.m. and after talking to the refugees for one hour, he would leave for his office. Next day, they went again to Nehru's residence and because Wasiq Hasan was wearing the battle dress of the navy, he was easily spotted. They described to Nehru the plight of the Panipat Muslims and he replied that was the reason why Gandhi had gone to Panipat, but the *sharnarthis* had pelted him with stones. He had now sent Lehri Singh to Panipat. Wasiq protested that Lehri Singh was a *pucca Jat*.

Instead of helping, he was bound to encourage more trouble. Nehru said that he could do no more, and it was a pity that he had no control either on the army or on the police. He was prime minister only in name.

On the way out of Nehru's house, some Sikhs started following Wasiq and Tasawwur. To escape, they entered a restaurant in Connaught Place which Wasiq used to frequent, but in which a Sikh was now running a *lassi* shop. Because Wasiq had lived in Campellpur when his father served there, he knew that lassi was sweetened not with sugar but with *peras* and he ordered peras for the two of them. For the life of him, the terrified Tasawwur could not drink that pera-filled lassi. Some Sikhs in the shop started questioning them and they pretended that Tasawwur was deaf and dumb. Wasiq told the Sikhs in Punjabi that he too was a refugee from Campellpur. A few days later, he contacted the Pakistan High Commission in Delhi and got a seat on a chartered flight to Quetta. From Quetta, he boarded the train to Lahore where he joined the Military Evacuation Organisation (MEO), which took Sikhs and Hindus to India and brought back Muslims to Pakistan.

In the search for his relatives, he went to Karnal where his uncle and other prominent citizens of Panipat were being held in prison. The deputy commissioner in Karnal told him he would free his uncle on one condition. He had written a book in Hindi, *Bal Gita*, which had been sent to Lahore for printing. If Wasiq could bring all the copies of that book to Karnal, his uncle would be set free. Wasiq travelled back to Lahore and tracked down the press whose ownership had, by now, been assumed by the former peon who sold the books by weight. Since *Bal Gita* was written in Devanagri, with great difficulty a Hindi-reading person was found who identified the book after many days. So *Bal Gita* was weighed, paid for, packed in sacks and transported to Karnal in the next trip. The deputy commissioner kept his word and released Wasiq's uncle, Iftikhar Ahmad Khan Ansari, and other prisoners. On the way back, they stopped at night in a camp of Pakistan army *jawans* in Panipat, sadly mourning their fate: their own houses, only a stone's throw away, were occupied by others while they were spending the night in tents in a military camp.

In the MEO, Wasiq Hasan became a commander of the convoys which plied between Pakistan and India and he evacuated many families from Panipat and Rohtak. The convoys which he escorted to Pakistan comprised marching columns as well as motor transport. There were never enough soldiers to protect them completely. Four trucks of armed men per convoy were allowed, which could consist of 200,000 to 250,000 souls. The convoy moved along the road and on both sides of it. If the armed trucks drove along the front of the convoy, the Sikhs attacked it from the rear; if the trucks travelled at the back, the Sikhs attacked it from the sides. There was simply no way to save people from being killed. Many old and sick people fell on the roadside and were unable to get up again, but the Sikhs used to stab them also.

When the motorised convoys evacuated people, priority was given to those whose names appeared on the lists which had been prepared in the Lahore office at the request of relatives and friends. It was a remarkable exercise in coordination in those turbulent times. Many of those whose names were not included in the lists waited beside the convoys, offering cash and jewellery held in their *jholis* and begging to be taken along. Wasiq recalled sadly that some of his colleagues accepted those jewels. Very often, he had to deal with the distress of desperate passengers and try to maintain sanity in his convoy. He refused to carry pets– or bearded clerics unless they shaved their beards.

The most difficult operations were conducted in the rural areas. The Pakistan army had set up camps in these areas to take out Muslims who had been forced to convert to Hinduism. This operation included rescuing women and girls who had been abducted. On learning about their whereabouts, the Pakistan army jawans brought them out from the villages. Rescuing women and girls was fraught with danger because the whole village turned hostile and tried to prevent the operation. The Indian army was responsible for helping the Pakistan army in this endeavour but always stalled, sometimes for hours on end. In the villages, people came out with arms and *lathis* to stop the operation. Once, in a Jat village in the Panipat area, Wasiq Hasan faced strong resistance and with great difficulty was he able to persuade an Indian army major to accompany him to the village. Only when the Jats saw the Indian army jawans did they return to their homes and he was able to save the converts.

In his only trip to Patiala, Wasiq had to deal with a former company mate at the Dehra Dun academy, Sukha Singh, a relative of the Maharaja of Patiala. The Maharaja had imprisoned many Muslims in a fort outside Patiala city. Some of the elders of these prisoners had been ministers in the service of his state. Wasiq had forty-two trucks at his disposal on that journey which probably meant that the prisoners were considered important people. Reaching Patiala, he parked his trucks in a line outside the fort. He then wrote a letter to Sukha Singh, reminding him of their association in Dehra Dun, to assure him that he was indeed Wasiq Hasan. Sukha Singh emerged from the fort and said he could do nothing against the Maharaja's wishes. But he did go to Patiala more than once to persuade the Maharaja who relented only to free a few men after a list of the prisoners was placed before him. Probably in collusion with Sukha Singh, the names of the prisoners were changed and they were all piled into those forty-two trucks. Sukha Singh was punished by the furious Maharaja by removal from his post.

Let us end this tale of savagery and fortitude on a gentler note. A certain Mirza Sahib, who sported a red beard and was a former minister in Kapurthala state, visited the MEO office in Lahore every day, pleading that his only daughter should be rescued from Kapurthala where she was being held by a Sikh advocate. It was impossible to spare a truck to rescue only a single person. Although the major in charge of the Lahore office pitied Mirza, all the convoy commanders refused to undertake this journey. Finally, Wasiq Hasan volunteered to go to Kapurthala. He was given a section of armed guard and two sub-machine guns. On reaching Kapurthala, he found that the Sikh advocate was not at home but his father, who was a judge, wanted the girl to return to her family. When the advocate came home, he refused to give up the girl because she was now his wife. Wasiq asked to speak to the girl himself. Resplendent in beautiful clothes, she came down the stairs like a queen, and on being told that her father had sent for her, she refused to leave. She was now the Sikh advocate's wife and if she returned to Pakistan, nobody would marry her. Wasiq assured her that, because she was lovely and belonged to a respectable family, she would find many suitors. 'Will *you* marry me,' she asked? His head whirled frantically, but he answered 'yes, I will marry you.' The girl was taken into the custody of the army jawans and the people who had gathered to prevent her departure moved away when they saw the sub-machine guns.

When the truck stopped, as all convoys did at the Wagah border, Wasiq Hasan related the whole story to the major on duty. He requested that the truck should be sent to Lahore under the command of another officer because he could not possibly marry the girl. In Lahore, the girl refused to descend from the truck unless the young commander who had promised to marry her, took her with him. Ultimately, however, she was persuaded to go home with her father.

Chapter 5

Fatehyab and the Anti-Ayub Movement

Fatehyab Ali Khan and I got married in the summer of 1969. His ancestors hailed from the principality of Jhunjhunu in Rajasthan. They were Qaimkhani Rajputs and traced their lineage to Prithviraj Chauhan who ruled over Ajmer and Delhi and was defeated and killed by Muhammad Ghori in 1247. One of Chauhan's descendants, Karamchand also known as Karam Karan Singh (1355–1419), son of Raja Motay Rai Chauhan of Doraya, and his two brothers converted to Islam during the reign of Feroz Shah Tughlaq (reigned 1351–88). Karamchand took the name of Qaim Khan and the descendants of all three brothers came to be known as Qaimkhanis. They were a warrior clan, much acclaimed for their valour and chivalry and claimed descent from the sun as *suryavanshis*, distinct from the lesser *chandravanshis* who had descended from the moon. With his radical ideas, Fatehyab did not believe in the virtues of lineage but when he was provoked, he would assert with some humour that he was a 'surajvansi'.

Fatehyab's grandfather migrated from Jhunjhunu to Karimnagar in Adilabad district of Hyderabad state and subsequently moved to Chinnoor, where he set up a zamindari which was inherited by his son, Fatehyab's father, Bakhtawar Khan. Chinnoor was one of the earliest settlements on the Godavri River and was located 273 kilometres north-east of Hyderabad. Today it boasts many banks, schools and degree colleges, but in Fatehyab's childhood it was a rather primitive place. Apart from owning thousands of acres of land, Bakhtawar Khan established many businesses and became the richest and most influential person in Chinnoor. He gathered his relatives around him and lived in feudal style in a lavish household, surrounded by many dependants and scores of impoverished *Bheel* servants. His children studied in the Nizam's schools but he sent his elder son, Mumtaz Ali Khan, to Lahore for higher studies. Because of his father's influence, Mumtaz was elected to the Hyderabad state assembly. He was a socialist and was influenced by the Marxist ideology of E.M.S. Namboodiripad (1909–98).

Outside the strict rules of the house, Fatehyab had a carefree childhood. Roaming freely, he became friends with the animals and birds in the thick forests surrounding Chinnoor. He wound wild snakes around his wrists and travelled deep into the forest in bullock carts. Chinnoor had a Hindu majority and was dotted with many temples into which Fatehyab ventured as a child. The popular temples around Chinnoor were the round temple, Jagannathalayam and Bada Hanuman. Apparently there was not much social or religious prejudice between the Hindu and Muslim communities in that small settlement. His father was sternly religious and Fatehyab had to call to prayer in the village mosque which his father had built. However, both his father and mother respected the Hindu festivals. Gifts and greetings were exchanged with their Hindu neighbours on Diwali and Eid.

After India was divided and the Nizam of Hyderabad struggled to keep his princely independence, Chinnoor became unsafe for the family. In 1948, they moved to Hyderabad city. They purchased part of a big *haveli* on Abid Road from Nawab Yusuf Jung and a few other houses, all in the name of his beautiful mother, Aziz Bano. His father was a follower of the Razakar leader, Qasim Razvi, and in the events leading to India's occupation of Hyderabad in 1949, he was wanted by the police. To avoid arrest and find a place for his family in Pakistan, he went to Karachi alone, leaving his brood behind him.

Fatehyab, his mother, siblings and their dependants – about thirty-five persons – travelled to Karachi by ship from Bombay. The journey, which they spent on the deck of the ship, lasted for three days. They settled down in cramped conditions in a small three-room flat on Elphinstone Street in Saddar which was purchased by Bakhtawar Khan on *pugree* from its Hindu owner. Fatehyab recalled that they reached Karachi on 3 January 1949 and disembarked from the ship at Keamari. They took the tram run by the Muhammadi Tramway Company (no longer in operation), from Keamari to Saddar with all their luggage and dependants. The area between Keamari and Boulton Market, apart from a few naval establishments, was not then populated. His father started his own business, an auction house near Naz Cinema on Bunder Road, and purchased a larger flat opposite Plaza Cinema into which the family shifted. In collaboration with a friend, he also started publishing an Urdu newspaper, *Awam*. Fatehyab was admitted to an English medium school in Saddar to which he went by tram every day from Plaza Cinema.

Eventually, Bakhtawar Khan sold his flats in Karachi and moved with his children to Shikarpur, in the interior of Sindh, where he had acquired some agricultural and urban property. They lived in the richest neighbourhood of Shikarpur, called Lakhidar. When the family shifted to Shikarpur in 1951, Fatehyab joined the government school there. But because the medium of instruction was Sindhi, he could not follow the curriculum. Therefore, he enrolled as a private student in Punjab University from where he took his Matric examinations.

Bakhtawar Khan died of a heart attack in Shikarpur in 1952. When her husband passed away, Aziz Bano was left to fend for herself with many unsettled young children, in a land in which she was a complete stranger. But she was a determined woman and boldly travelled to Hyderabad, alone. Her eldest son, Mumtaz, had stayed back because he was so engaged in politics and did not want to leave Hyderabad. She persuaded him to give up his political career and come to Karachi, much against his wishes, and perhaps to his utter regret. He became the head of the family and his word became law for all his siblings.[1]

After his father's death, Fatehyab studied for a couple of years in the famous C and S (Chellaram and Seetaldas) College in Shikarpur. It was named after its founders, the philanthropists Chela Singh Bajaj and Seetaldas Panjabi. Housed in a beautiful building, it was situated on the road to Sukkur, a few kilometres outside Shikarpur city. And it was here that the long history of Fatehyab's revolt against the establishment started.

Because of their poverty, the refugee students could not afford to cover the cost of their education. The government used to collect a tax to pay towards their fees and stipends. There were complaints that this money was not being spent on the education of refugee students and was diverted to other uses. Fatehyab stood up against this misuse of funds and led a procession of refugee students and some Sindhi colleagues, right up to the famous bazaar in Lakhidar where all roads converged. It was a small procession, the first of its kind in the history of Shikarpur, carrying a few placards. He recalled that the students who followed him were very poor but he was well off; he went to the college on a motorbike. The next day, he was called by the principal and asked to leave. As a favour, he was not rusticated, and on the basis of the certificate of study he managed to get admission in Islamia College in Karachi. He was scared and understood the seriousness of what he had done and, as he said, he had become 'notorious'. After he was reprimanded, his Sindhi friends stole his motorbike.[2]

Islamia College and the National Students Federation (NSF) were the crucibles in which Fatehyab's leadership skills were nurtured and his qualities of heart and mind blossomed. Islamia College, which he joined in 1954, was situated in a bungalow in the wealthiest part of Karachi, off Jamshed Road, near Guru Mandir. Many students who were migrants from India attended the college only a couple of times a week because, impoverished as they were, they worked during the daytime. Fatehyab also found a job in 1956 as an upper division clerk in the audit and accounts office, drawing a small monthly salary. Most of the regular students came from the elegant neighbourhood around Jamshed Road. Nearby, in an impressive old building, was located Green

Hotel, which was owned by a renowned singer. Fatehyab accompanied the senior students to Green Hotel which had a bar and had become the centre of music in Karachi. He recalled that he was not short of money, although little remained of the funds his father had brought from Hyderabad. His mother gave him the princely sum of one rupee for all his needs every day.

Fatehyab had pleasant memories of his early years in Islamia College. Men and women students socialised freely and the women were not enveloped in burqas – there was no *hijab* or *niqab*. They drank tea together in the same canteen. He remembered many attractive women colleagues, especially Shama Azam, the daughter of the acclaimed short story writer, Azam Barelvi, who became friendly with him. The prejudices which afflict us today did not then seem to exist. There was no gender discrimination, only 'gender respect'. Islamia College threw up many persons of distinction. The senior students who later became famous in the literary world, and about whom he spoke affectionately, were Sajjad Baqar Rizvi and Akhtar Faruqui – not forgetting Iqbal Afridi.[3]

Fatehyab's friend at Islamia College, Ahmad Zaheer Khan, wrote to me after Fatehyab passed away. In 1954–5, he wrote, in the college canteen he met Fatehyab, on whose face he discerned such wisdom and restraint that Zaheer felt compelled to seek his friendship. Wearing thick glasses, Fatehyab had a head full of hair, a broad forehead and his light brown eyes shone with intelligence and mischief. Urdu was, proverbially speaking, his own turf, and he excelled in debates, winning trophies in educational institutions all over the country. With his urbanity and networking skills he helped Zaheer to win elections in the college societies. Zaheer noticed that Fatehyab hardly ever lost his cool or his temper.[4]

It is difficult to capture in words the spirit of the times in which Fatehyab lived in the 1950s. Karachi was the capital of the country, the vibrant hub of all political activity. But it was also a time of confusion in which the state was struggling to find its moorings. He considered the mid-1950s as an unusual time in the political and social life of the city. The education system was functioning in the after-effects of the students' movement of 1953 which has been honoured publicly in recent years. It was led by the Democratic Students' Federation (DSF) which was founded as early as 1948 in Lahore and became the students' wing of the Communist Party of Pakistan. The movement had the support of fledgling socialist trade unions, with hardcore communist members, such as the Karachi Port Trust Union and the Biri Workers' Union. Many students, especially from Dow Medical College who later acquired fame as professionals and public figures, such as Adibul Hasan Rizvi and Haroon Ahmad,[5] were activists in this movement and were arrested. It may have passed peacefully had it not followed so quickly upon the heels of the sentences which were announced on 5 January 1953 against military personnel and civilians such as Faiz Ahmad Faiz, the celebrated progressive poet who was editor of *Pakistan Times* and Sajjad Zaheer, secretary of the Communist Party of Pakistan, in the infamous Rawalpindi Conspiracy Case.[6] It could have passed off only as a rowdy event if the district magistrate, Z.H. Hashmi, who was unable to control the mob with tear gas, had not lost his cool on 8 January 1953 and ordered the police to shoot.[7] Eleven people died (only one student among them) and scores were injured, including police officers and men. Interior minister Mushtaq Ahmed Gurmani barely escaped with his life. His Cadillac was sprinkled with kerosene oil, torched and reduced to ashes. Kerosene oil, it seems, was conveniently ready at hand. A dusk to dawn curfew was imposed in Karachi for several days.

The commissioner of Karachi, A.T. Naqvi, insisted on more than one occasion on the basis of intelligence sources that the rioting and arson were instigated by the communists who wanted to destabilise the government.[8] This was confirmed by Nazish Amrohi, the Marxist ideologue and secretary general of the Communist Party of Pakistan who gave me several interviews in 1990.[9] Notwithstanding the veracity of this allegation, which was denied by their leaders, a wave of sympathy for the students and their demands swept throughout the country. Messages of support poured in from schools, colleges, universities and professional institutions in all major cities. The largest demonstrations were held in Dacca where 20,000 students denounced the government in a public meeting, threatened a province-wise agitation, and all educational institutions were closed.[10] There were strikes in numerous educational institutions all over the country. And the politicians did not lag behind. With one voice, from the political right to the political left, they upbraided the government for mishandling the situation. The beleaguered prime minister, Khwaja Nazimuddin, addressed the students in a radio broadcast, promising a judicial inquiry.[11] The 'movement of 1953' was the first student agitation in Pakistan and its demands were considered justified even by a cautious newspaper like *Dawn,* which wrote in an editorial: 'The state of education in Karachi has been chronically disgraceful... The students were justified in seeking to ventilate their grievances in a spectacular manner.'[12] Ostensibly, their demands were simple enough: lower fees, more hostels and sports facilities, a separate ministry of education, no political victimisation of students.

To counter liberal and progressive trends among the students, the government sponsored the creation of the NSF. After the DSF fiasco and the Rawalpindi Conspiracy Case of 1953, the 'progressives' were on the run.

Most of the prominent DSF leaders went underground and the Communist Party of Pakistan was banned in 1954. Gradually and cautiously, however, they started joining the NSF and took over its organisation. They began participating in union elections and only when they won in many colleges, such as Dow Medical College, D.J. Science College and Islamia College, did the government wake up to the reality of their success. The administration and police were cautious and did not interfere directly in student activities; they became active only when a demonstration in favour of change was imminent. Thousands of students from East Pakistan studied on a part-time basis in Karachi and were also engaged in politics. Their presence strengthened the NSF. However, the NSF operated only in Karachi. It was supported by like-minded student organisations in the Punjab, but these were not branches of the NSF.[13]

Another organisation, the Inter-Collegiate Body (ICB) was, according to Fatehyab, a parliament of the students. All the winners in college union elections were members of ICB and worked for the welfare of students on issues such as their fees, teachers' problems, transport, books, the special problems of women students. The vice presidents and general secretaries of the winning unions participated in all ICB sessions which were held by rotation in different colleges so that the students should own their outcome. And the principals of colleges and the university's vice chancellor implemented these decisions or faced agitation. On the pattern of the NSF was also founded the Girls' Students' Congress, as the NSF had no women's wing, which spread to all the women's colleges, except the missionary colleges for women.[14]

Fatehyab made his first public speech in 1957 in Ram Bagh, renamed Aram Bagh after Partition, in a meeting of Huseyn Shaheed Suhrawardy's Awami League.[15] Nawabzada Nasrullah Khan, who was a member of this party, was also present in the meeting. Fatehyab was then only 21 years old. Suhrawardy had migrated to Pakistan from Calcutta in 1950. He was the leader of the Awami League (founded as the All Pakistan Awami Muslim League in 1949) on whose bandwagon the underground communists and progressives had jumped, finding a safe cover under which to operate. By and large, all prominent politicians who were not members of the Muslim League joined the Awami League and Suhrawardy emerged as a very important leader of the opposition. A.M. Qureshi, the founder of Islamia College, whose nemesis Fatehyab later became, decided to disrupt the meeting on behalf of the Muslim League. In his memoirs, Suhrawardy mentions this meeting and describes Qureshi as 'a shady character with a murky past who was proud of his associations with the underworld', and who organised a black flag demonstration against him. When Qureshi started inciting the students of Islamia College to disturb the gathering, Suhrawardy asked Fatehyab to speak and restrain them from violence. However, Suhrawardy stood no chance against the administration and 'the black flag trucks paraded the city in triumph'.[16]

Much has been written about the carnage and bloodshed of Partition, the miserable condition of the refugees, the utter lack of housing and civic amenities. But the burden of their presence on the limited educational facilities needs to be stated. Karachi did not have the number of schools and colleges needed to educate the young of the refugee population. 'There was nothing' said Fatehyab. The scholars who migrated to Pakistan found teaching jobs but facilities such as libraries, books, furniture, hostels, sports grounds and transport were sadly lacking.[17] Into this vacuum had stepped the Communist Party of Pakistan.

Fatehyab never became a member of the Communist Party of Pakistan, its factions or students' wing. His independent nature did not accept ideologues or the secrecy which surrounded their work. He participated in the annual meetings held to commemorate the 1953 movement but did not favour their 'underground' activities. Between 1954 and 1956, he came close to them, although he did not stand on the same platform with them. He was always against the concept of students' wings of political parties.

Fatehyab's emergence as a public figure can be linked to the election he contested to the post of vice president of the students' union in Islamia College in 1958. Earlier, in 1956, he had contested for this post against the NSF and lost. (The principal used to be the president of the union.) After Fatehyab lost the union elections in 1956, he joined the NSF on the understanding that he would not become a member of any underground party, would not accept any mandate, would openly state his views in committee meetings and exercise his right to oppose any policy.[18]

Ahmad Zaheer Khan describes Fatehyab's election in 1958 as vice president of Islamia College students' union from the platform of the NSF as 'revolutionary'.[19] His running mate as general secretary was Syed Saghir Ahmad Naqvi, a former member of DSF and, according to Fatehyab, probably a member of the underground Communist Party. Fearing the outcome, Qureshi tried to get the election postponed and put a padlock on the college gate – which was broken by the students and the election was held in defiance. Fatehyab and Saghir won with a very large majority, but were disappointed that the Bengali and Punjabi students had fielded candidates on an ethnic basis. Once elected to the union, Fatehyab and his team stirred the student community. It was a union with a difference which won the hearts of the students, teachers and some members of the administration. They arranged scholarships on merit and books for needy students and organised many literary sittings and all-Pakistan debates. One particular debate lasted for several days. These debates brought students from all over the country closer than they had ever been before.

Apart from bonding the students, the most significant achievement of Fatehyab's union was the acquisition of land for Islamia College. The plot on which the college stands today belonged to the city government where the Muslim League leader, Shabbir Ahmad Usmani, was buried. Fatehyab called a general body meeting of the students and they decided to walk to Karachi Municipal Corporation on Bunder Road on the day on which the mayor and his cabinet were meeting. On that day, Fatehyab led a huge procession comprising hundreds, if not thousands, of students to the mayor's office, shouting slogans and demanding that the plot of land on which Usmani was buried should be allotted to Islamia College on minimal payment. The mayor gave way before the enormous turnout and Islamia College now stands on land which Fatehyab and his colleagues procured for it by their activism.[20]

Fatehyab had an uneasy relationship with Qureshi and the more popular he became, the more the principal resented him. After his term was over, Qureshi placed a ban on Fatehyab's entry into the college premises, but Fatehyab held daily meetings on the roadside and his supporters stood by him. However, Fatehyab was generous in his opinion of Qureshi as an unusual person, an uneducated man who had founded a college. A member of the Muslim League, he liked to be addressed as Sir Syed the Second. He used the students to further his political aspirations and Fatehyab's confrontation with him came to a head when Qureshi took students to the airport to welcome Chaudhry Mohammad Ali and Iskander Mirza after the 1956 Constitution was adopted. Although he was uneducated, Qureshi employed distinguished persons as teachers, such as Hasan Askari, a scholar of Urdu literature and an expert in French, the principal A.M. Maulvi who was a great Arabic scholar, Karrar Husain, Kerawala the mathematics professor, Mumtaz Husain, Abul Khair Kashfi, Hasan Adil. These teachers kept in touch with students outside classroom hours and those interested in literature and poetry frequented the coffee houses of Karachi in the afternoons and evenings.[21]

The poets and writers who had migrated from India found literary space in the coffee houses and restaurants which dotted Saddar in Karachi. They were also frequented by the literati from other parts of the country. There were two well-known associations of writers at that time: Anjuman-i-Taraqqi Pasand Musannifin, whose members met in coffee houses, and Halqa-i-Arbab-i-Zauq who met either in private homes or in Fredrick's Cafeteria. The atmosphere in these coffee houses, Fatehyab recalled, was friendly, 'unusual' and welcoming. Faiz Ahmad Faiz used Metropole Hotel as a venue. Details of discussions in these gatherings, whether about politics, the problems of the youth or literary trends, spread throughout the country. Fatehyab frequented the old India Coffee House, which later became Zelin's Coffee House, and then Eastern Coffee House, from 1956–9. It was very popular and could accommodate up to fifty people. Even the waiters, he remembered, were so cultured. Students who were active in public life dragged out a single cup of tea the whole evening because they seldom had any money. Women rarely went to the coffee houses. All those who were interested in literature, poetry and politics sought the friendly environment of Eastern Coffee House; everybody came, including the popular poets Habib Jalib, Fareed Javed, Rasa Chughtai.[22]

Karachi was also famous for its restaurants – called 'hotels' in Urdu – owned and run by Iranians, mostly Bahais from Yezd, who have since left: Café George, known for its patties, Café Evelon opposite S.M. Arts College, another on the corner of Bohri Bazaar and Saddar and many others located in Pakistan Chowk. The cigarette and *paan* shops were run by South Indians who did not understand Urdu. Smoking was fashionable and was part of the coffee house culture: Bagla, King Stork, Diamond, K2, Red and White, Passing Show, Camel, and the more expensive brands such as Capstan, which Fatehyab smoked, Will's Navy Cut, Gold Flake, 555 and Players No. 3. And as B.M. Kutty, communist, compulsive activist and Moplah revolutionary has told me in his interviews, Karachi, especially the Saddar area, was dotted by bars which were frequented by the 'progressives'.

The Burns Road locality was taken over by migrants from India, mainly from Delhi and the United Provinces and every specialty of food from these areas in India was available in its eateries. The migrants from South India mainly lived near the central prison in Hyderabad Colony. Sindhi food was sold around Golimar. Fatehyab used to visit the old areas of the city, Mithadar, Kharadar, Lyari, Boulton Market and Merewether Tower, where some of his friends lived. Thus he got to know the city which he learnt to love so much. But the students who had migrated from India, he said, were not aware of the traditions of the city in which they had found shelter. They had no idea of the importance of Sind Madrasa or Jinnah's association with it. Their primary concern was the existential mire in which their lives were stuck.

Like all groups, the students had their toughs and musclemen who found favour with the government and were rewarded by it in the colonial tradition. A big name among them was Rana Azhar Ali Khan, often addressed as *thakur*. He dressed flamboyantly and was an impressive figure. He tried to bully Fatehyab in the 1958 elections to the students' union in Islamia College. Fatehyab reminded him that he had no *locus standi* because he was not a student of any college at all. Another tough was Shahinshah Husain, also backed by the administration, who used to control the Shia students. To continue to operate within the student community, Rana and Shahinshah had to eventually take admission in colleges and Rana later became chairman of ICB. They were intimidators who were armed with knives – pistols and guns were not in use then.[23]

The events of the 1950s and 1960s in which the students were involved, despite the role played by the Communist Party behind the scenes, were closely linked to the state of politics in Pakistan. The influence they wielded can be judged from the fact that the ICB and NSF led a huge procession along Bunder Road, joined by citizens and trade unions, against the attack on Egypt by Britain and France, after Nasser nationalised the Suez Canal.[24] Fatehyab had marched in that procession. The defining moment came, however, when Ayub Khan abrogated the 1956 Constitution and imposed martial law in the country. There was great resentment among 'thinking' people against Pakistan's accession to the western camp and western military pacts. The imposition of martial law was the last straw for the youth who could, until then, still agitate, assemble and press their demands. Now, a new kind of 'military' restriction was placed on the public. Political parties were banned by Ayub Khan and so, incidentally, was the NSF.

Later the NSF broke into factions, but the organisation which Fatehyab led in the University of Karachi was a remarkable nursery for political education and awareness. Thousands joined it and even today, in retrospect, they remember it wistfully and the bond still holds. It became a curious mixture of young people from different backgrounds: communists, socialists, Marxists, 'progressives' of all hues, nationalists, sympathisers of the poor, anti-establishment moderates, young professionals, writers and poets, it embraced them all. It was a mass front. Its hub was Karachi, although it spread to other cities. It gave space to students from all provinces, but was led inspirationally by those whose parents had migrated from India. Many of them lived in Pir Ilahi Bakhsh Colony, commonly known as PIB Colony, near the central prison. As Ehtisham has written, life as a scholar was very 'chaotic' but 'we had a vibrant social, intellectual and political life'.[25]

Several political leaders had welcomed Ayub Khan's coup and they were generally reluctant to defy martial law. After all, it was the first time that the commander-in-chief of the army had taken control of the country and the punishments for challenging his writ were very severe. But the NSF, and perhaps those who were advising it, were itching for confrontation. The communists were also stung by the death of Hasan Nasir, an icon of their movement, in Lahore Fort in 1959. He was secretary general of their party but because of the ban, like other communists, he had operated under cover of the

National Awami Party (NAP). Hasan Nasir was interrogated in Lahore Fort and apparently died under torture. If Nazish Amrohi is to be believed, he had sent a message – by whom, he would not say – asking his comrades for help because the physical pain had become intolerable. The party was relieved that he did not 'break' under torture or reveal any names, which would have led to an across-the-board swoop of communists in the country.[26]

Fatehyab enrolled in the political science department of the University of Karachi in 1960. He contested the election to the post of president of the students' union the same year. The establishment tried its best to make him lose the election, but he was a charismatic candidate, elegant in speech, refined in manner, a brilliant orator and a consensus builder. The election became a battleground and he won with a thumping majority, making him the first elected president of the union. His rival, Saeed Hasan, polled only two votes, though Safwanullah, the third contestant who was a very eloquent speaker, did a little better.

The NSF had won 90 per cent seats in elections to the college unions and felt it had the strength to take up the fight. Since it was banned, the students' activities were coordinated through the ICB, of which Fatehyab was the chairman. Because they were 'progressives', they decided to observe Lumumba day, after the brutal torture and execution on 17 January 1961 of the much-harassed and imprisoned Patrice Lumumba, the first prime minister of independent Congo. Lumumba, aged 35 years, was a hero of Africa and his execution, backed by Belgium and the United States, led to protests in many countries. However, not many people knew or cared about Lumumba in Karachi and the students' procession fizzled out. According to Ehtisham, in the streets of Karachi they were 'a forlorn group of about a hundred' carrying pro-Lumumba and anti-UN banners. It was 'a terrible let down' and even the policemen accompanying them slipped away.[27]

The next day, Dawn criticised the political priorities of the students. They were more concerned 'when cannibal makes cannibal bleed in darkest Africa' than 'bloodier massacres' of the Muslims of Jabalpur who were their 'nearer and dearer ones by killers brutalised by their hate of Islam' in neighbouring India. 'Our goose,' writes Ehtisham, 'was now properly cooked. We were damned if we did and damned if we did not.'[28] So ICB decided to observe Jabalpur day on 27 February 1961. Fatehyab called for a strike and presided over a huge meeting in the University of Karachi. In the city, thousands of students gathered near Pakistan Chowk and a procession was taken out from S.M. Arts College. After the successful protest, the district magistrate announced that the government would do everything possible to help the Indian Muslims and the students should disperse. A call for dispersal was given but an agent provocateur incited the students to rush at the police who responded with tear gas and a baton charge. The fight went as far as Burns Road whose residents had always supported the students and on this day, too, they gave them refuge and water to fight the tear gas fumes. About 200 persons were injured, including police constables and officers.[29] In the evening, Fatehyab and many of his supporters were arrested.

According to Ehtisham, about 160 students were brought to the central prison in Karachi. They were helped and protected by the notorious Abdullah Bhatti, a big smuggler, who was serving a prison sentence. The arrest of so many young men, ostensibly only because they had protested against the massacre of Indian Muslims, seems to have created a wave of sympathy for them among the citizens of Karachi. 'It seems,' writes Ehtisham, 'that the whole city was bent on bringing succour and comfort to us.' They spent time in singing, telling stories, teasing each other and in political indoctrination.[30]

Fatehyab and others who were considered dangerous, however, were not so lucky. Before they were lodged in the prison, they were moved as harassment, especially at night, from one police station to another. In Artillery Maidan police station, Fatehyab and Mairaj Mohammad Khan were mercilessly beaten. They were laid, face down, on a long table and whipped, taunted about their aspiration to leadership and accused of being Indian agents. Husain Naqi, who describes Fatehyab as the 'leaders' leader' and the first prominent student to become a victim of torture by Ayub Khan's fascist military dictatorship, told me that they were not given any medical aid and their friends fomented their bruises with the mugs in which hot tea was served.[31] Fatehyab remembered the name of the policeman who whipped him, but never divulged the name to me. His brother-in-law, Bashir Khan, who later rose to the rank of major general in the army, suggested that Fatehyab could be freed if an undertaking was given by the family that he would behave himself in future. Fatehyab's mother, a proud Rajput woman, dismissed this demand out of hand.

While in prison, bail applications were moved on behalf of Fatehyab and his co-accused before the sessions court on 7 March 1961.[32] Three applications were moved by Hassanali Abdul Rahman and nineteen by Talmiz Burney, including the one for Fatehyab, which stated that the additional district magistrate had erred in refusing bail because the purported offence was bailable. The students had only wanted to express their anger and grief at the brutal and cold-blooded massacre of Muslims in Madhya Pradesh, India. But the sessions court, like the additional district magistrate, Zakir Hussain, rejected these bail applications and the acting district and sessions judge, Mumtaz Ali Kazi, argued that he had no jurisdiction in the cases. Public prosecutor, H.T. Raymond, said the students would be arraigned in a military court. The press reported that 2,000 students, including a large number of girls, had gathered on that occasion outside the court premises. Therefore, the venue was shifted to the larger court of the district and sessions judge, but even this room could accommodate only 400 students.[33]

Fatehyab's trial as Accused Number One for violating martial law regulations 55 and 79 opened on 16 March 1961 in Summary Military Court No.1. He and his co-accused were brought in handcuffs to a building near Clifton Bridge where the trial was held. Of the sixteen students arrested, six were bailed out by the court, leaving ten students, including Fatehyab, facing charges.[34] In the military court, Fatehyab was not allowed a defence counsel but lawyers could be present as 'friends of the court'. The accused were permitted to cross-examine the prosecution witnesses. Talmiz Burney, Hassanali Abdul Rahman, Nuruddin Sarki, Ghulam Husain and Mahmood Dossa appeared as friends of the court throughout the trial. Talmiz Burney was tall, imposing and debonair; he looked like Gregory Peck.

Fatehyab was accused of jointly organising, with others, a procession of a political nature from S.M. Arts College and distributing banners and placards carrying slogans like *Nehru murdabad* (death to Nehru), *Jansangh hai hai* (death to Jansangh) and *Jabalpur mein Musalmanon ka qatle aam band karo* (stop the massacre of Muslims in Jabalpur). The procession was taken out without permission and in defiance of the orders of the district magistrate who had imposed Section 144 in the city. When the proceedings started, Fatehyab asked that they should be adjourned because he wanted to approach Ayub Khan to try their case in a special court. He pointed out that when the police first registered a case against them, he and his co-accused had been charged only with violating Section 144 of the Criminal Procedure Code, but later, the charge had been altered. They were given the charge sheet in prison, but no time or opportunity to consult their friends and prepare their defence properly. However, the trial continued.

As was to be expected, there was a world of difference between the version of events given by the administration and the accused. Briefly, the prosecution's case claimed that the meeting and procession were pre-planned. Large numbers of students converged on S.M. Arts College on 27 February and provocative speeches were made by Fatehyab and others. There were 7,000–8,000 students present when Fatehyab was making a speech. They carried stones in their pockets and bottles and brickbats with which they pelted the police personnel, many of whom were injured. They were repeatedly asked by senior members of the district administration to disperse because they were violating Martial Law Regulation 79 and Section 144 and warned not to proceed beyond the crossing at Ataturk and Strachan roads but they broke the police cordon. A mild *lathi* charge was ordered and when the situation became ugly, tear gas was used to disperse the crowd. When they crossed the red line at the traffic lights on Ataturk and Strachan roads, Fatehyab and some others were arrested on the spot.[35] M.A. Naqvi, station house officer of Artillery Maidan police station, Habib-ur-Rahman, superintendent of police East Division, Ahmadullah, sub-divisional magistrate and Mumtaz Ali Shah, sub-inspector CID appeared as prosecution witnesses. Mumtaz Ali Shah was a well-known figure in student circles. The prosecution also presented three 'history-sheeters' as witnesses who had been in and out of lock-ups and been useful to the police in the past. Two of them were hawkers, Bashir Ahmad and Anis-ur-Rahman, and the third was Saleemuddin, proprietor of Rashid Hotel on Somerset Street.[36]

Cross-examining the prosecution witnesses, Fatehyab was able to pick many holes in their testimony, but the decision had already been taken to punish him and his co-accused. They all pleaded not guilty and submitted that they were falsely implicated by the police. In his statement, Fatehyab said that the massacre of Muslims in Jabalpur had shocked the students and the 'editorials of local newspapers had added fire to the hay'. As chairman of ICB, he was approached by students to hold a meeting to condemn these massacres and it was proposed to call a general body meeting of ICB on 26 February, and a meeting of all students on 27 February at S.M. Arts College. Meanwhile, he learnt about the imposition of Section 144 and tried unsuccessfully to reach the district magistrate on the telephone. He also sought a meeting with the administrator of Karachi, which was refused. Ultimately, the district magistrate conveyed to him that the meeting should not be held. Accordingly, ICB decided to cancel both meetings and notices of cancellation were published in the *Pakistan Times*, *Morning News*, *Jang* and *Millat*, all of which Fatehyab produced in the court. The decision was also conveyed to the district magistrate but because 26 February was a Sunday, the students could not be properly informed about the cancellation of the meetings.

Fatehyab maintained that a large number of students, unaware that the meeting had been cancelled, had gathered at S.M. Arts College on 27 February. Also present, armed with lathis and rifles, were police personnel in large numbers who had surrounded the college. He persuaded the students to return home or go to their classes. As they started leaving, the police, under the erroneous impression that they were forming a procession, charged at them and threw tear gas shells at them indiscriminately. In the meantime, the crowd was joined by 'mischievous elements' and if there was any violence, it was between these elements and the police. Fatehyab must have had his tongue in his cheek when he said on the collective behalf of his followers: 'We have the most implicit faith in the present regime and we would be the last persons to cause (it) any embarrassment.'[37]

By and large, all the accused gave the same version of events as was given by Fatehyab. Mairaj Mohammad Khan pointed out that processions against the Jabalpur massacres had been taken out in other towns and cities in Pakistan.[38] And, in any case, this was an 'imaginary' procession since Fatehyab and he had done their best to persuade the students to disperse. He raised the issue of how Fatehyab and he were beaten mercilessly in the police lock-up. Ali Mukhtar Rizvi, who was a mesmerising speaker, pointed out that station house officer Naqvi had manhandled him and broken his wrist.

Only three defence witnesses were produced. The first witness, Shams Siddiqui, a reporter of *Morning News*, said he had seen students pelting stones at a police van but did not hear anybody instigating them. The only warning he heard over the loudspeaker was that no resident of the area should shelter the students, not that the procession should not be taken out. The other witnesses were Salahuddin Aslam, staff photographer of *Pakistan Times* and *Imroz* and Syed Asadullah of Raza Ali College.[39] The court examined two other witnesses: Syed Raza Karim Rizvi, principal of Raza Ali College and S.R. Ghauri, staff correspondent of *Dawn*.

During the trial, there was great unrest among the youth in Karachi. They presented a memorandum for the release of their colleagues to Brigadier Muzaffar Husain, martial law administrator of Zone A. They petitioned the vice chancellor of the University of Karachi, B.A. Hashmi, meeting him in several batches. They started a signature campaign for the withdrawal of criminal cases, agitated and kept away from classes and announced the formation of an action committee for the release of the detained students. There were some sympathisers. Baba-i-Urdu Maulvi Abdul Haq sent a telegram to Ayub Khan demanding the immediate and unconditional release of the detained students.[40]

The trial lasted from 16 to 26 March 1961. On 30 March, Fatehyab, Mairaj, Sher Afzal and Jauhar Hussain were handed down sentences of one year's rigorous imprisonment and C class in prison. Amir Haider Kazmi was given nine months and Ali Mukhtar Rizvi, Iqbal Memon and Anwar Ahsan Siddiqui six months' rigorous imprisonment and C class in prison. Agha Jafar and Mahboob Ali were acquitted.[41] All eight convicted students were sent north by train in a third-class compartment – Fatehyab, Mairaj, Sher Afzal and Jauhar Hussain to Bahawalpur District Jail, the other four to prison in Multan. Mairaj claimed they had become so popular that people recognised them at various railway stations, cheered them and fed them. They reached Bahawalpur in the dead of night after a long journey and were checked into separate cells in the ward in which death row prisoners were held, or *phansi ghat*. The prison was known for its harsh conditions and the heat in summer was intolerable.

Fatehyab was fortunate that the superintendent of Bahawalpur prison, Colonel Fakhruddin Mir, was a civilised man. He had fought in the Second World War and seems to have disliked Ayub Khan whose photograph he turned to the wall when the students entered his room. He was courteous but read all the letters received and sent out by them, including my letters to Fatehyab. Since the students had no money, he arranged for them to be provided with decent meals and sent for tea from his house when they visited him. His greatest help to them came during their formal interrogation by the intelligence agencies. To prevent them from being in contact with one another during the interrogation, only the one being interrogated remained in Bahawalpur, while the other three were shifted to prisons which were even more primitive than the one in Bahawalpur. The superintendent asked each one to write down the details of his interrogation, which he passed on to the next interviewee. Thus, they all told the same story. Apart from their ideological leanings, the team of interrogators comprising four to five persons, probed about their alleged links to India and the Soviet Union.

Fatehyab and his co-accused were released on 2 July 1961. They were transferred to Karachi prison in a police van from Bahawalpur. They reached it in the evening and found Mian Bashir, the inspector general of police, waiting for them. He insisted that the jail superintendent should lock them up and release them the next morning. The jail superintendent, one Mustafa, also known as Tiger, refused and said he had no orders to imprison them, his orders were for their release.[42] Finally, they were allowed to go home and to a magnificent welcome and many grand receptions in the university and local colleges.

The students thought that they had achieved the unthinkable – erased the public's fear of martial law and shattered the arrogance of its enforcers. Their freedom did not last long, however. In August 1961, they were thrown out of Karachi, not on account of any particular incident but because their popularity had become a nuisance for the administration. Fatehyab, Mairaj, Jauhar Hussain and Iqbal Memon went to Quetta, Anwar Ahsan Siddiqui, Ali Mukhtar Rizvi, Sher Afzal Malik and Saeed Hasan to other cities. In Quetta, they stayed in the house of Mairaj's venerable father and when the old gentleman became angry with them, he turned them out. So they put up in the vacant house of Mairaj's brother-in-law. They spent their time in fighting over the daily newspaper, walking down Anderson Road, taking tea in Café Farah and frequenting Dawn Hotel – the venue of all political discourse in

Quetta. They got to know the sardars of Balochistan, but their closest friend was Amanullah Gichki. However, as in Bahawalpur prison, none of their family members visited them in Quetta.

The political situation had changed during Fatehyab's expulsion to Quetta. Martial law was lifted on 8 June 1962. Political parties were revived and the ban on the NSF was also lifted. Fatehyab wrote to the administration to let him take his MA examinations and returned to Karachi. After the NSF became lawful again, its senior members met through the ICB network and decided to continue the fight. This time their target was the new University Ordinance and the Sharif Commission Report on education. Unlike the University Act of 1951, the University Ordinance restricted the autonomy of the universities and gave arbitrary powers to vice chancellors. The Sharif Commission Report was viewed as restricting education to the elite because it recommended three-year law and degree courses which poor students could ill afford to pay for.

The NSF chose a spectacular method to register its protest and demands. Three years after he grabbed power, Ayub Khan realised that he needed the support of a strong political party. A faction of the Muslim League decided to oblige him and hold a convention in Karachi on 4 and 5 September 1962. The Raja of Mahmudabad, then living in London, was invited to preside over the Muslim Leaguers' Convention. He sent a terse reply that the Muslim League had outlived its purpose after the creation of Pakistan and had 'died with honour', and that he wanted to see a non-communal party with a democratic and socialist outlook in Pakistan, whose salvation lay in a socialist economy and progressive values.[43] Choudhry Khaliquzzaman, ever willing to compromise and take office, was unanimously elected to preside over the convention. He supported a presidential system of government which was in line with 'Islamic' ideas and referred to Ayub Khan's takeover as the 'revolution' of 1959.[44] Jinnah must have turned in his grave to hear one of his close followers bestowing praise upon a dictator. Delegates poured in from all parts of the country, including a large contingent from East Pakistan.

The security of the meeting was the responsibility of two toughs from Lyari, Dad Rahim alias Dadal and Sher Muhammad known as Sheru who were protégées of Mahmoud Haroon, the publicity organiser of the convention. The NSF sent women students, dressed in white coats, from Dow Medical College to plead with these notorious characters, touch their feet and cajole them into giving them cards for entry to the meeting on the condition that there would be no disturbance. Dadal and Sheru may have wrecked the peace of many innocent people during their criminal careers, but could not ignore the coaxing of these young women.

Entering the mammoth meeting, the NSF members spread throughout the ground, chanting pro-Ayub slogans. Choudhry Khaliquzzaman refused to let them place their 'grievances' before the audience. At a snap of their fingers, Fatehyab and the others stormed the stage, took hold of the microphones and started making speeches. Still seated in his chair, Khaliquzzaman was lifted down to the ground from the stage. Zulfikar Ali Bhutto was also present on the stage; he was the secretary of the Convention Muslim League and came to blows with Saeed Hasan. In the pandemonium, the NSF passed its resolutions; the audience, including the ministers and leaders who had come from East Pakistan melted away. Pro-Ayub slogans turned into anti-Ayub slogans.[45] However, after an interruption of two hours, the convention continued its proceedings. Next morning, Fatehyab and eleven of his NSF colleagues were expelled from Karachi for one year again under the West Pakistan Public Order Ordinance 1960.[46] This time, the externment was more severe and they were banned from entering Islamabad, Rawalpindi, Lahore, Peshawar and Quetta.

The externment orders led to widespread resentment in the student community. They organised immediately and started observing 'demand' days and holding demonstrations almost on a daily basis to press the government to withdraw the orders.[47] Soon the unrest spread to other cities. The protests were coordinated by the ICB and were marked by strikes in the university, almost all colleges, and some schools. The movement gained encouragement from the massive demonstrations being held in Dacca to protest against police firing upon students. Demand days were observed through huge processions in Rawalpindi, Lahore, Peshawar, Lyallpur, Bahawalpur, Khairpur and Sukkur. The withdrawal of the orders against the twelve Karachi students was one of the main demands in all these protests.[48] And the situation only worsened by the firing in a high school in Chittagong in which two students were injured.[49]

Meanwhile, Fatehyab and Amir Haider Kazmi were prohibited from entry or residence in Lahore, Rawalpindi, Lyallpur and Peshawar districts. They were also directed to report their arrival to the police within twenty-four hours in any other district of West Pakistan where their entry or residence was not prohibited. In a statement, Fatehyab said he had come to Lahore to meet the governor and if the demands of the student community were not immediately accepted, finding a solution would become 'all the more difficult at a later stage'.[50] Finally, the students of Karachi went on an indefinite strike. They held a large meeting in Khaliqdina Hall, where Mohammad Ali Jauhar had been tried during the Khilafat movement.[51] Even the Pakistan Students' Federation in London condemned the police firing in East Pakistan and demanded the withdrawal of the orders against the twelve Karachi students.[52]

The land shrank for Fatehyab and his colleagues as they moved from place to place to seek shelter. They had no money but the people looked after them. They were also offered refuge in East Pakistan. In a three-page appeal to Ayub Khan, Fatehyab urged reduction in tuition fees, cheaper books, repeal of the University Ordinance, increase in allocation for education in the national budget, levy of an education tax on the higher income group, and a raise in the salaries of teachers. He said the externment orders had come as a 'rude shock' and they had been 'roaming from city to city and from town to town hunted and chased by the CID'.[53] That, after all, was exactly how the government wanted them to suffer. It had devised an education policy and was not willing to withdraw it in a hurry. Nor was it eager to cancel the orders under pressure from those whom it considered as 'professional agitators'. But the campuses were in turmoil and the mood of the street had changed. Therefore, the government held the three-year degree course in abeyance. Seventeen students, led by Nasir Ali of Dow Medical College and Iqbal Jaffrey of the Teachers Training College, went on hunger strike in D.J. Science College. The group included a 14-year-old school boy, Zobair Ahmad Ashrafi, and four girls who vowed to continue their fast until death if the Karachi students were not brought back. The presence of the fasting girls drew huge crowds. Later, they were all admitted to Civil Hospital for treatment. Baqar Askary, president of Dow Medical College students' union announced that if their twelve colleagues were not called back, the medical students would suspend their work in the city hospitals.

The turning point in this saga came when, during a clash with the police on 4 October 1962, Karamat Ali, a carpenter, was killed by a stray bullet, 200 people were injured and mounted police charged at the hunger strikers' camp.[54] Earlier that day, the industrialist Siddique Dawood, who was a member of the National Assembly, S.M. Sohail and Mohsin Siddiqui, members of the provincial assembly, and Khaliquzzaman requested the hunger strikers and their leaders to end the agitation to enable them to take up the matter with the government. The citizens of Karachi also stepped in. On the same day, a deputation comprising Mahmudul Haq Usmani, Z.H. Lari, Akhtar Ali Khan and Talmiz Burney called on the commissioner of Karachi, Afzal Agha, to condemn the unprovoked use of force against the students and impressed upon him the urgency of calling back the externed students and admitting them to educational institutions. Suhrawardy, who was the main opponent of the government at that time, expressed his shock at the police brutality. A ten-man citizens' committee was formed, led by Z.H. Lari, to negotiate a settlement and there was a clamour for holding a judicial inquiry. Even Ayub Khan's basic democrats threw in their lot with the students. All major newspapers splashed photographs of Karamat Ali and the protesting and hunger striking students in their editions.

The Karachi students suspended their hunger strike for ten days, and Fatehyab his hunger strike in Sukkur, on the assurance that their demands would soon be accepted. Dawood and Sohail played the key role in ending the agitation. They assured the students that they would resign from the assemblies if their demands were not accepted. They would not betray them and promised to bring back their leaders unconditionally in less than ten days and in one batch. The Karachi Electric Supply Corporation Workmen Welfare Union and the Burmah Shell Employees' Union condemned the use of force against the students and backed their demands. They were joined by the Bank Employees' Federation of Karachi and twenty-five other workers' unions.[55] The cleric, Ihtishamul Haq Thanvi, threw in his support for the students. It had become a cause célèbre. The Karachi High Court Bar Association adopted a resolution that the disturbances were directly traceable to the unhappy state of the law relating to externment which was not worthy of a civilised state. These orders were not challengeable on merits in a court of law and, therefore, the frustration and resentment among the students could not find a healthy outlet. The administration should enforce the rule of law.[56]

In the uproar which ripped the country, the other demands went into the background; the cancellation of the externment orders reigned supreme. Dawood and Sohail met the local administration and the governor of West Pakistan, the formidable Nawab of Kalabagh, in Rawalpindi. Meanwhile, the sword of Damocles hung over their heads as the ten-day deadline drew near and Baqar Askary and the NSF threatened to resume the strike on 15 October 1962. Seven students, Rana Azhar Ali Khan chairman of ICB, Baqar Askary, Khalid Mansoor, Mahmood Khan Modi, Mahboob Ali, Shafi Adabi and Saghir Ahmad, also travelled to Lahore to meet Kalabagh. The externment orders were lifted on 15 October 1962.[57]

And so it was that Fatehyab returned to Karachi thirty-six days after he was thrown out of the city.[58] They all returned together on 19 October 1962 by the Tezrau train. Jubilant and emotional scenes accompanied their arrival at Cantonment Station as people rushed to catch a glimpse of them. They were taken in processions through the streets of the city and the various colleges. Fatehyab demanded an open trial of students whom the government had described as traitors or foreign agents. If they were guilty, he said, they should be hanged and not a single voice would be raised from any quarter. If these charges could not be proved, an unconditional apology should be tendered. Later they condoled with the widow of the unfortunate Karamat Ali and visited his grave. Fatehyab proposed that Landhi railway station should be named after him.

What had started as a dramatic event in the Muslim Leaguers' Convention on 5 September 1962 had turned into nationwide turmoil. Never since has there been a movement of young people on the scale on which it occurred in the months of September and October 1962. It has been celebrated because Ayub Khan's dictatorship was challenged in educational campuses and the streets of Karachi and other cities.[59] Looking back at that amazing mobilisation almost sixty years later, one can see how the government's distance from reality threw up a new breed of leadership and brought together these young women and men whose fierce activism and friendship bonded them for future political movements in Pakistan.

Chapter 6

Education and Employment

The University of Karachi was established in 1951 in response to the need for higher education in the province of Sindh, whose population had swollen exponentially by migrants from India.[1] It was located in a lovely building in the old city on Princess Street. Student activism in the 1950s in Karachi, which was then the capital of the country had, as we have seen, raised many concerns for the administration. The building on Princess Street could hardly accommodate the growing student population and Ayub Khan was anxious that campuses should be shifted outside city centres so that there would be peace and governance would not be brought to a standstill. Therefore, a plot of land measuring 1,200 acres was allotted to the university miles away from the centre of the city, miles away also from the central prison, which was the last building on the city periphery. There was hardly any habitation along the road except for a path leading on the left to Farmhouse School. Beyond that, there was only wilderness and the Ojha Sanatorium.

For designing the buildings on the new campus, the government engaged the French architect and urban planner, Michel Ecochard (1905–85). He was not a stranger to Pakistan and had made a study for the settlement of refugees in 1953. He was a leading planner of Third World cities.[2] Much of his work was located in the Middle East and the Mediterranean and his public works in Damascus were specially acclaimed. Therefore, he was not unfamiliar with the nuances of the building traditions of Muslim countries. But he was also inspired by and was an admirer of the famous modernist French architect, Le Corbusier. His design for the campus took into account its vast sweep and also the climate of Karachi, of which he made a thorough study. All the buildings, including the staff quarters, had a constant flow of fresh air, making air-conditioning unnecessary in summer and they were warm in winter.

Ecochard's modernist and functional design for the university was neither understood nor appreciated. It was so different from traditional and colonial architecture. There were no domes, no arches, no grand reception rooms, no ornamental pathways. To his regret and bitterness, his concept was 'mauled' and abandoned by successive vice chancellors in the later buildings constructed on the campus. The urge to 'nativitise' was strong and the university settled for what it was comfortable with, the mundane and unpleasing architecture of the public works department. Moreover, he had designed a campus for 7,000 students, whereas today, 42,000 students are enrolled in the university. Almost sixty years later, the university is a hotchpotch of unpleasing buildings and vast stretches of unkempt land still exist. The Muslim landscaping and gardens we were promised are a distant fantasy, although they were part of the original plans. Architects who understand the modernist vision regard Ecochard's architecture at the university as far superior in terms of design and proportionality to anything produced in Pakistan to this day. It has been described as a universal heritage, not only Pakistan's heritage.[3]

The university moved to the new campus in 1960, the year I enrolled in the political science department. A small ribbon of a road, an apology for a highway, ran from the central prison to the campus through the sand dunes and prickly *babul* shrubs. The move was not particularly kind to the students. No provision was made in advance for transport to the campus and those who had no transport of their own were very often stranded in the evening and had to walk for miles as far as the prison roundabout. Gradually, some buses started plying but they were not sufficient to carry all the students. There was no academic facilitation either and no guidance counters. One had to grope one's way to find answers. It was with my friend, Farida Tapal, that I first met Fatehyab in the administration block when we went to get admission forms and there was not an official in sight anywhere. We were standing helplessly and about to turn away when Fatehyab appeared and got the forms for us. The cafeteria was not yet functioning and we often had tea from a dilapidated shack affectionately called *café de phoons*.

I had led a protected life and although I had frequently travelled in rickshaws, I had rarely taken the public bus. Farida, who lived on nearby Queens Road, and I experimented with reaching the campus by boarding a public bus from Empress Market, but soon gave up. Some of us, who lived in the same neighbourhood, started sharing our cars to go to the campus. To return home, Taj Abidi and I took the university bus into the city from where I hailed a rickshaw and she proceeded by another bus to her distant home in Hussain D' Silva Town. Our parents may have worried about us but did not show their concern. Karachi was a fairly safe city.

The distance of the campus from my home in Intelligence School and the long hours of travel did not detract from the novelty of my experience at the university. In those days there were no private universities. Our public sector university was a remarkable leveller in social terms. The rich had not yet opened their own private academies and young people from all backgrounds flocked to join its departments. Also, it was still easy to get admission. By and large, the more well-to-do refrained from participating in students' movements.

The two years I spent at the university were a great learning experience for me and taught me more about the people and problems of the country than any formal curriculum. So far, I had studied in the insulated atmosphere of missionary institutions. The year 1960 was unusual in that many women from St Joseph's College joined the university, raising female participation sharply. They came like a breath of fresh air to the rather inhibited female population and their presence added the colour and glamour which was lacking in the environment in Princess Street. They studied in all departments but were mainly enrolled in the English department and the arts faculty became a magnet for young men who converged there to look at them. Although many social barriers were breached, the women kept their distance and generally flocked together. Conversing in English and smartly turned out, their style offset the Spartan lines of Ecochard's architecture. Some young men dared to actually speak to them. But there were other attractive women too – Suraiya the Bengali girl, so lovely in her simplicity, Ayesha Riyasat, or Tashmeem Razzaki and my beloved friend in the political or science department, Taj Abidi.[4] Ayesha Riyasat became a silver-screen actress. Tashmeem Razzaki, a microbiologist, acquired recognition for her devotion to teaching at the university and for stem cell research.

My teachers were an uneven mixture of erudition and knowledge. I remember the brilliant lectures on political theory by Syed Adil Hussain, made more interesting by his handsome golden looks. World history was taught with so much enthusiasm by the eccentric Salahuddin who later lost his senses, climbed a tree and refused to come down unless he was recognised as a prophet, and Barkat Warsi, whose departure from the university reduced us all to tears and he wept also. One could confront one's teachers. In one lecture being delivered by Amir Hasan Siddiqui, my friend Taj could not tolerate what she regarded as his sectarian prejudice and stood up to challenge his views. He was very angry, walked out of the room and refused to teach us anymore. We cajoled him back, but Taj refused to attend his lectures. There were scholars of stature like Mahmud Husain,[5] dean of arts, experts in their fields like Abul Lais Siddiqui, Urdu critic and linguist, and Maya Jamil in the English department. But the professor whose dignity surpassed that of all others was Ilyas Ahmed, who was chairman of the department of political science. Always dressed in a *sherwani*, he was the embodiment of old world culture and tolerance and commanded absolute respect from everybody around him. I called on him in his modest house in PIB Colony when I was leaving to study at Cambridge. He was very unwell and could hardly rise from the *charpoy* on which he was lying. But he wished me well and asked if the degree I earned at Cambridge would be called 'Cantab'. Shortly afterwards, he passed away.

The political science department, which Taj and I joined, was a friendly place. There were no social barriers, but many conservative men students were still nervous and reluctant to speak to the women. It was my first experience of studying in a co-education institution and this was true for many of my male colleagues also. But those among us who became friends struck a fine balance between familiarity and respect, going together on picnics, attending debates, participating in sports, and studying in the department's library. We sat, ate, read and laughed together and there was no imposition of the ridiculous restrictions that are practised in some educational institutions today: Taj, Shafiq, Syed Mohsin Ali (who became a famous television producer), Fatehyab, Matloob Ahmed, Shamimuddin (who joined the air force) and Yaqinuddin. Outside the department, I remember the panache and style of Syed Jameel Akhtar, a reputed scholar of Urdu. He always dressed in a *chooridar* pyjama and sherwani. Not many women observed purdah on the campus; however, I do recall the mysterious Naghmana who was draped in black robes from head to foot with only her eyes showing, which she made up carefully. She died, unfortunately, in a car accident. The kind of hijab which is now so common, was simply unknown.

In a strange kind of way, the concept of social welfare prevailed. Education was not too expensive in those days, but it was still beyond the reach of the poor, therefore the students had agitated for lower fees and more facilities. Some of the richer students with an 'English medium' background came in their showy cars and aroused the envy of those who could not even afford to pay their fees. Apart from these issues, there was a pleasant atmosphere on the campus, even a romantic one, if one took into account the soulful walk of Ahmed Maqsood Hameedi up and down the corridors, the many friendships which sprang up, the budding talent of Waheed Murad (who became the future chocolate hero of the cinema), and the handsome looks of Jan-i-Alam. There was no violence in the university. The nearest to weapons was the knife which Wali Nizami was said to carry in his pocket.

There was a vibrant extracurricular life with many debating contests in both Urdu and English, organised by Fatehyab's union, in which students from all over the country participated. It may have been the dramatic increase in the number of women in the campus which produced the anonymous honours list for ten women students which Taj and I found one day, scattered on the floor in the seminar room. The couplet describing me has remained one of the most glowing compliments ever bestowed upon me:

> *har tajalli hai terey samne sharminda si*
> *chandni saya-i-deevar hui jati hai*

> all light shies away before your beauty
> even the moonlight hides behind a wall

Today I view this compliment to my beauty with gratitude and humour; in 1960 it was embarrassing and seemed to draw unnecessary attention to my person. My classmate, Mutahir, who was very fat and wore a burqa, but was a sincere and affectionate friend, was disturbed by this mischief. She suggested that we should pre-empt another list and so we secretly drew up our own the following year, getting it cyclostyled because there were no photocopiers in those days. We slid copies of the list under the doors of the seminar rooms and classrooms.

It was my father's dream that I should study at Cambridge, the university about which he was so nostalgic and where he had been so happy. Because I stood first in the MA examinations, I was given a merit scholarship by the government. However, I gained admission in Cambridge even before the MA result was announced, on the basis of a single handwritten essay on Socrates which I had posted to the university. When I left Karachi, my father was with our delegation at the United Nations and my brother Arif was in Oxford. My mother and some friends saw me off. I was very worried about Fatehyab's fate – he was living out his exile in Sukkur.

Many of my friends from the University of Karachi went to Cambridge: Tariq Jafar to Queens College, Javid Ali Khan to Fitzwilliam College and Qadir Sayeed to St John's. Fatehyab also tried to get away. Ilyas Ahmed gave him a glowing testimonial praising his qualities of head and heart, his courtesy towards his teachers, affection for other students and brilliant debating skills. If he could find a good supervisor, he wrote, he would do excellent research work.[6] Fitzwilliam College admitted Fatehyab but the government refused to give him a passport to travel. Later, he got admission in the Middle Temple to study for the Bar but was again refused a passport. Depriving Fatehyab of the opportunity to study at Cambridge was the cruellest of all the blows inflicted on him by Ayub Khan's government. To this day, I wonder why they were so obsessed with him – he was not even a member of any communist party. Perhaps their denial was an acknowledgement of his commitment to his principles and political convictions and his tremendous organising skills. It was easier to deal with the communists; some of them had learnt how to compromise and survive.

Girton, to which I was admitted, was the oldest women's college in Cambridge. It was established as an institution of 'higher education for women' in 1869 by Emily Davis, Barbara Bodichon and Lady Stanley of Alderley, but was not then recognised as a college of the university. So great was male prejudice against education for women that the college had to be located at Hitchin, at a convenient distance from Cambridge. However, the women insisted and persisted in fighting for their cause.[7] In 1873, it was relocated to its present site, a few miles outside Cambridge in the village of Girton, whose name it bears. It was, therefore, still far enough to prevent any socialising between women and men students. It did not receive the status of a college of the university until 1948, barely fourteen years before I joined. When I went to Cambridge, the two other women's colleges were Newnham (1872) and New Hall (1954) which I have always associated with Kaniz Sharif who read for the English tripos. The Lucy Cavendish College for women was established before I left in 1967.

I never occupied rooms in Girton. For the first two years I lived in the women graduates' club on 12 Mill Lane, a heritage building with a view from my room of the Cam where all the punts were parked, the scene of much liveliness in The Mill, the pub on the river. We must have been about ten women graduates in this heritage building, and I remember the lawyer from South Africa, Rowena Brett, with special affection. Cambridge is located in a hollow, completely exposed to the winds from the east which sweep over the Fens. The house was extremely cold. There were draughts under the doors and windows and only a small single-bar electricity heater, into which I had to keep pouring shillings, was available to beat the winter. We were not allowed to light a coal fire in the 'parlour' on the ground floor, although the winter was reported to be the severest of the century. The university library was huge and only slightly warmer. Finally, when I could not bear the cold anymore, I bought an electric blanket for myself. Every month I was paid the handsome amount of £50 for all my needs, including rent for the room. My parents never supplemented my scholarship with a contribution of their own.

For the better part of the rest of my stay, I lived on 11 Trumpington Street where Girton had a graduates' hostel. My room on the topmost floor was so tiny that my clothes had to be shifted to a cupboard on another floor. The room held only a bed, a small bookcase, a desk, a chair and a basin in one corner. That was my entire universe. On the landing there was a stove on which I could cook and which I shared with Leila Ahmed[8] from Egypt who lived across the staircase. Apart from Leila and me, all the other residents were scientists and left for their laboratories in the morning. The telephone was located on the ground floor, and since I was usually the only person in the house, I ran down several times a day to answer calls. That was one reason why I became so slim.

I went to Girton occasionally for dinners or to meet my tutor, Mary Ann Radzinowicz. She was the American wife of Leon Radzinowicz, the renowned criminologist and founder of the Institute of Criminology at Cambridge, but she was a scholar of English literature in her own right. The Mistress of Girton was Dame Mary Cartwright, a grand woman who was known as a genius in mathematics and held this position from 1949 to 1968. One of the early founders of the chaos theory in mathematics (which, as a lay person, I regard as the study of unpredictability) she contributed to the study of the oscillation of radio waves during the Second World War. She was the first woman mathematician to become a fellow of the Royal Society. I remember her declaring at the end of dinners at Girton: 'Ladies, you *may* smoke.' I made many friends, but only a few of them were English – Graham Castor, Gar Alperovitz, Irfanul Haque, Kaniz Sharif, Camellia Panjabi, Ted Margadant, Amit Bhaduri, Simon Schama – not forgetting Anil Seal whose support, friendship and encouragement sustained me during the trying days of thesis writing.[9]

Academically, Cambridge was a feast. The supervisor of my doctoral thesis was the celebrated historian, Nicholas Mansergh (1910–91). He was the historian of modern Ireland, the empire and the Commonwealth. Before he was 30 years old, he had published three books on his beloved Ireland. During the Second World War, he worked for the British government as an expert on Irish affairs but turned to scholarship after the war ended. His academic career took him to Chatham House where he distinguished himself by his classic surveys of Commonwealth history. He became the first Smuts Professor of the History of the Commonwealth at Cambridge in 1953 and Master of St John's College in 1969. He was a superb scholar, meticulous and elegant, and he wrote with lucid brilliance and subtle humour 'and a complete understanding of personalities and pressure of events'.[10] Through his scholarship he not only contributed to the historiography of the Commonwealth but also influenced the policy decisions by which the empire transited to a multiracial association 'based on shared values and perspectives, without the clutter of dated imperial terminology'.[11] His crowning achievement was as editor-in-chief of the masterly twelve volumes of declassified British records on the transfer of power in India, 1942–7.[12] Often, I dwell on his wisdom: 'Men who make revolutions are rarely in a predicament; men who find themselves in revolutionary situations very often are.'

I was not sure whether Mansergh would agree to supervise my thesis and I do not recall how the meeting with him was arranged. One cold evening, however, I found my way to his rooms in St John's College and knocked on the door. I heard a very deep voice saying calmly, 'come in'. I went in a little nervously. He was sitting in a huge armchair close to the fireplace – he was a tall and lanky person himself – and proceeded to interview me. I was probably not very coherent in my replies but he agreed to become my supervisor, although he was a historian, and I had been admitted to the faculty of economics and politics.

Before beginning to work on my thesis, I was required to take two papers, one a tripos paper in political sociology, a new subject at Cambridge, and the other a postgraduate paper in comparative government. Philip Abrams (1933–81), who had joined as a young lecturer that very year, was my tutor in political sociology. I found him rather self-conscious. He seemed to provide few answers and I felt completely out of my depth in the subject. Later in his academic career, however, he achieved distinction as a thinker in this discipline. His great contribution was the philosophy that there is no division between sociology and history, that they are essentially the same subject, not separate areas of study. His famous work, *Historical Sociology*,[13] was published posthumously after his death. I am not sure if he had ever heard of Ibn Khaldun's (1332–1406) *Muqaddima*, the universal history in which both areas of discourse were intertwined and about whom Toynbee wrote: 'He conceived and created a philosophy of history that was undoubtedly the greatest work ever created by a man of intelligence.' Ibn Khaldun did not figure in our syllabus. The course on comparative government was taught by the famous scholar, Denis Brogan, who was professor of political science; he always looked straight ahead of him when he spoke.

As the examinations approached, I became unsure about my ability to pass and confided in Mrs Radzinowicz. I found her sympathetic, but she brushed aside my fears. When the results were announced, I was utterly surprised that I had got a first. Denis Brogan, I heard, wrote a special note about my performance. I must have done well because, when I was interviewed to proceed with my thesis, the committee members asked me about my teachers at the University of Karachi. I told them about Syed Adil Hussain and Ilyas Ahmed, scholar and gentleman that he was.

Attending lectures was not compulsory because there was no course work and a PhD is a purely research degree at Cambridge. It is a loner's life, one lives with one's sources and material. But I did attend lectures by my supervisor, Nicholas Mansergh, Eric Stokes, Anil Seal, the orientalist A.J. Arberry, and Bernard Lewis when he visited. Ian Stephens, a great friend of Pakistan, who was winding up his affairs to leave this world, granted me a couple of interviews. Cambridge was rather conservative in its approach to history; what we regard as imperialism today was described as the 'expansion of Europe'. But I was fortunate in making the acquaintance of John Gallagher (1919–80), historian of the British empire and co-author with Ronald Robinson of *Africa and the Victorians: The Official Mind of Imperialism*.[14] This work is said to have caused a historiography revolution through its provocative ideas and brilliant writing. It proposed the notion of empire not only as the conquest of territory by European powers, but also as the response and collaboration of conquered people. And it viewed British imperialism as the interaction between Britain and its collaborators among the native population residing in its colonies.

However, it had its critics who pointed out exceptions to this rule, especially in Africa. Gallagher was then professor of history at Oxford and he frequently visited his favourite student, Anil Seal, in Trinity College. From 1971 until his death, he was professor of imperial and naval history at Cambridge. He was very gracious and took me to dinner at Le Jardin, the upmarket French restaurant, advising me never to co-author a book, an oblique reference to his differences with Ronald Robinson. Nicholas Mansergh was hospitable too – he always invited his students to high tea at his home in Little Shelford, a few miles outside Cambridge.

The controversy started by F.R. Leavis in his book *Two Cultures?*, a critique of C.P. Snow's 1959 lecture on 'The two cultures and the scientific revolution', still engaged his admiring followers and was a significant part of the academic debate at that time. Cambridge was famous for its school of Keynesian economics, studded with giants like Joan Robinson, Piero Sraffa, Austin Robinson, Nicholas Kaldor and Richard Kahn.[15] More superlatives have been heaped on John Maynard Keynes than upon any other economist, both for his theory and inspiring personality. He provided the economic rationale for the welfare state and by advocating public finance and government intervention in the economy, he may be considered as the saviour of capitalism. In my time, Joan Robinson was a fellow of Newnham College and later professor of economics and fellow of Girton College. She told me it would be ages before my country would find economic salvation (the expression is mine). She was an impressive figure on the streets of Cambridge, tall, handsome, dressed in a *shalwar kamiz*, draped in a shawl in the way of the women of the subcontinent, with her grey hair coiled back in a chignon, she could have been a Pathan woman in Pakistan. Her interest in developing economies led to her fascination with India and China which she visited several times. In her books on China, she praised the cultural revolution of Mao Zedong, which is considered today to have been a great disaster.

For one whole term, I travelled daily to London to read and research at the India Office Library, then housed in dark and crummy rooms in Whitehall. I took the 9 a.m. train to Liverpool Street and returned to Cambridge when the library closed, easily recognising the other commuters, only to rush to catch the train again next morning. I could have stayed overnight in London and nobody would have bothered, but Mansergh said 'keeping term' meant sleeping in Cambridge and I was honest about it. Since I did not know how to type, the chapters I gave Mansergh were all written in longhand by me. He read them and often discussed them with me, but never corrected anything I wrote. The only amendment he made was to the first few lines of the abstract of the thesis. He advised me to avoid using adjectives and I have tried to follow this advice in all my work. As the historian of the partition of Ireland, nobody understood better than Mansergh the conflict between nationalism and imperialism and he easily comprehended the forces behind Muslim separatism in India – about which I wrote in my thesis. He held liberal political views, and when I met him later in life he empathised with Fatehyab's political struggle. But he was an old-fashioned gentleman and never called me by my first name. I was always 'Miss Hasan'. Nor would I have dared to address him as 'Nicholas'.

In the academic year 1964–5, I went back home to collect material for my thesis on the transfer of power to Pakistan. I interviewed many people and was a little surprised at how easily doors opened, considering that nobody ever accompanied me. The cabinet division was then located in a nondescript building near the railway yards in Rawalpindi. Its senior officers let me see some of the confidential record on the canal waters dispute. But the real scoop came in Lahore. I sat, uncertain of how he would receive me, outside the office of the chief secretary of West Pakistan. In his grand office, he was aloof but not unfriendly. He sent me to Mian Sadullah, the keeper of the archives and from him I received the most affectionate support. He decided to give me access to the Punjab Boundary Commission records and trusted me enough to take the large maps in the records outside to get them copied. In the hot summer months of 1965, I sat in Anarkali's tomb in the Punjab secretariat, where the archives are housed, to read this fantastic record. Virtually, I copied it all out by hand.

Beside my seat in the tomb was the sarcophagus supposed to belong to Anarkali, the unfortunate courtesan whom Emperor Akbar was said to have condemned to death by suffocation between four walls because she flirted with his son, the heir apparent Salim, later Emperor Jahangir. On the sarcophagus a couplet in Persian is crafted in stone, attributed to Jahangir, which reads:

> *Could I behold the face of my beloved once more*
> *I would thank God until the day of resurrection*

But Anarkali was just a fictitious character created by the dramatist Imtiaz Ali Taj, although her story has delighted generations of literature, cinema and theatre fans. The grave probably belongs to Sahib-i-Jamal Begum, the third wife of Jahangir.[16] He fell passionately in love with her and she bore him a son, Parvez, and two daughters who died in infancy. She passed away in 1599 before Jahangir became the emperor. By then, a voracious lover and admirer of beauty, he had taken many other wives. She was so beautiful that Akbar himself bestowed the title of Sahib-i-Jamal upon her.

My romance with the Punjab Boundary Commission records and that lovely mausoleum ended all too soon. Mansergh was delighted with all the original source material I brought back to Cambridge, including the police record. I was the first scholar to ever use the Punjab Boundary Commission records in all their detail and to analyse them comprehensively. All the official documents were published by Mian Sadullah in 1983.[17] I was surprised and hurt, however, that for reasons unknown to me, he did not mention my name in the list of scholars who had used the records. I wonder why. However, that chapter of my thesis was published in a book dedicated to my father.[18] More than anyone else in my life, he deserved that tribute.

In the months in which I finally finished writing my thesis, a lot of affection and attention were showered upon me by the Raja of Mahmudabad – who was a friend of my father – and the members of his family. His son, Sulaiman, was reading mathematics at Pembroke College. Raja Sahib often visited him and invariably took us out to dinner. His nephews, Hussain Mehdi and Qasim Mehdi also came to see me. I was moved by the trauma of that family, which had been deprived not only of their vast estates but also lost their grandeur, trying to come to terms with the humdrum life in Karachi. Raja Sahib was a sad man. Once I saw him in tears at Heffer's bookshop, when he recalled how his private papers were burnt by his secretary after Partition because a raid was feared by the Indian police on his palaces in Lucknow. In those papers were all Jinnah's scribbling and doodles which the Raja used to collect after Muslim League meetings concluded.

Two events of importance occurred in my life in 1964–5. The first was my visit to the grave of my grandfather, Anwar Hasan, in Cairo. I stopped in Cairo on my way to Karachi and my father arranged for me to stay with our ambassador, S.K. Dehlavi, popularly known as Baba Sahib. The embassy residence is located in a palace donated to our government by the elder Aga Khan and is situated on the Nile. The embassy traced both the graveyard belonging to the family of Mishki Bey in which my grandfather was buried in the necropolis of Cairo, and also the grave itself. Considering that the tombstone was almost forty years old, it was in a fairly good condition. Had I been more mature and less afraid of showing emotion, I would have sat by his grave for a long time and talked to him, for he was the author of our good fortune and status in life. More than five decades later, I wonder if the tombstone still survives.

The other event was my journey to India in January 1965 when I accompanied my father to the unofficial Commonwealth relations conference in Delhi. Before we left Karachi, he said to me, 'you are my eldest child and you will understand.' For him it was a journey of pain in which he finally seemed to bid farewell to all that he had owned and cherished, his properties and possessions, his vision of a united India which never became reality, his love for every Muslim monument, his attachment to the neighbourhoods of old Delhi where his ancestors had lived and worked.

It started as soon as we landed at the airport in Delhi when he turned to me suddenly and said that the customs officer belonged to Panipat! He walked sadly through the grounds of the Red Fort and complained to Saiyidain about the shabby condition of its palaces. I saw the meeting between him and the friend of his youth, Tara Bai, when she came to Janpath Hotel to meet him – their restrained emotion, her moist eyes. Some of his furniture was still in her use in Lady Irwin College and she had had a beautiful little tea table polished for him to take back to Karachi. He refused and gave it as a gift to Sushila, the wife of his deceased friend, Sham Nath, whom we visited before we left Delhi.[19] Then Tara Bai asked him to pick up some other items in her care, but he turned away again.[20]

The conference was attended by many distinguished scholars from institutes of international affairs in Commonwealth countries, among them Norman Harper from Australia,[21] with whom I started a correspondence. According to George Masterman, another delegate from Australia, I was 'the girl at the conference' whom he would long remember.[22] With Kamal Hossain[23] who was a member of our delegation – Bangladesh had not yet happened – and his wife Hameeda, I took the Taj Express to Agra to see Fatehpur Sikri, the fort and the exquisite Taj Mahal. I have always associated Agra with Emperor Akbar who became my hero in history because of his religious tolerance, respect for diversity, attempts to abolish *sati* and raise the age of marriage, patronage of scholarship, and kindness and generosity to the women of his family. And also because he shaved his beard.

The most disturbing part of our journey was the visit to our ancestral home in Panipat. I am not aware of how and when my father made arrangements to go there. We were received by Rajeshwar, an industrialist whom my family knew before Partition, and he took us to my father's house in Mohalla Ansar, for the name still survives. There was a school in the premises, the children were very poor. The house was in a shabby condition; it needed repairs and the plaster was falling from the walls and the roof. As written earlier, the house opened on to two streets and had a chauburji. On the side street its façade was lined with lovely inset arches, the colour of the Mughal monuments in Delhi. I recalled the well in the courtyard, the red brick walls, the *devri* where my cousin Asima and I used to hide under *moras*. My father went from room to room as his former *munshi*, Chetan, burst into the house, clung to him and wept helplessly. We drove to my father's garden house, but he did not descend from the car. He took one look at the house, as though for the last time and said, 'let's go.' The Imambara Kalan or big imambara, had been turned into a Hindu temple with many glistening idols of gods and goddesses. Chetan tried to console my father by saying that it was still, after all, a place of worship, and he nodded sadly.

When we returned to Delhi, Kamal Hossain asked about our visit to Panipat. 'Don't ask him, don't ask him,' said chairman Haleem,[24] who had abandoned his own ancestral home in Bihar and understood what my father was going through. When we reached Karachi, the first words my father said to my mother were, 'Sughra *biwi*, yesterday we went to Panipat.' Only now, more than five decades later, do I truly understand the pathos of those words, the final snapping of a link which spanned seven centuries.

I went back to Cambridge in the wake of the Pakistan-India war of 1965 with all the precious material I had collected. My father left for New York as a member of Pakistan's delegation to the United Nations. The delegation was led by Bhutto and the session itself was stormy because of the war. For the rest of my stay, I shut myself up in the tiny room on the topmost floor of the hostel on 11 Trumpington Street to write my thesis. But I never lost touch with the beauty of Cambridge. I had lived with it every single day. I had walked on foot throughout its length and breadth in all seasons, photographing the Backs, admiring the blossoms, the daffodils in spring, the weeping willows, the copper beech, watching the swans nesting near the Cam, and the bright northern lights in the sky during the long summer nights. Cambridge shut down and was deserted, as always, over Christmas for several days during my last winter there. It was cold but the air was crisp, the skies were clear, the moon was shining and I could whistle as I walked alone, along the silent streets. Decent women, my friend Susan Haque[25] had told me, don't smoke – and perhaps don't whistle – in the streets. There was a feeling of total abandon.

Percival Spear and Hugh Tinker[26] examined my thesis. It was easy sailing. Hugh Tinker asked me how I felt, now that I had a PhD. When he got his PhD, he said, he felt that bands were playing for him outside. For me, it was time to go home. I packed my few belongings and books in a trunk and shipped it to Karachi and said goodbye to Mansergh in a gathering at his home in Little Shelford. I was to meet him again in Cambridge and London when he became editor of those truly monumental volumes on the transfer of power in India. The publication of my thesis was deferred because, somehow, life overtook me when I returned. But he said that he often had occasion to mention my thesis to his colleagues in the India Office Library. My whole family came to the airport to receive me in Karachi. They were proud of me but wondered who would be brave and liberal enough to marry a Muslim woman with a PhD degree?

*   *   *

After I returned to Karachi from Cambridge, I spent many years as a faculty member of the National Institute of Public Administration (NIPA). I had made two strategic decisions: one, not to work for the private sector and two, not to work abroad for any concern. My natural inclination was towards a teaching job at the university. With my PhD from Cambridge, I went to see I.H. Qureshi who was then vice chancellor of the University of Karachi. He was, himself, a PhD holder from Cambridge and I thought he would welcome my joining the university. I had known him since I was a child; he was a friend of my father, who was anxious that I should start working as soon as possible. In fact, my father had rather proudly made me recite to him from the Quran when I was just a little girl. However, he did not seem keen to recruit me and offered me a very junior position. I went home disappointed. There were very few options and I moped around until a vacancy was announced as a researcher in NIPA.

NIPA Karachi was one of the in-service training organisations set up in the public sector by Ayub Khan as part of his training policy for civil servants. It was a federal institution for mid-career civil servants and two provincial institutions were also established: in Lahore for West Pakistan and in Dacca for East Pakistan. All of them were set up with the technical assistance of the United States and some of the earliest faculty members were Americans. Training, research and consultancy were rolled together as their functions, in keeping with the thinking of the time. The concept of periodic training was new to the country and it was strongly resisted by the higher bureaucracy. This resistance was the result of the elitist structure of the bureaucracy, crowned as it was with the civil service of Pakistan (CSP), the members of which considered themselves successors to the prestigious Indian civil service (ICS), and by the foreign service of Pakistan. The members of other cadres were considered lesser mortals. The deputy commissioner was the lynchpin of the administrative system. The district was the crucible which prepared officers for the highest administrative and policymaking jobs. Members of all the cadre services were recruited through competitive examinations. It was almost impossible for non-cadre public servants to rise to the highest positions in the bureaucracy. Both the civil service and the foreign service were closed to women who gained entry mainly through the financial services.

When I started working at NIPA, I soon realised that it was a dump. It was situated in a residential house on Sharea Faisal. On my first morning in the office, I could not find a single soul anywhere; nobody bothered to come to work on time. A new building was constructed for the institution on University Road on a large plot of land. When we shifted to those premises, I was dismayed. I had imagined that the institution would acquire a state of the art building, designed by a qualified architect, in which all the facilities needed to educate civil servants in modern concepts and techniques of governance would be available. The building turned out to be worse than – or almost like – a government-constructed primary school. Its floors were made of cement, its window frames of iron and its doors of the cheapest wood available. There was no sense whatsoever in its design. Nobody ever asked where the money went. This is from where I started my long journey to the top of the civil service of my country.

Because of the indifferent attitude of policymakers to training, none of the directors appointed were men of vision or learning. The one exception, during my career, was Iftikhar Ahmad Khan, the son of Nawab Ismail Khan of Meerut. His inclinations, however, were literary; he was a writer and a poet. Qualified persons were not appointed as directors from outside the bureaucracy on the argument that they would be unfamiliar with the working of the government. In fact, the institution became a convenient parking place for officers in distress – those who were out of favour, had fallen out with their bosses, were not trusted or just wanted to be in Karachi for personal reasons. One mentally unbalanced director played havoc with the faculty. On compassionate grounds and because he was a member of the cadre civil service, he was not sent home and was posted as director. The faculty members had to close their ranks to get him removed. I remember, however, the dignity of Waris Ali Chaudhry from East Pakistan. Equally, it was difficult to get quality faculty because of limited career opportunities. While the organisation fell within the public sector, the faculty members stood no chance of moving laterally into the mainstream civil service, although my colleague Anwar Siddiqui tried hard and unsuccessfully to do so.

Notwithstanding all that I have written so far, I saw NIPA Karachi grow into a great institution. Some of the indifference to training gradually wore off and often very fine officers were sent – for whatever reason – to our programmes. It became, like its sister institutions, the official home of the discipline of public administration – if it can be called a discipline – in the government; the purveyor of management theories, skills and expertise. Of particular importance for most officers were courses in financial administration and project management because many of them were working in these fields, as the government undertook large infrastructure and development projects without any systematic understanding of their functions. But the notable achievement of the programmes was the elimination, for each individual participant, of the tunnel view of development as she or he learnt about the governance responsibilities and experience of their colleagues. By and large, there was considerable freedom of expression during discussions and many

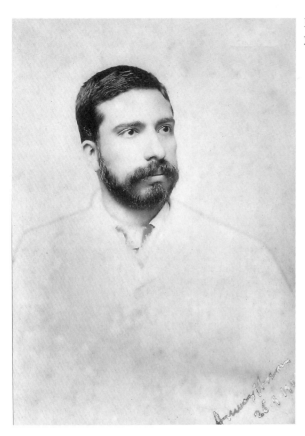

My grandfather, Anwar Hasan, in his youth.

My father, Sarwar Hasan, and mother, Sughra Begum, in London 1953.

Fatehyab Ali Khan when we got married in 1969.

In the Backs in Cambridge, 1965.

My sons, Hasan Ali Khan and Asad Ali Khan, 1993.

With Fatehyab Ali Khan in Pakistan's stall in the Women's Guild Bazaar in Vienna, 1997.

With Kurt Waldheim in Vienna, 1997.

With Saddam Hussein, President of Iraq, in Baghdad, February 2001.

In the General Conference of the International Atomic Energy Agency (IAEA), 1996. Ishfaq Ahmed, chairman, Pakistan Atomic Energy Commission (PAEC) is seated in the centre.

Meeting of the National Security Council, Islamabad, 2000.

Raising the flag on Pakistan's Republic Day in the embassy in Vienna, 1996.

In my office in the Pakistan embassy in Vienna, 1995.

With Thomas Klestil, president of Austria, in Hofburg Palace Vienna, after presenting my credentials as ambassador of Pakistan, 1995.

Fatehyab Ali Khan courting arrest on 18 August 1983 in Karachi during the Movement for Restoration of Democracy.

With my brother, Arif Hasan, 2020.

With my brother, Kazim Hasan (centre) and Fatehyab (far left), 1994.

Masuma Hasan.

officers were happy to get away from humdrum routine and the demands of their superiors

Although in-service training had not become mandatory for promotion, as it did later, one reason for its greater acceptance were the administrative reforms of Zulfikar Ali Bhutto in 1973. The administrative structure was manned by a profusion of services and it was estimated that more than 600 pay scales prevailed. Over the years, a great deal of resentment was generated against the elite services, especially the civil service of Pakistan, and the power they wielded. They were criticised for being inclusive and authoritarian generalists who were not equipped with the specialisations required for the development needs of a modern state. Many may have suffered from exclusion and one of them certainly was Vaqar Ahmad, a member of the audit and accounts service, who led the charge and was Bhutto's establishment secretary. But the intellectual substance of the reforms came from Bhutto's political party and its policymakers who had had enough of bureaucratic arrogance. There were others who supported a radical change, among them Hassan Habib who was, at that time, the principal of the Pakistan Administrative Staff College in Lahore, the apex training centre in the country. In him, Vaqar Ahmad found a willing partner.

Hassan Habib was associated with the founding of the Staff College and rose to the position of principal, from where he retired in 1976. He was handsome and refined, with a passion for reform.[27] He held my father in great respect and always affectionately encouraged me in my professional life. His ambition for me was to eventually step into his shoes. 'You must become the principal of the Staff College,' he would say. He was very hospitable. Even in later life, when he was very unwell, he always entertained me to lunch at the Gymkhana or dinner at a Chinese restaurant. He would don his peaked cap, pick up his walking stick, and sally forth.

Bhutto's administrative reforms had a tremendous levelling effect upon the public service. It was compressed into a few occupational groups which were supposed to be specialised and hundreds of pay scales were reduced to twenty-two 'grades' – still too many, I thought. This simplified the structure and the grades were gradually adopted by all public sector organisations, including the universities. The reforms also provided the opportunity for lateral entry – or entry for talented 'outsiders' – into the occupational groups and a system of combined pre-service training for probationers of all groups. Devising and implementing the reforms was a mammoth task. Subsequent changes led to the reversal of some of the steps which Bhutto took, and many of the occupational groups have been re-designated as services.

The first combined training programme, also called the 'first common', was held in Lahore in the winter of 1973. I was selected as a member of the faculty. My son, Hasan, was barely 2 years old at that time but I did not have the courage to refuse. I took him along with me to Lahore and my mother agreed to look after him during the day. The course was held both in the attractive civil services academy on the Mall in Lahore and in the huge campus of the finance services academy at Walton. There were only four or five women probationers in a large group of men. Bhutto had removed the ban on women's membership of the district management and foreign service groups. I was able to communicate well with my students, but the Walton group was both lively and raucous and decided to heckle me during the lectures. They had never had a comely young woman as a teacher before. After they had their fun, they bought a cake and held a party for me. Many of my students rose to the rank of federal secretary or held other important positions in the bureaucracy. Aftab Kohati, who joined the income tax group, was extremely tall but was soft-spoken and principled, with a charming sense of humour, and he was a superb singer. He was the son of Sattar Kohati, the legendary principal of S.M. Arts College Karachi from 1959 to 1972. When his mother passed away, he called me and always kept in touch with me until he passed away himself when I was ambassador in Vienna. His death was a tremendous blow to me.

How did I fare at NIPA Karachi? It was difficult, almost impossible, for a faculty member to rise beyond grade 20, almost equal to a joint secretary's position in remuneration, but not in importance. However, in 1984, when Fatehyab was facing Ziaul Haq's wrath, Ijlal Haider Zaidi, the establishment secretary, agreed that I should be promoted. My educational attainments may have played a part in this success and I had already become the deputy director of the institution. Beyond that was a red line which could never be crossed. I made representations for grade 21 which were stalled by the finance secretary, Rafiq Akhund, and the prime minister's principal secretary, U.A.G Isani; I did not belong to an elite group, I was not a member of any cadre. But ultimately, the tide changed and this grade was bestowed upon me in 1990. A couple of years later, I became the first woman and first faculty member and professional to head any management development institution. Although this was considered a great achievement, it brought me no peace. I was very bored and wanted to move out but did not know how to go about it.

I continued to work in NIPA Karachi because I needed a secure job to keep the family afloat. Fatehyab's political engagements kept us on financial tenterhooks and I would never have left my mother to take up employment abroad. Once I became the director, however, I put my heart and soul into my work and there was a tremendous response from the professional community. Since the faculty was sparse, we depended on experts from the field and the institution flourished because of their support and contribution. My colleagues and I pulled the programmes out of the bureaucratic fold and took the participants closer to the community. The women who flocked to our seminars from grassroots communities were especially expressive and eloquent about their priorities and problems. The largest city in the country, a megapolis, Karachi was developing an assertive civil society. Many innovative solutions to civic problems were being debated – some even adopted – and we opened our doors to all original ideas. One famous self-help approach which was later replicated in many countries of the world was the Orangi experiment fathered by Akhtar Hameed Khan. His first office was next to mine and a visit to the Orangi project became a regular part of our programmes. He was not able to draw me into the actual work of his project but he gave me his books of poetry and prose to read and paid me a glorious compliment: 'I consider you,' he said, 'the *itr* of all that is good in the elite of this country.'

I tried to keep the institution abreast of technology, developed a large computer laboratory and organised focused computer programmes which were over-subscribed. The faculty also reached out to the private sector and the organisation hummed with activity. NIPA Karachi was a small empire. Its physical infrastructure had been developed by Iftikhar Ahmad Khan during his long tenure as director and I had added to it. I conceived, and edited for many years, the *Pakistan Journal of Public Administration*, but it petered out because nobody else was willing to undertake that painstaking task. When I left, the institution's coffers were full of funds which were spent lavishly by my successors.

Whatever his earlier reservations may have been, cadre and non-cadre, about my promotion to higher levels, Isani seemed to overcome them when he came to know me as the director of NIPA Karachi in his capacity as chairman of its board of governors. He was the powerful secretary general in the establishment division at that time. He supported my efforts and gave me good advice when the clerks' association went on a rampage against me. They struck work and held noisy demonstrations with black flags and banners, but I did not budge before their unfair demands. They went to the press saying that a really cruel officer had taken charge of the institution. They even compared my attitude to the labour-friendly leanings of Fatehyab and went to see him to complain about me. Although Isani advised me not to become unpopular, he stood by me.

Isani was principal secretary when Moeenuddin Qureshi became the caretaker prime minister in 1993. He put up a summary for promotion to the highest grade 22 of three officers, including me, which the prime minister approved. Conservative bureaucrat he may have been, but all the three officers he recommended can be described as 'technocrats'. I was promoted to grade 22 on 10 October 1993. I had broken the glass ceiling. After Benazir Bhutto won the elections and became prime minister again a few days later, she questioned him about these promotions. A senior police officer who was present on the occasion is reported to have raised an objection and said about me: 'how can she be given the highest pay scale? She is married to Fatehyab Ali Khan.' That had been an issue of concern about me for all governments.

Through my long association with NIPA Karachi, I learnt about the distant reaches of the government and developed a holistic view of actual governance. Civil servants from all parts of the country, from different backgrounds and professions, doctors, engineers, geologists, scientists, planners, members of the armed forces and intelligence agencies, many occupational groups and even elected representatives passed through its portals. The camaraderie they developed often lasted for a lifetime. Interacting with them gave me a broad perspective of public policy. Because there was so much reliance on outside expertise, I was able to learn also from outstanding specialists in different fields. I lectured at many academies and universities, attended numerous conferences at home and abroad and travelled to many countries. I am very grateful for that experience.

The continuing concern of all governments was reforms in the public sector and I was a member of many committees. The major commission was the Services Reforms Commission set up in 1989 which was headed by Justice Dorab Patel, former judge of the Supreme Court of Pakistan. It was a privilege to work with him.[28] He upheld the highest traditions of independence in the judiciary, refused to take the oath as a judge under the dictator, Ziaul Haq, in 1981 and resigned. He was very calm, patient and focused in conducting the proceedings of the commission, which travelled to all provincial capitals and heard all stakeholders. A lot of money was spent on its travels and proceedings. But, as with most commissions, nothing came of it, and after Benazir Bhutto's government was dismissed in 1990, everybody lost interest in its work. It was wound up in 1994 and, to the best of my knowledge, its recommendations were not made public.

Chapter 7

The Bhutto Years

The loss of East Pakistan was a monumental tragedy which left my family both shocked and shaken. For my parents' generation, which had sacrificed so much for a new homeland, it was a betrayal with which they could not come to terms. Some people in West Pakistan were more unhappy about the defeat and humiliation suffered by the army than with the loss of territory. My father had found comfort in the false news of success in the eastern theatre and the individual acts of heroism which were reported in the press. However, all hope collapsed when Dacca fell on 16 December 1971. A couple of years earlier, when I was in Dacca to do research for a book, I had sensed the Bengalis' resentment, whether in my interview of Abul Hashem[1] or conversations with that most respected of mentors, Abdul Razzak of Dacca University, who was interested in my work and took me under his wing. In fact, in a post office in the city, I had found it impossible to buy stamps because I could not speak Bengali. The staff was amused at my confusion and I had to leave the post office in embarrassment. But the time I spent in Hameeda and Kamal Hossain's home, on the boat journeys with Abdul Razzak on the Ganges, and on the road to Mymensingh and Rajshahi, were among the happiest moments of my life.

In our public memory, Zulfikar Ali Bhutto is regarded as both a saviour and spoiler in the events leading to the secession of East Pakistan. In my youth, he shot like a meteor across the political firmament of Pakistan and my story would be incomplete without a reference to the impact of his politics and personality on the times in which I lived. My father came close to Bhutto because of his expertise in foreign policy, wrote briefs for him, worked with him as a member of our delegations to the United Nations, and edited and published his speeches. He was impressed by Bhutto's political panache, his spirited projection of Pakistan's image abroad and the respect he commanded in the capitals of the world. When Bhutto was sacked as foreign minister by Ayub Khan in 1966, my father was one of the few persons who went to receive him at the airport in Karachi. Bhutto repaid this admiration by making a move to remove my father from his position in The Pakistan Institute of International Affairs.

Towards the end of 1972, Bhutto sent an emissary from the foreign office, asking that both my father and chairman Haleem should resign and 'new blood' should be inducted at the helm of the Institute's affairs. He had no *locus standi* to dictate these terms, as the Institute was a non-official private members' association and not a government organisation and apart from a paltry grant of a few thousand rupees annually, it was not even partially funded by the government. Actually, he was seeking a place for a member of his constituency, the Pakistan Peoples Party (PPP) and for diplomats who had retired from the foreign service. My father was not as upset with his likely removal as he was with the fact that he was not even consulted about who should succeed him. He was the builder of the Institute that had gained prestige from his own status as a scholar and expert in foreign policy and diplomacy. As Mahmud Husain[2] said in the memorial meeting held after my father passed away, he '*was* the Institute'.

My father died of a heart attack on 12 February 1973, before he could resign, and his health had, no doubt, been affected by the distress he had suffered. It seemed then, that the whole world had turned out to mourn for him, so large were the gatherings at his funeral and *soyem*. But there was not a word of comfort or condolence from Bhutto. When I went to collect my father's private papers from his office, I remember Haleem Sahib sitting at my father's desk with tears in his eyes, for their partnership had stretched over twenty-five years. '*Beti,*' he said to me, 'have you heard from Bhutto?' I saw Bhutto on many occasions in public meetings and when he spoke at the Institute as foreign minister, but I never actually met him.

Whatever his follies and mistakes, when Bhutto embarked on his new political journey after his removal by Ayub Khan, against whose martial law so many had struggled and taken to the streets, sufficient political space had been created for a vigorous opposition to emerge. All the important political leaders of that time had been in conversation with Ayub Khan at one time or another. Bhutto capitalised on the tenuous political landscape to form his own PPP with a socialist agenda, but recognised reality by asserting that 'Islam is our faith'. No doubt he also rode on the crest of the revolutionary wave for change which was sweeping throughout the world towards the end of the 1960s.

Bhutto was a new kind of phenomenon on Pakistan's political stage. His oratory, which has always been an important element in the political culture of the subcontinent, was a departure from the traditional style of public speaking followed by Muslim leaders whose sophisticated speeches sometimes created an intellectual distance between them and their audience. For the life of him, he could not have quoted from the scriptures or from Iqbal but he appealed to the poverty of the people and his personal flair and fearless expression created the atmosphere in which the barriers erected by social oppression seemed to crumble. He spoke in the language of the people and the street and the huge crowds in his public meetings responded vibrantly, as he raised question after question, through which he made them partners in his own policy decisions. After the stifling years of martial law, a new freedom seemed to emerge.

Leftist forces had gained some strength and credibility during the struggle against Ayub Khan. They now felt that they could, with their rhetoric, influence Bhutto or, as they said, 'use' Bhutto to advance their socialist ideology, and some of them decided to throw in their lot with him. Bhutto had personally asked many people, including Fatehyab, to join his party. For a long time, Fatehyab was in two minds about what to do. He was not a member of any political party and his activism and integrity would have won him a prominent place in the new party. In the end, he decided not to participate in the convention in which the PPP was launched in Lahore on 30 November 1967. Mairaj[3] believed that Fatehyab may have seen far beyond what other leftists did and come to the conclusion that Bhutto was no socialist and would never be able to sustain a socialist agenda. But the PPP was the party of the future and people belonging to many shades of political opinion and backgrounds converged in its ranks.

Bhutto has been accused of the worst follies in Pakistan's history. He posed as a great democrat but his own entry into politics, it is said, was made through the murky channels of Ayub Khan's martial law. He was obsequious towards Ayub Khan and flattered Iskander Mirza to the extent of calling him a greater leader than Jinnah.[4] He encouraged Ayub Khan to embark upon an ill-prepared operation in 1965 into Indian-held Kashmir and misled him by assuring him that India would not strike across the international frontier. In fact, it has even been suggested that Bhutto deliberately engineered the war so that Ayub Khan's government should fall and he should come into power himself.[5] He has been criticised for contributing to the break-up of Pakistan; some hold him solely responsible. He was in league with the army and his violent public statements clearly indicated his intentions.[6] His own unbridled ambition, they say, led Bhutto to his violent death. In fact, the famous palmist, Ibrahim, who was an educated man unlike many other palmists, had predicted at great risk to himself that eventually Bhutto would lose both his mind and his head![7]

Bhutto's detractors have given him no quarter. The choicest abuse has come from Lieutenant General Gul Hassan who, along with Air Marshal Rahim Khan, has been credited with bringing Bhutto to power,[8] which he has denied in his memoir. Only four days after the fall of Dacca, he was 'astonished' to find that Bhutto had already taken over as president and chief martial law administrator. He was 'more or less coerced'[9] by Bhutto to 'take over' the army but insisted that neither Bhutto nor his ministers would interfere in his work. He soon discovered that, in spite of the stupendous chaos Bhutto had inherited, he found time 'to get up to his tricks'. Their mutual mistrust increased as Gul Hassan refused to let the army be used during the labour unrest in Karachi and the police strike in Peshawar and some Punjab cities which Bhutto described as a 'mutiny'.[10] Gul Hassan felt that he was 'dealing with a person who thrived on mischief' and 'was hell-bent on wrecking the Army'.[11] Gul Hassan and Rahim Khan were dismissed for refusing to help the government, in an amusing and amazing cloak and dagger 'drama', and sent abroad as ambassadors.[12]

Gul Hassan criticises Bhutto's prodigious public meetings as managed by government agencies and the press, and the radio and television were at his command. 'The nation was fed Bhutto for breakfast, lunch and dinner', and any space or time left over 'was devoted to defaming Yahya Khan'. A 'showman of high calibre',[13] his 'devotion to democracy was an utter façade. He was an out and out autocrat and thrived on subterfuge, threats, vindictiveness, and was a master in the art of over-awing people' and his speeches were 'reminiscent of Hitler'.[14] He dwells on Bhutto's vanity, 'his utter lust for absolute power, and his unqualified abhorrence of any type of opposition',[15] his 'volcanic ambition and unbounded egoism' and in a way, he 'was his own Rasputin'.[16] Gul Hassan resigned as ambassador through a virulent telegram sent to Bhutto in April 1977[17] but was anguished by the fate he suffered.

Bhutto is the villain of the piece in Mazari's autobiography. He considers him a liar and deceiver whose sole aim was to further his own ambition, who persecuted his political rivals and brutally suppressed the aspirations of the people of Balochistan and the Frontier.[18] Bhutto was 'a man driven by naked ambition alone' and in his 'avid pursuit of power, basic concepts such as truth, loyalty and integrity had become largely foreign to his nature' writes Mazari.[19] In public statements he sank to crude forms of abuse, was a 'premeditated last-minute spoiler' in negotiations in the East Pakistan crisis, took pleasure in making people suffer and was a 'civilian despot' who loved 'flattery and sycophancy'. A creation of martial law, to him 'lying, double dealing and deceit were normal means of attaining and keeping power', and 'his selfish and brutal pursuit of absolute power had led to his undoing. He had engineered his own doom.'[20]

Contempt for Bhutto runs through all the writings of Asghar Khan, who was considered Bhutto's main political rival and was a popular leader of the Pakistan National Alliance (PNA) whose agitation triggered Bhutto's downfall. He was a rather stern politician. When Ayub Khan handed over power to Yahya Khan, he claims his was the 'lone voice of protest' while, on the other hand, Bhutto welcomed the imposition of martial law for the sole end of capturing power for which he was willing to use every stratagem.[21] In fact, during the East Pakistan crisis, Bhutto suggested to Yahya Khan that they would both make a very good team to run the country and all would be well in East Pakistan if 20,000 people were killed there.[22] Earlier, in 1970, when Asghar Khan toyed with the idea of joining the PPP, he discovered that Bhutto had scant respect for the people. He told Asghar Khan that they could rule together: 'The people are stupid and I know how to fool them. I will have the "danda" (stick) in my hand and no one will be able to remove us for twenty years.'[23] He threatened to break the legs of his party members who attended the session of the National Assembly which was to be convened in Dacca on 3 March 1971, though Bhutto denied having said this. The following day, Yahya Khan postponed the session. As a result, Mujibur Rahman's attitude, which had shown some chinks of flexibility, hardened and he described military action as 'the end of Pakistan'.[24] Asghar Khan even implies that Bhutto was responsible for the blowing up of the aircraft, Ganga, hijacked from Jammu to Lahore which gave India the excuse to prohibit flights over its territory between the two wings of Pakistan.[25] He bitterly criticises Bhutto's role in the Security Council, where he went as Yahya Khan's foreign minister, in rejecting Poland's resolution in December 1971 'which would have prevented the surrender of the Pakistan army six days later'.[26]

Asghar Khan gives many instances of how he and the members of his family and party were hounded, harassed and victimised after Bhutto came to power and how his party, Tehrik-i-Istiqlal, in its early life 'had to fight its way through fire and brimstone'.[27] But he has been fair to Bhutto on some counts. After the fall of Dacca, he publicly stated that there was no alternative but to hand over power to Bhutto and his party, although he believed that would be a tragedy. He recognises Bhutto's charisma, wit and charm, but says he had 'the arrogance and vindictiveness of the worst in our feudal aristocracy' and believed in the 'concept of absolute power'.[28] However, in his desire to impose one party rule, 'he did not abandon or deny the sanctity or supremacy of the law' but rather made constitutional amendments even though they changed the spirit of the 1973 Constitution.[29] The framing of the 1973 Constitution was a landmark in Pakistan's history, but Bhutto extracted a price in agreeing to a parliamentary system by insisting on the insertion of clauses which made the removal of the prime minister virtually impossible. He admits that during the first five years of Bhutto's rule, he had enjoyed 'a special licence' to move around with reasonable freedom.[30] As Ziaul Haq kept faltering on his promise to hold elections, Asghar Khan claims that, in a meeting with him on 3 May

1978, he asked that Bhutto should be released and he and his party should be permitted to take part in the elections.[31] It appears that, in the end, he did not plead for Bhutto's life to be saved.

There is no doubt that Bhutto inherited a colossal mess when he came to power and he and his ministers worked relentlessly to put the country again on an even keel. There were many achievements, especially in setting up financial and educational institutions and in restructuring the economy. The legislative programme and achievements were impressive, the most outstanding being the 1973 Constitution itself, although the earlier amendments to the Constitution were disappointing and Bhutto's preference for a presidential system had to be countered. Many pro-people and pro-labour laws were adopted, but there were some failures such as the generic medicines scheme which was sabotaged by the big pharmaceutical companies. Bhutto's nationalisation of industry, insurance, banking and education have been increasingly criticised in recent years. However, all those who held radical beliefs at that time were pleased with these decisions. He also introduced anti-elitist policies within the civil service and opened all occupational groups and the foreign service of Pakistan to women, a historic decision. He toured the country extensively, making his presence felt in the remotest regions where no political leader had ever ventured. Thus, even today, his name and visits are remembered and PPP offices can be found in these distant areas.

From the narratives of his own associates, however, he emerges as a whimsical ruler who indulged in theatrics,[32] showed scant respect for his colleagues and was contemptuous towards many of them. He could sack somebody one day and re-appoint the same person to an important position the next day. He accused them of laying plans to assassinate him and felt threatened by their popularity,[33] and he could sulk like a petulant beloved. He constantly tested their loyalty, feared their ambition and imprisoned them[34] or humiliated them[35] and got them beaten up, like the venerable party founder, J.A.Rahim, was beaten.[36]

In its early years, Bhutto's government was besieged by many problems: a police strike; widespread labour unrest; an unstable economy; a restive press, the language controversy in Sindh in which many lives were lost; and also the hostility of those whose businesses had been nationalised. He was keen on quick nationalisation and announced land reforms, but gradually veered towards the feudal elements which jumped on his apparent success and he moved away from his socialist agenda. He had 'taken another path' to 'rely on the traditional establishment of Pakistan, its colluders and collaborators'.[37] It was convenient, in these circumstances, for Bhutto's associates to blame the establishment and the intelligence services for all that went wrong.

Bhutto was an unfortunate leader whose close associates abandoned him in his hour of need. All his political colleagues owed their own importance to him and the wave of populism on which he rode, to his charisma and demagoguery. He attributed his downfall to their desertion, but they had seen the writing on the wall (which he failed to see) and had gradually started distancing themselves from him.[38] Some felt that he had betrayed his socialist mandate and emerged in his true feudal colours, some chafed at being suspected of disloyalty and being spied upon, and still others were unhappy with his contemptuous leadership style within the party. They considered him a 'rare political animal' but lived in constant fear of displeasing him. Many of them have written their own accounts after Bhutto's death and have squarely laid the blame for his downfall upon his suspicious nature, impulsive behaviour and failure to heed sincere advice. All these accounts are attempts by these writers to absolve themselves from the charge of contributing to Bhutto's downfall.

Rafi Raza's version is the most informed and coherent. He was Bhutto's personal friend and special assistant and was, therefore, in constant touch with him, accompanying him on his diplomatic trips abroad, including the journey to Simla to negotiate the return of Pakistan's prisoners of war with Indira Gandhi. He describes Bhutto's fall in terms of a Shakespearean tragedy, of a man of distinction brought down by his personal flaws, political errors and misjudgements. Let him have the last word in unravelling this enigma, for his words are worth quoting:

> He was full of complexes and contradictions: a feudal lord with socialist ideas, an educated man whose language was demotic, a populist with aristrocratic and autocratic attitudes who sought popular acclaim and adulation yet viewed individual human beings with regrettable contempt. He had a great belief in his own capacity, though at times he showed a surprising inability to see the reality of a situation.[39]

It is now generally agreed that the results of the general elections held in March 1977, which led to Bhutto's downfall, were manipulated. The PNA movement spread throughout the country, although the alliance itself was a marriage of disparate, even opposing, political elements.[40] To this day, many wonder from where the PNA got the funds to mobilise so many people. Had it not been for the number of casualties and deaths, the movement might not have garnered so much support.[41] As with all broad-based political protests, it was joined by many groups of dissidents who had their own complaints against Bhutto's regime. Foremost among them must have been former owners of business and trading concerns whose economic interests Bhutto had hurt by nationalisation. Foreign powers which were unhappy with Bhutto's nationalist foreign policy would have been happy to see him exit from the political scene, although they may not have wanted to go so far as to see him hanged.[42] Fatehyab and I watched his last late-night appearance on the television on 4 July 1977; he was a lonely and forlorn figure.

* * *

Fatehyab contested the 1977 elections to the National Assembly from two constituencies in Landhi-Korangi from the platform of the Pakistan Workers Party (PWP)[43] which he had joined and of which he was senior vice president. But in the face of the surging sea of support for the PPP and the opposing PNA, he did not stand a chance, although he campaigned bravely. His election symbol was the candle. He knew that he would not win, isolated as he was, but felt that he had to make a political statement. Fatehyab stood aside from the PNA movement against Bhutto, although we waited by the roadside to watch their impressive processions, and Fatehyab waved to the frontline leaders as they marched towards Jinnah's mausoleum. Instead of agreeing to a re-election in which he would not have fared badly, Bhutto clung to power and was ousted by Ziaul Haq in a military coup on 5 July 1977. Even here, his judgement had faltered.

After Ziaul Haq proclaimed martial law and detained Bhutto, a constitution petition challenging his detention and the imposition of martial law, R I of 1977, was filed by Nusrat Bhutto against the chief of army staff before the Supreme Court of Pakistan. The federation sought to become a party in the case and in his lengthy rejoinder, Bhutto described Ziaul Haq's reply as 'political pornography', wrote that a Nero could not become a hero and that Islam was not the monopoly of *mullahs*.[44] In its judgement in this case, the Supreme Court ultimately validated Ziaul Haq's martial law under the doctrine of necessity.[45]

While this petition was being heard, Fatehyab sent a telegram to all the judges of the Supreme Court asking to be made a party in Nusrat Bhutto's petition with regard to the detention of Bhutto and ten others. He wrote that he was an advocate, a patriot and a democrat and as a victim of a previous martial law in 1958, he knew that if the present martial law was validated, all his fundamental rights would disappear. He wanted to address public meetings on the supremacy of the Constitution and the rule of law but could not do so because of martial law orders and regulations. The question of public importance before the Court, he wrote boldly, was 'whether high treason had been committed and by whom'. He prayed that he may be allowed to address the Court in person as the questions being agitated were of grave public importance and affected him as a citizen, lawyer and politician. Subsequently, on 22 October 1977, he filed a constitution petition, R II of 1977, challenging the imposition of martial law, in the concluding stages of Nusrat Bhutto's petition.

Constitution petition R II of 1977 was a very hard hitting document.[46] Challenging Ziaul Haq's imposition of martial law, Fatehyab stated that it was the very antithesis of the rule of law and civil rights and liberties and was against the ideology of Pakistan which had been won through enormous sacrifices so that its people could live as free citizens in a democratic society. He recognised the crucial role of the armed forces but could not shut his eyes to the fact that, since 1958, over 150 senior officers of the armed forces had been directly or indirectly involved in politics in Pakistan. Ziaul Haq had also dragged the judiciary into politics and lowered the prestige of the army. Moreover, he had recently threatened to act harshly against 5 per cent of the population who opposed him, which came to a staggering 3.5 million people. He was prolonging his hold on power through a constitutional deviation, but did not enjoy a mandate from the people or authority from the Constitution. Democracy, the rule of law and Jinnah's vision for Pakistan had been thrown to the winds. He sought a declaration that Ziaul Haq's proclamation of 5 July 1977 was not valid and a direction for holding general elections. Since the Supreme Court validated the imposition of martial law on 10 November 1977, Fatehyab amended his petition in March 1978 but in spite of reminders, it went unheard.[47]

Fatehyab believed that these stands had to be taken and these views recorded, even if they were not considered and met with failure. They were rare acts of courage in those politically vindictive times. From his papers, it seems that he travelled to Rawalpindi and appeared in person before the Supreme Court to pursue his case. I remember him telling me that Bhutto and his wife were present in the Supreme Court when he appeared. Bhutto was surprised to see him and talked to him during the recess. On this occasion, Sharifuddin Pirzada, who was the attorney general and law officer assisting the Supreme Court, made a statement at the Bar that six months were needed to complete accountability, after which it would be possible to hold elections within two months. Fatehyab did not rest on this information. Much later, on 21 January 1979, he sent a contempt application to the Supreme Court, praying that since Sharifuddin Pirzada had misled the superior courts in the matter of holding elections, he had become ineligible to assist them and his presence and assistance should be dispensed with.[48]

Bhutto's trial for the murder of Mohammad Ahmed Khan Kasuri during Ziaul Haq's rule was a great test of the patience and political resilience of the people of my country. He has been accused of being responsible for the murder of political opponents and of browbeating and terrorising them, but few people in the circle in which I moved really believed that he had ordered Kasuri's assassination. Ziaul Haq's rule was so barbaric, however, that political activists did not easily dare to confront him openly. In a desperate attempt to draw attention to Bhutto's case, to everybody's astonishment, thirteen people burnt themselves to death. There is no responsible reckoning of all Ziaul Haq's barbarities, but he arrested thousands of workers of all protesting political parties and according to one estimate, the total number of lashes awarded by military courts was 45,000, including whipping for social crimes and taking part in political activities.[49] Even women were flogged.[50] It was disgusting then, as it is now in retrospect, that so many people used to turn up to watch the spectacle of flogging. All those spectators seemed to have had a thirst for blood.

The political worker or foot soldier in politics in a poor country, with an unhappy human rights record, is a particularly helpless and vulnerable creature. Since he is poor, as he usually is, he does not have the social status to avoid the infliction of cruelty or the financial resources to buy himself out of harsh treatment at police stations and by other agencies. He leaves his wife, children and other dependants with scant means to survive and puts his family members at the risk of harassment, and dispossession. Yet we expect him to rise above his fears and, it is surprising, how many actually do. Only faith in a cherished political leader or ideology keeps him afloat. However, some well-organised and well-endowed political outfits do provide funds and other kinds of assistance to their committed political workers.

Bhutto was condemned to death by the Lahore High Court for the murder of Mohammad Ahmed Khan Kasuri, on 18 March 1978. He went into appeal against the conviction before the Supreme Court of Pakistan. Shortly after that, the government started a campaign against him on the radio and television called 'Zulm ki Dastanain'. In this programme, people who had been incarcerated illegally by Bhutto narrated on the radio and television how they had been harassed and victimised. The list included some prominent politicians, such as Khawaja Khairuddin, a Muslim League leader from the former East Pakistan. Fatehyab viewed the programme as a vicious method of trying to influence public opinion and the judgment of the Supreme Court. His sense of justice was outraged and he was very disturbed by the programme. Therefore, he filed a contempt application and wrote to all the judges of the Supreme Court to stop the programme from being aired.

In his telegram to the judges of the Supreme Court, on 4 January 1979, Fatehyab stated that he had been in the vanguard of all democratic movements in the country and was one of the first persons to not only oppose the constitutional amendments made by Bhutto's government, but to come out openly against the imposition of the present martial law in his constitution petition, R II of 1977, which was still pending adjudication. 'Zulm ki Dastanain' merited judicial notice because, in Bhutto's appeal versus the State against being condemned to death by the Lahore High Court, the judgement was due to be announced soon and the case had attracted wide attention nationally and internationally. Therefore, even the slightest doubt that justice had not been done would strike at the very foundation of the administration of justice and the image of the judiciary. The programme amounted to contempt of court because, if Bhutto's appeal was dismissed, an impression would be created that the government had already taken a decision and through this programme it was preparing the people to accept Bhutto's punishment in terms of the forthcoming judgement. If the appeal was allowed at this juncture, it would make the judgement controversial in the eyes of the public. Therefore, he prayed that contempt proceedings should be initiated against Pakistan Television Corporation, Pakistan Broadcasting Corporation, the Minister of Information and Broadcasting, and the participants of the programme which should be stayed.[51] Fatehyab appeared in person before the Supreme Court on 21 January 1979. The programme was stayed by the Supreme Court which issued contempt notices to three respondents.[52] But it took up the matter after the dismissal of Bhutto's appeal.

Fatehyab's intervention in this matter was courageous because martial law was harsh and merciless. He had no political constituency and no political backing for this action which should have been taken by the members of Bhutto's own party. He had no welcoming place to stay in Rawalpindi or friends who would support him in those troubled times but he ventured forth, along with rare books on law from my father's library, some of which were retained by the judges and never returned. He was accompanied by my brother Kazim, who had recently returned to Pakistan after being admitted to the Bar at the Middle Temple. Kazim also helped Fatehyab to draw up the arguments. Thus he made his debut in the legal profession by appearing before the Supreme Court of Pakistan.

Bhutto's life hung by a thread as he waited for the judgement of the Supreme Court in the appeal filed against the sentence of the Lahore High Court. The Supreme Court dismissed Bhutto's appeal on 6 February 1979 and two days later, on 8 February 1979, Fatehyab sent a telegram to the Supreme Court which he described as communication in 'an unusual manner' in view of justice and urgency. He stated that the national and international reaction to the judgement had proved beyond any shadow of doubt that it had become controversial and would remain the subject of fierce judicial and political controversies for a long time to come. He pointed out the irregularities and flouting of principles in the composition of the court and stated further that: 'If the judgement delivered in appeal was unanimous the judicial controversy would not have arisen but the split majority judgement rendered the court *corum-non-judice* because there are constitutional provisions relating to quorum and filling of vacancies that were not observed.' Further, a review, if filed by Bhutto, could only lie before the permanent eligible judges of the Supreme Court of Pakistan.[53]

A petition for review of the Supreme Court's judgement was filed by Bhutto's lawyers, and Fatehyab sent another telegram to the Supreme Court submitting his 'short reasoning in the contention of lack of quorum for record and posterity lest it be regretted in judicial history that this anomaly was never pointed out to the Court'. He gave reasons why the number of judges in full court could not be reduced to less than eleven and, therefore, the judgement delivered on 6 February 1979 was *corum-non-judice*. With the rejection of Bhutto's appeal, the lack of quorum had become 'too glaring to be ignored by any jurist' and the Supreme Court should have considered the matter *suo moto*.[54]

Fatehyab's journey in this case did not end here. On 11 February 1979, he addressed Ziaul Haq as the chief martial law administrator, asking that the infliction of capital punishment be suspended during the current period of constitutional deviation. The Supreme Court had declared that the 1973 Constitution was still the supreme law of the land and the current period was, therefore, in the nature of a constitutional deviation. Ziaul Haq's own elevation to the office of president was also in the nature of a constitutional deviation because he was not eligible to become a member of the National Assembly and he was in the service of Pakistan. He must not, thus, exercise the president's prerogative to grant or refuse pardon and capital punishment should remain suspended until the country was back on a constitutional path.[55] If more people, perhaps a flood of people, had approached the Supreme Court, could there have been a reprieve for Bhutto?

* * *

Many rumours and conjectures were in circulation about how shabbily Bhutto was being treated in prison in Rawalpindi and also about what transpired in the last moments before he was hanged. These concerns have been laid to rest somewhat by the book written by Colonel Rafiuddin, who was the Special Security Superintendent in Rawalpindi District Jail, where Bhutto was held from 17 May 1978. He was an army officer who had served for eight years in the Special Services Group and had fought in the wars against India in 1965 and 1971. Later, he also served as military attaché in Pakistan's embassies in Indonesia and Malaysia and did a tour of duty in the Inter-Services Intelligence (ISI) directorate during the Afghan jihad. Thus he was highly trusted by the martial law authorities. In the last 323 days of Bhutto's life, in Rawalpindi District Jail, Rafiuddin was almost in daily contact with him and he seems to have developed an empathy for his prisoner. He has given an account of Bhutto's daily routine, lists of his daily visitors, details of Bhutto's conversations with him, his views on important national and international issues and his opinion about his colleagues and world leaders. Rafiuddin claims that he regarded Bhutto's hanging as a great national tragedy, and decided to publish his story thirty years after Bhutto was hanged, although he had starting writing it down immediately after his execution.[56]

From Rafiuddin's account it is clear that Ziaul Haq made detailed plans and took every possible precaution to prevent his prey from escaping from the prison in any manner whatsoever. The security force installed in the prison was kept alert to deal with any emergency and accident relating to Bhutto's attempt to commit suicide, attempts to murder him by poisoning him, blowing him up on his way to and from the Supreme Court, killing him in a traffic accident or by setting fire to the prison. The likely methods of escape considered were through a tunnel leading out of his cell, abduction through a ground attack led by commandos or an air attack with or without external help, inciting a mutiny within the prison to facilitate his escape or trying to free him through an attack by a huge public demonstration in front of the prison, the Supreme Court or on the road between the two. Before his arrival, the floor of his cell was dismantled, re-laid and fortified and the roof was reconstructed with iron sheets.[57]

All airlines, including Pakistan International Airlines (PIA), were prohibited from flying over the prison. A battery to bring down helicopters and aircraft flying over the prison was also installed and instructions given to the army aviation base at Dhamyal to shoot down any aircraft flying over the prison.[58] Around the security ward, machine guns and rocket launchers were installed which were manned day and night. Plans were put in place to deal with attempts to abduct Bhutto or the likelihood of his walking out in the *burqa* worn by his first wife, Ameer Begum, when she visited him in prison.[59] Sensitive instruments were installed in his cell to monitor his conversations and movements. All the conversations he had with his lawyers and other visitors were recorded, and the prison staff were given instructions to note in writing his behaviour and every word he said from the time he was told about his imminent hanging on the evening of 3 April 1979 until the last words he uttered, if at all, at the gallows. Rafiuddin writes that Bhutto's personality and public popularity had so terrorised his jailers that, in spite of these precautious, they feared he would somehow manage to escape.[60] One would think that Carlos the Jackal was on the prowl to take out Bhutto and set him free.

Inside the prison, Bhutto fought bravely to get relief from intrusive surveillance and restrictions on his movements against which he went on his first hunger strike from 18 to 22 May 1978. His living quarters comprised four cells, of which Rafiuddin has included a sketch in his book, and a courtyard where Bhutto was eventually permitted to sit in the evenings. This area was cordoned with rolls of barbed wire. Rafiuddin gives details of the facilities which he was allowed, like the furniture in his cell, food from outside, a *nawar* bed, a lamp, a fan and heater, personal bedding, linen and clothes. He was given two newspapers, *Pakistan Times* and *Jang* every day and the journals and magazines brought for him by his wife and daughter. But, after all, a prison cell is a prison cell.

When I interviewed Saleem Cheema on 20 November 2009 about his participation in the Pakistan movement, I was not aware that he had attended to Bhutto in Rawalpindi District Jail.[61] He flattered me by saying that more than anybody he knew, I understood the reason for the creation of Pakistan. Towards the end of the interview, he decided to trust me with recollections of his association with Bhutto which, he said, he had not yet shared with anybody else. He told me that he had provided dental care to Bhutto five times in prison but Rafiuddin's list of Bhutto's visitors shows that Cheema met him four times, on 3, 10 and 25 December 1978 and 3 February 1979. Cheema was a dental consultant to many important persons including Chief Justice Anwarul Haq who, on one occasion, asked him for a favour. Anwarul Haq was concerned about the reputation of the judiciary in the light of rumours floating around about Bhutto's deteriorating condition and he requested Cheema to look after Bhutto's health. Subsequently, Cheema received a letter from the Registrar of the Supreme Court, asking him to visit Bhutto. Before his first visit, he called on the Punjab home secretary, S.K. Mahmood, whose sterling qualities he admired, and who warned him to be careful. 'You are young,' he said, 'be careful, the place is bugged.'

Cheema was not a stranger to prisons. His father had been, at one stage in his career, medical officer in Lahore prison. He had some difficulty in getting access to Bhutto, as the jail superintendent, Yar Mohammad, had no prior notice of his arrival. When he met Bhutto, he greeted him as prime minister. Bhutto was pleased and asked, 'do you still consider me prime minister?' He was even more pleased when he discovered that Cheema, who had dressed in one of his best suits and a tie for the occasion, was not a *desi munda,* but had been educated in England and had taught in New York. He agreed to let Cheema examine his teeth, and a small dental unit was set up near Bhutto's room, including an X-ray facility and other equipment. Cheema found nothing particularly wrong with Bhutto's teeth.

Bhutto was hospitable. He had many facilities – books, newspapers, writing equipment, a Schaffer pen with a broad nib and black ink, hot and cold water for ablutions, a refrigerator, a kitchen. When he had guests, he could order food from outside. He was fond of chicken sandwiches, which he offered with coffee, and coaxed Cheema to stay longer over 'another cup of coffee'.

In the course of these visits, Cheema was able to sum up his patient. Bhutto was mentally alert, able and eloquent, with an excellent memory – in fact, a photographic memory – very well read, but distrustful and suspicious. He was upbeat in his attitude and distant from reality. He was critical of all his party colleagues; he never mentioned his sons but had kind words for Benazir. 'She will do well,' he said. He was extremely bitter about the way his mother had been treated and there was no forgiveness for the relatives who had refused to accept him and her legitimately into the family fold. Moreover, he was convinced that he could not be hanged.

'How can they hang me,' he would say, 'when the whole world, kings, queens, presidents and prime ministers are asking for my life to be spared?' On one occasion, he asked Cheema, 'do you know what I am writing? I am writing the speech I will make at *Mochi Darwaza*. My people will take me from here and drive me to Lahore and I will make this speech at Mochi Darwaza.' On another occasion, Cheema noticed that Bhutto wrote page after page and threw the pages behind his bed which, he thought, he used to pass on to his visitors. Yar Mohammad, the jail superintendent, had strict orders to ensure that Bhutto should not commit suicide and he sought Cheema's advice on the matter after Bhutto's appeal was rejected by the Supreme Court.

Cheema thought that Bhutto was extremely unwise in his utterances and brought his doom upon himself. He should have known that his prison cell was bugged but he was unrestrained in his expression, abused the generals and said he would make shoe laces from their hides. He swore at Ziaul Haq, regretting that he had not known that the general had a beard in his stomach, an Urdu metaphor implying that he was a covert mullah. Before his appeal to the Supreme Court was dismissed, Cheema met him for the last time. 'Do you think they will hang me,' he asked? Cheema could bring himself only to say, 'No Sir, they can't hang you.' He could hardly have said anything else.

Looking back, and on the basis of recollections and revelations, it is apparent that Ziaul Haq would have 'eliminated' Bhutto irrespective of the verdict of the Supreme Court. His crowded press conference, on 1 March 1979, was particularly telling and convinced us that he would not spare Bhutto. He said that it was his prerogative to reject or accept mercy petitions, but he saw no justification for a head of state to come in the way of a case after it had been duly decided by the superior courts and, in such a criminal case, there appeared no room for the prerogative to be used against the judgement. During the last eighteen months, he added, his government had sent 400 convicts to death and this criminal case was no different, implying that Bhutto would be hanged.[62]

Rafiuddin had been instructed not to release Bhutto even if the Supreme Court acquitted him and gave orders to set him free.[63] He also heard later that, in the event of Bhutto's acquittal, a special military court had been nominated to try him on other charges. Bhutto, however, did not believe, or hoped against hope, that he would not be hanged. He thought that a drama, a political stunt,[64] was being enacted to cut him down to size and that a former foreign minister, prime minister and president of the country could not be eliminated so easily. He was also the chairman of the Islamic Summit and was on good personal terms with the leaders of many countries. However, the Supreme Court rejected his appeal on 6 February 1979 and his review petition was also dismissed on 24 March 1979.

On 1 April 1979, Ziaul Haq signed on the decision to execute Bhutto. On 20 March 1979, Malik Ghulam Jilani's petition, praying that Bhutto's execution should be stayed and offering to pay blood money had been dismissed *in limini* by the Lahore High Court.[65] There was a last-minute desperate attempt by his close associates, led by Abdul Hafeez Pirzada, to save Bhutto's life through the courts of law. But his petitions, as well as the habeas corpus petitions filed by Bhutto himself and his daughter, Benazir, were dismissed by the Sindh High Court and Pirzada could only say that 'the legal battle was over'.[66] According to Pirzada, a message was sent by Bhutto to his family members not to make mercy appeals for him 'because he was ready to meet his Creator with a clear conscience and he would like the people to see how a brave man, a leader of the people, Chairman of the Islamic Conference, advocate of the unity of the Third World, goes to meet his Creator'.[67]

Contrary to Bhutto's wish, appeals for mercy were filed by some of his relatives and associates, and the helpless central executive committee of the PPP, which met for three futile days, sent a two-page unanimous representation to Ziaul Haq to commute the death sentence.[68] A last-minute unsuccessful personal appeal was made by Nusrat Bhutto to Ziaul Haq. Appeals for clemency poured in from all parts of the world, from heads of state and government, including three private appeals by British prime minister James Callaghan,[69] parliaments of different countries, human rights' bodies, jurists, international organisations, religious leaders including the Pope and the Archbishop of Canterbury, associations of lawyers and many ordinary citizens. Most touching and well reasoned was the letter written to Ziaul Haq by former president Fazal Elahi Chaudhry, pointing out the ethnic divide among the judges of the Supreme Court and asking for Bhutto's death sentence to be commuted.[70]

Rafiuddin gives a blow by blow account of how the noose was tightened around Bhutto's neck. After his review petition was dismissed, he was treated like an ordinary criminal and all his facilities were withdrawn. His visitors were allowed only half an hour with him; they were to be thoroughly searched and could speak to him only from behind iron bars. The food which was sent from the house of Zafar Niazi, his friend and dental consultant, was stopped and the refrigerator was withdrawn. The electricity switches inside his cell were shifted outside and his medicines and toiletries were also removed, although he tried to resist this. His bed was taken away, but he was allowed to spread his mattress on the floor and was permitted to walk for half an hour in the courtyard under strict surveillance. He continued to receive newspapers.[71]He was watched physically day and night. The prison was cut off from the rest of the world.

Bhutto reacted angrily at these restrictions. He was hurt also by the insolent attitude of the prison staff whose behaviour changed after the Supreme Court dismissed his appeal. He fought for small concessions and went on another hunger strike from 24 March to 1 April. By the time the black warrant for his execution was received in the prison on 2 April 1979, he had become, physically, a shadow of himself. When it was read out to him, he clung to lapses in legal procedure, such as not being informed about his execution, according to rules, twenty-four hours in advance, and being given only seven hours' notice. And not being allowed to have a last meeting with his relatives, including his cousin Mumtaz Bhutto, who were present in Rawalpindi. He complained that no written order for his execution had been shown to him and also asked to see Zafar Niazi and his lawyers immediately.

Rafiuddin paints a poignant picture of Bhutto's last hours in this world and his final meeting with his wife and daughter. Benazir Bhutto had the presence of mind to tell the prison staff that Bhutto would have wanted to be buried in Larkana. Nusrat Bhutto said that she and her daughter would like to accompany his dead body on its last journey, but this request was denied. Bhutto's last broken words, before he was moved to the gallows on a stretcher, according to Rafiuddin, were about his wife: 'I pity my wife…' [72] He was hanged in contravention of the jail manual in the dead of night, instead of the early hours of the morning. It is sickening to read about the macabre arrangements made with detailed precision about the logistics of moving his body to his family graveyard in Garhi Khuda Bakhsh where his grave had already been dug, the provision of a coffin, flowers and rosewater. Worse still is the indignity of his body being photographed after the hanging to ascertain if he had been properly circumcised and how the executioner, Tara Masih, had stolen Bhutto's ring. Tara Masih belonged to a family of long-standing professional hangmen who are still in business with the prisons today. It is said that his father had been the executioner of the young revolutionary, Bhagat Singh, and his comrades Sukhdev and Rajguru, in Lahore prison on 23 March 1931.

Cheema's interest in the fate of his patient continued even after he had passed away. He met Yar Mohammad after the hanging to ask whether the stories about Bhutto being tortured were true, which Yar Mohammad denied. He told Cheema how all of Bhutto's facilities were withdrawn after the death warrant was signed. Bhutto declined to make a last wish and towards the evening the prison doctor gave him a strong dose of Valium, but this is not recorded by Rafiuddin. He did not utter a word as he was taken to the gallows; when the hood was pulled over his face, he merely said, 'make it quick.' Again, this is not corroborated by Rafiuddin's account. But he does reveal that when Bhutto's gold ring went missing from his finger, it was found in Tara Masih's pocket!

On 4 April 1979, the day of Bhutto's hanging, Fatehyab and I were in Lahore, where we had gone a few days earlier to give ourselves and our children a break. We were staying with my cousin, Wasima, whose husband, Zafar Askree was in the army. Early that morning, Zafar returned from a meeting to tell us that all was over. Fatehyab had just woken up and said in utter disbelief, 'No.' He asked me to pack up because he wanted to leave for Karachi immediately. I murmured something about the children's holiday being cut short. 'There will never be any holidays in this country again,' he replied. We took the flight back to Karachi on the same day. Strange, I said to myself, that everybody in the aircraft appeared to be so calm.

I have written in some detail about Bhutto's execution because it was a tragedy which has scarred the politics of Pakistan. As he said himself, the country needed a dead Bhutto, and not a living one. In the following years, in which we struggled against Ziaul Haq's martial law, we did so in the shadow of his assassination. Some of the political parties in the PNA had asked Ziaul Haq to postpone the elections and take Bhutto to task. Thus he found a perfectly valid reason to keep postponing the elections. Some parties had also contributed members to his cabinet, such as the Jamaat-i-Islami, which supported him all the way, and Nasrullah Khan's Pakistan Democratic Party (PDP). None of the PNA parties asked for clemency for Bhutto. Nobody in Bhutto's own party had the calibre or following to lead a successful agitation on a national scale to prevent his hanging, especially in the politically crippling circumstances of that time. Some of his colleagues had fled abroad. A mass movement was needed, legal battles were not enough.

The main argument advanced by Bhutto's party colleagues who met Ziaul Haq[73] to plead for clemency for their leader, was that his execution would cause widespread disturbances and the country would disintegrate. There were some disturbances and demonstrations after Bhutto was hanged – there may have been many which were not reported in the press because of strict censorship – but they were not on a scale which the martial law regime could not suppress. And the country has not disintegrated to this day. For his followers and admirers, however, the catharsis came on his first death anniversary on 4 April 1980.

Bhutto's first death anniversary was the scene of an intense outpouring of grief and emotion. People travelled to Garhi Khuda Bakhsh from every nook and corner of the country on every conceivable means of transport. The roads leading to the graveyard were choked with pedestrians and traffic. It was a moment of truth in which the PPP workers demanded answers from their leaders, grabbing some of them by their collars and physically assaulting them. Leaders and members of other political parties also flocked to his grave. Fatehyab spoke at the anniversary gathering and was overwhelmed by the collective grief of the people. Khawaja Khairuddin said in his speech that, after participating in the programme 'Zulm ki Dastanain' against him, he had come to salute the late Bhutto.

Popular leaders have been removed by military juntas through violent means in other countries also. In May 1960, the military junta in Turkey overthrew the government of Adnan Menderes and he and his associates were charged with violating the Constitution. He was tried by a military court and executed on 17 September 1961 on the island of Imrali, in the Sea of Marmara, where an open-air prison had existed since 1935. Executed along with him were foreign minister, Fatin Rustu, and finance minister, Hasan Polatkan. Pleas for forgiveness by President Cemal Gursel, opposition leader Ismet Inonu and world leaders, including John F. Kennedy and Elizabeth II, fell on deaf ears. Menderes was, however, posthumously pardoned by the Turkish parliament in 1990.

Salvador Allende of Chile suffered a similar fate. The military coup against his government on 11 September 1973 was preceded by extreme public unrest similar to that prevailing in Pakistan in 1977. Before the military's capture of the presidential palace, Allende made his farewell speech, reminiscent of Bhutto's last appearance on the television in Pakistan. Then he faced the gang which attacked him and died fighting, although the government of Chile has always insisted that he committed suicide during the attack. The difference between the violent deaths of these leaders is that Bhutto was tried by civilian courts, and not by a military court, and his death had the stamp of the judiciary which had validated Ziaul Haq's martial law.

Chapter 8

Movement for Restoration of Democracy

The old woman sat on her haunches, native style, under a tree in the compound of Central Jail Karachi. I was sitting under the same tree, on a stone, waiting for the tiffin carrier to be returned to me. She was a small woman, poorly dressed, with teeth stained by *paan* and tobacco, her uncombed hair twisted into a tiny plait. Just as in hospitals and clinics, patients in waiting rooms are curious about one another's illnesses, the relatives of prisoners are also inquisitive. She had come to visit her son and had apparently lost another son to crime. After pleading before the 'sahibs' running the prison, she had managed to meet him across a grilled window. Unaware of the procedure for getting permission to see her son, like most marginalised persons, she could only beg and plead. Rubbing the palms of her hands together, she said: 'When I finally met him, he asked me, mother have you brought *roti salan* for me? And when I answered no, I haven't, he burst into sobs.' In despair she wailed, 'how would I know that he wanted roti salan?' How could she have known, really, that the food served in prison was inedible? Her anguish broke my heart because I had gone to the prison to take roti salan for Fatehyab. The Movement for Restoration of Democracy (MRD) had been launched.

Many politicians have taken credit for inspiring the movement after it became evident that Ziaul Haq's appetite for power was unrelenting. They met him when he called them, received his messengers, attended banquets he hosted for foreign visitors, and tried to 'persuade' him to hold elections. They could hardly have manoeuvred a showdown with the army under the brutal terms of martial law. Ziaul Haq easily found collaborators among the parties which could not resist the lure of power. Members of the Muslim League, Jamaat-i-Islami (JI), Mufti Mahmood's Jamiat Ulema-i-Islam (JUI) and Nasrullah Khan's PDP were sworn into his cabinet on 23 August 1978 and sent packing eight months later on 21 April 1979.

Two prominent politicians, Sherbaz Khan Mazari and Asghar Khan, have written their memoirs and both used this 'lull' to go abroad on holiday. The former records several meetings with Ziaul Haq and participation in state banquets for the British prime minister James Callaghan, the Shah of Iran and president Sardar Daoud Khan of Afghanistan in 1978 and his surprise at finding other politicians like Ghulam Mustafa Jatoi and Kausar Niazi also present. He often received Lieutenant General Fazle Haq in 'his unofficial capacity as one of my oldest friends'[1] who briefed him on political happenings and tried to convince him to join Ziaul Haq's nominated cabinet, which he refused. However, on 4 February 1978, he attended Ziaul Haq's special conference on national issues, as did others, which he described as 'a grand and artful exercise'.[2]

Asghar Khan, who had long aspired to become the prime minister[3] and considered his Tehrik-i-Istiqlal as the real opposition – and it was, indeed, studded with many famous names in public life[4] – also met Ziaul Haq, in the fantasy that he could be persuaded not to hold the local bodies' elections or tinker with the Constitution. Ziaul Haq, on the other hand, found one excuse after another for postponing the elections he had promised for October 1978, and told him that his own PNA colleagues had 'begged' for this postponement.[5] Asghar Khan dined with Ziaul Haq, attended banquets for foreign dignitaries, and flew with him for the opening of the Thakot Bridge on the Karakoram Highway. He liaised with Ziaul Haq through lieutenant generals Faiz Ali Chishti and Fazle Haq.

It is difficult to assess what turn events would have taken if the leading politicians had refused to have any dealings with Ziaul Haq. Both Mazari and Asghar Khan had close friends in the army and hoped, no doubt, that their own parties would gain in a future political dispensation. However, the Jamaat-i-Islami was firmly behind Ziaul Haq and so was Pir Pagaro; Nasrullah Khan had collaborated, and Wali Khan openly cooperated with Ziaul Haq and advised him not to hold elections. He and his wife had 'a good understanding with Ziaul Haq'.[6] In his 'real' martial law, Ziaul Haq banned all political activity, imposed strict censorship and cruel punishments for even minor acts of a political nature. He had already terrorised the people with his regime of whipping, lashing and fear of amputations.[7] The people of Pakistan had never been subjected to such systematic savagery.

In desperation, these politicians turned to one another and to Bhutto's widow to form a common front against martial law. It took many months and the process can be followed in the memoirs of Benazir Bhutto, Sherbaz Mazari and Asghar Khan. Fear of martial law and lack of courage had, as Asghar Khan said, prevented them from sinking their differences. They were probably encouraged by the first lawyers' movement which started in August 1980 and led to the arrest of many lawyers who were tried by military courts.[8] Asghar Khan even considered accepting an interim government in which Ziaul Haq could continue as the 'constitutional president' until elections were held.[9]

According to Mazari, the first step towards the formation of the MRD was the initiative his National Democratic Party (NDP) took to contact other parties for a joint programme for the revival of democracy in August 1980.[10] They proposed that the movement should have four basic demands: lifting of martial law, restoration of the 1973 Constitution in its original form, elections under this Constitution, and greater provincial autonomy. The PPP, which had given the first draft agreement through Pyar Ali Allana in December 1980, tried to hang on to Bhutto's controversial constitutional amendments but had to give in. On 5 February 1981, Mazari received Nusrat Bhutto's signature on the document and affixed his own and so, he writes, 'the MRD was formed'.[11]

In the meeting on 6 February 1981, at Bhutto's residence in 70 Clifton, Nusrat Bhutto requested that Fatehyab Ali Khan of the Mazdoor Kissan Party and Mairaj Mohammad Khan of Qaumi Mahaz-i-Azadi should be allowed to participate. They had 'to sit outside all through the duration of the meeting while their case was argued'.[12] After the leaders affixed their signatures on MRD's declaration, Mazari writes dismissively: 'Even Mairaj Muhammad Khan and Fatehyab Ali were now invited to sign the document.'[13]

Having failed to motivate or bribe her party members to launch a popular movement against Ziaul Haq,[14] Nusrat Bhutto turned to the men who had not lifted a finger to save her husband's life. Indeed, they had scant respect for him and many of them had been victims of Bhutto's oppression. As we have seen, the choicest epithets are used for Bhutto in Mazari's memoirs. Asghar Khan's views about Bhutto were no less flattering. Apparently they did not doubt the fairness of the death sentence handed down to Bhutto by the Lahore High Court. Asghar Khan had met Ziaul Haq on 12 March 1979, three weeks before Bhutto was hanged, but did not plead for his life. He did, however, on one occasion, have the grace to attend Bhutto's trial in the Supreme Court.

The senior politicians who signed the MRD declaration did not have much love lost for one another either. Mazari considered Nasrullah Khan as an expert in the intrigue of backroom politics with 'an abundant store of political guile'.[15] He had met Bhutto clandestinely during the PNA movement and always had 'a personal agenda'.[16] Asghar Khan thought that if left alone, Nasrullah Khan would have agreed to all Bhutto's conditions for an agreement with the PNA. He had no real party, survived on political alliances and parleys, was not politically reliable, suffered from complexes and was a reactionary.[17] On the other hand, Mufti Mahmood of the JUI was not strongly opposed to Ziaul Haq, was flexible in his approach and would stay with any grouping so long as he was made the leader.[18] Asghar Khan wrote that although Mazari was anti-Zia, his party would play to the tune of the military government.[19]

Benazir Bhutto mentions the feelers sent by the PNA leaders to her mother, who had become chairperson of the PPP.[20] It was a difficult decision for Nusrat Bhutto to take. How could she forget Asghar Khan's words at a PNA rally: 'Shall I hang Bhutto from the Attock Bridge or from a Lahore lamp post?'[21] The senior leaders of her own party had deserted her. 'Today it is Jatoi,' she told her daughter, 'tomorrow it will be somebody else.' Although her rigid handling of the initial PPP movement against Ziaul Haq has been criticised, joining the MRD was a resolute act as well as a bid for survival, even if the PPP was just a 'rabble'.[22] The irony was not lost on Benazir who watched the politicians drinking coffee out of her father's china, sitting on his sofa, using his telephone. The PNA was riven by internal fissures and 'betrayals' by its leaders who were deeply suspicious of one another and talked only through emissaries.[23]

Whatever these differences, the MRD charter was signed on 6 February 1981 on a four-point programme: lifting of martial law, restoration of the 1973 Constitution, holding of general elections, and release of all political prisoners. There were nine signatories to the declaration: Nusrat Bhutto for the Pakistan Peoples Party, Sherbaz Mazari for the National Democratic Party, Mahmud Ali Kasuri for Tehrik-i-Istiqlal, Nasrullah Khan for Pakistan Democratic Party, Fatehyab Ali Khan for Pakistan Mazdoor Kissan Party, Fazlur Rahman for Jamiat Ulema-i-Islam, Mohammad Abdul Qayyum for Azad Jammu and Kashmir Muslim Conference, Mairaj Mohammad Khan for Qaumi Mahaz-i-Azadi and Khawaja Khairuddin for one faction of the Muslim League. Following the hijacking of a PIA aircraft to Kabul on 2 March 1981 by Salamullah Tipu, the Al-Zulfikar agent, there was a severe crackdown on the MRD and thousands of people were arrested across the country.

However disdainful the old guard may have been about the leftist parties in the MRD, Fatehyab's signature on its declaration brought the Pakistan Mazdoor Kissan Party (PMKP) (popularly known as MKP) into mainstream national politics for the first time. A word about the party itself. It was founded on 1 May 1968 by Afzal Bangash after he quit the National Awami Party. In 1970, Major Ishaq Mohammad of the Bhashani NAP faction in West Pakistan merged his group with the MKP. Its mobilisation focus was the peasantry which had risen in armed revolt in the 1960s and 1970s in North-West Frontier Province (NWFP) against the private armies of landlords and the repression of successive governments in that province. The confrontation in Mandani in July 1971 is regarded by the party as its glorious defining event. Although it led to the death of twenty peasants in a day-long pitched battle against 1,500 armed police, the peasants were victorious.

The party gradually enlarged its base among the peasants in Peshawar and Mardan districts, Malakand Agency, Swat and Dir and in parts of Kaghan and established links with peasants in southern and western Punjab. It participated in the movement against Ayub Khan in 1968–9. Its first national congress was held in Shergarh in Mardan District where 5,000 delegates assembled, in spite of the presence of armed security forces. It considered the PNA movement as reactionary and warned that it would lead to a military takeover. But soon internal differences arose on strategy and the party split into three factions led by Afzal Bangash, Sher Ali and Ishaq Mohammad. However, its continuity was best represented by Afzal Bangash's group which was generally recognised as the MKP.

The second or unity congress, also held at Mandani in July 1979, was a historic event in which over 5,000 delegates again participated from all over the country, in spite of martial law restrictions. Earlier, the PWP, led by the veteran trade unionist, Mirza Ibrahim, had merged with the MKP. By this merger, the MKP became a real peasants' and workers' party. The Mandani congress was attended by observers from numerous leftist parties and a message was also received from Benazir Bhutto. At this congress, Afzal Bangash was elected as president, Fatehyab as vice president and Sardar Shaukat Ali as secretary general. Fatehyab had joined the PWP when it was established in 1972. Eventually, other leftist groups like Mazdoor Majlis-i-Amal, Punjab Jamhoori Front and Mutehda Mazdoor Mahaz merged with the MKP in the Punjab, further broadening its base.

The MKP had a genuine grassroots base among the peasantry, different from that of liberal parties whose following in NWFP consisted mostly of landlords. Its political programme called for a 'people's democratic system in Pakistan', leading to socialism. It viewed Pakistan as a federation of provinces which had come together in an equal and voluntary union and in which the provinces would have complete autonomy. Its economic programme with respect to landholdings and industry was similar to that of other socialist parties. Different nationalities and ethnic groups would be given equal rights and fundamental rights would be universal, irrespective of nationality, religion, sect, caste, race, colour or gender. Women had a special place in its programme, although the party's base in NWFP was among very conservative peasantry. Women would have equal rights with men and no political or official position, employment or profession would be closed to them. The MKP published extensively in Urdu and the regional languages. The popular struggles led by the party gave birth to a large volume of literature, song and music. No other party paid so much attention to political education as the MKP. Under its leadership, the peasants won many battles against the state machinery and landlords, against evictions, rent-racking and unpaid labour, and hundreds of its leaders, cadres and supporters laid down their lives in this struggle.[24]

After the clampdown on the MRD, Fatehyab was arrested near Naudero on 4 April 1981, travelling with my brother Arif and our friend, Aftab Manghi, and brought to the Central Jail Karachi. He had gone underground in interior Sindh on 9 March 1981 and proceeded to Garhi Khuda Bakhsh for Bhutto's death anniversary at a mammoth gathering. The Central Jail Karachi was established in 1899. Many prominent leaders had been held there, the most famous being Mohammad Ali Jauhar of the Khilafat movement. Today, a ward is named after him in the prison. Bhutto was imprisoned there, and later many MRD leaders, including Bhutto's wife and daughter.

The social ostracism which I encountered after Fatehyab's arrest was incredible but not unexpected. My friends stopped contacting me and inviting me to their homes. Even if they were concerned about my welfare, it was not in their interest to be seen in my company. Their husbands had jobs, property and business interests to protect. They saw no reason to expose themselves to harassment for the sake of friendship. Gradually, but surely, they moved me out of their lives. Some even advised me to leave Fatehyab for good. The situation in my office also changed dramatically. My colleagues stopped recognising me. Except for my private secretary, Rahmatullah Baig and my peon, Mannu, who were perturbed but caring, for the others I had ceased to exist. My colleague Amjad Ali Saqib, to whose friendship I owe a great deal in life, was cautious in the office but met me often at home. There was, I have heard, a barrage of anonymous and not so anonymous letters to the establishment in Islamabad about my complicity in the movement against Ziaul Haq when, in truth, I was so busy trying to hold my family together that I was quite unaware of the outside world.

Matters came to a head on 31 March 1981 when I was sitting with the director, Iftikhar Ahmad Khan, in his office. He was blessed with a sense of humour and often discussed political issues with me. A few minutes later, there was a telephone call from Islamabad from Ijlal Haider Zaidi, the establishment secretary. The expression on the director's face changed and he asked me to leave the room. Shortly afterwards, he summoned me to say that Zaidi was furious and could no longer deal with the stream of complaints pouring into Islamabad against me. He asked me to apply for leave. I believe this was called 'forced leave'. He insisted on six months' leave but I did not agree to more than three months.

My removal from the official scene may have eased the tension that Zaidi claimed he suffered on my account. He hailed from Shahbad which was close to Panipat and had formed part of the constituency from which my father contested the elections in 1937. As establishment secretary, he was trusted by Ziaul Haq but he also held my father in great esteem. Although making me inconspicuous may have played its part, I was probably not dismissed from service because of the regard which A.K. Brohi, who was Ziaul Haq's trusted adviser, had for me. Brohi was closer to Ziaul Haq than Zaidi. And, in any case, a faculty position in a training institution was hardly an important job.

In a sense, the 'forced leave' gave me respite, more time to spend with the children and look after Fatehyab from outside the prison. Our lives settled into a regular pattern. After the children went to school, I bought provisions and cooked for Fatehyab and some of his fellow prisoners. It was improper to send food for only one person, as all the political prisoners took their meals together. I took the food to the prison gate and waited for the tiffin carrier from the previous day's delivery to be returned to me. In the beginning, I prepared both lunch and dinner, but later an agreement was reached among the prisoners' families to divide the task.

Some of my most vivid memories of those days relate to the time I spent at the prison gate, waiting for the tiffin carrier. In contrast to the attitude of my friends, colleagues and neighbours, the ordinary people were kind to me. Shopkeepers and tradesmen in our neighbourhood enquired about Fatehyab, and the owners of Gharib Nawaz hotel, where I purchased food when I was too tired to cook, always asked about his health, although they blasted their employees if the portions handed out to me were large. The police guards at the prison were Sindhis who were all sympathetic to the PPP. Nusrat Bhutto was also detained in prison at that time and her staff drove with her food right up to the main gate. A really stylish constable oversaw the movement in and out of the compound, twirling his thick moustache and frequently blowing his whistle. 'Why,' I asked him one day, 'do you let Nusrat Bhutto's car drive straight to the main gate, while I have to walk all the way from the road?' 'Because,' he answered, 'her husband was a *badshah*, when your husband becomes a badshah, I will let in your car also.' I understood his simple logic.

My sons, Hasan and Asad, and I lived in a rented house in KDA Scheme One. The house opened on an unpaved dirt street along which ran a deep stretch of water full of weeds which the odd angler frequented. In winter, Siberian cranes rested on the water. It was the darkest path in the entire neighbourhood. There were no street lights and people were afraid of entering it after dusk, but we had got used to its spookiness. Often we had no domestic help because the police harassed our employees so much that they ran away. The *chowkidar* of the neighbouring house knew that Fatehyab was in prison and the children and I were all alone. He told me not to worry and that he would patrol the street a few times during the night. Often, as I lay awake, I could hear him thumping his heavy stick on the ground as he made his rounds outside. Whoever he was, I am grateful for his kindness.

In those times, so treacherous for my sons and me, my mother's house was a haven of peace and tranquillity. She provided the stability in my children's lives which I could scarcely muster in running around to look after Fatehyab's welfare. She loved Fatehyab, his decency, cultivated manners, restraint and integrity and she believed in his political mission. Never once did she suggest that he should give up his political engagements. She was the mainstay of our lives. Never failing in his affection and care, my brother Arif was a formidable source of strength and became a father figure to my sons. My in-laws made some appearances although they were so numerous that, if they had only taken turns, my life would have been easier. Other relatives were either scared or unable to express their concern, except my cousin Asima and her husband, Naqi Zamin Ali, who stood by me through it all. There was also the sympathy of some of my father's friends, such as Ali Maqsood Hameedi, who were anxious about Fatehyab's welfare.

Political prisoners were allowed visits from family members or friends once in two weeks, other prisoners could be visited once a week. But this facility was not automatic and permission had to be obtained from the home secretary each time. During Fatehyab's detentions and imprisonments, I dealt with a number of home secretaries, including Mazhar Rafi, Nazar Abbas Siddiqui, and Ahmad Sadik. I was fortunate that they met me and were courteous to me. The relatives of less-known and poor prisoners were not so lucky; it was not easy to get past the bureaucratic barriers in Sindh secretariat, but they persisted. One person whose kindness touched me was the deputy home secretary, Ghulam Husain Soomro, who always granted permission 'according to rules' immediately and assured me that I was his 'sweet sister'.

The first time the children and I met Fatehyab after he was arrested was in Bahadurabad police station and later in the prison on 9 April 1981. We went into the outer portion of the prison, or *mari*, with our small parcels of provisions and the cigarettes he could not do without. A warden sat in the meeting room with us as Fatehyab came from the inner prison. Fatehyab entered with a smile on his face and addressing me said, 'Now don't unload yourself here.' We had to smile, there could be no complaints, no tears. One person who endeared himself to the children was Colonel Shamim Alvi who stayed with us for a few days when Fatehyab was in prison. I came upon him walking on my leaf-strewn lawn, dressed in *khaddar*, with tears in his eyes and a book in his hands. He was going through a great emotional crisis and our home provided him with some comfort. He insisted on accompanying us to meet Fatehyab whom he admired, saying he wished he had the courage to follow in his footsteps. He took the children for outings and to expensive restaurants, and gave Hasan his entire collection of rare maps from the Survey of India.

When we visited Fatehyab, one of our dearest friends, Khawaja Humayun Akhtar, was also in prison and arranged tea to be served.[25] However, the visits left a lasting painful impact on the children who saw the seamy side of prison life. Prisoners emerging from the prison van, so suffocating that it was called *kutta gari*, had to squat *jori jori* and didn't dare to look up, and men in bar fetters with mangled ankles, who were considered dangerous criminals. Once we even saw from the window of the jail superintendent's room a prisoner tied to a *tiktiky*, ready to be lashed as punishment for some misdemeanour.

Fatehyab's bravado was a façade. Although the political prisoners incarcerated with him at that time were a force to be reckoned with, life in prison was tough and demoralising. Since Fatehyab was a graduate and an advocate, he was entitled to B class, even A class in prison, but he was always held in C class. He slept on the floor on a thin mat; in the morning there was a rush on the limited bathroom facilities. There was no wire netting on the windows, the cells were full of mosquitoes and smelt of perspiration. Before dusk, the prisoners were locked up and if anyone fell ill, the guards rarely unlocked the cell. There were no facilities like newspapers, radios, the television, public call offices, computers and intercoms which are available in prison today. I had read about the terrible conditions in which Nelson Mandela was imprisoned in Robben Island. When I saw his cell during a visit to Robben Island, I was surprised that he did not share it with anybody and it contained not only a bed, but also a table and chair. However, Mandela was an icon, had spent twenty-nine long years behind the bars and was surely entitled to the use of a table and chair.

When the food taken for a prisoner is returned, it means he is no longer within the prison premises and has been shifted elsewhere. This happened on 26 June 1981. The prison authorities professed ignorance of Fatehyab's whereabouts, only that he was no longer with them. Before Fatehyab was arrested, he told me that if he was interrogated, he would go on a hunger strike. After running around frantically for a few days and finally reaching Mazhar Rafi, I discovered that he was being held at an interrogation centre in Hub, a few miles outside Karachi. I pleaded unsuccessfully with the young military officer in the martial law outfit, Colonel Matiur Rahman, to let me meet him, for I feared the worst. At night, I would lie awake, sometimes holding little Asad for comfort. Finally, there was a call from one Inspector Maqbool, asking for a small transistor and some toiletries for Fatehyab which I had to deliver at the police headquarters. Later, I learnt that Fatehyab and B.M. Kutty[26] were lodged in the interrogation centre in harsh conditions and were not allowed to communicate with each other. They whispered a few words when they crossed each other to use the facilities. Fatehyab's hunger strike apparently won him some concessions which were his conditions for answering questions. I wish I could read the text of that interrogation. Kutty was soon released from Hub and came to see me. That was the first time I met him and it was the beginning of our friendship, based on mutual respect and affection.

Fatehyab was sent back to prison from Hub on 2 July 1981 and his detention was extended on 2 September 1981. He had fallen seriously sick and I had to move heaven and earth to get him shifted to a filthy room in Civil Hospital on 7 September 1981. However, because he was hospitalised, the children and I could meet him every day. He was released on 24 September 1981. After he came home, our lives became, if anything, more hectic. There was a stream of visitors every day – both from the MRD and well-wishers – who had to be entertained. But our family peace did not last long. On 14 December 1981, I received orders that, in the public interest, I was transferred to the public administration research centre in Islamabad, an even greater wilderness than NIPA Karachi. Apparently, no ministry wanted me, but Tariq Siddiqi agreed to give me a post in the O&M (Organisation and Methods) division. Looking back, it would have been wiser for me to take indefinite unpaid leave. But the mood was to show defiance and say 'boo' to the dictator.

I went to Islamabad on 2 January 1982, leaving my children in my mother's care and Fatehyab to the vagaries of the political situation. My own period of externment, as it were, had started. I stayed in various government hostels. Most people avoided my company, but there were others who looked after me and I can never thank them enough for their support. Imtiaz Ahmad and his wife, Talat, opened their home to me and I frequently stayed at their place. Imtiaz was a handsome man, a fine human being, a loyal friend and an upright and honest civil servant. Iftikhar Ahmad and his wife, Farida, did not bother about the political fallout of their hospitality either, both in Quetta and Islamabad. When the MRD was formed and was much in the news, Iftikhar was the comptroller of revenues in Quetta; he and Farida gave me space in their home and I left the children with them when I went on official assignments.

Nor can I forget the warmth with which Saeed Malik and his entire family, including his gracious mother, welcomed me in their midst. Very often, as I sat alone in the hostel room, Anis Chowdhury, a Bengali intellectual I had met long ago in Dacca, then posted in the Bangladesh embassy, came to see me or took me home for a meal. Tariq Siddiqi, my boss, understood Fatehyab's struggle and I struck a friendship with his wife, Nigar Ahmad, which matured over the next three decades into my collaboration with her in *Aurat Foundation*, the women's empowerment organisation she founded in

1986. And my relatives in Islamabad, Wasima and Zafar Askree, Sabiah and Muzaffar Askari, Shahida and Izhar Kazmi did not let me down. Izhar Kazmi was a learned man and a famous broadcaster, and Shahida was my childhood friend.[27] They were ardent Bhutto supporters. At their home I met that giant of a poet, writer and intellectual, Ilyas Ishqi, whose dignity and old world culture were so exceptional. Ijlal Haider Zaidi made his peace with me on 2 June 1982 when he came to see me with his wife at Khawaja Masrur Hussain's house. Khawaja Masrur Hussain, who hailed from Panipat, was then Ziaul Haq's intelligence chief and I was in Islamabad, safely beyond the reach of my husband's evil influence.

Although I went to Karachi occasionally, the separation from my children was agonising. Once, as I was leaving, Asad clung to me and said, 'Ammi, please don't go.' Later, when I applied to go home, I told Tariq Siddiqi that I would not return to Islamabad. He understood my anguish and posted me to Karachi to work on the project financing of the Hilton hotels. I was based in the Pakistan Secretariat in Saddar, an historic complex of barracks and rudimentary buildings in which the bureaucracy had started functioning in primitive conditions in August 1947. My room was very basic and its window opened on a *katchi abadi* in which angry mothers regularly thrashed their helpless children. I developed an attachment to the tacky premises and the mediocre staff and spent the next few years in relative peace.

The years 1982–5 were probably the worst years of my life. They were packed with activity on numerous fronts, Fatehyab's political engagements, attending to him and even some of his colleagues in prison, trying to shield the children from being hurt, looking after their schooling and illnesses and the uncertainty of it all. When Fatehyab was not in prison, he was busy attending meetings of the MRD's central action committee, subcommittees and even so-called secret committees which did not remain secret because the government had many informers and usually got wind of them. Also, he frequently travelled out of the city. Many orders restricting his movement to interior Sindh and other provinces were served on him. On these occasions, he travelled incognito. In that rough and tumble, Hasan earned his black belt in karate; he was only 10 years old. Asad was a little behind with a blue belt.

Even the slightest rumour of MRD meetings led to arrests and expulsions and Fatehyab went through many mini detentions, too numerous to list. When he was free, there was a constant flow of people in and out of our house, political leaders and workers, journalists, well-wishers, and some relatives. In my diary, I have noted many names but cannot do justice to their numbers. The telephone rang all the time, mostly from journalists asking for news. We had guests for lunch and dinner every day and tea was served to all, even to the intelligence agents who watched us from the street outside or trailed our movements. Some visitors came daily, sometimes more than once, such as Khawaja Khairuddin who was secretary general of the MRD and Mairaj Mohammad Khan who was the joint secretary. They always moved together and we genially referred to them as 'Khawaja Pia' and 'Chanda Mian'. Since they usually stopped for a meal, the children asked if there were no kitchens in their own homes! The numbers were highest when Fatehyab became the MRD convenor or when he was released from prison, or when scores of his party members visited from the north. Since Fatehyab was not a Baloch sardar or Sindhi wadera, there was no retinue of loyal retainers and servants at our disposal. There was only one domestic help.

The first important MRD meeting held at our house was on 16 March 1982 when Fatehyab was the convenor. It was attended by Nusrat Bhutto, Sherbaz Mazari, Khawaja Khairuddin, Mustafa Jatoi, Mairaj, and also by Abid Zuberi, Qari Sher Afzal and Nafees Siddiqi. Fatehyab made elaborate arrangements to seat these important visitors in our small living room and serve them lunch. Peering at them for a moment from a slit in the window, I was struck by the dignity of Nusrat Bhutto. Later, Fatehyab arranged to take her to a trade union meeting which was a rare public appearance for her. Before leaving for the venue, as a decoy Fatehyab brought her to my mother's house. She told my mother, 'you know, I do get nervous' and 'we must flood the streets with people against Zia, only then will he go.'

That flood came, if at all, when she left the country for medical treatment abroad. Her departure has been viewed as a kind of let down by some MRD leaders.[28] Fatehyab, who met her often, developed great sympathy for her suffering. Like many others, he campaigned for her to go abroad – in fact, there was an international campaign on her behalf. Like hundreds of others, he went to see her off at Karachi airport on 19 November 1982.[29] Her departure put Benazir at the centre of the MRD's struggle because the PPP had the largest political base in the country and also a martyr to mourn for.

On 5 April 1983, Fatehyab piled the children and me into the car and drove to Quetta. After a few days in Quetta, we went to Khuzdar and stayed at Amanullah Gichki's house. Fatehyab had known Amanullah since he was exiled to Quetta in 1962. The mission was to persuade Mir Ghaus Bakhsh Bizenjo to join the MRD. Fatehyab had great respect for Bizenjo and was unhappy that the MRD was deprived of his wisdom and experience.

As I wrote in my obituary[30] of Bizenjo, he was the grand old man of Pakistan's politics and a great statesman. He strode across the two worlds of socialism and Baloch nationalism. His political career saw many changes but, in spite of bitterness at the ruthless military action in Balochistan by Ayub Khan and

Bhutto, he remained a staunch supporter of the unity of Pakistan.[31] Critical of the Sardari system and cruel social customs in Balochistan, he joined the Kalat National Party while still a student at Aligarh, the Communist Party of India in 1937, established Ustman Gul in Kalat in 1955 and the Pakistan National Party (PNP) in 1956, which was a merger of many radical groups. In the NAP, which was the first large coalition of leftist and nationalist forces in Pakistan, he wielded great power until it split into two in 1967. When the NAP was banned by Bhutto in 1975, he joined Mazari's NDP. He spent one-quarter of his life in prison, the last spell for almost five years in the Hyderabad conspiracy case under Bhutto. He was released in 1979 by Ziaul Haq.

There was a great sense of disquiet about Bizenjo among some leaders of the MRD. Mazari, himself a Baloch, regarded him as a 'shrewd political operator...with a gifted tongue' and 'an over consummate politician' whose 'ambitions would leave even his colleagues momentarily speechless'.[32] Akbar Bugti considered him as an 'arch-intriguer'.[33] However, Bizenjo was an accomplished politician who preferred negotiation to confrontation. Because he wanted to keep the door of dialogue open, he had wanted the PNA to accept Bhutto's offer – a 'betrayal' which led to his ostracism by his colleagues during the incarceration of the NAP leaders in Hyderabad jail, and doubts were raised about his loyalties.[34] Some leaders were wary of him because he had been a member of the Communist Party of India, but the communists in Pakistan let him down on several occasions.[35] Others were unhappy because of his support for the Saur Revolution in Afghanistan. He had refused to join the MRD as its charter did not address the issue so close to his heart –the autonomy of the federating units. Nor did the MRD declaration demand an open struggle through rallies and public meetings.[36]

While the children and I stayed in Khuzdar, Fatehyab and Amanullah Gichki drove in pouring rain on the difficult road to Nal, Bizenjo's village. In his memoir, Kutty has written:

> I may make a special mention here of the monumental personal effort made by Fatehyab Ali Khan of the Mazdoor Kisan Party to persuade Mir Saheb to sign the Declaration ... Fatehyab went all the way by road to Khuzdar incognito (as the police was on his trail), where he enlisted the help of Mir Amanullah Gichki and the two then braved the heavy rains and dangerous potholes on the crack-filled track that was the Khuzdar-Nal road to meet Mir Saheb at his residence.[37]

The PNP formally joined the MRD on 28 September 1983 but Bizenjo had already courted arrest on 2 September 1983 from Chakiwara in Karachi.[38]

When it became evident that the MRD's meetings, resolutions and observance of black days would not compel Ziaul Haq to budge, it was decided to launch a civil disobedience movement from 14 August 1983 from Jinnah's mausoleum. According to the arrangement, every day some members of the MRD parties would seek arrest at a public place. Fatehyab and Qari Sher Afzal, central information secretary of JUI, were to court arrest on 18 August 1983 from Empress Market in the heart of Karachi. To avoid being arrested prior to this event, Fatehyab went underground on 13 August and emerged to have tea with me in Shezan that evening. He spoke at Jinnah's mausoleum the following day at the MRD rally which became violent.[39] He dodged the police and even held a press conference at a Chinese restaurant, Chung Wah. On 17 August, he attended the meeting in which the MRD directed its coalescing parties to break the seals on their offices and start operating normally. On 18 August, I stayed with him the whole day and drove him to Karachi Bar Association where he made a speech while I sat outside in the car. We had our last lunch together before his arrest at Seagull restaurant in Saddar, and he held a brief press conference at Gulf Hotel at 4.30p.m. Then I drove Fatehyab, Qari Sher Afzal and Iqbal Haider towards Empress Market.

All roads leading to Empress Market had been sealed off by the police and thousands of people had gathered to witness the arrest. It seemed impossible to break the police cordon. Fatehyab had, however, bought a megaphone and as we drove towards Empress Market from Regal Chowk, he switched on the siren. People thought it was a police hooter and moved away and we found an opening in the road. I drove at top speed and stopped bang outside the steps of the market where I had accompanied my mother to buy provisions since I was a child. It was 5.15 p.m. As Fatehyab and Qari Sher Afzal got out of the car, scores of policemen pounced upon them and in the confusion I drove away quickly. Iqbal Haider, who sat in the back seat, kept shouting 'hurry, hurry!' I had thrown all caution to the winds and, in any case, the police were so busy gloating at 'catching' those who had volunteered to get caught, that they could hardly have bothered about me.[40] Next day, I took Fatehyab's clothes and food to the prison and applied to Mazhar Rafi to meet him. The drill had started again.

Fatehyab was the only signatory of the MRD declaration who was tried and convicted under martial law. Most of the others were held in their homes or rest houses, although some were occasionally held in prison. Fatehyab was charged under martial law regulations 18 and 33. I went to the provincial assembly hostel in Saddar, where the trial was conducted, the first time with Nuruddin Sarki and the journalist, Iqbal Jaffery, and later by myself. Sometimes he was not produced in court and I waited in vain, but I met him on 23 August in the prison, along with the children. It was a short trial; he was convicted for one year on 3 September. After the sentence was announced inside the prison, Fatehyab distributed sweets among the other prisoners, recalling his first conviction under Ayub Khan's dictatorship in 1961. Soon our house became the venue of clandestine MRD meetings which shifted also to the residence of my brother Arif. Iqbal Haider was MRD's chief organiser in those days and he frequently came for a meal. It is a mystery that throughout the early years of the movement he was never arrested, in spite of his numerous public pronouncements.

Even from outside the prison walls, one can sometimes follow the fortunes of one's prisoner. If the food is returned, it means he has been shifted to another prison, perhaps to a hospital in an emergency, or he is dead. On 23 September, Fatehyab's lunch was returned untouched. I asked at the gate about where he had been sent, but nobody gave me an answer, only that he was no longer in Karachi prison. I was devastated. Where could I find him, how would I keep in touch with him? After running from pillar to post, I discovered a few days later that he had been moved to Sukkur, 300 kilometres north of Karachi, along with Qari Sher Afzal and Ali Mukhtar Naqvi. I started the process of getting permission to meet him.

Sukkur barrage is any viewer's delight. Its majestic stretch is lined on either side, as far as the eye can see, with vast expanses of gushing or still water. At one end of the barrage was located Sukkur district jail where Fatehyab was imprisoned, at the other was Inter-Pak Inn where I stayed when I went to meet him. In happier times, we had sojourned there with the children on our cross-country car journeys. With the permission letter in my hand, I would take a tonga across the barrage to the prison, waiting to be let in. The Sindhi personnel were usually courteous and Fatehyab slightly embarrassed by my presence. I went alone on the Fokker flight from Karachi, except when my brother Arif drove me and the children to meet Fatehyab. My visits were a welcome occasion for the other prisoners from Karachi, because I carried pillows which they were denied, cigarettes, letters, clothes, cheques for children's fees and even Ali Mukhtar's wristwatch for repair. Once, in the airport lounge, I ran into Humayun Farshori who was the deputy commissioner of Sukkur. He was my student at the civil services academy and a more gracious man would have paused to speak to me, but he simply turned away.

The period of Fatehyab's incarceration at Sukkur was very distressing for my whole family. Apart from close relatives, the journalists Mahmud Sham and Majeed Abbasi frequently dropped by in the evening, travelling on a motorbike. Mahmud Sham usually started using my telephone while Majeed Abbasi waited patiently. Razzak Tabani, Saeed Malik, Amjad Ali Saqib, Julia and Sulaiman Ghanchi, Shaheen and Anwar Abbas Naqvi with their children also came occasionally. Anwar Abbas belonged to Nasrullah Khan's PDP and courted arrest on 19 August 1983 but soon became disillusioned with the movement. Mushahid Hussain Sayed, editor of *The Muslim*, visited a couple of times, sitting beside me on the terrace on a cushion on the floor. Mir Bizenjo and Shah Mohammad Amroti also came to see me, groping their way in the darkness which surrounded my house. Sadly, these visits were very few and far between. And my children were definitely the worst sufferers in this saga.

After a few visits, Fatehyab told me not to come to Sukkur again. Hundreds of MRD prisoners were held at Sukkur, including some influential Sindhi landlords. There is a list of over 400 prisoners in Fatehyab's papers, but he reckoned that there were over 1,000. True to their feudal tradition, the Sindhis were hospitable and looked after their fellow sufferers. But I could not rest in peace, and riots in Sukkur prison, in which there were some casualties, upset me further. I applied for Fatehyab's transfer to Karachi to Mazhar Rafi on 6 December 1983, but my request was not entertained. In the meantime, on one visit I purchased paper and pens from the clocktower shops in Sukkur and urged Fatehyab to write about the movement. He wrote about sixty pages and one fine morning they were all found to be missing. A search was made in all corners of the prison, but they could not be traced. His handwritten manuscript probably landed in the custody of the intelligence outfit.

To Nazar Abbas Siddiqui, who became the home secretary and was my contemporary at the University of Karachi, I owe Fatehyab's transfer from Sukkur to Karachi. He had a stiff upper lip and we fondly called him the 'brown sahib'. On the morning of 21 March 1984, Fatehyab was brought to Karachi by Sukkur Express in a third-class compartment. I went with my brother, Kazim, and Iqbal Jaffery to meet him at the Cantonment Station. He had become a shadow of himself. Along with him also travelled some wretchedly poor prisoners who were ordered to sit jori jori on the platform and were too scared to look up. He was lodged in the prison in Karachi. Fatehyab's article on federalism and democracy was published in *The Muslim* in Islamabad on 4 May 1984.[41] It caused a great stir and Mushahid Hussain was questioned by the intelligence agencies about how it reached him. He told them it had come in the post, whereas I was the culprit who had sent it to him. It is a testament to Fatehyab's vision of the original concept of Pakistani statehood. Fatehyab was released on 31 May 1984.

After Ziaul Haq's ridiculous referendum on 19 December 1984, the stage was set for the 'party-less' general elections he had promised, in February 1985. Fatehyab went underground in the third week of January 1985 and a really distressing period began for my whole family. He shifted his hideout several times. The police searched for him everywhere and were incensed that he managed to slip away from the press club at poet Habib Jalib's function. That evening, the police surrounded our house and the station house officer warned me that he would take away Hasan and Asad, who were 13 years and 11 years old. Surely, he said, that would bring Fatehyab to his senses. Mujahida Manto, my brother Arif's wife, came running to say that the police had also surrounded my mother's house and threatened to pick up her daughters, Tahera 11 years and Salma 9 years old, the little girls who had made ammonia prints of MRD letterheads when no press dared to print them. Finally, in desperation, the police took away my brother Kazim, my cousin Naqi who was visiting me and all my mother's servants. In the dead of night, I received a very aggressive and threatening call from the superintendent of police, asking why Fatehyab was afraid of giving himself up. 'What do you mean,' I replied, 'give himself up? He is not a criminal. Why can't you arrest him yourself?' The police mobiles kept watch throughout the night. Fatehyab was arrested a couple of days later.

On 3 March 1985, Fatehyab was suddenly transferred again from Karachi to Sukkur. When I protested to Ahmad Sadik, the home secretary, he told me Fatehyab was shifted because Nasir Baloch was to be hanged. 'But what,' I blurted out, 'has Nasir Baloch's hanging to do with Fatehyab?' He answered: 'you don't understand, these are not rational decisions. Fatehyab is a very influential prisoner so we can't take the risk of having him here at that time.' Also, he said, they might have to hang Ayaz Samoo. I went away dismayed, hoping no more young people would be sent to the gallows.

Before Fatehyab was transferred to Sukkur, Nasir Baloch wrote to him from his death cell on the back of silver foils of cigarette packs, thanking him for his support, wishing him well and expressing resignation to his fate. He was a PPP activist, accused of being a member of Al-Zulfikar and an abettor in the PIA hijacking in March 1981. His trial was held in camera and he was always produced in handcuffs and with bar fetters on his legs, so he could not even sip water during the hearing, nor was he allowed a counsel of his choice. Fatehyab always cherished the foils on which he had scribbled. His fate was sealed when Ziaul Haq signed, on 26 October 1984, the sentence condemning him to 'suffer death by being hanged by the neck until he be dead'.[42] He was 40 years old. On the eve of his hanging, his relatives, friends and community members spread out in the space in front of Central Jail Karachi and held a night-long vigil for him. It is said that he met death bravely and raised political slogans on the way to the gallows, which were echoed by other prisoners from their barracks and cells. He was accorded a grand funeral in his village.[43]

As the papers of Rao Sulaiman reveal, PPP activists suspected of being members of Al-Zulfikar were shown no mercy in Ziaul Haq's prisons. Rao Sulaiman, a lifelong and committed socialist, was Fatehyab's comrade and secretary general of the MKP. He was based in Multan and gave these young prisoners, kept in pitiful conditions, legal assistance, food and reading material. Since they were shackled day and night, their primary concern was to get their shackles removed and their wounds treated. Some of them wanted to take university examinations while they were in prison. Their letters to Rao Sulaiman are full of expressions of gratitude to him and his wife for their help and compassion.[44] How many of them were really members of Al-Zulfikar and how many were just swept into prison is not known.

Fatehyab was brought to Karachi by Sukkur Express on 20 March 1985 and lodged in the juvenile jail in Landhi, 20 kilometres outside the city. Ahmad Sadik said they could not take the risk of lodging him in the Central Jail Karachi. When he was released on 9 April 1985, the children and I went to fetch him as the last rays of the sun fell on the prison complex in Landhi. Although Benazir Bhutto lobbied fervently to save his life, Ayaz Samoo was hanged on 26 June 1985.[45] He was 22 years old.

Many coalescing MRD parties went through great internal stress during the movement in 1986; some broke into factions. Foremost among them was the PPP when Ghulam Mustafa Jatoi challenged Benazir's leadership, acrimoniously parted ways with the Bhutto family after almost thirty years' association and formed his own party, the 'angry uncles' National Peoples Party (NPP). Mazari resigned from the NDP which he had himself established when his colleagues rejected MRD's demand to hold elections under the 1973 Constitution; in fact they rejected the 1973 Constitution altogether.[46] Asghar Khan writes stoically in his diary about how one colleague after another left Tehrik-i-Istiqlal for greener pastures. A big chunk of Bizenjo's PNP broke off to join the Awami National Party (ANP) launched in Karachi on 26 July 1986.[47] Khawaja Khairuddin's Muslim League fractured into two and led to his own expulsion from the MRD.[48] Even Nasrullah Khan's tiny PDP lost some of its members.

The MKP also had its trials. Afzal Bangash, the founder of the party, had lived in self-imposed exile for many years after being framed in a murder case. He corresponded with Fatehyab under various names, often writing under the name of 'Khalid'. His long letters were full of praise for Fatehyab's leadership of the party, his own political analysis and his personal problems. When he returned to Pakistan, to the utter surprise of many of his party members, he joined the Sindhi-Baloch-Pushtoon Front (SBPF) headed by Mumtaz Bhutto, becoming its vice president. The SBPF stood for a confederation in Pakistan and its ideology was, therefore, opposed to the four-point programme of the MRD. Fatehyab was a staunch believer in the federal system and could not countenance the idea of a confederation for the country. Therefore, he removed Bangash from membership of the MKP.[49]

A crisis developed in the MKP when Rasool Bux Palijo of the Awami Tehreek became the MRD convenor. He was released from prison after many years in detention and was much celebrated, feted and garlanded. He was charming, learned, an eloquent speaker and a smooth operator. Bizenjo had mooted the idea of the merger of four leftist parties, his own PNP, the NDP led by Wali Khan, Awami Tehreek led by Palijo and the MKP. Fatehyab sent Shaukat Ali to negotiate on behalf of the MKP in Quetta. Shaukat Ali had a shady past as a squealer and had been thrown out of the Communist Party of Pakistan for that sin.[50] At this meeting, with Palijo's connivance, he negotiated Fatehyab's expulsion from his party. On 19 July 1986, a big PNP contingent came to our house to brief Fatehyab about the conspiracy against him in the Quetta meeting. Fatehyab tided over this crisis with the help of Rao Sulaiman and the working committee members who supported him. Since Bangash refused to leave the SBPF and Fatehyab stuck to his allegiance to MRD's four-point programme, his credentials were accepted by the heads of the MRD parties as the president of the MKP and signatory of its declaration.[51] The new party, the ANP, was admitted as a member of the MRD although Bizenjo, who had proposed the merger of leftist parties in the first place, pulled out of the merger, describing it as an alliance of opportunists.[52] The landmark MRD session held in Lahore on 2 August 1986, adopted unanimously the historic Lahore declaration on provincial autonomy, the result of five years' work, for which Fatehyab and his colleagues in the radical parties had lobbied and struggled.[53]

Fatehyab was arrested again in October 1985 while I was in London. The big event the following year was Benazir Bhutto's return to Pakistan. She was given a magnificent welcome wherever she went. On 3 May 1986, thousands of people turned out to welcome her in Karachi; Fatehyab and I waited for hours to see her procession pass by on Sharea Faisal. Later, with four children, Hasan, Tahera, Asad and Salma, we went to Jinnah's mausoleum where she addressed an enormous public meeting. The area all around the mausoleum was overflowing with people, trucks, buses, cars, rickshaws and motorbikes. We heard her speech in the early hours of the morning. The fervour and passion of the public response cannot be described in words when she concluded: *aj to ho gai Bhutto Bhutto* (today there is only Bhutto Bhutto).[54]

Benazir Bhutto was so impatient with the old men in the MRD that she foisted the ill-prepared civil disobedience movement of 1986 on the alliance.

She thought that the large public turnout at her meetings would compel Ziaul Haq to hold party-based elections and transfer power. But Ziaul Haq was removed from the scene only when somebody –we don't know who – blew him up in the air on 17 August 1988. On her insistence, the alliance decided to hold rallies throughout the country on 14 August 1986, but all meetings were banned and fifty-five top MRD leaders, including Fatehyab, were arrested in Karachi.[55] There were processions and clashes, especially in Sindh, where forty people lost their lives and many were killed in the police firing in Lahore.[56] My brother, Kazim, filed a constitution petition against Fatehyab's arrest which was admitted by the Sindh High Court. P.K. Shahani accompanied Hasan and me to the court when it was taken up for hearing on 1 and 2 September by a division bench comprising justices Mamoon Kazi and Nasir Aslam Zahid. As I watched, the justices appeared so impressive, almost superhuman in their dignity. Fatehyab was very composed when he argued before them and, on 3 September 1986, they ordered his release.[57] That evening, our house was full of slogans, flowers, garlands, incessant telephone calls and total exhaustion for me. Like the civil disobedience movement of 1983, after a few weeks this movement also fizzled out.

Fatehyab was the convenor of the MRD for three months from May to July 1987. The heads of parties and central action committee meetings were held in our house in June that year. Leaders, workers, journalists and other visitors flooded our house for many days. A really colourful ANP procession, waving red flags, drove to our gate on 19 July. Arrangements for lunch and dinner for hundreds of people wore me out but there were lighter moments.[58] Since I never ventured near the meeting, as a courtesy Benazir Bhutto met me in another room. Suddenly, she turned to Fatehyab and said: 'Fatehyab Sahib, people tell me that your wife is even more brilliant than you are. Why don't you give her to my party?' Nothing was secret in those days and when Bizenjo heard about this offer – or demand – he sent word that if I was to join any political party, it should be his PNP! On that occasion, Lord Ennals, the British politician who campaigned for human rights, pleaded with Benazir Bhutto to lend her support to bring back the poor 'Biharis' stranded in Bangladesh to Pakistan, but she was adamantly against it and did not relent.

Next year, on 5 and 6 March 1988, Prime Minister Muhammad Khan Junejo[59] convened a round table conference of all political parties to discuss Pakistan's position at the Geneva talks, now that the Soviet Union had agreed to pull out of Afghanistan. Ziaul Haq was against the signing of any accord until a framework for a future Afghan government was in place and he did not relish the independent policy of his prime minister. However, in the round table conference, Junejo got a political consensus to sign the Geneva

Accords. Fatehyab attended the conference; I was thrilled to watch him on the television. Ziaul Haq sacked Junejo a couple of months later.

All the MRD leaders contested the general elections held in November 1988 after Ziaul Haq's departure and only a few of them won. They felt betrayed by the PPP, which did not honour the understanding that the elections would be contested as an alliance, but they believed that their sacrifices for democracy would be recognised by the people. Fatehyab also contested from a constituency in Karachi and lost. The Muhajir Qaumi Movement (MQM) swept the elections in the city. The big names among the losers were Bizenjo, Asghar Khan and Mazari, and Jatoi and Shah Ahmad Noorani outside the MRD. The PPP won enough seats for Benazir to make her political compromise with the establishment and become the prime minister. Her colleagues in the MRD felt that, had she honoured the election alliance, she would have emerged stronger and no compromises could have been imposed upon her. The MRD had ceased to exist.

The history of the MRD, full of courage and pathos, success and failure, has yet to be written. I have told the story as I saw it through the lens of Fatehyab's role in the struggle. Although it failed to get rid of Ziaul Haq, it was a great movement, if only for the sheer mobilisation of thousands of people in all the provinces. It was most successful in every corner of Sindh where the anger at Bhutto's hanging was an important motivating factor. Both in 1983 and 1986, thousands of people, including women, courted arrest for many weeks and came out in processions. The movement created political links at the grassroots, introduced the idiom of democracy, and threw up new political leadership at many levels of society. People throughout the country were arrested, imprisoned, tried by military courts and flogged; many were put to death.[60] This solidarity in pain bound them together in the decades ahead. The subcommittees of the alliance did excellent work on the Constitution, provincial autonomy, organisation and structure, and their reports should be published.

One can pause to consider some of the weaknesses of the movement. Although it tried to remain united, its members did not always concur with one another. Asghar Khan was sceptical about it from the beginning and his stalling tactics have been described as one reason for its attrition.[61] He left the alliance in October 1986. Wali Khan's conflicting statements about the 1973 Constitution and his negative public pronouncements about Jinnah and the creation of Pakistan alienated many. The more conservative parties, such as Fazlur Rahman's JUI, were unhappy with the support to the Soviet Union in Afghanistan by Wali Khan and Bizenjo. Some members were critical about the ANP's tilt towards the idea of a confederation. And although the PPP's mass base was important, all the others were angry with Benazir's attempt to monopolise the MRD and impose the slogan of 'Bhuttoism' upon it.[62] The parties in the alliance, therefore, had to keep publicly reiterating their loyalty to MRD's four-point programme.

The alliance was large but Ziaul Haq's martial law was so cruel that it required considerable personal courage to challenge it. Many families, especially poor families and their children, were totally destroyed in the process. Since the leaders were arrested at every significant political moment, the struggle was carried on by second–or third-tier activists who were less experienced. Restrictions placed on the leaders' movements prevented them from organising and reaching out to their followers. Also, some politicians were tempted to open a dialogue with Ziaul Haq. For example, Khawaja Khairuddin never made a secret of his links with the army. Eventually he was expelled from the alliance for being an agent of the rulers.[63]

*   *   *

Since I was a child I had a dislocating knee cap which caused excruciating pain. None of the famous surgeons in Karachi took these episodes seriously until the slightest push would throw me to the ground in agony. Finally, some doctors, Ehtisham among them, advised surgery. David Dandy was the star of orthopaedic surgery in Cambridge, also the pioneer of arthroscopy and I reasoned that I would be comfortable in the city that I knew. But I did not know what was in store for me. I went at my own expense in July 1988 for surgery at the Evelyn, a private clinic on Trumpington Road. My brother Kazim and my sons, Hasan and Asad, went with me. Fatehyab could not accompany me because he was again refused a passport by the government which claimed that my illness was just a pretence. When I met David Dandy, he said my knee cap was very unstable and an operation was essential. All seemed to go well until the final X-ray showed that the operation had been unsuccessful. A few days later, Dandy opened the joint again. As I came out of anaesthesia, I saw him standing beside me. 'There you are,' he said, 'entirely stable'. But I was in terrible pain all along.

From the clinic, I shifted to the flat we had rented and waited for Fatehyab who had petitioned the high court in Karachi for a passport. Here my ordeal started. My leg swelled to enormous proportions and in spite of repeated requests, Dandy did not see me. Finally, as a great favour he visited me at the physiotherapist's, Mrs Nye was her name, and exclaimed 'a clot, jinxed twice?' He rushed me barefoot to the radiologist and the venogram showed that my leg was full of clots – I had suffered a massive deep vein thrombosis. Mercifully,

I was not aware of the seriousness of a DVT. Poh Sim Plowright, my friend since 1963, called me every day while I was in hospital and also came to see me. I had many visitors from London and Cambridge: Anil Seal and Debbie Swallow, Farzana Shaikh and Patrick Chabal, Husain Naqi, Ahmad Zaheer and my dear friend, Zahid Saeed. Fatehyab was given a passport on the orders of the high court and joined me. He took me away to London and Dandy was relieved to see me disappear into the care of the vascular physician, Anthony Goldstone. I shall be ever grateful to Salim Siddiqui, Fatehyab's friend at the Bank of Credit and Commerce International (BCCI), who let us use a flat in St John's Wood. We settled down there as a family.

On 17 August 1988, Ziaul Haq was blown up in mid-air over Bahawalpur. We heard the news on the television and just then, Khawaja Masrur Hussain and his nephew, Asad Abbas, came to see us. Masrur Hussain, as I have written earlier, was Ziaul Haq's intelligence chief. He was stunned by the news and Asad said to Fatehyab, 'let us embrace'. Word got round that an MRD leader was in London and Fatehyab became the centre of media attention. The broadcasting and television services besieged the flat. I sensed that Fatehyab wanted to be where the action was, in Pakistan, following Ziaul Haq's death. I was still on crutches and had to go to the laboratory in University College London Hospital for frequent blood tests to adjust the dose of blood thinners, but I encouraged him to leave. Before he left, he held a press conference in Westminster under the aegis of the Society for Restoration of Human Rights in Pakistan.

I was left alone in the flat because the children had also gone home. Poh Sim and her husband, Piers, looked after me during the rest of my stay in London. At night I fell asleep praying there should be no further complications. Often I went alone by taxi to the laboratory, struggling along on my crutches. Goldstone told me that I should consult a vascular surgeon and thus Mohankumar Adiseshiah came into my life. When he first saw me, he said, 'you have been very ill.' I have always considered him my saviour and consulted him every few years. Fatehyab's friends in London stood by us at that difficult time, Irtiqa Shaikh, Muhammad Arif and his wife Siriani, Sibghatullah Kadri and Karita, and Shahbaz Rana. The lawyers among them suggested that I should sue David Dandy and he really deserved to be sued for negligence.[64] But I wanted to recover and not waste my energy, money and time in lawsuits in a foreign country. When Poh Sim and Piers saw me off at Heathrow in Ali Mehmood's Bentley Turbo, on 31 August 1988, I threw away the crutches. My colleagues from the management services division welcomed me warmly at Karachi airport.

Chapter 9

Vienna

In the winter of 1994, Benazir Bhutto appointed me as Pakistan's ambassador to Vienna. To her, I owe this fascinating turn in my career. When she came to power in 1993 in her second term as prime minister, I was very senior in the larger civil service and the only woman in the highest grade. There were no women even far down in the level below me. Everyone thought that, as a woman prime minister, she would appoint me as secretary in one of the ministries, but it was not to be. The elite civil service had probably warned her that this was their turf. Malik Qasim reminded her about an appointment for me and he called me after meeting her. 'She won't make you federal secretary,' he told me. 'Why?' I asked, and I will always remember his reply: 'These are the ways of *badshahs*.' She sent word that I should, if I wanted, become secretary of the women's division. While I had always supported the empowerment of women, I thought this suggestion was gender discrimination in reverse. It amounted to saying, 'since you are a woman, you can head the women's ministry only.' So I demurred, arguing that if I was not qualified to head mainstream ministries like finance, production and petroleum, there were social sector ministries to which the government attached less importance, anyway, like education, health, population or the environment. Surely I was competent and experienced enough to lead one of them?

Eventually, Benazir decided to send me abroad as ambassador. She could not really have continued to ignore my seniority. Like the elite civil service, the foreign service of Pakistan also jealously guarded its interests, but traditionally, heads of government have made their own appointments to about 40 per cent of the ambassadorial posts. So Benazir would not really be ruffling too many feathers. But the choice of the capital became an issue. Word got around that I was being considered for an ambassadorship. At one event, I met Sardar Asif Ahmad Ali, who was the foreign minister and he ticked me off. 'People think,' he said, 'that they can take up any job. Diplomacy requires professionalism and experience. We might consider you for a lesser mission.'

The first offer made to me was for Athens. Greece is a beautiful country, but it could hardly be considered an important posting in terms of its relations with Pakistan and I did not want to simply issue visas. Benazir also suggested Brazil or Mexico where relations were 'virtually non-existent' and I would have an empty canvas to make of it what I could with my 'considerable talents'. The countries of Latin America had a lot of diplomatic and economic potential but they were also diplomatic outposts. They were so far away that I could never have afforded to travel back home. So I stalled again, much to Fatehyab's annoyance. 'Look,' he warned, 'she is the prime minister.' 'I know,' I replied, 'but she is large-hearted enough to understand and respect my reservations.' And so she did. She decided to send me to Vienna. To give her credit, she had made the same suggestion before her first government was dismissed on 6 August 1990.

To familiarise me with multilateral diplomacy, I was sent as a delegate to the UN General Assembly session for a few weeks in November 1994. I spoke in the General Assembly plenary sessions and in the Fourth Committee and introduced resolutions in the First Committee on disarmament and a nuclear weapon-free zone in South Asia. And I sat through meetings of the Security Council and the OIC Contact Group. This exposure to the UN system prepared me for my assignment in Vienna. Fatehyab was also a delegate and we spent time with Nawabzada Nasrullah Khan, chairman of the parliamentary committee on Kashmir. Much to Nawabzada's regret, Pakistan did not table a resolution on Kashmir in the First Committee that year. He was very upset and left New York in the days following.

To prepare for my assignment in Vienna, I spent a few days being briefed in the foreign office in Islamabad. Najmuddin Shaikh was the foreign secretary and from him I received both courtesy and support. But there was hardly any 'briefing'. The only person who spoke to me at length about policy matters and our diplomacy with the West was Munir Akram.[1] Kausar Ahsan[2] came to my rescue and helped to hasten the administrative work about my departure. There were some lighter moments when I discovered that the credentials described me as 'he' and not 'she'. I took them to Najmuddin Shaikh and said I did not mind being referred to in the masculine if that was the usual practice; he was amazed at the error and ordered a change immediately.

There may have been less administrative support than is extended to career diplomats, but my appointment was well received by the general public, my colleagues, and the members of the women's movement. I made the usual calls on secretaries of various ministries and met Ishfaq Ahmed, chairman of the Pakistan Atomic Energy Commission (PAEC) for the first time. An impressive and dedicated scientist, he took me on a tour of the Pakistan Institute of Nuclear Science and Technology and introduced me to many scientists in that facility and he gave me a comprehensive briefing on our national interests in the International Atomic Energy Agency (IAEA). I also received advice in my personal meetings with former ambassadors Qamrul Islam and Mahdi

Masud. Munir Ahmad Khan, former chairman of PAEC, took me under his wing, but more about that later.

I made a last dash to Islamabad to call on the president, Farooq Leghari, and pick up my credentials – 'she' this time. He kept me waiting for twenty-five minutes. The atmosphere in the presidential office was rather stuffy. His principal secretary and another officer were present and he was very formal during the conversation. When I told him that the mission in Vienna had only two diplomats but was both bilateral and multilateral, he said the ambassador would have to do most of the work. In that stuffy room he appeared to be somewhat of a prisoner. To my eternal regret, a meeting could not be arranged with Benazir before I left.

Many of my friends and the members of The Pakistan Institute of International Affairs held farewell dinners and receptions for me; however, nothing compared with the grand send-off accorded to me by my colleagues at NIPA Karachi. They had prepared for it secretly under Waqar Hussain's guidance and had invited my friends and former teachers. When I reached the campus, I was astonished by the welcoming police band; there were lights, flowers, gifts and a music programme. The auditorium was packed with about 200 people and many speeches were made by my colleagues and friends. A touching tribute was paid by my teacher at the University of Karachi, Syed Adil Hussain, whom I had always admired.

Nobody had told me how an embassy was run. But with some knowledge of global politics, administrative experience and the interactive skills which I had acquired during my career, I ventured towards Vienna. Hasan and Asad travelled with me. As is customary, I stopped on the way for a week in another capital, Paris, which I had visited frequently when I was studying at Cambridge. Saeed Dehlavi was our ambassador in Paris. I knew him since my visit to Cairo in 1964, when his father, S.K. Dehlavi, was ambassador there. Saeed had accompanied me to my grandfather's grave and shown me around the city. He sent his staff to receive us but my brother Arif's first wife, Natalie and his son Sikandar insisted on taking us home with them. Natalie and I had always been friends and so affectionate was she that I gave in to her wish. 'We are family,' she insisted.

Hasan and Asad had proceeded from Paris to Vienna before me and I travelled alone to that 'city of dreams' on 30 January 1995.[3] The embassy staff and members of the Pakistani community received me warmly at the airport. The embassy residence was being repaired, so we had to start living at the Hilton hotel. It was bitterly cold, a Viennese winter. The Foreign Office conveyed that I should move into the embassy residence, but it was unusable and had no heating, running water or protection from the severe winter winds.

Next morning, I went to the embassy, situated in Hofzeile, in the upmarket 19th district.

The embassy building was small compared to the huge ornate edifices in which the missions of other countries were housed, but it was owned by our government. The furniture, fixtures, upholstery and carpets in the office and the residence were somewhat worn out and the foreign office agreed to provide funds to purchase some furniture and furnishings, silver from Karachi and flatware from Kings of Sheffield. The embassy residence, which was being repaired, was a lovely turn-of-the-century mansion located in the 18th district. It had high roofs, grand windows, large reception rooms, chandeliers owned by us, and a polished wooden staircase leading to the first floor on which only three rooms were located. Behind the house was a sloping, unkempt and charming garden with trees, ferns, grass and tulips which bloomed in summer, but which we never had enough funds to look after. On top of the first floor there was a huge loft where my predecessor, Samuel Joshua, had stored unused furniture and objects, and in which there was frequent movement at night. The basement ran under the entire ground floor and the cellar could have accommodated hundreds of bottles; however, it was cold and damp. Within walking distance was Potzleinsdorfer Schlosspark (Palace Park) with its winding paths and vistas, magnificent giant sequoia trees, streams and statues.

In the same district was located Vienna's largest park, Turkenschanz, built between 1885 and 1888. It drew its name from the Turkish entrenchments found at the site, probably belonging to Suleiman the Magnificent's abandoned siege of Vienna in 1526. The Ottomans had knocked at the doors of Vienna and had they succeeded in that siege or in their later ambitious push in 1683 under Kara Mustafa Pasha, the history of Europe would have been different. They were already masters of Hungary and central Europe. But the Holy Roman Empire and later the Habsburgs fought back, and eventually the Ottomans lost their hold on much of Hungary. After the failure of the siege in 1683, Kara Mustafa Pasha was punished by the powerful janissaries and put to death in Belgrade. In the traditional manner for nobles and aristocrats, he was strangled with a silken cord.

I started work almost immediately, calling on the chief of protocol, Gustav Ortner, and secretary general of foreign affairs, Wolfgang Schallenberg, in very pleasant meetings. On 15 February 1995, I presented my credentials to President Thomas Klestil in the Hofburg, the former imperial palace which was built in the thirteenth century and has since remained the seat of the Austrian government. A lot of colour and glamour accompanied this ceremony. Gustav Ortner collected me from the hotel in a state car. The road to the Hofburg had been closed to traffic, so that the state car, with its pilot and outriders, could drive through smoothly. Many people lined the streets on both sides. The weather was cold but sunny and when I descended, there was a guard of honour with a band and I remembered to bow to the flag. Inside the palace we went through many grand rooms, the doors of which were manned by soldiers who presented arms and finally into a large gilded room at the far end of which stood Thomas Klestil, flanked by Schallenberg and his chef de cabinet. Klestil belonged to the conservative Austrian People's Party (OVP). He was a former civil servant and diplomat and had been ambassador of Austria to the United Nations and the United States.

After I had presented my credentials, Klestil made a short speech in German. We then settled down to talk beneath a large portrait of Maria Theresa in a heavily adorned golden frame. The furniture was gilded, the upholstery was maroon. It was a very pleasant and relaxed conversation in which I brought up the need for peace in our region which would not be achieved unless the Kashmir dispute was resolved. When I walked out of the Hofburg, the national anthems of Austria and Pakistan were played and there was a final salute. My chauffeur, Nisar, was thrilled that we could then fly the national flag on the embassy car, which is allowed only on special occasions in Austria. Later in the month, I presented my credentials to Hans Blix,[4] director general of the IAEA, Mauricio Campos, director general of the United Nations Industrial Development Organisation (UNIDO) and Giorgio Giacomelli, head of the United Nations Office in Vienna (UNOV).

Vienna provided a rare combination of multilateral and bilateral work. Apart from being a United Nations headquarters, it was the seat of intergovernmental organisations such as the Organisation of Petroleum Exporting Countries (OPEC) and the OPEC Fund for International Development. Because of Vienna's importance as a diplomatic posting, many countries appointed more than one ambassador there, one to Austria and another to the multilateral agencies. Most European countries also sent a separate ambassador to the Organisation of Security and Cooperation in Europe (OSCE). Turkey had three representatives and so did Iran. But the less-developed countries had only one ambassador. Our mission in Vienna was both multilateral and bilateral, and to deal with the workload, there were only two other diplomats and one representative of PAEC.

Critical to our nuclear interests in Vienna was our work at the IAEA. After the carnage caused by the atom bombs dropped by the Americans on Hiroshima and Nagasaki, the world – and the Americans – woke up to the horror of nuclear power and the diverse uses of nuclear technology. The IAEA was created as a specialised and autonomous organisation within the UN family in July 1957 and reports to the UN General Assembly and the

Security Council. In Article 11 of its statute, it was mandated to work with member states to accelerate and enlarge the contribution of atomic energy to peace, health and prosperity throughout the world, and also to ensure that the assistance it provided was not used in such a way as to further any military purpose. Today, in common parlance, the IAEA is described as a 'nuclear watchdog'. Its work revolves around safety and security, science and technology, and safeguards and verification. The IAEA has 172 member states. Pakistan became a member of the agency in 1957, the year it was established.

The IAEA seemed to be in constant session. If we were not actually attending its meetings, we were preparing to attend them. The board of governors met five times a year and there was a general conference of all member states, usually in September each year. There were also many ancillary meetings such as those on the financing of safeguards. Ishfaq Ahmed came from Islamabad to attend these sessions and I benefited as much from his knowledge and expertise as his support and understanding. He was my mentor on all nuclear issues. But I also received advice and affection from Munir Ahmad Khan, the former chairman of PAEC. He had 'briefed' me, as it were, before I left for Vienna. He often visited that city because of his former association with the agency and because his wife was Austrian. In the summer of 1996, he told me at great length about how Pakistan's nuclear programme had evolved, taking me to all the places where he had met Zulfikar Ali Bhutto in Vienna and convinced him to opt for the nuclear path, including the celebrated restaurant, Drei Husaren, in Weinburggasse. I suggested that he should write his memoir for posterity. He also showed me the splendid presidential suite in Imperial Hotel where Bhutto had stayed. Pakistan's nuclear programme was Bhutto's greatest gift to his country.

As is well known, Pakistan's concern was to seek more permanent representation and, therefore, make a greater contribution in the board of governors – which is one of the leading policymaking bodies of the IAEA – from the Middle East and South Asia (MESA) region. There were eight regional groupings in all.[5] The only designated member from the MESA group was India. The president of the board of governors for 1994–5 was the Indian physicist, Rajagopala Chidambaram. He was a former chairman of India's atomic energy commission and was known for his contribution to India's nuclear programme. In 1995–6, the chair was held by William G. Padolina from the Philippines, a famous scientist. The board comprised thirty-five members and its composition covered all regions globally, but because of the procedure adopted, for more than two decades Pakistan was an elected member of the board for two out of every three years, generally (but not always) by consensus in the MESA group. In its meeting in September 1994, before

I arrived in Vienna, the general conference of the IAEA had, by consensus, requested the board to continue consultations with member states to devise a mechanism for amendments to Article VI of its statute which could lead to the enlargement of the board's membership, and place them for approval at the next general conference in September 1995. An open-ended consultative group was established with Fugen Ok, the permanent representative of Turkey, as the chair.

With the ambassadors of other interested countries, our mission participated in the open-ended consultative group's meetings to consider the revision of Article VI of the IAEA statute to raise the membership of the board to forty-one. This was the maximum number to which the western countries and Japan would then agree, but it could open a window for Pakistan to acquire a designated seat on the board. The question of the expansion of the board had been the concern of the IAEA's policymaking bodies for almost two decades. The expansion was opposed by the advanced countries, ostensibly on the basis of the argument that it would affect the board's efficiency. But like other developing countries, our mission argued that the board should reflect the existing international realities in the nuclear community in all regions, the enlarged membership of the IAEA, and the acquisition of nuclear technology for peaceful uses by many countries since the board was first constituted.

A group of member states, otherwise referred to as the 'Sherry Group', which included Pakistan, worked out a proposal for the modification of Article VI. The Sherry Group's proposal was based on the argument that the regional groupings contained in the IAEA statute and the criteria for their classification were established thirty-eight years ago and were no longer valid. Further, the current size and composition of the board did not correspond to global realities because of the increase in the membership of the IAEA. Member states who opposed the Sherry Group's proposal argued that – much as the permanent members of the UN Security Council contend with respect to its expansion today – both the composition of the board and the criteria for the eight-area regional classification were adequate. Subsequently, the Sherry Group put forward a revised proposal. Ambassador Ben Moussa of Morocco, who was a very active diplomat, also tabled a formal proposal, inter alia, on the size and distribution of seats on the board.

The United States had made it clear that it would oppose any proposal for the expansion of the board unless Israel was accepted as a member of the MESA group. Israel's membership of this group had been opposed all along by all its members and it was generally agreed that it could not be imposed on them against their wishes. In fact, Israel was a kind of regional outcast. It did not belong to any group at all and had itself tabled a proposal which placed it in the MESA group. This issue came up in the general conference of the IAEA in September 1996 when we were still fighting for the revision of Article VI of the IAEA statute for which we had lobbied throughout the year, both from our mission's platform and from that of the Group of 77. My nominee as chairman of the committee of the whole, Sadegh Ayatollahi of Iran, fought valiantly in the general conference and so did Ben Moussa. But we were sidelined by the Arabs in their negotiations with the US delegate, Robert Einhorn, then deputy assistant secretary in the US State Department. He negotiated with them throughout the day, ignoring other member states in the MESA group. When we took him to task, he pretended he was not aware that he had shut us out. My diary entry for 20 September 1996 reads:

> Spent whole day in IAEA General Conference. The Arabs let us down in their negotiations with Einhorn. Spent morning battling for the amendment of Article VI and the whole evening against Israeli's membership of MESA. Our negotiations held up the Conference plenary. Returned home exhausted and broken hearted at what the Americans can do.

Three years later, in 1999, sustained effort and consistent diplomacy by Pakistan and other countries seeking representation led to the tabling of a formal proposal to amend Article VI of the IAEA statute whereby the size of the board would be raised from thirty-five to forty-three members. This was a tremendous achievement and brought Pakistan conceptually to the threshold of a designated seat. However, the revision has to be accepted by two-thirds of the IAEA membership before the amended statute can be adopted. Pakistan accepted the amendment in June 2000. Israel is still not a member of any regional group.

Although Pakistan was well on the way to becoming a declared nuclear power, its most urgent need was technical assistance in the peaceful uses of nuclear applications. For this purpose, we sought the transfer of technology and access to training programmes, which were often denied to us by the more advanced countries. There were also embargoes on the transfer of scientific equipment and material. Since this need was common to many developing countries, a mechanism was devised to advise the director general of the IAEA on its technical cooperation strategy and policies and review its technical cooperation programmes. I went with other permanent representatives and the Chinese ambassador to present the report on setting up the Standing Advisory Committee on Technical Cooperation (SAGTAC) to Hans Blix on 23 March 1995, and later to request that PAEC chairman, Ishfaq Ahmed, be included in the SAGTAC experts committee. Eventually, he was elected to the chair of SAGTAC, which was established in 1996, comprising representatives of both developing and developed countries. They were drawn from the sciences, academia and the development sector.

The other major intergovernmental organisation, which was a specialised agency, was the United Nations Industrial Development Organisation. During my stay in Vienna, UNIDO went through a crisis of survival and our mission worked to save it with the help of assertive colleagues from other developing countries and China, as well as from the platform of the Group of 77. Created in 1966, it was converted into a specialised agency in 1985 to promote and accelerate industrialisation in developing countries and encourage industrial development cooperation. However, the advanced countries, led by the United States, thought that industrial development could be more effectively achieved through assistance by the private sector and some of them withheld support from UNIDO. The United States, which was the largest donor, withdrew from UNIDO in 1995, followed by notices of withdrawal by the United Kingdom and Australia. Canada had withdrawn in 1993. All this resulted in a drastic cut in the organisation's budget. The advanced countries argued that the organisation had become irrelevant in the current global economic situation. They shifted their interest to the private sector in developing countries, arguing that most of them had achieved a fair level of industrialisation and UNIDO must, therefore, redefine its role. This was not an honest argument. While there may have been some industrial tigers in the developing world, many countries in Africa and the least developed countries were heavily indebted, did not have organised private sectors, and needed state intervention for industrial growth.

The developing countries went through a tense period of negotiations as they closed their ranks to save UNIDO from extinction. Our success in keeping the organisation alive owed much to the vision and leadership of Fugen Ok. She chaired the Industrial Development Board of UNIDO and although she worked under great pressure, she did not waiver in her mission. The director general of UNIDO, Mauricio Campos, a Mexican with many Latin American advisers, did not come across as a forceful leader. In 1997, the member states designed a business plan to salvage the organisation and it was implemented in the following years.

In contrast to the regular professional support provided to our diplomatic initiatives by the PAEC, the other institutions and ministries in Pakistan were less responsive. No delegation from Pakistan attended the sessions of UNIDO's Industrial Development Board, programme and budget committee or general conference while I was ambassador. Our mission kept the ministry of industries informed of developments in that agency, but the briefs we received did not adequately address the issues facing the organisation. We were able to play a prominent role during the crisis in UNIDO only because of the knowledge I had acquired during my career about the industrial sector in Pakistan. I had suggested the holding of an Intechmart in Pakistan but that did not materialise either.

In October 1995, I led our delegation to UNIDO's Global Forum on Industry and the Meeting of the Ministers of Industry in Asia and the Pacific in Delhi. When the plane circled over Delhi, I could not hold back my tears as I thought of the centuries' old association of my ancestors with that city. I was sitting alone in the front row of the plane and thought that nobody had noticed, but soon found the cabin steward standing beside me. 'Have you come in peace?' he asked. In the Ashok Hotel, where I stayed, the Indian government posted two armed personnel round the clock outside the door of my room. And one man in mufti accompanied me like a shadow wherever I went, probably to keep an eye on my movements. He did not let me out of his sight. I teased him: 'How can you protect me, if you are not armed?' He touched his pocket and said his weapon was ready.

As always, I was drawn to Humayun's tomb. A few young girls, glamorously dressed and made up, engaged me in conversation as I sat on the platform of the tomb. When they heard I came from Karachi, they tried to identify the Karachi neighbourhood in which I lived: Nazimabad, Liaquatabad, Federal B Area, Saddar, they knew all these names. Before leaving the tomb, I stopped at Arab Serai where Bahadur Shah Zafar, the last Mughal emperor, had waited for his doom.

Riaz Khokhar was our high commissioner in Delhi. He invited me in Gul-i-Raana, the house which Liaquat Ali Khan had fondly built in Delhi and named after his beloved wife, Raana. He had left behind vast estates in the United Provinces and bequeathed the house to the Pakistan government after Partition. Shahid Malik was deputy chief of mission and I met, after a long time, my contemporary at the University of Karachi, Mufti Jamiluddin.

I could not restrain myself from searching for my roots and looking for the house in which my parents had lived near the University of Delhi. The last address in my father's papers was 4 Cavalry Lines. On a road which seemed familiar, I drove into many houses, only to rush out in embarrassment; they were all built on the same Lutyens design. Finally, somebody pointed towards a house and said: 'that is 4 Cavalry Lines'. I knocked on the door of the house with some hesitation. A man came out and looked at me inquiringly. When I explained the purpose of my visit, he invited me inside. I did not recognise the house. My memory, like the memory of any child recalled larger spaces, bigger rooms. The house was occupied by a young couple. They were kind and friendly. The woman was a sculptor and sensing that I must be a Muslim because I came from Pakistan, the man told his wife, 'show her the book'. The woman then brought out a sculpture of the Quran. I left their house with mixed feelings, not knowing whether I had indeed found my parents' residence. There were flat sites all around; perhaps 4 Cavalry Lines had been converted into a block of flats.

There were many other important organisations in Vienna, such as the Commission on Narcotic Drugs, Commission on Crime Prevention and Criminal Justice,[6] and the Committee on the Peaceful Uses of Outer Space. The International Narcotics Control Board also operated from Vienna and in 1997 it became home to the Comprehensive Test Ban Treaty Organisation. In the European context, it was the seat of the Organisation for Security and Cooperation in Europe, which then had more than fifty members, including the Central Asian Republics in the Commonwealth of Independent States. Pakistan was a member of all United Nations bodies in Vienna and had observer status at the UN Commission in International Trade Law.

The organisations in Vienna provided a platform to define and promote issues which were fast becoming the new currency of international politics. The commissions on Narcotic Drugs and Crime Prevention and Criminal Justice explored relatively new issues such as standards and norms, illicit production and trafficking in drugs, terrorism, smuggling of aliens, control of firearms, violence against women and children. These were universal concerns and new aspects of security emerged to ensure investment and the free movement of capital while restricting the free movement of labour which was part of the West's vision of globalisation. The former socialist states of Eastern Europe were partners in this endeavour. The Russian Federation was ambivalent in that it sought western economic assistance, but wanted to retain its influence on the former eastern bloc nations.

Pakistan had an important stake in the work of both the commissions on Narcotic Drugs and Crime Prevention and Criminal Justice. The United Nations Drug Control Program (UNDCP) conducted surveys of poppy cultivation and the illicit production, trafficking and use of drugs in Pakistan. We did not agree with all their conclusions. During my tenure, we successfully liaised with UNDCP and were frequently consulted by the executive director of the UNOV. Pakistan was elected as vice chair (the ambassador) of the regular session of the Commission on Crime Prevention and Criminal Justice in 1995. Repeated reminders did not result in any briefs from Pakistan to the sessions of this commission. In the absence of an authorised brief, our mission could not make a statement in the plenary in 1996 although Pakistan's record on many items on the agenda, especially in the field of legislation, was impressive. We did our best to compensate by participating in the informal consultations.

The Committee on the Peaceful Uses of Outer Space (COPUOS) was established by the UN General Assembly in 1959 to govern the exploration and use of space for peaceful purposes, security and development, for the benefit of all humanity. Its purpose was also to promote greater internal collaboration in outer space. We were able to negotiate successfully with the advanced countries to adopt the UN practice of rotating posts in its bureau and subcommittees among the regional groups which, for decades, had revolved only between Austria, Romania and Brazil. Pakistan had always played an important role in the Scientific and Technical Subcommittee of COPUOS and we influenced the decision in favour of holding Unispace III in July 1999. This conference created a blueprint for the peaceful uses of outer space in the twenty-first century and stressed upon increasing access for developing countries to the benefits of space science. COPUOS was headed, since 1991, by the forceful and gifted Austrian diplomat, Peter Hohenfellner. In the meetings he chaired, it was usually difficult to speak, because he dominated the space and time. This prompted the Indian ambassador, Doshi, to say that an ambassador is an honest person who is sent abroad to get bored for his country, a twist to the famous expression that an ambassador is an honest person sent abroad to lie for his country.

I was elected to the chair of the Group of 77 in 1996, making me the first woman diplomat to hold the chair of any chapter of the Group of 77. It was a reflection of confidence in the work of our mission and a great personal honour for me. After my election to the chair of the Group of 77, I requested the foreign office to send one more diplomat to our mission because an additional parallel stream of work had been created, but my request was not granted. 'You will manage', I was told. Since there was so much emphasis on 'economic diplomacy', I had also asked for an economic counsellor and drew another blank. It was an eventful year for the Group of 77, especially with respect to UNIDO and COPUOS. The Group of 77 rallied around UNIDO although its performance and the style of its top management came in for criticism. In my opening statement in the first plenary meeting, I emphasised that the concept of globalisation had changed the nature and priority of concerns for the developed world, but poverty remained a continuing concern for the Group of 77 countries.

All the international organisations in Vienna operated from the Vienna International Centre (VIC), also known as UNO City, a large, multi-storey, modern building on the left bank of the Danube. It was constructed by the Austrian government as an international centre to be used by the organisations of the United Nations' system. A global competition was floated for the design of the building which attracted 288 architects. The Austrian architect, Johann Staber, was declared the winner and the VIC started functioning in 1979.

*   *   *

Austria is a small country with a glorious past. At the bilateral level, Vienna acquired a new dimension in diplomacy after Austria joined the European Union on 1 January 1995. The Austrian government was a coalition of two parties, the conservative Austrian People's Party (OVP) and the socialist Social Democratic Party (SPO). The SPO took inspiration from the government of the charismatic Bruno Kreisky (1911–90) who was chancellor of Austria from 1970–83. He was an ardent socialist and introduced truly wide-ranging reforms and welfare measures in a country of conservative Roman Catholics. These reforms related to family laws, prisons, decriminalisation of abortion and homosexuality, and discrimination against illegitimate children. Progressive reforms were carried out about labour benefits, working conditions, equality for women, sex equality, the penal code, maturity benefits, widows' pensions, education, free medical treatment, compensation for health damages, social security, and housing supplements. Kreisky actually introduced a widower's pension. This system of support provided by the state has endured and is one reason for the social stability in Austrian society and the confidence found among Austrian citizens.

When I was ambassador in Vienna, Franz Vranitsky of SPO was chancellor of Austria, followed by Victor Klima. Vienna has traditionally voted for the socialists and was often described in the past as 'Red Vienna'. But Austrian politics also saw the rise of Jörg Haider, leader of the ultra-right Freedom Party. Haider was known for his populist, anti-immigration, anti-EU and anti-Islam views. His rhetoric did not bring comfort to the substantially large Turkish population in Austria, the single largest immigrant group. They came initially as guest workers for the construction and export industries. I noticed a strong feeling of exclusion and superiority among ordinary Austrians who were intolerant of Turkish labour, although it was recognised that they filled a significant gap in the Austrian economy. In 1997, a more restrictive immigration system was introduced. Austria was vehemently opposed to Turkey joining the European Union.[7]

Located in the centre of Europe, with a population in 1996 of about 8 million and a common border with eight countries,[8] Austria offered a welcoming environment for trade and investment. Multinational companies and firms which started operations in Eastern Europe usually first established themselves in Vienna. The balance of trade with Austria was slightly in Pakistan's favour. The Joint Commission on Trade and Economic Cooperation between Pakistan and Austria, which had lingered on, was finalised and held its first meeting in Islamabad in 1996. We were in regular contact with the Federal Economic Chamber in Vienna and liaised with the two giant Austrian companies with important business interests in Pakistan: VA Technology and OMV. I visited VA Technology's production plant in Linz and was impressed by their steel manufacturing technology and precision units.

Austria favoured an early resolution of the Kashmir issue, but adhered to the neutral collective policy decisions of the European Union. Because of our forceful demarches, Austria spoke out against human rights violations in Kashmir in the EU sessions. I briefed the president, foreign minister, members of the Federal Economic Chamber, speaker and members of parliament, leaders of political parties, editors of major newspapers, governors of provinces and academic and research institutions about the Indian oppression in Kashmir. A demonstration on Kashmir was held outside the Indian embassy in Vienna's city centre in 1995 by the Pakistani community to protest against the desecration of the mosque in Charar Sharif.

The year 1996 was celebrated throughout Austria to mark 1,000 years of its history. Our mission was one of the few embassies in Vienna to arrange cultural events to honour Austria's millennium celebrations. We organised *kathak* performances based on the poetry of Ameer Khusrau by the famous artist, Nahid Siddiqui and her group. Nahid considered herself – and was regarded by many– as the finest kathak dancer in the world. She danced in Salzburg, Innsbruck and Lustenau and her audiences were held spellbound. For the general public in Vienna, she performed before a packed audience in the Kongressaal. The performance for the Austrian government and diplomatic corps was held in the stunning marble hall of the Museum of Ethnology (Museum für Völkerkunde) in Vienna, so reminiscent of Mughal courtyards with their pools of water in the centre. Funds for these events had been promised by Kishwar Naheed from the Pakistan National Council of the Arts and at the last minute she backed out, leaving our mission in the lurch. It was only due to the ingenuity of Zaheer Parvez Khan, second secretary in our mission, that we were able to go ahead with these celebratory events.

There was a small Pakistani community in Austria, assessments varied from 3,000 to 6,000 persons. Islam is the second most widely practised religion in Austria and Muslims were given the status of a recognised religious community after the Austro-Hungarian occupation of Bosnia-Herzegovina. The Pakistanis were a devout community and worshipped at the Vienna Islamic Centre which had been functioning since 1979. But there were two

Pakistani mosques, the foremost being the Madni mosque. Most of the other mosques in Vienna belonged to the Turks.

Many of the Pakistanis had their own businesses or were 'place' workers, selling newspapers in the streets and squares of various cities. Most of them were located in Salzburg and Tirol provinces because of which an honorary consul, Anwar Azeem, had been appointed in Innsbruck. Anwar Azeem owned the Wald Hotel in the small Alpine town of Seefeld in Tirol. Seefeld, with a population of less than 3,000 persons, is a millionaire's paradise known for its cross-country skiing and casino. Azeem accompanied me in the calls I made on governors and other officials in Salzburg, Innsbruck and Tirol and also to meet the billionaire, Gernot Langes-Swarovski, one of the heirs to the Swarovski empire. The Swarovski museum in Wattens, Crystal World, was breath taking. It was studded, room after room, path after path, with a limitless sea of sparkling multi-coloured crystal.

Many distinguished Pakistani scientists worked for the IAEA and some professionals for other international organisations. They were urbane and dignified and stood together: Jamshed Hashmi, Arshad Muhammad Khan, Javed Aslam, Shameem Chaudhry, Mazhar Saieed, and Sajjad Ajmal. M.A. Majid, the brother of Nobel laureate Abdus Salam, who had retired from UNIDO, also lived in Vienna. I was deeply moved by the support extended by the members of the Pakistani community to our mission's initiatives. For the first time, an open invitation was extended to the community to gather on Independence Day on 14 August. There was a huge turnout in 1995 and 1996. The wives of the Pakistani professionals working in Vienna cooked and transported masses of food to these events. They were wonderful women, friendly, happy and confident: Tasneem (Ruhi) Hashmi, Jayyada Saieed, Kausar Jameel, Nayyara Chaudhry, Naheed Ajmal, Tasneem Arshad, Zahida Majid, and the lovely Nasreen Tanvir from OPEC. And they willingly gave their suggestions, time and energy to the exhibitions we organised of Pakistani fabrics and artefacts in which the pure silk scarves hand painted by Talat Qureshi and the crafts brought by Farzana Rahman from Karachi were put on sale.[9] The proceeds of the sales went to the UN Women's Guild Bazaar.

To celebrate Pakistan's golden jubilee in 1997, I wrote a long article about Pakistan's history, culture, geography, natural wealth, irrigation systems, economic development, foreign relations, tourism facilities, and arts and crafts. It was published and circulated by the Diplomatic Press Agency in Vienna on the occasion of our national day on 23 March 1997. We shared the article with other Pakistani missions in Europe which photocopied and distributed it without bothering to acknowledge the source. If the size of the gathering is any reckoning, our golden jubilee national day reception on 23

March 1997 was the finest hour for our mission. The reception was held in the hall of that jewel of a building, the golden Festaal of Wiener Borse (Vienna Stock Exchange), which has been described as an 'exceptional masterpiece'.

Compared to the emoluments drawn by the members of other embassies, our staff in Vienna were paid peanuts and found it difficult to make ends meet. Many embassies were very well endowed because Vienna is an extremely expensive city. The members of our mission drove to Bratislava in Slovakia to buy cheaper provisions and milk for their children. Bratislava, the capital of Slovakia, to which I was accredited, was just emerging from the effects of Soviet occupation. Slovakia had separated from Czechoslovakia only a few years earlier. Bratislava was a rundown gloomy city, a seemingly sad place, from where one could purchase some quality crystal. It was also very unsafe and our vehicles could not be left unattended for a single moment. Gradually, however, it emerged from the shadows and sleek shops and restaurants started lining its streets and squares.

On the other hand, Ljubljana, the capital of Slovenia to which I was also accredited, was a much more affluent city. Slovenia is one of the breakaway republics of the former Yugoslavia. As part of the Austro-Hungarian empire, the Habsburgs constructed many buildings in the Viennese style and in some places it looked like a mini Vienna. It has some fascinating sites – Postojna Cave, formed over millions of years by the Pivka River – trickling water, chirping sounds – complete with a train and a large space in the cave which can accommodate 10,000 people for concerts and solo performances. And the massive Bled castle, the oldest castle in Slovenia, rising sheer on a high cliff on the shores of the pristine blue waters of Lake Bled.

Because Vienna is both a bilateral and multilateral centre, there was a very large diplomatic community. Austria's association with its historic Catholic past can be gauged from the fact that the dean of the diplomatic corps in Vienna is always the representative of the Pope, the Apostolic Nuncio, and not the senior-most diplomat. When I arrived in Vienna, there were about four women ambassadors and when I left, that number had risen to twenty, the largest gathering of women ambassadors in any country. Their presence changed the diplomatic landscape. We complemented each other's efforts, like the way in which, led by Fugen Ok of Turkey, we worked to save UNIDO. And some of us travelled together on that memorable trip that Filiz Dinçmen of Turkey, Katja Boh of Slovenia, Eva-Christina Mäkeläinen of Finland, Thelma Doran of Ireland and I took to Prague. In Prague we walked to the castle, down Neruda Street, across Charles Bridge – which was very dirty – to the old town square and then into the big square, surrounded by countless crystal shops. In Karlovy Vary (Karlsbad) we visited the outlet of Moser, glass makers since 1857, who are described as the 'kings of crystal' and their products as the 'crystal of kings'. Like many other countries, Pakistan orders its gold-embossed glassware from Moser.

Most of the women ambassadors were accomplished diplomats. Some represented the countries of eastern and central Europe where, after the unravelling of the Soviet Union, there was not much professional diplomatic talent to draw upon. Therefore, they came from other professions and included Daniela Rozgonova from Slovakia, Katja Boh from Slovenia and Tatjana Mijatovic from Bosnia. Tatjana's words often ring in my ears: 'You are the only person in Vienna who understands what has happened to my country,' she said, referring to the break-up of Yugoslavia. I understood, I told her, because of what happened when India was divided in 1947. Ana Marija Besker of Croatia had a distinguished career in the foreign service of former Yugoslavia. Fugen Ok and Filiz Dinçmen belonged to the first generation of women ambassadors in Turkey.[10] By contrast, although the foreign service was not formally opened to women until 1973, Pakistan had started appointing eminent women as ambassadors in the early 1950s. Eva-Christina from Finland – so elegant and graceful – and Thelma Doran from Ireland were career diplomats. Swanee Hunt from the United States and Ursula Seiler-Albring from Germany were political appointees, but their diplomatic missions were professionally well manned. The US mission was fortunate that it had as deputy chief, a diplomat of the calibre and standing of Joan Corbett.

The government of Austria were generous hosts and the beauty of their country enhanced the elegance of their hospitality. Every year they organised a ski trip for foreign diplomats in the Austrian mountains. In 1996, a ski excursion was arranged for diplomats in Maria Alm in Salzburg state. A dinner was hosted by Vice Chancellor Wolfgang Schussel and a grand reception was held in the freezing marble hall of Mirabell Palace in Salzburg city. The following year, the excursion went to Schruns. A mountain resort famous for hiking and climbing, it was the favourite ski resort of Ernest Hemingway. The tour of the town was rounded off with a reception in one of the castles around Schruns. East of Salzburg lies the lake district, Salzkammergut, literally meaning the 'estate of the salt chamber'. It is a series of interconnected lakes, including Wolfgangsee, on the shores of which the picturesque St Wolfgang town is located. There were spectacular sights, stillness and peace, as I saw the mist rise over the blue green waters of Wolfgangsee and settle again in the evening in a veil of indigo.

In the summer of 1995, the Austrian foreign ministry organised a diplomatic seminar at Hellbrunn Palace near Salzburg. Hellbrunn, built by Markus Sittikus, who was both prince and archbishop, is truly a pleasure palace and is famous for its trick fountains. Many palaces and mansions were built in Austria by archbishops for their mistresses. The keynote speaker at the seminar was the Iraqi diplomat Ismat Kittani, but I was surprised that two of my countrymen, Moeenuddin Qureshi and Mahbub ul Haq were also included in the list of speakers.[11] Apparently, a lot of importance was attached to this seminar because all the top brass of the foreign ministry were present, and so was Kurt Waldheim.

Culturally, Vienna was delightful and I was grateful for the experience. Although one could always watch symphonies and ballets on the big screen outside the Rathaus, listening to the Vienna Philharmonic Orchestra in the Musikverein was like a dream which had come true. A special box in the Musikverein was reserved for foreign diplomats. The seats in the main Golden Hall, surrounded by statues inside this neoclassical building, are upholstered in plush red velvet and the ceiling and walls are worked in ornate gold. It is the venue of the annual New Year concert for which Vienna is famous. In the Musikverein, I was able to hear Zubin Mehta conducting the Vienna Philharmonic Orchestra.

Over 400 balls are staged in Vienna each winter. In that festival of culture, the women ambassadors went to many Viennese balls. Katja Boh, Daniela Rozgonova and I went to the Opera Ball which is an official event, running up and down various levels of the grand Opera House, calling on the president in the imperial gallery and ministers in their boxes. The same year we attended the equally impressive Lawyers' Association Ball at the Hofburg, the following year the Teckniker Cercle Ball in a dazzling setting in the Musikverein, and the Juristen Ball at the Hofburg where I was accompanied by my son Asad, and Thelma Doran. The captivating atmosphere of these balls was the stuff of fairytales, with the long lines of debutantes in their flowing white gowns, their young partners in formal dress, the glittering crystal chandeliers, the gleaming dance floor, the music of the Austrian maestros. The last dance of the debutantes in the Opera Ball is always Johann Strauss' waltz, *Blue Danube*.

Vienna is an exquisite city steeped in history. It is difficult – almost futile – to describe its beauty in words. The fortress walls around the city were razed and converted by Emperor Franz Joseph (1830–1916) into a boulevard called the Ringstrasse which circles the inner city (Innere Stadt). Along this route were constructed, at the beginning of the twentieth century, the magnificent public buildings, private mansions and parks which give the city its distinctive character. The embellishments and décor, especially in the palaces and public rooms, are overpowering. The board room of the OPEC building is so dazzling that, as the saying goes in Urdu, my gaze could not settle.

In the centre of the inner city stands St Stephen's Cathedral, which was dedicated to the saint as early as 1147. St Stephen is considered as the first martyr of Christianity. He was accused of blasphemy and stoned to death by the Jewish authorities in Jerusalem in CE 36. Within the cathedral many celebrities are buried, including Emperor Frederick III (1415–93), the first emperor of the Habsburgs and Prince Eugene of Savoy (1663–1736) whom the Austrians revere as a hero because of his military victories, especially the defeat of the Ottomans in the Great Turkish War and at the battle of Zenta in the latter half of the seventeenth century. The cathedral's crypt and catacombs contain the remains, skulls and bones of many religious figures. It has been used for the funerals of Kurt Waldheim and Thomas Klestil. Many great cities have patron saints. Lahore has Data Ganj Bakhsh, Islamabad has Bari Imam, London has St Paul, Moscow has St Peter, Delhi has Nizamuddin Auliya, and Karachi has now acquired Abdullah Shah Ghazi. I have always respected the mystique associated with their names. St Stephen can be considered as the patron saint of Vienna although it was not officially so declared. One could sit in peace inside the cathedral as the rays of the sun slanted through its stained glass windows. And it was here that I mourned in silence for Aftab Kohati. Respecting the religious traditions of my hosts, I attended Christmas and Easter mass at the Augustine Church. And I paused at the peace-giving grotto in the Vienna Woods (Weinerwald), a copy of the Marian Cave at Lourdes, in reverence for the Virgin Mary who is honoured above all women in Islam and is the only woman mentioned in the Quran by name.

While the buildings in the inner city and museum quarter are a combination of many architectural styles, from classical to art nouveau, a striking departure is Hundertwasser Haus designed by Friedensreich Hundertwasser.[12] Painter and architect, he opposed the straight line and regular forms, and has left behind this extraordinary block of apartments and offices, irregular, colourful, unconventional, an expressionist landmark. He was a passionate believer in many causes, to draw attention to which he would appear in the nude in public. Sometimes I found a few moments to visit the Belvedere palace to admire the golden period paintings of Gustav Klimt, especially 'The Kiss' which must surely be the most celebrated modern erotic painting in the world. If I was not working on Sunday, Ruhi Jamshed and I stole time to admire the tulips in bloom in Schonbrunn, the summer palace of the Habsburgs. I took my guests to the historic Café Central which had been patronised by Adolf Hitler, Vladimir Lenin, Leon Trotsky, Josip Tito and Sigmund Freud. Our mission entertained diplomats also in Vienna's fine restaurants, such as the Griechenbeisl, one of the oldest inns, founded in 1447.

There was a stream of important visitors to Vienna. Many of them stayed in the embassy residence. The most important visitor was Abdul Waheed Kakar, chief of the army staff, who came with his wife, Yasmin, and a military entourage early during my posting. With his usual skill, Zaheer Parvez Khan arranged a faultless programme. We drove the chief to Durnstein on the Danube River in the wine growing Wachau region. In Durnstein Castle, Richard the Lion Heart was held captive during the Crusades and the restaurant, Richard Lowenherz, is named after him. Kakar talked to me at great length about political conditions in Pakistan. When he returned to Rawalpindi, he wrote to thank me for what he graciously described as my 'deep insight regarding international affairs'.[13]

Although Vienna dominated the urban landscape of Austria, the other towns were no less lovely. Salzburg – with its annual music festival – has been admired universally. Getreidegasse, on which Mozart's house is located in Salzburg, is described as the most beautiful street in the world. But I found Innsbruck equally charming, and to a lesser extent Melk and Graz. In the pink and golden opera house in Graz, in our rare moments together, Fatehyab and I watched Swan Lake, before he left for home after an all-too-short visit.

In the end, I was equally drawn to Budapest. One can travel by hydrofoil from Vienna to the pier in Budapest, along the picturesque Danube valley. Unlike Vienna, it has the advantage of being built on the river on whose banks its neo-Gothic parliament building is located. At night, the lighted contours of the parliament building shimmer in the waters of the Danube. The walls of that gem, the Matthias Church in the Castle district in Buda, are embellished with work which reminded me of the gold leaf on the chalices of Mughal emperors and *kundan* jewellery which is so famous in the subcontinent. And Andrassy Avenue, like the Ringstrasse in Vienna, linking squares and monuments and lined with spectacular palaces and mansions. The Ottomans ruled over Hungary for almost one and a half centuries. One of the first monuments we visited in Budapest was the small octagonal tomb of Gul Baba (d. 1541), a Bektashi dervish who was a poet and companion of Suleiman the Magnificent. When he died, during the Turkish occupation, Suleiman declared him as the patron saint of the city and legend has it that he helped to carry his coffin. His tomb is a national monument and is the property of the Turkish republic.

On 23 June 1997, I left Vienna. A truly elegant reception was held for me by Albert Rohann, general secretary in the foreign ministry. Many ambassadors, including the women ambassadors, and Kurt Waldheim attended the event. The same evening, I held a farewell reception at the residence and there were speeches of praise and regret at my departure. Kurt Waldheim took the trouble to attend this reception also – the second for him on the same day. The Diplomatic Press Service wrote with some concern:

Unfortunately it turned out that this invitation will bring a severe loss for the entire foreign diplomatic corps in Vienna...In the farewell speeches we found out how popular this ambassador was among all her colleagues ... and in experts issues her highly resolute and competent way was appreciated. Therefore, it is completely incomprehensible for us all why such a recognised representative of her country has been recalled ... In case there should be political reasons behind it, this would be a sad reflection for the leadership there. The only excuse, however, for this recall would be if Dr Hasan would take over the foreign ministry. Thus, the success for Pakistan would be certain.

I made a last call on Vice Chancellor Wolfgang Schussel before I left for the airport. To see me off, most of the women ambassadors arrived at the airport lounge. It was a splendid farewell by them and the Austrian protocol.

There were suggestions from the developing countries, especially from the African and Arab blocs, that I should become a candidate for the post of director general of UNIDO to which elections were to be held in December 1997. But I was aware that Nawaz Sharif's government would not sponsor a candidate who had been appointed as ambassador by Benazir Bhutto. Her government was dismissed by Farooq Leghari in November 1996 and the next general election brought Nawaz Sharif to power in February 1997. Although the period of my deputation was over, strangely enough a question was raised in the Senate on 20 May 1997 about my presence in Vienna. I was surprised that Akram Zaki,[14] whom I knew so well, had taken it upon himself to table that question. During the debate, one senator pointed out that my appointment could not be considered as political because I was a serving civil servant. But Abida Hussain, who was the answering minister was apparently not sure that NIPA Karachi, from where I was on deputation, was a government institution.

When I returned to Islamabad, I called on the president, Farooq Leghari. The warm welcome he accorded me was so different from his aloof demeanour before I left for Vienna. He said: 'Everybody recognises how successful you were. What a pity that your appointment was considered as political.' Fatehyab hosted a splendid homecoming party for me on the lawns of our residence which was swarming with guests. He lit up the house and invited our friends, relatives and all my colleagues. I was honoured by the presence of two wonderful women who had always encouraged me in my career, Shaista Ikramullah and Khanum Qamar Ispahani, wives of two of my father's close friends. Khanum had often raised me to the seventh heaven of delight by saying, 'she is the pride of Pakistan'.

Chapter 10

Last Posting

My appointment as cabinet secretary to the Pakistan government was as much a surprise for me as for many other people. I had never met Parvez Musharraf, although my friend Saad Ashraf reminds me that he was present at the dinner Saad hosted for me before I left for Vienna. I have no recollection of that meeting. When Musharraf seized power on 12 October 1999 after the high drama in the skies, sad as it was for democracy, many democrats rejoiced. They had thought that after the long struggle against Ziaul Haq and his ignominious exit from this world, there would be no dictators in their lives again. But there was so much disenchantment with Nawaz Sharif's government that a general welcome was given to the man on horseback. We waited for many hours for him to appear on the television on 13 October 1999, looking very cross, to tell us how he was compelled by circumstances to step in.[1] He continued the emergency but did not abrogate the Constitution or impose martial law, so there were no martial law courts or regulations. He appeared somewhat different from previous dictators – urbane, liberal, broad-minded.

There was no public outcry at Nawaz Sharif's exit nor did the political parties, including his own party, stage demonstrations against the military takeover. He had frittered away the advantages he had gained by his landslide victory against Benazir Bhutto in 1997. He was accused of corruption, pushing through constitutional amendments arbitrarily and wanting to be designated as *Ameerul Momineen*. In fact, there was a movement afoot to dislodge him even before Musharraf stepped in. The nineteen-party Grand Democratic Alliance (GDA) was set up specifically to oust him. Its chief, Nasrullah Khan, had announced only a day earlier that the alliance would stage a 'long march' in Rawalpindi and the GDA parties would hold rallies to protest against the failure of foreign policy, dismal economic situation, increasing unemployment, deteriorating law and order and sectarian violence.[2] They also demanded fresh polls and the formation of an independent election commission.

With one voice, all political parties blamed Nawaz Sharif for being his own nemesis, trying to politicise and divide the army and destroying every state institution. Most religious parties welcomed Musharraf's coup: Jamaat-i-Islami, Jamiat Ulema-i-Islam, Tehreek-i-Jafaria, Pakistan Awami Tehreek.

All parties called for a tough process of accountability before the next polls were held and many suggestions were thrown at Musharraf about the time frame for holding elections – some as long as two years – and the composition of his cabinet. From Kabul, Mullah Omar expressed his desire to establish good ties with Musharraf's government.[3]

Benazir Bhutto, living in exile, did not welcome the coup but described Nawaz Sharif as a hated despot who was responsible for creating the situation leading to his ousting. She had known Musharraf as director general of military operations during her premiership and thought he was not ambitious enough to 'hang on to power'. She wanted a limited time frame but was willing to give Musharraf enough time to put the 'house in order' and conduct across-the-board accountability.[4]

On 17 October 1999, Musharraf made another speech in which he announced a seven-point programme, including the much demanded 'across-the-board accountability'. Accountability would be directed especially towards tax evaders, loan defaulters and those guilty of plundering and looting national wealth. Obviously, even if the process was transparent, as he had promised, it would require far more than the three months given to an interim government in the Constitution. And the Constitution had already been temporarily held 'in abeyance'. In this speech, while he pledged 'unflinching moral, political and diplomatic support' to the people of Kashmir, he offered dialogue and an olive branch to India.[5] The savvy politicians who heard him loud and clear were familiar with army coups and must have realised that he would need a long time to 'fix' everything. They settled down to expressing pious hopes for early elections and a return to democracy. The GDA, for instance, welcomed Musharraf's seven-point priorities and the dismissal of the 'dictatorial' Nawaz Sharif government. It looked forward to transparent and even-handed accountability and a return to 'true and genuine' democracy but refrained from pressing for any time frame.[6]

The Supreme Court of Pakistan validated the military takeover, giving the regime three years to hold elections and restraining it from making structural changes in the Constitution. Musharraf had wanted five years. Had Musharraf honoured the three-year time frame, held transparent elections and transferred power to whichever party won in the elections, he would have been acclaimed in the history of Pakistan. As it was, he clung to power for several years and had to eventually flee the country in 2008 under threat of impeachment.

The international community was less impressed with the army's action– the days of dictators were over. France, Japan, Canada and the UN secretary general criticised the coup. The United States slapped sanctions on Pakistan under the Foreign Operations Appropriations Act[7] and its ambassador in

Islamabad expressed disappointment that no time frame was given to hold elections. Pakistan was suspended from all councils of the Commonwealth pending the restoration of democracy, and the 'unconstitutional overthrow' of Nawaz Sharif's government was condemned.[8] The European Union also denounced the coup and urged an early return to civilian rule.

In this situation of international isolation and domestic uncertainty, Musharraf appointed his lean cabinet of ten members, with 'an impeccable reputation and a successful track record'. Before being appointed, they were interviewed by a committee of top army officers and by himself.[9] Federal secretaries were chosen with the same circumspection and some of those selected were intensely interviewed by top generals. Omer Asghar Khan was given the portfolio for environment in the cabinet and he discussed the possibility of my being appointed as secretary in his ministry. I knew it would be very difficult, even in that relatively unimportant ministry, to overcome the reservations of the mainstream bureaucracy. However, one day, Tariq Aziz, who was Musharraf's principal secretary as well as his trusted confidante, asked me to show him my résumé in Islamabad. He read the first page and put down the document and said, 'can we make you the cabinet secretary?' I was utterly amazed at his suggestion.

My name may have been under consideration even before this meeting with Tariq Aziz. The notification appointing me as cabinet secretary was faxed to me on 16 February 2000 and later in the evening, Tariq Aziz called to tell me about an awkward development. He was very apologetic and Tariq Saeed Haroon, the establishment secretary, also called to apologise. News had spread that a notification had been issued and suspended and the media gleefully badgered me about what had happened. I stayed out of the house the following day and when I returned in the evening, Fatehyab said the phone had not stopped ringing.

From what I gathered later, Musharraf had announced at a dinner one evening that he was appointing me as cabinet secretary. Two of his guests, in particular, let him have it, Attiya Inayatullah and Imtiaz Ahmad Sahibzada. Attiya recounted my misdeeds as Fatehyab's wife and how I had been punished by Ziaul Haq. Imtiaz Sahibzada could not countenance that the prized posting should be given not only to a woman who was not a member of an elite occupational group but, even worse, was an ex-cadre officer. That would surely destroy the dignity and prestige of the 'service'. How could Musharraf have blundered so?

Musharraf was baffled and pulled up the establishment secretary for sending him the summary for my appointment. To give him credit, Tariq Saeed Haroon stood up for the decision. He said I was the builder of NIPA

Karachi and Musharraf would see the change after my appointment. Above all, he pointed out that I was the senior-most government servant in the entire country at that time, having been promoted to the highest grade as early as 1993. Apparently, Tariq Aziz also said that the decision should be honoured. So I flew to Islamabad to take up the assignment on 21 February 2000 from my predecessor, Zaheer Sajjad, whose foresight I must compliment because he told me there would be no democracy in our country for many years to come.

When I met Imtiaz Sahibzada at my first session of the National Security Council on 24 February 2000, he had the grace to say that although he had opposed my appointment, he would now support me – 'Cambridge and all' – and as an elder brother would happily advise me, should I consult him on any matter. He had served as Benazir Bhutto's cabinet secretary during her first term as prime minister. Attiya Inayatullah's recognition, if any, was expressed only after I had retired. She wrote to me graciously that during our association in the cabinet, she had made 'a discovery of Masuma Hasan, one which made me proud'.[10]

The brief period I spent as cabinet secretary was the most rewarding part of my career. As the highest position in the public service, it brought its own importance, but I was fortunate that my colleagues cooperated with me throughout. Because the cabinet division is an empire, with a myriad responsibilities apart from cabinet affairs, it was possible to make a contribution in many ways. It was also home to many regulatory authorities. Whenever there was a problem in placing departments and agencies, they were parked in the cabinet division. The establishment secretary kept posting officers who had fallen from grace, whom no ministry accepted or those who needed to keep a low profile, but I found them all excellent colleagues.

Conventionally, cabinet secretaries were awesome and aloof and stepped out of their offices only on important occasions. Throughout my career, I had kept my door open and I continued to do so now. My office was beautiful but badly cluttered. I removed all the clutter and created comfortable seating spaces. Also, I replaced the photograph of Quaid-i-Azam which graced most offices and did no justice to his handsome looks, with a striking photograph I had borrowed from Khanum Qamar Ispahani and had enlarged and filled with colour by my friend, the famous photographer, Shaukat Mahmood. From my desk I could look out on a lovely vista all the way down Jinnah Avenue, now destroyed by the ugly stations of the metro bus.

I lived in Suite 205 A in Parliament Lodges, a sprawling and unattractive structure of no architectural significance which had cost billions of rupees to construct, unaccounted billions, they say. A modern, functional, cost-effective set of buildings would have been kinder to our poor country. Since there was no parliament and therefore no parliamentarians, the suites were occupied by all manner of military and civilian officials. The members of parliament had used public funds to furnish the suites with expensive gilded furniture, some of it hand painted, most of which I removed. In spite of the unforgivable extravagance in space and furnishing which should have been avoided, the ambience in the Lodges had its own charm. I arrived from work very late in the evening to the delight of scores of children playing in the gardens and the driveway. From my window I could see the cabinet block, the lighted façade of the unused parliament building, and the fountains playing in the moonlight.

Most of my work was confidential, but I was not lonely. Fatehyab came to see me often and the time we spent together compensated for the separation inflicted upon us in the past. There were three families which always welcomed me. My cousin Sabiah and her husband, Muzaffar Askari had always given Fatehyab and me a place in their home. The hospitality of my maternal aunt, Maimoona Kulsoom and her husband, Mahmud Salim Jillani was well known. She had been raised in Panipat by my mother and her table reminded me of my mother's establishment. Salim Jillani became federal secretary, but before joining the service, he had taught sociology at the University of Karachi. He was one of the most civilised persons I have met and I was guided in many of my decisions by his advice and wisdom. Then there is my debt to Aftab Ahmad, writer and poet, who had retired as additional secretary to the government and to his wife, Shamima. From Aftab Ahmad's chaste Urdu, excellent prose and knowledge of the masters of Urdu poetry, I learnt a lot. I shall always hold dear the letters and poems of support he wrote to me when I was posted in Vienna.

Nobody had interviewed me for the job, so my credentials must have been acceptable. I met Musharraf for the first time at the meeting of the National Security Council on 24 February 2000 which was held in the prime minister's secretariat, an imposing building on Constitution Avenue with mixed architectural styles and much waste of space. When he entered, baton in hand, I moved forward to greet him and he asked me, 'are you Dr Masuma Hasan?' When I replied that I was, he said, 'I will speak to you later, first let me look at the grandeur of this building.' As the meeting started, he welcomed and formally introduced me in words of appreciation and praise. Whoever had briefed him, had got the details of my life and career right. After a few days, I was able to call on him in his office.

During that meeting, I told him about my family background and Fatehyab's political struggle and commitments which had always come in the way of my career. I said that I understood the importance of my appointment. When I informed him that my family had lived in Panipat for 700 years before migrating to Pakistan in 1947, he said, 'from Panipat, how can that be, my father was from Panipat?' That came as a complete surprise to me because he was said to belong to Delhi and Meerut. Later, I heard that his father had probably served in Panipat before Partition. I described Fatehyab as a freedom fighter and he seemed to like that description. Also, I requested that if he heard anything negative about me, he should speak to me directly. He put me at ease immediately, assuring me that nothing would go wrong.

Musharraf had chosen the title of chief executive, not that of president; he became president much later, on 20 June 2001. By then I had retired from public service. 'Chief executive' was a more neutral and corporate description of what he considered as his responsibilities. His cabinet was small and consisted of some 'technocrats', not the large assembly which passes for a cabinet today, because he was under no pressure to oblige a political constituency. It was well balanced between the provinces, although the inclusion of some immature members was surprising, but he was patient with them. Cabinet meetings lasted for several hours. There were lengthy PowerPoint presentations and he was quick to grasp the figure work; his concentration never wavered. Later, long presentations were made by various ministries and divisions, as he tried to understand the nitty-gritty of governance, all of which I was required to attend. For me, therefore, the files had to be read late in the evening; there was no time to call it a day.

Some colleagues stand out in my memory of those days. Lieutenant General Ghulam Ahmad, popularly known as GA, was Musharraf's chief of staff. His previous posting had been in the ISI. He was a fine officer and a fine man. Sometimes, I would climb the flight of stairs to his office and talk to him. He was convinced that the army should relinquish power as soon as possible; however, other considerations prevailed and Musharraf became the president. GA was a family man and often spoke affectionately about his wife and children. Unfortunately, he was killed in a road accident in 2002 – some people say it was not an accident – and the government was deprived of a voice of wisdom and restraint.

Omer Asghar Khan and I worked together to honour the people's heroes. Although the civil awards were routed through me, the names had to be proposed by a department, ministry or provincial government. I requested Omer to propose the names of Haidar Bakhsh Jatoi, the hari leader, and Mirza Ibrahim who had fought for the rights of industrial labour. But only Jatoi's name went through. Also honoured at my suggestion were the poets Rasa Chughtai, Jaun Ailya and Kishwar Naheed. Most of Musharraf's federal secretaries were competent men – I was the only woman in the group – but Yunus Khan was more prominent than the others. He held the difficult post of finance secretary as the government faced a financial crisis and went through an economic transition. He was handsome and during the long PowerPoint presentations, it was a pleasure to sit across the table from him.

In terms of the greatest public good, the designing and approval of the Urdu code plate for computer applications was the most significant achievement of my time as cabinet secretary. The National Language Authority (NLA) functioned under the cabinet division and the scholars in its Urdu informatics department, which was set up in 1998, had designed the keyboard and code plate. A host of software specialists, vendors and companies had their own versions of the code plate and their vested interest in the outcome. To create a consensus appeared virtually impossible. I stole time from my daily schedule to hold long meetings to bridge the gap between their opposing interests and persuade them to arrive at a consensus code plate. The cabinet approved the proposal on 23 August 2000, but few people at that time understood its significance and far-reaching importance. Because of the code plate, millions of people across the world became computer literate in Urdu. It became possible to type, develop software, post material on the internet and create data bases for research and development in Urdu. This keyboard was adopted by the national database in Pakistan and by Microsoft in Windows XP English and Urdu versions. Later, it was universally adopted.

After approval was accorded, there was an attempt to shift Urdu informatics to the ministry of science and technology, but I fought to let it remain in the cabinet division where the code plate had been envisioned and constructed. It was decided that the development of standards for the use of Urdu for computer applications shall continue to be the responsibility of the cabinet division.[11] Subsequently, I moved to put Urdu on Unicode, which is the international code for language processing, and when I saw it on their banner, it was the proudest moment of my life. The NLA became a full corporate member of the Unicode Consortium and the code plate has gone through many revisions.

Musharraf's government gave a big boost to women's rights. Let us not forget that the Taliban were ruling in Afghanistan at that time and women had all but vanished from public space in that unfortunate country. The Taliban had partners in ideology in our own country whose obsession with women focused on motherhood, misogyny and sexism. Musharraf had devised, on the plan developed by Lieutenant General Tanvir Naqvi, his own system of a multi-tiered local government – union, tehsil and district – and the question of women's representation came up. In its advocacy campaigns, the women's movement had always demanded a reservation of 33 per cent of seats at the political level in all elected bodies, but the demand was considered far-fetched and was not taken seriously by political parties and previous governments. Musharraf, however, was willing to give 50 per cent of seats to women at the local level until it was explained to him that since women won on general seats also, their number could exceed 50 per cent. The mullahs were absolutely horrified, so we settled for a reservation of 33 per cent of seats for women in the union councils by direct election and the same percentage in other tiers by indirect election. It was a unique achievement in women's rights which was reversed in Sindh and Punjab after Musharraf's exit. It led to the empowerment of 36,000 women councillors on the basis of direct elections by men and women voters when the local government elections took place in 2002 and created a template for further advancement. Musharraf also reserved 17 per cent of seats for women in both houses of parliament – a big jump – and almost 18 per cent in the provincial assemblies.

In the autumn of 2000, I asked Musharraf for a few days' leave to travel to Kashgar in Chinese Xinjiang by road. In my childhood, I had heard about the beautiful city of Kashgar from my aunt, Butul Begum, and had dreamt of making that journey along the Karakoram Highway into China ever since the road was opened. I wanted to take Hasan and Asad with me, but they had both gone abroad for higher studies. It was a private trip and I had heard that public transport was available between Sust, our border town, and Kashgar. Naively, I thought I would hire transport for myself, as if I was travelling from Islamabad to Lahore. It was the chance of a lifetime and realising that I should not travel alone, I invited Waqar Hussain, my NIPA Karachi colleague, and Shahid Butt from the cabinet division to accompany me.

We flew to Gilgit on 24 September 2000 instead of driving, to save time. It turned out that Subhan Memon, a former student of mine, was posted as chief secretary at Gilgit. From him I learnt that nobody travels in a single vehicle on the lonely and risky road to Kashgar; people travel in a convoy of at least two vehicles. He arranged an interpreter and transport for me and a pickup proceeding on the same journey joined us. Subhan issued the *parvana-i-rahdari* –that was all that was needed to go to China –and travelled with us as far as Gulmit. On the journey we were also joined by Zafar Iqbal, the managing director of the northern areas transportation company. Like so many people in the northern areas – in fact, in the whole country – he had studied and lived in Karachi and had a soft corner for the NSF.

It was the most beautiful journey of my life. The mountains were so magnificent, the glaciers took away my breath, the highway was majestic. I had merely read about and seen photographs of the Karakoram Range, largely because of Hasan's obsession with mountain peaks. We had good weather, but for miles and miles there was not a soul to be seen; the stillness and silence were uncanny. On leaving Sust, we were held up by a landslide at Dehi. At Khunjerab Pass, I remembered to move very slowly and did not feel breathless.

Khunjerab stands at 4,700 metres as the highest paved mountain pass in the world. The driver of our vehicle was a veteran of this journey and seemed to know the soldiers manning the check posts on both sides of the border.

When we entered China, the landscape changed. Except for one very high mountain, probably Muztagh Ata, we drove past Karakul Lake, through miles of lush green rolling country and for the first time I saw yaks and double humped camels. We stopped for official formalities in Tashkurgan, which was a major post in days gone by on the Silk Road. Tashkurgan customs sent a woman officer to accompany us to Kashgar which we reached late at night. In Kashgar, we checked into the 'Russian consulate', which formerly housed the Russian diplomatic mission and was now used as a hotel. The Uyghurs are a very handsome people. Next morning, at breakfast, I was amazed at the beauty of the women who were serving us. Dainty, and with lovely features, they were really the bewitching fairies of *Koh-i-Qaf* about whom I had heard in my childhood. Their devotion to their religion was touching and some of them were saving money to perform Hajj. Word went round that important visitors had come from Pakistan and we were much feted and entertained. We were also received by representatives of the foreign office and tourism department and attended a song and dance show at Chinibagh Hotel. I found peace in walking along the tree-lined avenue outside the hotel on the other side of the world. The sky was clear, the stars shone radiantly, and I learnt to spot the Pole Star.

Kashgar, with a rich history going back 2,000 years, was ruled by a series of dynasties, including three centuries of Buddhist rule. It was an important city on the Silk Road between China, the Middle East and Europe. Islam came to Kashgar in the tenth century. It became part of the dynasty of Genghis Khan's grandson, Chagatai Khan, and one of the Chagatai khans who ruled Kashgar converted to Islam, thus establishing the religion formally. Marco Polo visited Kashgar in the later thirteenth century and Timur ravaged and sacked it in 1389. In contemporary times, Indian Muslims belonging to my father's generation were nostalgic about the short-lived Islamic Republic of East Turkistan (1933–4).

Kashgar is a modern city, with modern amenities, and I was able to call Fatehyab by telephone. Among its many historic monuments, the Id Kah mosque stands out; built in 1442, it is the largest mosque in China. Some of the old structures of the city, it was said, were on their way to extinction and the new buildings were covered by boring grey tiles. In the famous Oriental Bazaar, ceramics and pottery were spread out in the middle of the road and I bought beautiful blue pottery, some written inside in the Persian script. We took a day trip to Yarkand, a few hours drive from Kashgar, stopping on the way to shop for knives in the stunning roadside knives bazaar in Yengisar. In Yarkand, an oasis city fed by the fabled Yarkand River, we visited the tombs of the khans, the royal graveyard and the Altyn mosque. We returned to Islamabad after spending a delightful evening with Subhan Memon and his family in Gilgit. To him and to Zafar Iqbal I owe this most fascinating interlude in my life – seven days.

Some memories stand out in my mind. Bill Clinton came calling on Musharraf on 25 March 2000. After an extended visit to India, he stopped for six hours in Islamabad to scold Musharraf. In the security measures taken for his embarrassing visit, the whole city and its surroundings were shut down. Nobody went to work or study that day. He flew in an unmarked aircraft and his own Air Force One preceded it as a decoy. He brought his own automobiles and his fleet of cars drove on the right side of the road, as in the United States. I did not meet him; only a few persons had been selected for that honour. But I was glued to the television like everybody else that day. He also lectured to the people of Pakistan on the national television that the answer to flawed democracy was not to end it, but improve upon it. He could not and would not mediate on Kashmir and criticised attacks on civilians across the Line of Control. I was pleased to learn later – if it was true – that President Tarrar arrived a few minutes late to receive him. We all heaved a sigh of relief when he left unscathed. According to Shaukat Aziz, then finance minister, the sole purpose of Clinton's visit was to save Nawaz Sharif's life; he was eventually given a life sentence and not sent to the gallows.[12]

A dramatic turn of events led to the declassification of the Report of the Commission of Inquiry 1971 – War, popularly known as the Hamoodur Rahman Commission report. The Indian weekly, *India Today*, carried excerpts from the supplementary report of the Commission on 13 August 2000 which were reprinted in *Dawn* on 14 August 2000. The publication so close to 14 August, Independence Day, led to speculation that it was timed to divert attention from human rights violations in Indian-occupied Kashmir which had become the focus of attention of many rights organisations, including Amnesty International. It was difficult to pin the blame for the disclosure. A few politicians had borrowed copies of the report and never returned them. Whoever was responsible for this disclosure, the appearance of the report caused distress and embarrassment in Pakistan which, perhaps, was its very purpose.

In spite of the sensation which gripped the country following the appearance of parts of the report, wisely the government did not get pushed into declassifying the report immediately. A committee was formed, comprising interior minister Moinuddin Haider, foreign secretary Inam-ul-Haq, and myself, to study the report and recommend what action should be taken. Reading the entire report was the most soul shaking experience of my life. As I sat alone, going through those pages night after night and well into the early hours of the morning, my tears did not stop flowing. Often I paused to wonder at how much the members of the Commission themselves must have suffered.

The committee recommended that the report should be declassified and Musharraf gave his consent to our recommendation. It was a brave decision, since the report was so critical of his own constituency, the army, but it could hardly have been otherwise. On reading the report, I could understand why Bhutto had not made it public. A bewildered nation was surely entitled to know how and why its country had been catastrophically split into two, but equally, it was necessary not to further shatter the morale of an army which had surrendered so that it could be rebuilt into an effective fighting force. Whether the report should have been kept under wraps for so many years later, is another matter.

The report was declassified in its entirety except for some passages dealing with our relations with foreign countries. To quell impatience and some criticism in the media, the cabinet division issued a press release on 20 December 2000 stating that, because there was a long-standing demand that the Report of the Commission of Inquiry – 1971 War should be made available to the public, the chief executive had constituted a committee comprising the minister of interior and the cabinet and foreign secretaries to study the report and make recommendations about its declassification. The chief executive had accepted their recommendation that the report should be declassified with effect from 30 December 2000.[13]

The timing of releasing the report was a matter of concern. We avoided declassification close to the Eid holidays and during the December days when full-fledged war had been fought in East Pakistan in 1971, leading to the fall of Dacca on 16 December 1971. There was some confusion also about the manner in which the report should be made available. It was suggested that photocopies of the report should be distributed to the media. That, I thought, would be inappropriate because not only is the report very voluminous but the media were not the only party interested in its contents or entitled to have access to it. So copies of the report were placed in the cabinet division, making them available to anyone who was interested in reading it, in the manner in which restricted documents and records are declassified in archives all over the world.

Let me now turn to the report itself. Within a week after he was sworn in as president on 20 December 1971, Bhutto appointed a three-member commission of inquiry into the 1971 war, with Justice Hamoodur Rahman, then chief justice of Pakistan as president and Chief Justice Anwarul Haq of the Lahore High Court and Chief Justice Tufail Ali Abdur Rahman of the High Court of Sind and Baluchistan as members. They were required to inquire 'into the circumstances in which the Commander, Eastern Command, surrendered and the members of the Armed Forces of Pakistan under his command laid down their arms and a cease-fire was ordered along the borders of West Pakistan and India and along the cease-fire line in the State of Jammu and Kashmir.'[14] First, the views of the public were invited. A public announcement was published in the newspapers on 1 January 1972 that all statements made to the Commission would be privileged and would not lead to any civil or criminal proceedings, except when they were false. The proceedings were held in camera. The Commission examined 213 persons, including members of the army, air force and navy, political leaders, serving and retired civil servants, journalists and members of the public.[15] The main report was submitted to Bhutto on 12 July 1972.

Since some of the major players in the catastrophe in East Pakistan were prisoners of war in India, the Commission tried to interview them through the International Committee of the Red Cross but the attempt failed. When the prisoners of war and civil internees were repatriated from India to Pakistan after the Simla Agreement in 1974, the Commission was re-activated[16] and it examined the evidence of seventy-two persons including that of Lieutenant General A.A.K. Niazi, Commander Eastern Command.[17] Based on this evidence, the supplementary report which was partly published by *India Today*, was completed before the end of 1974.

It is difficult to contain the substance of the main and supplementary reports within a few paragraphs. In the main report, the principal culprits are Yahya Khan and the coterie of generals who surrounded him. Yahya Khan, however, is the chief culprit and the most damning words are reserved for him. The report declares that he did not take over the country in order to restore normalcy and democracy but to obtain personal power and those who assisted him had full knowledge of his intentions and were equally guilty. His decision to postpone the meeting of the National Assembly on 1 March 1971 was a move calculated to precipitate a deadlock. His calculation that no single party would emerge victorious in the elections in East Pakistan in 1970 and he and his colleagues would continue to rule, had backfired. Sheikh Mujibur Rahman had contested the elections on the basis of his Six Points programme which really meant a confederation, but Yahya Khan never challenged him on this issue nor had Bhutto made it an election issue. On the contrary, he entered into 'fraudulent' negotiations with the Sheikh.

The report gives a graphic account of the Awami League's civil disobedience movement which was really a 'reign of terror' and criticises the officers in command for neglecting to maintain law and order. The 'punitive' military action taken on 25 March 1971, after Yahya Khan secretly flew back to Karachi from Dacca, both in nature and execution was unwise and lacking in political foresight and would 'inevitably seal the doom of East Pakistan'.[18] The army, which had been at the receiving end of the Awami League's civil disobedience movement, cut off even from food supplies, reacted violently. It should have been apparent to Yahya Khan and his advisers that a military solution could not be forced upon one's own people, and that military action was 'immoral'. But he was insensible to the need for any solution and unaware of the danger of armed intervention by a hostile neighbour, India.[19] Moreover, it was 'sheer madness' to think that driving out Hindus from East Pakistan would solve the political problem. That 'brutal action' resulted in the migration of two million refugees to India. All sections of Indian society had declared that such a chance to break up Pakistan was not likely to occur again[20] and India had the sympathy of several big nations, including the Soviet Union. But naively, Yahya Khan believed that since the Indians were training and arming the Mukti Bahini, they would not themselves invade our territory.[21] Pakistan must be the only country in the world which did not take the invasion of its territory to the Security Council when the Indians attacked East Pakistan on 21 November 1971. 'This was a war', the justices wrote, 'in which everything went wrong' for Pakistan's armed forces. 'They were not only outnumbered but also out-weaponed and out-Generaled.'[22]

The supplementary report, which was written after the returning commanders from East Pakistan were examined, makes more painful reading than the main report. It is harsher in its indictments since it deals with the surrender of the armed forces. It dwells again on the 'fraudulent manner' in which Yahya Khan conducted negotiations, the Awami League's parallel government and the reign of terror it unleashed, leading to military action on 25 March 1971.[23] Every witness deposed that a political solution was needed and there were many opportunities for seeking such a solution and many windows of opportunity which were closed. But the 'declared purpose of General Yahya, right from the start was to do no such thing'.[24] The amnesty offered to those who had crossed into India was 'delayed, ill-conceived in design, dishonest in intention and thoroughly bungled in implementation'.[25]

The report criticises the state of preparedness of the armed forces and some aspects of military strategy. The defence of East Pakistan was built around the concept of 'fortresses' and strong points. There were twenty-five fortresses and nine strong points built around district and sub-divisional headquarters, towns, large villages and cantonments on the assumption that they would be defended 'to the last man and last round' and would be so dispersed as to engage the enemy at multiple points. But these fortresses did not have adequate reserves, were not located to support each other and were, furthermore, based in areas where the population was hostile and the troops had, for eight months, been engaged in counter-insurgency and were exhausted.[26] Dacca was a fortress to be defended at all costs but it was denuded of regular troops between May and August 1971 to save the situation on other fronts. Jessore, Laksham and Brahman Baria fortresses were abandoned without a fight, the loss of Jessore being particularly distressing.[27] If the purpose, the justices wrote 'was that troops should remain in isolation while the enemy effectively occupied the rest of the country and established its government over it, then the plan did succeed'.[28] The failure in which Niazi displayed an 'utter lack of understanding of even the rudiments of military planning' was shared by general headquarters. There was no plan at all for the defence of Dacca.[29]

The report also points out the fallacy of the military concept that the defence of East Pakistan lay in West Pakistan and that the eastern command would never have to fight any major battle with the Indians. They would only have to keep the Indian forces involved so that they would not be withdrawn to face the west. If this was so, the second front in West Pakistan should have been opened much earlier. Above all, however, was the 'delusion' from which Niazi suffered, and so did general headquarters, that the Indians would not cross the international frontier in East Pakistan. As the report shows, the whole world had warned Pakistan against the Indian threat. Had the Indians amassed eight divisions, three armoured regiments, two additional detached brigades, a parachute brigade, artillery brigades, thirty-five battalions of border security forces, eleven air force squadrons – we had only one – two naval submarines, an aircraft carrier, landing craft, frigates and destroyers, only to fight a proxy war? Did the hawks in general headquarters think that such an opportunity to settle scores with India on the western front, where near parity prevailed, would never arise again, so why not take advantage of it, even though in the bargain East Pakistan might have to be written off? The justices were completely 'astounded' by the immorality and perversity of such an idea.[30]

The narrative is balanced about the 'terror let loose' by the Awami League and its military wing, Sangram Parishad, before military action was taken on 25 March 1971 which led to the mass exodus of non-Bengalis, and the reaction of the army after military action actually started. Our troops went out in anger during the military action and sweep operations; they lived 'off the land' which led to two million people crossing the border into India. Some of these people used guerrilla tactics to return and fight again. Precise figures of the atrocities perpetrated on Bengalis by the Pakistan army have never been reached and it is, indeed, impossible to do so. According to Bangladesh, three million Bengalis were killed and 200,000 women were raped. 'So much damage,' writes the Commission, 'could not have been caused by the entire strength of the Pakistan Army then stationed in East Pakistan, even if it had nothing else to do.'[31] It accepts the general headquarters' figures that only 26,000 persons were killed during the army action.

The supplementary report examines the war sector by sector in detail from 3 December 1971 onwards when the second front was opened in West Pakistan. It records the confusion, incidents of panic, dereliction of duty and concern for personal safety as well as the many acts of heroism such as the brave defence put up by our forces in the battle of Hilli. Some commanders may have lost the will to fight, but the junior officers and their men fought bravely and would have continued to do so to the last if they had been properly led.[32]

The most poignant part of the supplementary report relates to the surrender in East Pakistan. The justices seem to fight their own war on paper, as they thought it should have been fought. For this purpose they made a thorough study of the signals which were exchanged between general headquarters and Niazi from 21 November 1971 onwards when Indian troops invaded East Pakistan. And the assessments sent by the governor, D.M. Malik, which were more realistic than those of the commander, citing the desperate military situation, lack of food, fuel, oil, complete paralysis of life, and the butchery of pro-Pakistan elements by the rebels; and begging for a ceasefire and a negotiated solution.[33] As a result of Yahya Khan's signal to the governor to ensure 'safety of armed forces by all means that you will adopt with our opponent', Malik sent the controversial message for a ceasefire – but not of surrender – through Rao Farman Ali to the assistant secretary general of the United Nations, Paul Mark Henry, which was said to have compromised our case in the Security Council.[34]

The report raises the question: 'Was General Niazi bound to obey an order to surrender?' Their own analysis of the exchange of signals in those last days of the tragedy in East Pakistan led the justices to conclude that Niazi was not given an order to surrender but only permission to surrender, further resistance being no longer humanly possible.[35] Niazi himself stated in his evidence that a suggestion by a superior is a courteous way of giving an order. Was the order to surrender a lawful act within the provisions of the Army Act? Different witnesses gave different replies, some quoting instances in history where such orders had been disobeyed. In fact, a few commanders in the theatre had advised against the surrender. Along with their officers, some commanders were found missing, and it was presumed that they did not surrender and had died fighting.

The Commission further raised the question whether it was necessary for Niazi to surrender? It arrived at the conclusion that 'the will to fight had snapped long before the actual surrender' and that Niazi had lost control of the situation and was 'in a state of almost complete mental paralysis'.[36] There was no need at all to surrender at this stage. Contrary to his signals that the Indians were at the outskirts of Dacca, it would have required at least two weeks for the Indians to take Dacca. He over-estimated the threat of the Indian bombardment of Dacca, to which India would not have resorted, as it was moving in its perceived role as the saviour of the Bengali people. Niazi had 26,000 troops in Dacca under his control. If he had held out, it was likely that a ceasefire would have been negotiated in the Security Council. Even after he sent out the command to surrender, there was no compulsion to agree to the ceremony in Race Course Maidan in Dacca on 16 December 1971. And anyway, why was it necessary for him to receive General Arora at the airport and present a guard of honour? Even at the final stage he does not 'emerge with the dignity of a gallant but defeated soldier who faced odds too high to overcome'. He need not have contributed to the picture which India wanted to present to the world.[37]

The Commission recommended that Lieutenant General A.A.K. Niazi and other officers in the field and at headquarters should be tried for their role in the conduct of the war. It also recommended that a high-powered court or commission should be set up to inquire into the allegations of atrocities committed during army action from March to December 1971.[38] Needless to say, no trials were held.[39]

The Hamoodur Rahman Commission report has been criticised by many people who have never actually read the report. Bhutto's detractors have found fault with it for not holding him equally responsible with the generals for the loss of East Pakistan, and the terms of reference for including only the military, and not the political aspects of the tragedy, although the report deals decisively with the political circumstances prevailing at that time. Together with its supporting material, it is a remarkable document and the range of evidence it sifts and examines can only be described as monumental. The question is still asked as to why the top army commanders refused to negotiate with Mujibur Rahman even when defeat stared them in the face. As Rao Farman Ali deposed before the Commission, the hawks were not willing to accept the domination of East Pakistanis in future political arrangements in Pakistan.[40]

I want to end my oblique association with this chapter of our national life with the tributes paid to our troops by the enemy, especially in the battle of

Hilli. As Brigadier Tajammul Hussain, who fought to the end at Hilli with his pistol before he was captured, stated, for a self-respecting soldier, surrender is 'another form of death'. D.K. Palit dismisses the argument that there was a general collapse of the Pakistan army. He writes about 'the bitter resistance' put up by the Pakistani forces at Hilli, Jamalpur, Khulna and other strongholds, 'often having to be physically destroyed' before the posts could be taken. In the battle of Hilli:

> The Pakistani garrison virtually had to be annihilated before the post could be taken... Whenever the Pakistanis decided to hold out they fought ferociously. At Hilli they held their ground with admirable tenacity, though it was the courage of a desperate, doomed, beleaguered garrison left with no other alternative than to fight to the last man. Indeed, it would be correct to say that whenever the Pakistanis were fighting from prepared positions, they fought with grim determination.[41]

Many years later, in a television interview to Karan Thapar, the Indian army chief, Field Marshal Sam Manekshaw, said:

> The Pakistan army in East Pakistan fought very gallantly but they had no chance. They were a thousand miles away from their base; I had eight or nine months to make my preparations. I had the superiority of almost 50 to 1. They just had no chance but they fought very gallantly.[42]

The war was, above all, an unequal fight, man to man, weapon to weapon, aircraft to aircraft, warship to warship and not enough homage can be paid to the nameless soldiers who laid down their lives. Anyone who had even the vaguest idea of the distress that Partition had caused to the Hindus of India and the Congress Party would have realised that India would never forego any opportunity to break up Pakistan. Hence Indira Gandhi's triumphant reference to history after the surrender at Dacca. Garlanded profusely in the Indian parliament, she described her victory as 'a deed well done'. And even forty-seven years later, Narendra Modi could not refrain from mentioning it during his visit to Bangladesh.

In January 2001, there was a massive earthquake in Ahmedabad, India, causing destruction and death. When I heard about it, I suggested that we should send medical and other relief supplies to India as soon as possible. Providing relief fell within the mandate of the cabinet division. Brigadier Ilyas, who worked in the military wing of the cabinet division, led this mission. When he reached Ahmedabad, the entire media shifted its attention to the relief mission from Pakistan and he was surrounded by hundreds of people. He made a very dignified speech to the Indian media. I went to base Chaklala to see off the C-130 aircraft which carried the first lot of supplies and shook hands with the pilot before he took off. Relief supplies were also sent to Afghanistan and were received by the Afghan ambassador, Abdul Salam Zaeef. He would never have shaken hands with me. Most diplomats in Islamabad shunned the Afghan ambassadors, representatives of Mullah Omar, although they were courteous and offered to facilitate my journey to visit the grave of my ancestor, Abdullah Pir of Herat, which did not happen. In 2001, Zaeef was handed over by Pakistan to the Americans who sent him to Guantanamo Bay where he was held until 2005.[43]

In the first week of February 2001, I called on Saddam Hussein in Baghdad. Saddam was hated by the West and by his own people also for being so despotic, but Iraq had suffered terribly under sanctions and Musharraf decided to send a humanitarian flight to Iraq with medical and surgical supplies. It was a very sensibly constituted mission with media people and businessmen, led by Abdul Malik Kasi, minister for health, and included Sher Afgan Khan, additional foreign secretary, and me. Since there was a no-fly zone over Iraq, we had to get a waiver to fly to Baghdad airport which was completely deserted as no flights had landed there for ages. We were received, apart from Iraqi officials, by our ambassador Manzar Shafiq, who had been my student in the 'first common'. We checked into Hotel Rasheed where every visitor had to step on the image of George Bush which was woven on the mat at the entrance of the hotel. As I looked out of the window at those wide roads and impressive infrastructure, I thought of my father and how he had made me memorise Iqbal's odes to Muslim triumphs on the Tigris and Euphrates. And the book, *Baghdad: The City of Peace* from his library which I had kept for myself.

In Baghdad, we visited all the sacred shrines – Imam Musa al-Kazim and Imam Ali al-Taqi at Kazimayn, Abd al-Qadir Gilani and Abu Hanifa. Since ours was a medical mission, we were taken to a couple of large hospitals, all well equipped. Saddam was a great supporter of the Palestinian intifada and provided medical care and treatment to the young men who were injured by Israeli aggression and retaliation. Some of their injuries were so gruesome that I have not been able to wipe them from my memory. One young man's skull was crushed so badly that it had settled into curves. Another fighter had both his legs amputated below the hip; he was smiling and exercising his arms. We were also taken to a basement where children had sought shelter from bombing raids. The shelter was not impervious to the deadly bombs dropped by the Americans. As the bombs exploded deep into the shelter, their tiny bodies and limbs flew out in all directions and some of them were still stuck to the walls and roof of the shelter.

According to the protocol chief, three names – Kasi, Sher Afgan and myself – were sent to Saddam for a meeting. He hardly ever received visitors – not even the credentials of ambassadors. I brooded that if he decided to see us at noon next day, how would I perform *ziarat* in Najaf and Karbala and return to Baghdad in time to meet Tariq Aziz in the evening? I saw my ziarat vanishing into thin air, but consoled myself that the Imam would surely 'call' me.

Next morning, we were told that the president would receive us. A Mercedes Benz car each had been placed at the disposal of Kasi, Sher Afgan and me. However, a new fleet of cars, a different pilot and outriders drove us nearby to a quiet street and we were taken into an unpretentious building. We trooped into a rather dull lobby with a huge chandelier and gilded chairs, in one corner of which sat Tariq Aziz and Mubarak, the minister for health. We made small talk about the religious and cultural ties binding our two countries and Kasi tried desperately to sell our rice to our hosts, who smiled politely. Eventually, a man turned up and said we were 'ready' but this was a decoy and instead of being led into Saddam's presence, we travelled miles out of Baghdad, finally entering a road on the right with no entry sign.

It could have been the road to Thatta in my childhood, everything merged into the colour of the earth. Twice we were stopped by guards who stood in front of Kasi's car and then drew back to stamp into a salute. Finally, we arrived at a building, and yet another interpreter introduced himself. As we sat on gilded chairs, a few drops of coffee were offered to us from a traditional urn. And then a man turned up, with a proud look and a bushy moustache, wearing an army coat, who was introduced as the president's personal secretary. He was Abid Hamid Mahmud al-Tikriti who was hanged on 7 June 2012 after the occupation of Iraq for the killing of members of banned political parties. The room was painted white. It had many pillars and the floor was made of white marble, the texture of Peshawar marble. However, parts of the roof and some walls had been worked in blue. On our left there was a gaudy mirror in a golden frame; in the centre was a dining table surrounded by chairs. Somebody came to fetch us. We had barely crossed the room and gone down two steps when we saw Saddam Hussein coming forward to greet Kasi.

The room we entered was also white; it had a very high roof and no visible doors except the entrance through which we had stepped. There were roof to floor elegant curtains made of a fine silky fabric and a beautiful large blue and beige carpet was spread in the centre of the glistening floor – probably a Hareke. There were smaller carpets at the feet of sofas and chairs – upholstered and semi-gilded. And there was the inevitable chandelier. It pleased me to see a western painting on one of the walls. Saddam greeted Kasi, then me, then Sher Afgan. He said words of welcome, holding my hand, but I couldn't say much. The television crew clicked all the time – our own crew was not allowed to cover the event. They had left for the holy shrines early in the morning.

Saddam sat at the far end of the room on a large ornate chair with a tall flag of Iraq beside him. Kasi sat on a chair on his right and at some distance Tariq Aziz, Sher Afgan and I sat on one sofa. Mubarak sat on a chair to my right. Four people took notes – Saddam's secretary, another official, Sher Afgan and Mubarak – apart from the two interpreters. Saddam was a very tall man, neither his hair nor moustache were grey. He sat comfortably, with his legs at ease. He was dressed casually in shirt, sweater, checked tie and mouchoir, all in different shades of blue, and the most casual blue moccasins. I was struck by his absolute composure. He did not appear to be the devil of the West and the reincarnation of Satan. We were offered water and tea, and cigars were brought in. Saddam offered one to Tariq Aziz, lit one himself and since Kasi did not smoke, he said, 'It is good that neither of the ministers of health smokes,' referring to Kasi and Mubarak.

Saddam took his time to read the letter from Musharraf which had been translated for him into Arabic. And then he started speaking in Arabic, in an even tenor, about the relations between Pakistan and Iraq and the saga of his country, the victory of justice, the way his people had rebuilt their country, their tenacity and patriotism. We had come with medicines, but his people did not need our help. Because he understood we needed a reason to come to Iraq, he had accepted our supplies; however, such reasons were not required to draw our countries together and he hoped they would not be necessary in the future. From their ordeal, the Iraqi people had learnt to become self-reliant. They had rallied around him to reconstruct their bombed-out offices, hospitals, schools, homes and roads. Iraq did not need tears, it needed recognition of its capacity to regenerate itself and improve upon its past. He spoke of the destruction caused by Zionism for 6,000 years on the rubble of which Iraq had rebuilt itself. I never did understand why he mentioned 6,000 years.

Kasi spoke of the dips in the relations between Iraq and Pakistan, pointing out that irrespective of which government was in power, the people of Pakistan had always supported Iraq and stood by it during the Gulf War. Saddam replied that the people understood one another and we should never forget that the people were always ahead of their rulers. Referring to disputes between Muslim countries, he said that if a third Muslim country could not assist in resolving a dispute it should, at least, remain neutral.

At one point, Kasi praised the Iraqi ambassador in Islamabad for organising an exhibition of photographs showing the destruction caused by bombing and the sanctions imposed on Iraq, and how all the visitors were moved by the photographs. A look of displeasure flitted across Saddam's face and he said his ambassador was wrong. Far from making a show of destruction, the exhibition should have conveyed how the people had rebuilt their country.

Sometimes the president seemed to gaze reflectively into the distance. I thought of his remarkable career and his acts of cruelty, how he had hounded the Shias, crushed dissent and was accused of even arranging the assassination of his sons-in-law. As a young man, barely in his twenties, he had been hounded himself and sentenced to death *in absentia*. They fell into place then, these acts of cruelty, which carried their own momentum. Surely, the most important attribute for him must have been that of loyalty.

I will not refer to the rest of the conversation. Kasi looked at me, and I nodded. It was time to leave. Because the foreign office had forgotten to send a gift for Saddam, our ambassador had rustled up a carpet from his stock which was ceremoniously rolled out before Saddam as the meeting concluded. He smiled and said it was *jamila* – actually it was not so beautiful – and he asked if it was Iranian. Kasi hastily informed him about our worldwide monopoly in the carpet industry and he smiled, and perhaps tongue in cheek, said that the Iranians are good businessmen. After Kasi, I said goodbye to him. Dictator he may have been, but I told him about how impressed I was by the resilience of the Iraqi people who had risen from the ashes, and how I would always remember this meeting. Saddam had given us about fifty-five minutes of his time. We then hastily took the road to Karbala. The Imam had 'called' me but that is another story. Tariq Aziz and Mubarak hosted a grand reception for us that evening and we flew home from that deserted airport in Baghdad next day.

By the time Saddam was hanged by the Americans and Iraqis, some of the hatred against him had worn off because of the sheer savagery of the Anglo-American invasion of Iraq in 2003. Fatehyab and I had watched on television that unbelievable blitz which flattened out so much of the 'City of Peace'. A superpower bombing on false pretences a country which could never have fought back. Saddam became an instant hero for those who hated the Americans. He cut such a pathetic figure when he was captured out of the hole in which he was hiding, in December 2003. He warned his interrogators that they would fail in Iraq because they did not know its language and history and did not understand the Arab mind.[44] As his interrogator, the CIA leadership analyst John Nixon has disclosed, everything the US thought it knew about Iraq and even about Saddam's personal life and habits, was wrong. But the American establishment would not give up its delusions and the myths it had created about Saddam, even apart from the phantom weapons of mass destruction.

Hanged on 30 December 2006, Saddam died bravely, with the *kalima* on his lips. His trial by the Iraqi Special Tribunal has been described as flawed by human rights groups and the process of hanging itself was marred by the indignity of the insults hurled at him. According to one witness to the execution, before the noose was put around his neck, he shouted that the Muslim *ummah* would be victorious and that Palestine was Arab.[45] Nixon has also revealed that before the invasion Saddam had stopped taking an interest in the governance of Iraq, delegating much of it to his top aides. He was busy in writing a novel and had written four novels before the invasion of Iraq. During his incarceration, as he waited for his trial and death, all he wanted to do was to finish writing his novel. 'You must understand, I am a writer, and what you are doing by depriving me of pen and paper amounts to human rights abuse,' he told his interrogators.[46]

Chapter 11

For Fatehyab

After retiring from public service, I turned my attention to The Pakistan Institute of International Affairs, the story of which needs to be written. The association of my family with this institution has always been recognised and its members have nurtured and protected it. My father brought it from Delhi, established it and watched over it. He represented Pakistan at the United Nations and numerous international forums and his name was linked to the Institute throughout the diplomatic and academic world but, as we shall see, other family members had to step in to save the institution.

The founding members of the Institute were some of the most eminent citizens of our country. Some of them, like Shaista Ikramullah, Jahan Ara Shahnawaz, Mahmud Husain, I.H. Qureshi, were members of the Constituent Assembly of Pakistan. Others were prominent men like Altaf Husain, editor of *Dawn*, Mumtaz Hasan, Shahid Suharwardy, M. Ayub, Hemendas Wadhwani; the young Agha Shahi and the young Rashid Ibrahim from the public service; Yusuf Haroon, Jamshed Nusserwanjee, Mirza Mohommad Rafi and D.M. Malik from the business community and A.B.A. Haleem, vice chancellor of Sind University. The prime minister, Liaquat Ali Khan, inaugurated the Institute on 26 March 1948 and his speech made headlines in the press.[1]

The first few years of the Institute's life were vigorous. No other organisation in the capital, Karachi, provided a platform for discussion on Pakistan's evolving foreign policy, especially its disputes with India, including Kashmir. The fledgling foreign office, housed in Mohatta Palace, had scant access to material and sources, and turned to the Institute to prepare its briefs and analyses. Shifting from my father's drawing room in the barrack in Intelligence School which was our first home, the Institute moved to rented rooms in the iconic Frere Hall. My brother, Arif, and I roamed around its beautiful gardens – there was a statue of Queen Victoria in the centre, later removed – as we waited for our father to finish his work. Our parents told us not to talk to strangers, but apparently nobody feared that we would be harmed. Lectures and discussions were held in an equally elegant building, Somerset House, on Somerset Street, now occupied by paramilitary forces. Zafrulla Khan, who was Pakistan's foreign minister and distinguished himself at the United

Nations and later at the International Court of Justice, was a great friend of the Institute and often spoke there.

I am not sure about the Institute's financial resources. The government, which was short of funds itself, could hardly have contributed much to its coffers. However, the government advanced a sum towards the construction of a new building which the Institute repaid with interest. With his usual foresight, my father chose this central plot of land in the heart of Karachi, and enthusiastically started getting the building designed.

The first sketches were made on our dining table; then he poured over the blueprints night after night. The elevations were designed by a Spanish architect who had come to Karachi to advise the government on a new capital for the country. My father made sure that the building reflected Muslim architecture in the subcontinent and the Spanish architect's Moorish arches were changed into imposing Mughal arches. Hence also the sandy pink colour which has become its landmark. In the end, there was a shell of a building with graceful arches and a pink façade in colour crete, mirroring the colour of the Muslim monuments in Delhi. The now famous library and some offices were completed and space was let out on either side to augment the Institute's income. Many important institutions began their journey in this building, such as the celebrated Institute of Business Administration. Due to shortage of funds, the interior and auditorium remained incomplete. However, the edifice which my father raised, brought grief to the Institute.

Chairman Haleem and my father had always jealously guarded the Institute's independent status. The foreign office, which did not have its own research outfit at that time, tried unsuccessfully to place some of its officers on the governing council. When my father died, there was a crisis in the Institute. Who could fill his place? In a series of long conversations, Fatehyab persuaded the lawyer and scholar, Kemal Faruki, to become the honorary secretary. But the foreign office returned with counter proposals. It may have been Bhutto's desire to control institutions, he may have been encouraged by the foreign office, or he may simply have wanted a post for his party men. Whatever the reason, he coerced the council to appoint as secretary, A.A. Akmut, a member of his party, who agreed not to bring politics into the affairs of the Institute. In the meantime, Haleem co-opted me as a member of the council.

Akmut could not keep his word and the Institute was flooded with Bhutto's party workers and their problems. All this, to Haleem's horror. As vice chancellor of the University of Karachi, he had been a past master at managing conflict and he confided in each council member that Akmut should be removed. He called me too, and made me promise to attend the next council meeting on 9 August 1974. After the regular business was concluded in the meeting, to his utter surprise, Akmut was asked to leave the room so that we could discuss his case. 'We must remove him,' Haleem told us. He had signed Akmut's salary cheque, so handed it to him, and asked him to leave. It was a resolute act on his part as he would not, in normal circumstances, have taken on the government. The annual general meeting after Akmut's dismissal was one of the stormiest I have attended, with poor Mrs Akmut unsuccessfully trying to get in a word.

The shadow of the foreign office, however, did not recede. It appears to have been part of the understanding that Haleem would vacate both his seat on the council and his position as chairman, as Bhutto had wanted. In recognition of the forceful role he had played during this crisis, Haleem co-opted Fatehyab to the seat he was vacating. Bhutto – or the foreign office – insisted that a retired ambassador, M. Masood, should be appointed as paid secretary of the Institute.

Haleem's departure as chairman created another crisis. For twenty-six years he had held the reins of power. Who was to succeed him? Most of the other members of the council were his cronies. There were men of stature such as Ehsan Rashid[2] and Kemal Faruki who may have aspired to his position, but would they be able or willing to withstand pressure? Kemal Faruki, in fact, told me that the Institute should shift to Islamabad where 'the ambassadors are', an absurd argument. Fatehyab searched in the membership list for an eminent person and persuaded Justice Noorul Arfeen[3] to accept the chair. He was widely respected, dignified and decisive. But to our consternation, he resigned as chairman when a certain martial law regulation was promulgated.

One day, Aftab Alam Kizilbash came to see me. He was the Institute's legal adviser and a member of the council. 'Do you,' he asked me, 'want your father's life work to be reduced to dust?' I was taken aback by his question and even more surprised when he suggested that I should become the chairman of the Institute. I was young, and as my critics rightly said, just the equivalent of a deputy secretary. 'But,' I protested, 'I lack experience and nobody will accept me.' Kizilbash said, 'leave that to me. If you don't agree, the building of the Institute will be sold for a song and the books in the library dumped on the footpaths. And the Institute will be shifted to Islamabad. Nobody will care or dare to take a stand.' I was overwhelmed by this suggestion and after Kizilbash proposed my name in the next council meeting, I said I would consult my department first. When I put the proposition to my director, Iftikhar Ahmad Khan, he was delighted and told me to go ahead and accept the challenge.

With hindsight, I can see that the election of a young and inexperienced woman suited many people. In particular, it suited a developer who sat in the council and was also a tenant in the building. A clear conflict of interest, but

Haleem trusted him and depended on him for his election as chairman. In the end, they fell out acrimoniously and Haleem saw through his ruse. Dealing with the developer gave me my first brush with the arrogance and ruthlessness of big business. He was an entrepreneur and builder of many large housing complexes. More than anybody else, he understood the value of the building of the Institute.

He moved methodically to pocket the organisation, suggesting that council meetings should be held in his office because he would serve excellent coffee; the tea served in the Institute was insipid. Then he asked that the unfinished auditorium should be let out to him. He was our largest tenant and the vast auditorium space would have made him into a super tenant. So I declined, saying we would eventually complete the auditorium. Finally, he said he would get an amenity plot allotted for the Institute – which he could have done easily with the clout he wielded – and construct a building for us, and the Institute's building should be sold to him. Since the Institute's property was not my personal asset, I told him it was not up for sale. He then warned that the chief of army staff, General Ziaul Haq, was his personal friend and he would get the Institute shifted to Islamabad. He tried to intimidate me by saying, 'do you think you are Indira Gandhi,' and 'Bhutto also thought his chair was strong.' There was some sense of the ridiculous in his assertions. Before this open confrontation, he had paid for hundreds of membership applications through the secretary, who was probably in league with him in this venture. However, all these applications were rejected by the council.

In the last stages of this confrontation, the developer manoeuvred to get the annual general meeting of the Institute stayed through a court order, although there was a good turnout of members on that occasion. Then he pushed his relatives and employees to file one case after another against me in the lower courts. It was thanks to Waheed Farooqui, a family friend and distinguished lawyer, that these cases were dismissed and to the integrity of Mirza Arshad Ali Baig, the district judge of Karachi, whom he could not influence. These were very distressing times for me and I am surprised that I found the courage to carry on. While the cases were in progress, he bullied the members of the council, threatening our venerable treasurer with dire consequences. A stream of anonymous and not so anonymous complaints to the foreign office led to Ambassador Najmus Saqib's visit to inquire into the state of our affairs. His report may have paved the way for the next development.

One morning in April 1980, when I thought the storm was over, Enver Inayatullah, a well-known journalist, called to ask if I had read the newspapers. A presidential ordinance had been published, taking over the Institute, dissolving the council, and appointing an administrator.[4] I was at a complete loss and decided to consult A.K. Brohi. He was considered Ziaul Haq's *éminence grise* but as I have written, he had known my father well and had always been affectionate towards me. He said he would take me to meet Ziaul Haq. In Islamabad, I had lunch with Brohi at his residence on School Road before we drove towards Army House in Rawalpindi. On the way, Brohi told me, 'Masuma, don't be on the defensive when you talk to the president. You have done nothing wrong.'

I do not remember how long my meeting with Ziaul Haq lasted, but I do remember how aggressive and abrasive he was. Popping nuts into his mouth, he inquired why I had turned up to see him. I said I was surprised at the presidential ordinance and did not know the reasons for its promulgation. Brohi intervened to say 'Masuma had the right to be heard.' Ziaul Haq replied, 'did nobody consult her, did nobody hear her?' And then he indicated that I had been quarrelling with this developer. I told him that he was our tenant and wanted to buy the building which I had resisted and if he would hear me, I would tell him the history of the Institute. He heard me out and concluded by saying that he did not have a false ego and would get the matter re-investigated; however, if he found that there was any anti-government activity in the Institute, he would 'get those people hanged upside down'. In fact, the propaganda had succeeded and when I tried to counter it by asking Zafar Ahmad Ansari and Colonel Hashim[5] to talk to him, Ziaul Haq had shown his displeasure with Fatehyab. 'Her husband,' Brohi told him, 'is inconvenient for you.'

On the way back from Army House, Brohi advised me to challenge the presidential ordinance, which I would have done in any case. Three administrators were appointed for the Institute by Ziaul Haq. The first administrator was Justice Qadeeruddin Ahmed who, as a man of law, should have known better than to take up the appointment. He was a former law student of my father in Delhi and called me to meet him. He did not stay long in this position and the next administrator, Air Marshal Nur Khan, also summoned me and hinted at the presence of 'subversive' elements in the Institute. He gave up the assignment too; perhaps it was too small for him. After all, he had been commander-in-chief of the air force and had also led the national airline. The next administrator was Major General Ghulam Umar who was one of the persons held responsible by the Hamoodur Rahman Commission for the break-up of the country. Although he did not summon me to his presence, his loyalty to Ziaul Haq prompted him to publish his benefactor's photograph in *Pakistan Horizon,* the scholarly journal of the Institute. The founders of the Institute must have turned in their graves.

Fighting in the courts of law to get the independent status of the Institute restored was a saga spread over thirteen years. My brother Kazim worked long hours to draft the constitution petitions and had it not been for Fatehyab's courage and determination, the struggle would have been long lost. Because of the severity of martial law, the members sometimes withdrew their petitions. Also, the law kept changing and the petitions were dismissed because of the provisional constitutional order.[6] When Muhammad Khan Junejo became the prime minister in 1985, some members of the Institute made a representation to him, but there was no response.

After Benazir Bhutto was elected as prime minister in 1988, I ran from pillar to post to contact as many members as possible, some of whom agreed to write to her. We thought she would repeal the ordinance, but her party colleagues had other fanciful plans for the Institute. Ultimately, Fatehyab approached Yahya Bakhtiar who was her attorney general.[7] During 1989, I called on him several times in his office in the Supreme Court building in Rawalpindi and he worked out a *via media*. He persuaded Benazir to appoint me – as the chairman dismissed by Ziaul Haq – as the administrator in place of Umar. He treated me with great respect, was very dignified and said, 'don't thank me until I have actually helped you.' Nusrat Bhutto also threw her weight behind us. She met me on 19 September 1989 and when I told her that there was a silver lining and thanked her, she said, 'they don't usually listen to me.' I remember how excited she was at the prospect of meeting her grandchildren. We were helped also by the editorial written by I.A. Rehman in *Pakistan Times*.[8]

On 2 September 1989, Yahya Bakhtiar called to say that the order appointing me as administrator had been signed and I took over on 4 September 1989. There appears to have been genuine satisfaction among its members and all those who were happy about Ziaul Haq's exit from our lives, when I took charge of the Institute. But how were we to get rid of this ordinance which still hung around our necks? Strangely, the fate of the Institute was linked to the vicissitudes of Pakistan's politics. It is a case study in bureaucratic decision making.

Whatever her reasons – it was not a priority in her political agenda – Benazir Bhutto did not repeal the ordinance promulgated by Ziaul Haq, although I met Yahya Bakhtiar several times in this connection. After her government was dismissed by the president, Ghulam Ishaq Khan, on 6 August 1990, I continued liaising with the foreign office to press for the repeal of the ordinance. She was succeeded by the caretaker prime minister, Ghulam Mustafa Jatoi. I learnt later that Jatoi came under great pressure from the developer to remove me, but he held and cherished feudal values and I was saved, perhaps for the first time, because I was Fatehyab's wife.

Nawaz Sharif's government did not interfere in the affairs of the Institute; after all, it was still a government department. In fact, some of its leading diplomats spoke at large gatherings at the Institute: Akram Zaki, Shahryar Khan.[9] Finally, persistence prevailed and on 27 May 1991 the federal cabinet gave its approval to repeal the ordinance through a bill in parliament, and on 18 October 1992 it also approved the text of the bill. Mehboob Ali Khan, Aneesuddin Ahmed and I celebrated this victory over lunch on 19 October 1992.[10] However, the bill could not be moved in parliament because Nawaz Sharif's government was dismissed by the president on 18 April 1993. After his government was restored by the Supreme Court on 26 May 1993, I started my campaign again. On 2 October 1993, foreign secretary Shahryar Khan signed a summary for the prime minister which reached the president's secretariat on what would be the last lap of its journey, after which I lost track of the case. In the meantime, the Supreme Court had admitted a constitution petition in appeal of three of the Institute's members.

The appeal was filed in the Supreme Court of Pakistan against the dismissal by the High Court of Sindh of a constitution petition filed in 1988 by Rasheed Razvi, Mazharul Jameel and Arif Hasan.[11] When the case came up for hearing, I made the task of the justices easier by conceding the petition. On 19 October 1993, Chief Justice Nasim Hasan Shah heard the case and reserved judgement. I was miserable as I waited for the announcement of the order for this was the last court of appeal. And thus it was that on 21 November 1993, the Supreme Court of Pakistan declared Ziaul Haq's ordinance as a violation of fundamental rights in the Constitution of 1973 and restored the Institute to its original independent status.[12] An extraordinary general meeting of the members was convened which decided to hold an annual general meeting to elect the governing council.

But the future in store for the 'speaking building' still troubled me. What was to prevent another builder, another adventurer, a high stakeholder, from eyeing its location and multi-million value? So to prevent its demolition for all times to come – however long that takes – I moved to get the building declared as 'protected heritage'. With the support of Kaleemullah Lashari[13] and my brother Arif Hasan, who are members of the Sindh Heritage Committee, this was done in 2016. The conspiracy to grab the Institute's property had not, after all, succeeded.

*   *   *

When I look back at the times in which I lived, I am grieved by the violence which pervaded the world: wars and war crimes, genocide, public rage, racial prejudice, and the helplessness of the marginalised and deprived. Also civil strife and the relentless appetite of major powers to kill and destroy. I have tried to recollect the sensitivities of my childhood and the factors which influenced my upbringing. First, there was the violence of Partition which remained the defining event in our existence. After the first few years of the trauma, it receded in conversation but never quite faded away. In the discussions in our home, my father wanted to get the historical narrative right, the fate of the Muslims who were butchered or escaped in trains and foot convoys in the villages and towns near Panipat, around his beloved Delhi, and in the other cities and princely states which he knew. He never talked about the preparations he had made for our own escape. But when Pakistan became a republic on 23 March 1956, he told me emotionally, 'For you, I gave up everything I possessed.' He implied that he could have lived with the disastrous consequences for his community in a united India, but he wanted a different future for his children. So he gave up everything. I was moved by his emotion, but was too young to understand its deeper implications for our lives.

Now I pause to reflect on the choice he made – for unlike his relatives, he was not physically pushed out. Even if the rabble had attacked our house, even if Delhi reeked with blood in August and September 1947, he could have sought shelter. He had many friends– Tara Bai, Sham Nath– who would have helped him to stay. But he believed in the Muslim League's understanding of the communal conflict in India and, above all, he had absolute faith in the leadership of Mohammad Ali Jinnah. He packed his bags and left with his young family and with the institution which he cherished.

Pakistan was my father's passion, he was obsessively patriotic. He represented his country throughout the world and what he had lost in worldly possessions, he gained in reputation and stature. He hardly complained that he had gleaned only a fraction of what he had abandoned, but his papers reveal the facts. Perhaps like the other thinking – or unthinking – Muslims of his generation, he hoped a day would come when he would cross the frontier freely and show his children the great Muslim monuments in Delhi and Agra on which his ancestors had gazed for centuries. After the Partition riots, that had become impossible. Well had Shaista Ikramullah written in anguish to her husband, his friend Ikramullah, 'how can there be a Pakistan without Delhi?'[14] Sometimes he drove me over the sand dunes in Clifton and gazed silently at the sea, watching the sunset, uttering not a word. I was impatient, just a small child who wanted to go home.

For my father, the battle lay in the domain of culture. His ancestors wrote and corresponded in Persian, the language of the Mughal court; the handwritten manuscripts in his father's archives were in Turkish and Persian. His mother was educated in Persian and Urdu, he had studied at Aligarh Muslim University before proceeding to Cambridge. With Iqbal, he was sentimental about a universal Muslim culture and longed for a great future for the Muslims of the subcontinent. He could never have accepted modern India's symbols of nationhood, the tricolour, the Jana Gana Mana anthem, Asoka's wheel. Saffron was not his colour. Nor could he have come to terms with symbols of recognition like Bharat Ratna and Padma Bhushan, or the universal use of the Devanagari script.[15] His greatest concern was for Urdu, the language which he spoke and wrote beautifully.

My mother, on the other hand, was less restrained in dwelling on the past. All my knowledge about Panipat, my father's life and career in Delhi, his property, the names of his friends, anecdotes about the election he lost, family disputes, her education at Queen Mary College, Lahore, came from her. In the hot summer afternoons we listened to her, spellbound, as she took us through the narrow streets of Panipat and talked about her family elders, their struggle, their aspirations. She created a cultural continuity when she related the fairytales and stories which she had heard in her own childhood – and also taught me the dirges she had recited in that lost city.

In our neighbourhood in Intelligence School, we were surrounded by uprooted families. Rich and poor, they were partners in distress and understood each other's pain, so few words were needed to express that pain. But we were isolated from the larger city and only slowly came to understand its diversity. It amazes me how the refugees who came from different directions in different ways, some in trains, others in trucks or on foot, searched for and found their separated family members in the sprawling refugee camps, simply by word of mouth. My father's employees in Delhi somehow landed in his office in Karachi. Many women and men volunteers worked in the refugee camps in those days of confusion and hope.

My parents took easily to the official and social life in Karachi, but their link with the land did not go beyond Thatta. It took many years for them to make friends in other cities who were not migrants from India. Their knowledge of the rural areas was limited to their acquaintance with some feudal families of Sindh, whose culture was different from that of the landowners of northern India. The Baloch sardars were beyond their acquaintance. Over time, however, they saw the assertion of Sindhi interests – Karachi was their city, after all, and became more so when Ayub Khan shifted the capital to Islamabad, reducing us all to tears. After Ayub Khan grabbed power, there was a systematic flow of Pathans into Karachi. The Pathans came initially as labourers, became petty shopkeepers and transporters and their culture, with its tribal code, jirga system and rigid patriarchy, sat uneasily with the culture of the uprooted. They brought with them the guns and weapons whose ownership was part of their tradition. My father knew and respected the leaders of East Pakistan, but our interaction with ordinary Bengalis was mostly limited to their work as domestic help.

The first great painful event after Partition was the civil war in East Pakistan. Although we were not directly affected by the violence, it tainted our history with blood. For the thousands who were directly involved on both sides, civilians and military personnel, it was a brutal experience, completely senseless, which could have been avoided. Very few people in the history of the modern world would have seen their homeland so torn apart. For my parents' generation on whose dreams our country was built, it was a tragedy without parallel, and their sense of shock was severe. There were political protests throughout the country and calls for accountability,[16] but East Pakistan was so far away that people carried on in numbed silence. Some justified the defeat by saying that we were well rid of the Bengalis.

The violence inflicted by dictators filled our public space, repression by Ayub Khan, cruelty by Ziaul Haq. Ayub Khan is lionised because of his economic and social reforms and green revolution. But he was ruthless in suppressing dissent and set the clock back for democracy by many decades. Ziaul Haq dragged brutality into the arena, as people watched the spectacle of political workers and petty criminals being lashed and whipped. He thought he could cleanse the system of crime and crush political dissent by inflicting barbaric punishments. So many people were hanged and lashed, and the western world was silent because it needed his support for the war in Afghanistan. We cannot even recall the names of the young activists who languished for years in various prisons and, therefore, do not celebrate their struggle.

Often, as I waited for Fatehyab to be released from prison, I wondered what drove the foot soldier in politics to his acts of defiance. The political worker is a helpless creature, thrown into the fray with few resources and under a dictatorship, with no hope for justice. What drove Fatehyab's party colleague, S.M. Altaf,[17] to run from one clandestine meeting to another during the movement for restoration of democracy, with no personal transport and no money in his pocket? What motivated the semi-educated Pathan workers of his party in Karachi to paste anti-Zia slogans under cover of darkness? And who was that wit who scrawled on the outer wall of a graveyard, *Ya Allah, ab to Ziaul Haq ko bhi utha le*? (Oh God, please now take away even Ziaul Haq.) Attacks against both leader and worker could lead to death. In the early days of the movement against Ziaul Haq, an attempt was made on Fatehyab's life. On the main artery, Sharea Faisal, a vehicle so powerful rammed into his old Mercedes that it was crushed like a match box. He hailed a motorcycle rider and pursued the vehicle which picked up speed and disappeared. After the accident, Fatehyab's political associates and friends gathered at our house. Khawaja Khairuddin, who had witnessed political crime in East Pakistan said, 'I have lived long enough to know that this was not an accident.'

There were many political assassinations in Pakistan. The most high profile killing was that of Benazir Bhutto. She returned to Pakistan in October 2007, after reaching an understanding with Parvez Musharraf, in a blaze of political fervour and media publicity. From experience we knew that the journey from the airport to her house would take several hours. A grand welcome had been planned for her. The truck in which she was travelling was specially designed for comfort and security. It was surrounded and escorted by more than 100 of her hand-picked young followers, the *jiyalas* of her party. Her procession would travel along Sharea Faisal, about 1 kilometre from our house. I persuaded Fatehyab to leave the comfort of his chair and accompany me to watch the procession. There was a carnival on the road –camps, lights, buntings, flags and music and dancing. We stood on the pavement along with hundreds of people as night fell. While we waited, the street lights suddenly went off and a policeman told us that there had been a bomb blast. We called Mudassir Mirza[18] in *Jang* newspaper and he confirmed that there had, indeed, been an explosion. Scores of ambulances screeched past us, sirens blowing, loaded with bodies. I had no idea there were so many ambulances in Karachi. Within no time, the carnival collapsed. A man wearing a peaked cap, who had been walking up and down the pavement, told somebody on his mobile phone to switch on the street lights. The road was absolutely deserted. Another man, apparently of some importance, came up to us saying 'they will pay for this, they will pay this.' He advised Fatehyab and me to go home. When we reached our car, we found the whole area absolutely deserted.

If this experience was startling, Benazir Bhutto's assassination after her last speech in Liaquat Bagh in Rawalpindi on 27 December 2007, was an event of utter helplessness. I was visiting friends in north Karachi when the woman of the house said she feared somebody important had died. She switched on the television and we heard that Benazir Bhutto had been killed. No more than fifteen minutes later, I left the house to find fires blazing along all roads. Fortunately, I had a chauffeur and was driving in a small car, a Suzuki FX. The city sank into mayhem and arson. When flames did not block our path, ferocious young men with huge stones in their hands did, threatening to smash the windscreen of the car. Patiently weaving our way from street to street, we approached Hasan Square only to be confronted with more blazing fires. There was no option but to drive into the low-income Catholic colony, Isa Nagri. Hundreds of people were on the move in those narrow streets, some pleading for a lift in my car, but my chauffeur refused. After driving over ditches, dumps and open sewers, we entered a gridlock. There was no way to move forward or to move backwards. But the stream of people emerging from nowhere did not stop. A young man approached me and offered to take me home – he assured me his mother and sisters would be present. 'Do you know who has been killed,' he asked? 'Benazir Bhutto. *Khala*, how will you spend the night in this little car?'

The mobile service had stopped working and after ages, it seemed, was I able to contact Niaz Siddiki[19] who said he would try to unlock the traffic gridlock. Finally, the long line of buses, pickups, vans, cars, rickshaws and scooters drove over more ditches and open sewers. When we reached University Road, we ran into scores of buses and trucks which had been set on fire. More angry men were leering and watching the spectacle. How was so much fuel so easily available in such a short span of time to torch so many vehicles? Almost as if they had been waiting for this moment. For the next few days, the city was shut down completely and there was no food or water, at least in my immediate neighbourhood. One large shop on Stadium Road opened its doors partially to sell provisions. My friend, Ana Marija Besker, called from Croatia to ask if she could help in any way!

Perhaps it is too early in time to assess the true legacy of Benazir Bhutto. She was a brilliant star on the political horizon of Pakistan. Millions adored and followed her, contradicting the belief that the men of Pakistan do not want a woman leader. In the defining elections of 1988, which made her the first woman prime minister in Pakistan and the entire Muslim world, she came to power mainly on the strength of male voters. Women were not registered in such large numbers as voters and on election day their access to polling stations has always been difficult. That a woman was prime minister gave women even in remote areas a sense of pride, although it may not have improved their domestic situation.

Benazir has been criticised for abandoning her allies in the MRD because she was in a hurry to assume power. In doing so, she compromised with the military establishment and their protégé, President Ghulam Ishaq Khan, which curtailed her power and curbed the journey towards democracy. She disregarded the understanding that the 1988 elections would be contested by the MRD parties from a common platform. As written earlier, their leaders believed that if they had all stood together, the establishment could not have dictated its terms. But she did not trust the leaders of other parties. Had she allowed the venerable Nasrullah Khan to become president in 1988, he would probably not have dismissed her government.[20]

The apparent haste in which Benazir became prime minister should be viewed in the light of her unusual political experience as well as her suffering. As we all know, she could never have made it without the Bhutto name, the Bhutto mystique. For her followers, her victory was a vindication of her father's innocence in a false murder case. She did not have long political struggles behind her, like those of Nasrullah, Bizenjo or Asghar Khan. But none of these leaders had lived in such tragic circumstances. She was a very young woman who had inherited a great political responsibility. After she got rid of her 'uncles', the old guard of her party who had deserted her father, she only had second level political advisers and the jiyalas who loved her, but had little political experience. In fact, after she came to power, all manner of people solicited her for positions, favours and rewards.

In any event, Benazir's assumption of power was an electric moment for the whole country; it was charged with wonder, emotion and hope. The world watched her on television taking the oath from Ghulam Ishaq Khan, as the politicians who had done nothing to save her father from the gallows looked on, as well as many political non-entities. In her moment of glory, she had forgotten to invite Fatehyab to the event. He was deeply moved by the ceremony as he also watched it on the television.

* * *

It is painful to profile the violence which gripped Karachi in the 1990s. During the war in Afghanistan, our streets were awash with arms and sophisticated weapons. Easy access to weapons as well as the very need to counter violence, probably led political parties to create militant wings. The political culture in which popular leaders spoke in chaste language, their speeches interspersed with verses of Urdu poetry, became a 'kalashnikov culture'. People were targetted in the houses and alleys of various neighbourhoods and police stations, but every passer-by could become a random target. Surely governments knew what was happening; the ordinary citizen was simply bewildered by the chaos in the city of lights. There were curfews, schools shut down, markets were closed, life was paralysed by strikes. In my youth I had driven alone at night and was never threatened or molested. Now I paused at the entrance of my house to see whether anyone was lurking at the corner of the street. New words entered our vocabulary, like 'no-go areas', where the writ of the state did not prevail. It was often said that you knew when you left your house, but were not sure if you would ever return. The verses of the young poets of the city began to reflect their confusion and despair.

The turf wars of political parties and criminal gangs affected different parts of the city differently. People residing in less affluent areas found no escape from the bullying and learnt to live with their tormentors. Those living in well-to-do areas, who were compelled to pay large sums of money, moved their businesses out of the province or even abroad. They sent their children away to avoid being kidnapped and held for ransom, one way in which the gangs acquired funds, apart from extorting protection money. They started employing security guards and security companies have since become a booming business. Because there was no operation against these excesses, everybody who could make a quick buck jumped into the fray. The shopkeepers in my neighbourhood paid money to many groups. These conditions encouraged the suppression of political and social dissent. Fatehyab received threats to his life on the telephone and so did my brother Arif, for his superb work on the troubles of the city. But we never found out who was calling.

One interesting incident occurred on our doorstep. I was walking in the garden and through the slit in the gate saw a white car with an official number plate pause in the street outside. I wondered who could have come calling on us in an official car. By the time I opened the gate, the car had driven away and a rather bewildered man was left standing in the middle of the street. He asked me where he was and how he could get a taxi to go home. He was Jamil Dadabhoy, a well-known businessman, who was kidnapped and now set free in the secluded street in which our house stands. Fatehyab brought him inside and gave him tea and then drove him to his residence. He told me Dadabhoy's house was crowded with people who were praying that his life should be spared and he should return home unharmed. We did not know if a ransom was paid by his family, but God had listened to their prayers.

No ordinary effort was needed to crush this disorder, but somehow the anxiety it inflicted on the people had just become a way of life for them. By the time Operation Blue Fox was launched in 1992–4 to 'clean up', it was already too late. The brutality of that operation, in which thousands were killed and injured, may have brought temporary peace, but the targeted people regrouped to take revenge and fight another day. Violence knows no boundaries and conditions deteriorated in other parts of the country also, particularly in the interior of Sindh, where we had to move in convoys on the highway for safety.

Upon the heels of the troubles in Karachi came the curse of organised terrorism. My concern is only with the effect it had on our lives. Every analyst has traced the origins of terrorism in Pakistan to the jihad in Afghanistan, the fighters and students who were left clueless after the war in Afghanistan seemed to conclude, and who regrouped to form the Taliban. Everyone was not, however, upset with their rise to power. In some quarters they were regarded as 'good', if religious people, who had brought peace to Afghanistan in 1996. We were said to wield influence over them and failed even to persuade them not to blow up the historic sixth-century monumental Buddhas in Bamiyan in 2001. They suppressed all dissent, hacked down the Shias, veiled and restricted women to their homes and did not accept the Durand Line as our frontier with Afghanistan. Their crude justice sent shivers down our spines but they were far enough away not to bother us directly.

Just as violence knows no borders, the philosophy of the Afghan Taliban was sympathetically received in some religious and political circles on our side of the border and the Tehrik-i-Taliban Pakistan (TTP) was formed in 2007. They were organised, armed and aggressive enough to occupy the beautiful valley of Swat. Through 'a truce', they governed Swat as if they had won an election, and they introduced their own version of Shariat in the governance of the areas they occupied. They unleashed their oppressive rule and only when they broke the truce did our troops take back the occupied areas. The government also entered into an agreement with the tribal elders in Waziristan where the Afghan Taliban were said to have safe havens, to prevent attacks on Afghan and NATO forces across the porous borders. This was seen as an initial attempt to introduce the writ of the state in the remote tribal areas of Waziristan.

Eventually, there were many militants operating on the ground. The principal groups appeared to work along two tracks. One, they attacked important security installations, the army, navy and air force establishments, police stations, check posts, and paramilitary forces. Two, they blew up non-Wahabi places of worship, mosques, imambargahs, churches. The suicide bomber, man or woman – could strike anywhere and we got used to the term 'non-state actors'. Only after the TTP slaughtered, on 16 December 2014, the young pupils and teachers of the Army Public School in Peshawar was Operation Zarb-i-Azb launched by the troops and there was respite from the fear of imminent suicide attacks. In my neighbourhood, the trades-people said the roads were safe again and there were no takers for protection money. All the killers of the students of the Army Public School and the attack on Karachi airport[21] in 2014 were foreign fighters – Chechens, Arabs, Afghans, Uzbeks. They had operated on our soil. Pakistan has lost more citizens to terrorism than any other country in the world.

The answers to my questions lie in the domain of high policy to which I was not privy. It is interesting, however, that although Karachi was dubbed as a most dangerous city, we found a way, poor and not so poor, to carry on with the business of life. There was a lot of resilience in society, augmented by the social change which had taken place in the country since independence. Many foreign analysts fail to understand this social change because their analysis is based on academic models fashioned for developed countries. I recognise two important catalysts of change: urbanisation and the women's revolution.

At school, I was taught that Pakistan was an agricultural country where 80 per cent of the population lived off the land in rural areas. This was particularly true because of the dependence on agriculture in East Pakistan. Karachi was the great magnet which drew people in search of livelihood from both parts of the country. It was described as *gharib parwar*, a 'poor friendly' or 'poor nurturing' city. They found employment in its industries, transport sector and sprawling urban infrastructure. As one family dug its roots here, it became a hub for attracting other families from the home district or village. Because the government built roads and highways, it became easier for people to travel to urban centres. But the phenomenon was not restricted to Karachi. Many other towns developed and it is estimated that about 50 per cent of the population lives in urban areas. The pull of Karachi continues, however; it is one of the fastest growing cities in the world.

When the rurals came to Karachi, they were dazzled by its wide roads and high-rise buildings, at the inner city distances. The young men may have felt liberated by a new-found freedom of expression and movement, but initially their elders were reluctant to bring their women to the city for fear that they would become too 'free'. Eventually, after the first generation of migrants settled down, their families became *Karachi wallas*. They wanted to stay in this megacity where they found not only livelihood but also medical facilities, education for their children, and entertainment. Even in the remotest parts of the country, one comes across people who have lived, worked and studied in Karachi and relate to it emotionally. As we discovered during Fatehyab's election campaigns, people of many nationalities have found shelter here, even from Myanmar (Burma) and far away Vietnam.

Why do I write that there has been a women's revolution? This in a country where crimes against women are reported almost daily in the media? When I was a child, my parents did not discriminate against me to favour my brothers. My family had a tradition of educating its women. When I was at college and university, they did not place restrictions on my movement. However, very early I realised that other women and girls did not enjoy the same freedom or protection. I knew that their distraught and misogynist men hurt them physically. I heard their cries.

I remember poor Sarwari sitting on the floor and sobbing silently in front of my father. She had merely tried to raise a few pennies for herself by doing domestic work. There was nobody to console her except my father who gave her a couple of rupees to buy soap for herself. And Sanobar Khan, who lived in a shack with his family opposite our house and threatened to punish his wife if she dared to step out in his absence. Or the burly domestic who said he had to beat his wife otherwise she would not behave herself. Or the elderly man with a sparse beard, employed in my office, who had treated his orphaned child wife so cruelly. Or the macho Buledi from Balochistan who told my sons that it was a curse to be born a woman. But I realised also that Partition had liberated many women who had migrated and lived in my neighbourhood. At the community level, some emerged as leaders because they had to find work to make ends meet.

The urge to find work to make ends meet was the compelling factor which encouraged women to step out of their homes. In the rural areas they had always worked in the fields – the elite women stayed veiled indoors – while in some areas the men sat in tea houses and smoked. But their work was not counted as labour either by their men or by the state. In the urban areas, they ventured first into the informal sector, exploited by middlemen – although some started working in factories. As the informal economy spread, so did the contribution they made from their homes and 'safe' places of work. Initially, the economic policies of governments did not specifically target women, but they gained from the positive development trends. The official statistics did no justice to their contribution.

My first contact with the women's movement came when Nigar Ahmad asked me to become a member of the board of governors of Aurat Foundation which she and Shahla Zia had founded in 1986.[22] I was its treasurer for a number of years and have been president of the board since 2011. Over time, it became the leading women's empowerment organisation in Pakistan with an outreach in every district. My association with Aurat Foundation opened my eyes to the women's struggle at the community level which I had viewed largely from a bureaucrat's perch. The progress we made was incremental – and there were many setbacks – as is true of any social movement. We realised that while advocacy was the bedrock of our struggle, it was necessary to work in sync with the government.

And governments responded. There was considerable initial scepticism in the bureaucracy, but the international environment favoured women, especially the initiatives taken by the United Nations.[23] Nor can one overlook the space created for women by an increasingly vibrant media. It would be puerile to divide empowerment into different segments, and if it can be done, political empowerment is its most important element. The affirmative policies of various governments and quotas for women in legislative bodies strengthened their political empowerment. From merely two women in the Constituent Assembly of Pakistan in 1947, today quotas ensure that women number 17 per cent in all legislative assemblies and in the Senate of Pakistan. But women's representation is much higher than the quotas and will keep increasing – about 22 per cent today – because they will continue to win elections on general seats also. This representation is below that of many African and Latin American countries, but it is higher than in India (14 per cent) and even Japan (merely 10 per cent).

Whatever the criticism about women being nominated, rather than being elected by political parties to the assemblies, their presence was a boon to the women's movement. Their most important contribution has been to law making. By and large, they have joined hands across political divides to get numerous pro-women laws passed over the last fifteen years. These laws relate to domestic violence, harassment at the workplace, rape and sexual harassment, anti-women practices such as forced marriage and denial of inheritance, punishment for acid throwing. All these laws were passed unanimously, even the clerics voted for them. The punishments should have been harsher, but a consensus was necessary to get the laws approved.

The young activists of Aurat Foundation lobbied tirelessly to get these laws adopted. Critics argue, what is the use of laws which are not implemented? The answer is that laws are the first line of defence. Facilitating women's participation in the election process as voters, political workers and candidates has been a slow but rewarding process. The women who have fought for their rights in all professions – politics, law, education, the media, business, the services and arts and culture – and the men who have supported them in the face of patriarchy and prejudice, are outstanding people.

There has been a revolution because women are now seen everywhere in the public space and on all platforms where, in a gathering of 200 men, I would be the only woman a few decades ago. We are well past the 'awareness raising' stage on which so much money is spent. As cabinet secretary, I attended the famous Kalash festivals in Chitral.[24] The road to Chitral was so perilous that, at every bend, I feared the car would fall into the valley below. In the evening, I called on the village headman. There was an air of tolerance in his house, for some women of his family who had converted to Islam, lived side by side with those who retained their original Kalash identity. I asked him if the government could help his community in any manner. I was sure he would ask for the construction of a safe road. But he said, 'please build a school for the girls. The boys can go to study in Peshawar, it is difficult for the girls to do so.' However, access to Chitral itself was important, so when I returned to Islamabad I tried, with whatever little influence I had, to press for the completion of the Lowari tunnel.[25]

Pakistan is placed almost at the bottom of all gender indices, but these indices reflect only averages and not the differentials between regions, social levels, urban and rural areas. I am moved when I see the women's contingents of the armed forces marching in the republic day parade, when women soldiers take over guard duties at Jinnah's mausoleum, when they participate in the colourful flag lowering ceremony at Wagah border, when women scientists and artists win international recognition, when Malala Yusufzai becomes a Nobel laureate and Samina Baig scales Mount Everest and all the Seven Summits.[26] These are all barriers broken in my lifetime. My only prayer now is that they should find the courage and strength to counter the conservative backlash which draws strength from the ideology of fundamentalists.

*   *   *

I have written about my family, my life and the times in which I lived, the story as I know and understand it. I want to conclude this narrative with a tribute to Fatehyab Ali Khan, my friend and companion for fifty years. When he passed away on 26 September 2010, I felt that a veil between me and the world had been lifted. Born in a conservative family, he was remarkably free of the prejudices which afflict people in cultures all over the world. He was discerning of the differences in the society in which we lived. When he led the youth in the agitation against Ayub Khan, he became a public figure at a very young age, but the glory did not make him arrogant. He was a teacher and passed his knowledge – and his ideals – to his young colleagues and admirers. In later life, when he entered mainstream politics, he took many brave stands on principle, but he was also a consensus builder. He never compromised with the reactionary forces in our country.

Fatehyab was a very civilised and refined person, in thought, expression and behaviour. In the large public meetings he addressed during the movement for restoration of democracy and of his own party, he spoke forcefully but he was not a rabble rouser. He had suffered at the hands of governments which tortured and imprisoned him and denied him education abroad. However, he never complained about his suffering either publicly or in private. He kept his pain to himself – for there must have been pain – covering it in a cloak of dignity and humour. Throughout his political career he fought for democracy, justice, the rule of law and decency in public life both from the platform of his party and through the constitution petitions he filed in the superior courts. He was a fearless fighter when others stepped back or sought refuge abroad. In the 'buy and compromise' political system, he could have got any ministry or position but he rebuffed all overtures. He was very hurt by the fragmentation of the left in our country and was sceptical of all efforts to achieve a united front because so many attempts had failed.

At a personal level, there are no words which can describe Fatehyab's devotion to me or mine to him. He was the anchor of my life and I tried to stand with him in all his endeavours and tribulations. Few husbands could be as tolerant and proud of their wife's career as he was of mine. He patiently created the space for me to function, and because of my frequent absences, lived alone for long periods of time. At every step, he supported me with his wisdom and foresight. Nobody knows what happens after death, but when he was being taken away for burial, I prayed that he would go to a happier and more peaceful world than the one in which he had lived.

Glossary

ajrak	block printed cotton shawl, symbol of Sindhi culture
alam	flag, here the standard of Husayn ibn Ali, the third Shia Imam
Allahus Samad	He is Allah, the Unique One
Ameerul Momineen	leader or commander of the faithful
anar	literally pomegranate, here a kind of firework
ashraf	belonging to the nobility or a respectable family
ashrafi	gold coin used in medieval India
ashurkhana	imambargah in Hyderabad Deccan
auliya	plural of wali, master or protector, often used to designate the status of a saint
Aurat Foundation	Women's Foundation
ayahs	women employed to look after children
babul	tree full of thorns
badshah	king or monarch
baithak	traditional seating area, particularly for men
bara	big
begar	unpaid labour
Bektashi	Sufi dervish order
beti	daughter
Bheel	indigenous ethnic tribal caste in India
biradari	clan or community
biwi	literally wife, also a word of respect for a woman
boni	first sale of the day
bulbuls	nightingales
burqa	concealing head to foot covering worn by some Muslim women
café de phoons	café made of straw
chaat	savoury snack
charpoy	bed strung with ropes
chauburji	four towers
chhinkas	containers for food held high on the roof
chhota	small
chirki billa	game played in squares on the ground
chooridar	tight fitting trousers worn both by men and women
chowkidar	watchman, guard
darbar	audience hall, court or reception

dargahs	shrines built over the graves of revered religious figures
dawakhanas	pharmacies
dervishi	act of living a simple life of poverty and austerity
desi munda	native boy
devdasis	female dancers dedicated to serve a Hindu deity in a temple
devrhi	outer part of the main entrance to a house, antechamber
dewan	prime minister in a princely state in India
dhobi	person whose occupation is washing clothes
diwan	collection of poems by a single author
doli	palanquin
Dom	community who express their culture through music, poetry and dance
Fakhr-i-Pakistan	pride of Pakistan
faqa shikni	breaking the fast, to be distinguished here from breaking the fast in Ramadan
fateha	Islamic funeral prayer
fatwa	ruling on a point of Islamic law given by a recognised authority
fiqh	Islamic jurisprudence or any school thereof
firman	sovereign's edict, grant or permit
gaddi	literally seat, here spiritual succession
ganj shikan	fort breaker
ghararas	flowing divided skirts traditionally worn by Muslim women in the subcontinent
gharib parwar	sheltering and providing livelihood to the poor
ghazals	lyrical poems
gol kamra	literally round room, drawing room
goras	pejorative for white men
Hadith	sayings of the Prophet
hakim	physician practising traditional medicine
hakimwalas	belonging to the family of practising physicians
hamds	poems in praise of God
har mal wala	seller of all kinds of goods
haris	peasants or cultivators of land in Sindh
haveli	traditional mansion
hawais	fireworks rising up towards the sky
hijab	headscarf worn by some Muslim women
hikmat	literally wisdom, here medicine
imambara kalan	big congregation hall of mourning for the martyrs of Karbala
itr	perfume
jagir	estate or feudal land grant with powers to collect public revenues

jamila	beautiful
Jat	member of a people living across northern India and in Pakistan
jathas	armed bodies of Sikhs
jawans	literally the youth, here young soldiers
jholis	bags usually made of cloth
jhonpri	thatched hut
jiyalas	devotees or passionate admirers and followers
jori jori	side by side, in pairs
julahas	community of weavers
kahars	men who carry palanquins, usually four in number
kala chhapra	black hangar
kala pani	literally black water, here the prison in the Andaman Islands
kalima	declaration of faith in Islam
Karachi wallas	residents of Karachi
katchi abadis	informal or temporary settlements
kathak	one of eight major forms of classical dance in the subcontinent
khaddar	homespun cotton cloth
khala	mother's sister
khanazads	Nizam's adopted sons and daughters
khanqah	Sufi lodge
khilafat	spiritual authority bestowed by a Sufi master on a disciple
khus	fragrant grass with a sweet aroma
khutba	sermon on a formal religious occasion
khwaja	honorific title used in the Muslim world
kirpans	curved swords or knives carried traditionally and legally by Sikhs
Koh-i-Qaf	legendary mountain in mythology of the Middle East
kufr	denial of the truth or article of faith in Islam
kundan	traditional form of gemstone jewellery
kutta gari	vehicle meant for transporting dogs
lakhs	one hundred thousand
lassi	yogurt drink
lathi	heavy iron bound stick used as a weapon
lathi charge	baton charge to disperse a crowd
majzub	one who is possessed by spirituality
manqabats	devotional poems in praise of Ali ibn Abi Talib, the first Shia Imam, or of a Sufi saint
mansur-i-mun	victory of my heart
maqsud-i-mun	intended, proposed of my heart
mari	entrance or outer part of the prison
marifat	mystical intuitive knowledge of spiritual truth

marsiyas	elegiac poems written to commemorate the martyrdom of Husayn ibn Ali, his family members and followers at Karbala in 680 CE
mashaikh	plural of shaykh, spiritual guide after the Prophet
mashqs	traditional water carrying bags made of goatskin
masnavi	poem written in rhyming couplets
mastanas	persons driven by intense emotions
maunds	forty kilos
mehndi	henna
mian log	gentry
minars	towers, milestones
mitti	mud
Mochi Darwaza	gate in Lahore city where large political gatherings are held
mohalla	neighbourhood
moras	round seats or stools made of bamboos
mullah	Islamic religious teacher or leader
munshi	secretary or clerk
murshid	guide or teacher
musaddas	genre of Urdu poetry
mynahs	birds of the starling family in South Asia
naats	poems in praise of the Prophet
Nahajul Balagha	collection of sermons, sayings and teachings of Imam Ali
naimat khana	cupboard with netting to store food
namak haram	ungrateful, not true to one's salt
naqqar khana	area where ceremonial drums are kept and played in a shrine
nauha khwani	reciting a dirge about the martyrdom of Husayn ibn Ali and his family members
nawar	broad tape made of thick cotton used to weave a bed
nazrs	offerings as gifts and tokens of fealty
niqab	veil worn by some Muslim women covering the whole face except the eyes
paan	betel leaf
palki	palanquin
parao ki zamin	land used by the army for encampment
pargana	former administrative unit introduced by the Delhi Sultanate
parwana	literally a moth circling a candle, a devotee
parwana-i-rahdari	permission to travel, passport
patakhas	fire crackers
peras	sweet made of flour, sugar and milk
peshkar	court clerk
phansi ghat	death cell

phuljharis	sparklers
piri muridi	link between a spiritual master and his disciple
pithu	game played by hitting a pile of stones with a ball
pucca	strong, solid
pugree	interest free refundable security deposit given to landlords
purdah	the practice of veiling or secluding women
qalandar	adherent of a non-Sharia Sufi order, the Qalandariyya
qaris	reciters of *qir'at*
qawwali	form of devotional music and singing, usually associated with Sufis
qazi	judge
qir'at	recitation of the Quran according to the styles recognised by various schools of recitation
roshnai	black ink
roti salan	bread and curry
sakar	spiritual intoxication
salaams	poetical salutations to Husayn ibn Ali and the members of his family
sam'a	devotional Sufi recitation accompanied by ecstatic dance and music
saqqas	water carriers
sarais	resting places for travellers
Sarak-i-Azam	Grand Trunk Road
sarangi nawaz	one who plays the sarangi, a musical instrument
sati	a Hindu practice in which a widow burns herself on her husband's funeral pyre
Shab-i-Barat	commemorated between 14 and 15 Sha'ban, the eighth month of the Islamic calendar, it is a night of prayer and salvation
shalwar kamiz	loose-fitting trousers worn by men and women in the subcontinent, and a shirt
shams	sun
Shariat	Islamic law based on the Quran and the teachings of the Prophet
sharnarthis	refugees
sherwani	buttoned knee length coat with a high collar
shuhada	martyrs
silsila	literally chain or link, for Sufis the chain of succession for spiritual knowledge
soyem	third day of mourning
soz	chanting of a dirge or lament, especially for the martyrdom of Husayn ibn Ali, his family members and followers
subedar	mid-level junior commissioned officer

takhti	writing tablet made of wood
taluqdar	large landholder responsible for collecting taxes
tamashas	grand shows or performances
tarafs	sides or quarters
tariqat	Sufi doctrine or path of spiritual learning
tazia	replica of the tombs of the martyrs of Karbala
tehsil	administrative unit or subdivision of a district
tehsildar	land revenue officer in a tehsil
tehzeeb	culture, refinement
thakur	feudal title for a landowner
tiktiki	sloping wooden platform to which a prisoner is strapped for whipping or lashing
tonga	single horse drawn two-wheeled carriage
ulema	plural of alim or scholar, here a recognised authority in Islamic law and doctrine
uncha chabutra	high platform
urs	literally wedding, the death anniversary of a Sufi saint signifying the union of his soul with his Maker
waderas	feudal lords or landowners
zakir	preacher on religious issues
zamindar	owner of an agricultural land holding
Zeba adab baja lata hai	Zeba offers his salutation
zenanas	women's living quarters
ziarat	pilgrimage to holy sites, especially associated with the Prophet and his descendants

Acknowledgements

Many people encouraged and assisted me in writing this memoir, for which I had started collecting material many years ago. My greatest debt is to the renowned historian, Francis Robinson, who read the entire manuscript. His critical and sensitive appraisal gave me confidence and I am very grateful to him for the suggestions he made to improve the manuscript.

Some friends and relatives read a few chapters of the manuscript. Among them was Poh Sim Plowright, formerly of Royal Holloway, University of London, whom I met many decades ago in the cafeteria of the British Museum when I was studying at Cambridge, and her husband, the famous BBC Radio producer, Piers Plowright. Ana Marija Besker, a colleague from my time as ambassador in Vienna, supported and followed the progress of this endeavour all along. She was Croatia's representative at the United Nations in Vienna, when I first met her.

Since this is the story of our shared upbringing, lives and experience, I was encouraged by my brother, Arif Hasan, who read many chapters of the manuscript. Often I consulted him about past events, drawing upon his memory, and I am thankful to him, as also to Sabiah Askari, both for her suggestions and her appreciation of my work. I want to acknowledge the encouragement and support provided by Khwaja Wasiq Hasan and Khwaja Rafat Ali through their recollections, in a series of extensive interviews, about our family's departure from Panipat during Partition. Unfortunately, they have both passed away. My gratitude also to my uncles, Mehdi Hasan and Jafar Hasan, for giving me original material on the history of our family. I thank all those who gave of their time and patience to share their knowledge and experience with me about the political events in my country: B.M.Kutty, Imam Ali Nazish, Husain Naqi, Mairaj Mohammad Khan, Saleem Cheema and, of course, Fatehyab himself. Many of them have not lived to see this memoir published.

When I was researching for this memoir, I spent many happy summers over a number of years in the British Library in London in different reading rooms, including the Asian and African Studies Reading Room, and thank their librarians and staff for their unfailing help and courtesy. My thanks also to the librarian and staff of the National Documentation Centre of the Cabinet Division in Islamabad who provided valuable material, and to Ishratullah Siddiqui, the librarian of The Pakistan Institute of International Affairs for giving me access to back issues of *Dawn* newspaper.

To my great regret, Yaman Raza has not lived to see the publication of this memoir; he passed away in 2019. With patience, sobriety and some humour, he typed revised versions of the manuscript, sometimes offering his own opinion. However, I recognise the assistance provided by Syed Rashid Ali and Khalid Hussain Khurram.

I could not have wished for a more professional editor than Gaynor Haliday and thank her for her very methodical, patient and friendly editing. At Pen & Sword Books, my thanks are due to Harriet Fielding for overseeing the production of the book and most of all, my gratitude to Lester Crook, the commissioning editor, for his subtle understanding of my narrative's ambience and historical setting and the consistent interest he has shown in my work.

Notes

Chapter 1: Panipat and My Family

1. Shaikh Muhammad Akram, *Aab-i-Kausar* (Lahore: Muhammad Ashraf, 1945, 7th ed.), p. 103.
2. ibid., pp. 137–9.
3. This account about my family is based on the history written by my ancestor, Khwaja Fazle Ali Khan, *Tarikh-o-Nasb Khwajgan-i-Panipat*. The manuscript is in Persian and excerpts have been compiled and translated into Urdu by Khwaja Jafar Hasan.
4. *Gazetteer of the Karnal District 1883–84 (*Reprint, Lahore: Sang-e-Meel Publications, 2001), p. 153.
5. *The Encyclopedia of Islam*, Volume I (Leiden: EJ Brill, 1960), p.109.
6. Khwaja Abdullah Ansari, *Intimate Conversations (Munajat)*, Introduction and translation by W.M. Thackerson Jr. (New York: Paulist Press, 1978), p. 172.
7. Sardar Sir Jogendra Singh, *The Persian Mystics: The Invocations of Sheikh Abdullah Ansari of Herat: A.D.1005–1090* (London: John Murray, 1939), p. 19.
8. Serge de Laugier de Beaurecueil, 'Abdullah Ansari: A Profile', in *Abdullah Ansari and Other Sufis of Afghanistan* (Kabul: Ministry of Information and Culture, 1976). Beaurecueil, a Dominican friar, has written extensively on Abdullah Ansari.
9. Abu-l-Fadl al Maybodi, *Kashf al-Asrar*, as quoted in A.G. Ravan Farhadi, *Abdullah Ansari of Herat (1006–1089 C.E.): An Early Sufi Master* (London: Curzon Press, 1996), p. 5.
10. ibid., p. 12.
11. *Nasbnama-i-Ansar-i-Panipat*, also known as *Nasbnama-i-Haideriya*, p. 21.
12. ibid., and Khwaja Fazle Ali Khan, *Tarikh-o-Nasb Khwajgan-i-Panipat*.
13. *Nasbnama-i-Ansar-i-Panipat*, p. 21.
14. 'Tark' means to give up or renounce. However, he is generally described as 'Turk' since he had migrated from Turkistan.
15. Khwaja Fazle Ali Khan, *Tarikh-o-Nasb Khwajgan-i-Panipat*.
16. Syed Muhammad Mian, *Panipat aur Buzurgan-i-Panipat* (Panipat: 1995), p. 35.
17. Khwaja Fazle Ali Khan, *Tarikh-o-Nasb Khwajgan-i-Panipat*.
18. ibid.
19. Syed Muhammad Mian, *Panipat aur Buzurgan-i-Panipat*, pp. 117–119.
20. Khwaja Fazle Ali Khan, *Tarikh-o-Nasb Khwajgan-i-Panipat*.
21. Khwaja Azhar Hasan, *Tazkira-i-Shehr-i-Marhum* (Lahore: 1991), pp. 20–3. It is probably erroneously stated in other works that he is buried in Panipat.
22. ibid., pp. 145–6.
23. Khwaja Malak Ali, *Tajalli-i-Nur* (Delhi: Hali Publishing House, 1939), Vol.1. The manuscript had been in my family since it was written, but was published only in 1939 and the original has since disappeared.

24. Khwaja Azhar Hasan, *Tazkira-i-Shehr-i-Marhum*, pp. 147–8.
25. *Gazetteer of the Karnal District 1883–84,* p. 22.
26. 'He who is powerful is the qalandar', Khwaja Azhar Hasan, *Tazkira-i-Shehr-i-Marhum*, p. 69.
27. *Gazetteer of the Karnal District 1883–1884*, pp. 28–9.
28. ibid., p. 27.
29. ibid., p. 257.
30. Ramesh Chandr Puhal Panipati, *Dastan-i-Hali* (Panipat: 2010), p. 149.
31. The names of these fifteen gates are given in ibid., pp. 149–55. One of these gates was Darwaza Ansar which was built by my (Ansari) family.
32. *Gazetteer of the Karnal District 1883–84,* p. 258.
33. Victor Jacquemont, *Letters from India: Describing a Journey in the British Dominions of India, Tibet, Lahore, and Cashmere During the Years 1828, 1829, 1830, 1831* (London: Edward Churton, 1834), Vol.1, p. 358.
34. Anjuman-i-Ahbab-i-Panipat in Karachi have given a list of sixty-six renowned personalities, all Muslims, buried in Panipat in their calendar for 2013. A list can also be found in Ramesh Chandr Puhal Panipati, *Dastan-i-Hali*, pp. 166–76.
35. *haidaryam qalandaram mastam, banda-i-Murtuza Ali hastam, peshwa-i-tamam rindanam, ke sag-i-ku-i shehr-i-Yazdanam*: I am the qalandar of Haider, the slave of Ali, the leader of all those who are intoxicated, because I am the dog of the lane of God's city. This quatrain is often wrongly attributed to Shahbaz Qalandar.
36. Abul Fazl, *Ain-i-Akbari*, Urdu translation by Muhammad Fida Ali Talib (Reprint, Lahore: Sang-e-Meel Publications, 2007), Vol. 2, p. 334.
37. Shaikh Muhammad Akram, *Aab-i-Kausar*, pp. 251–2.
38. Khwaja Fazle Ali Khan, *Tarikh-o-Nasb Khwajgan-i-Panipat*.
39. Shaikh Muhammad Akram writes that there were many occasions on which Bu Ali's behaviour did not conform to worldly standards of decency but the world, which he had abandoned, recognised him as a qalandar, *Aab-i-Kausar*, p. 251.
40. *Gazetteer of the Karnal District 1883–84,* p. 25.
41. Khwaja Fazle Ali Khan, *Tarikh-o-Nasb Khwajgan-i-Panipat*.
42. *Gazetteer of the Karnal District 1883–84*, p. 34. For an interesting sketch of Begum Samru, who was the leader of a mercenary force, see William Dalrymple, *The Last Mughal: The Fall of a Dynasty. Delhi. 1857* (London: Bloomsbury, 2006*),* pp. 238–9.
43. *Gazetteer of the Karnal District 1883–1884*, p. 30.
44. ibid., 35.
45. ibid., pp. 220–3.
46. ibid., p. 23.
47. V. D. Savarkar is credited with first describing the mutiny as the war of independence. For an account of his incarceration in the Andaman Islands, see S.N. Aggarwal, *The Heroes of Cellular Jail* (Delhi: Rupa & Co, 2007).
48. *Gazetteer of the Karnal District 1883–84*, p. 46.
49. For an early account of looting from Indian homes in Delhi by British officers, see Charles John Griffiths, *A Narrative of the Siege of Delhi* (London: John Murray, 1910). Details are also found in Christopher Hibbert, *The Great Mutiny: India 1857* (London: Penguin Books, 1982).

50. Sir John Kaye, *The History of Indian Mutiny: A detailed account of the synchronous incidents at Mirath, Delhi, Culcutta, Banaras, Allahabad, Kanpur, Punjab, N.W.F.P. and Kashmir during 1856–57* (Reprint, Lahore: Sang-e-Meel Publications, 2005), p. 153.
51. ibid., p. 145.
52. *Gazetteer of the Karnal District 1883–84*, p. 47.
53. Ghalib to Majruh, 7 March 1859, *Urdu-i-Mualla*, compiled by Syed Murtuza Hussain Fazil (Lahore: Majlis Taraqqi-i-Adab, 1969), Vol. 1, p. 373.
54. Zaheer Dehlavi, *Dastan-i-Ghadr (*Reprint, Lahore: Sang-e-Meel Publications, 2005), pp. 103–104.
55. Ramesh Chandr Puhal Panipati, *Dastan-i-Hali*, p. 278.
56. Lists of these qaris and qarias are given in Khwaja Azhar Hasan, *Tazkira-i-Shehr-i-Marhum*, pp.102–40.
57. The narrative about Muharram in Panipat is based on interviews of Khwaja Rafat Ali, my father's cousin, who was a famous marsiya and nauha reciter, on 23 May, 25 May, 26 May and 25 July in 1999.
58. Khwaja Ghulam Saiyidain (1904–71) was a close friend of my father. His family stayed in India after Partition. He became secretary, ministry of education in India after Partition.
59. Abdul Ghaffar Madholi, *Jamia Ki Kahani* (New Delhi: Qaumi Consil Bara'i Urdu Zaban, 2004), pp. 212–13.

Chapter 2: Hyderabad Interlude

1. Sarwar Hasan Archives (hereafter SHA) testimonial, Allahabad, 11 November 1899.
2. Testimonial, Allahabad, 11 November 1899, ibid.
3. Testimonial, Dhuri, 26 January 1901, ibid.
4. Testimonial, Dhuri, 11 February 1901, ibid.
5. Testimonial, Maymyo, 28 July 1902, ibid.
6. Testimonial, Rangoon, 9 September 1907, ibid.
7. Testimonial, Maymyo, 11 September 1907, ibid.
8. Letter of resignation, 22 July 1907, ibid.
9. Letter, 14 August, 1907, ibid.
10. Narendra Luther, *Hyderabad: Memoirs of a City* (Hyderabad: Orient Longman Limited, 1995), p. 67.
11. Omar Khalidi, *Romance of the Golconda Diamonds* (Ahmedabad: Mapin Publishing Private Limited, 1999), pp. 21–5.
12. Omar Khalidi gives a list of famous diamonds from these mines in ibid.
13. V.K. Bawa, *The Last Nizam: The Life and Times of Mir Osman Ali Khan* (New Delhi: Viking, 1992), p. 57.
14. Ramesh Chandr Puhal Panipati, *Dastan-i-Hali*, p. 87.
15. John Zubrzycki, *The Last Nizam: The Rise and Fall of India's Greatest Princely State* (London: Picador, 2006), pp. 20–1.
16. V.K. Bawa, *The Last Nizam*, p. 4.
17. John Zubrzycki, *The Last Nizam*, p. 29.
18. ibid., p. 34.
19. ibid., p. 42.

20. Edward Thomson, *The Making of the Indian Princes* (London: Oxford University Press, 1943), p. 6.
21. John Zubrzycki, *The Last Nizam*, p. 45.
22. ibid., p. 51.
23. Quoted in ibid., p. 73.
24. ibid., p. 86.
25. ibid., p. 69.
26. ibid., p. 88.
27. Harriet Ronken Lynton and Mohini Rajan, *The Days of the Beloved* (Berkeley and Los Angeles : University of California Press, 1974), p. 67.
28. ibid., p. 71.
29. John Zubrzycki, *The Last Nizam*, p. 102.
30. D. F. Karaka, *Fabulous Mogul: Nizam VII of Hyderabad* (London: D. Verschoyle, 1955) p. 90.
31. Narendra Luther, *Hyderabad: Memoirs of a City*, p. 251.
32. Lynton and Rajan, *The Days of the Beloved*, p. 72.
33. ibid., p. 79.
34. Quoted in V.K. Bawa, *The Last Nizam*, p. 72.
35. ibid., p. 317.
36. ibid., p. 79.
37. ibid., p. 91.
38. D.F. Karaka, *Fabulous Mogul*, p. 97.
39. V.K Bawa, *The Last Nizam*, p. 119.
40. John Zubrzycki, *The Last Nizam*, p. 119.
41. Mushtaq Ahmad Khan, *Karvan-i-Hayat* (Lahore: 1974), p. 72.
42. ibid., p. 70.
43. Anwar Hasan, Charge List on handing over charge at Raichur, 12 January 1912, SHA.
44. Extracts from ASE's Inspection Notes of Raichur Distt in Isfander & Furwardi 1321, ibid.
45. Letter, 10 April 1910, ibid.
46. Letter, 10 October 1910, ibid.
47. Mushtaq Ahmad Khan, *Karvan-i-Hayat*, p. 57.
48. Omar Khalidi, *A Guide to Architecture in Hyderabad, Deccan, India* (MIT: Aga Khan Program for Islamic Architecture, 2008), p. 70.
49. Nawab Ali Yavar Jung (1905–76) was India's ambassador to many countries after Partition, vice chancellor of Aligarh Muslim University 1965–8, and governor of Maharashtra 1971–6.
50. Omar Khalidi, *A Guide to Architecture in Hyderabad, Deccan, India*, p. 122.
51. Details of the Hyderabad monuments are based on ibid.
52. ibid., p. 235. Omar Khalidi wrote to my family on 7 November 2006: 'I would never have known that your grandfather was the architect of this majestic building but for a one-line reference in a non-architecture article by Nawab Ali Yavar Jung.'
53. ibid.
54. Details of the construction of the house are found in SHA.

55. Abdullah remained with our family for the rest of his life. He passed away in 1996 in Karachi.
56. Sarwar Hasan to Saiyidain, 18 May 1920, SHA.
57. ibid.
58. Saiyidain to Sarwar Hasan, 23 May 1920, ibid.
59. Unfortunately copies of only two of my father's letters to Saiyidain are available in his archive. I have been unsuccessful in gaining access to his own letters from Saiyidain's family in Delhi, if they have survived.
60. Saiyidain to Sarwar Hasan, n.d., ibid.
61. Saiyidain to Sarwar Hasan, 24 October 1920, ibid.
62. Saiyidain to Sarwar Hasan, 3 November 1920, ibid.
63. Narendra Luther, *Hyderabad: Memoirs of a City*, p. 213.
64. Notes by Sarwar Hasan on the ship's stationery, probably October 1922, SHA.
65. Mushtaq Ahmad Khan (1903–2005) became agent general for Hyderabad in Pakistan after Partition.
66. A.R. Cornelius (1903–91) was studying at Selwyn College. He became the chief justice of Pakistan, 1960–8.
67. Hashim Mohommed Ali (b.1895) was a scientist and great-grandson of Sir Syed Ahmad Khan. He kept in touch with us long after my father passed away.
68. Text of Sarwar Hasan's speech, SHA.
69. Ali Maqsood Hameedi, artist and intellectual, was my father's contemporary at Aligarh.
70. *The Granta*, 22 May 1925, p. 440.
71. ibid., 20 November 1925, p. 114.
72. Testimonial, 7 September 1928, SHA. E. Carey Francis was a fellow of Peterhouse and university lecturer.
73. See Saeed Naqvi, *Being the Other: The Muslim in India* (New Delhi: Adelph Book Company, 2016).
74. Saiyidain to Sarwar Hasan, 13 September 1924, SHA.

Chapter 3: Life in Intelligence School

1. The Indian Institute of International Affairs was located at 6, King Edward Road, Delhi. By 1945, it had shifted to 8A Kashi House, Connaught Place, New Delhi.
2. The following account of how the Indian Institute of International Affairs was shifted from Delhi to Karachi is based on K. Sarwar Hasan, 'The Pakistan Institute of International Affairs: How it was Established', SHA. Also published in *Pakistan Horizon*, Vol. 61, Nos 1–2, 2008.
3. Ishtiaq Hussain Qureshi (1903–81) was a historian, member of the Constituent Assembly of Pakistan, deputy minister of refugee rehabilitation and minister of education in Pakistan, and vice chancellor of the University of Karachi, 1961–71.
4. Mumtaz Hasan (1907–74) became Pakistan's finance secretary, officiating governor of the State Bank of Pakistan, deputy chairman of the Planning Commission and managing director of the National Bank of Pakistan. Chaudhry Mohammad Ali (1905–80) rose to become the finance secretary, establishment secretary, finance minister and briefly, prime minister of Pakistan.

5. K. Sarwar Hasan, *Pakistan and the United Nations* (New York: Manhattan Publishing Company, 1960).
6. Taqi Ahsan eventually migrated to Canada with his family.

Chapter 4: Farewell to Panipat
1. 'Quaid-i-Azam, the great leader, has declared that we will definitely achieve Pakistan', Mehdi Hasan, interview and note to the author, February 2015.
2. Khwaja Rafat Ali, interview, 23 May 1999.
3. *Civil and Military Gazette* (Lahore), 13 August 1947, also *The Statesman* (Calcutta), 15 August 1947.
4. *The Statesman*, 5 June 1947. The same views on reunion were expressed by Acharya Kripalani, Abul Kalam Azad, Sarojini Naidu, Rajendra Prasad, Rajagopalachari and the All India Congress Committee. References in Masuma Hasan, 'The Transfer of Power to Pakistan and its Consequences', PhD dissertation, University of Cambridge, 1967, p. 93.
5. Leonard Mosely, *The Last Days of the British Raj* (London: Weidenfeld and Nicolson, 1962), p. 248.
6. Mountbatten of Burma, *Time Only to Look Forward* (London: Nicholas Kaye, 1949), p. 22.
7. Based on Jinnah's negotiations with the Sikh leaders and his offer as dealt with in detail in Masuma Hasan, 'The Transfer of Power to Pakistan and its Consequences', pp. 122–8. See also Jamil-ud-Din Ahmad (ed.), *Speeches and Writings of Mr Jinnah* (Lahore: Ashraf, 6th ed., 1960), Vol. I., p. 167.
8. M.A.H. Ispahani, *Qaid-e-Azam Jinnah As I Knew Him* (Karachi: Forward Publications Trust, 1966), p. 219.
9. Details of all these preparations are found in Police Abstracts of Intelligence, Government of the Punjab, Lahore, 1946–7.
10. *Dawn* (Karachi), 14 April 1960.
11. ibid., 24 July 1959, extracts from the Maharaja of Patiala's published reminiscences.
12. Nicholas Mansergh, editor-in-chief, *The Transfer of Power 1942–7* (London: HMSO, 1983, hereafter ToP), Vol. XII, p. 65.
13. ibid., pp. 117–18.
14. Copy of D.O. dated 28th July 1947 from the Central Intelligence Officer, Lahore, to the Deputy Director (A), I.B., H.D, Government of India, New Delhi.
15. ToP, Vol. XII, p. 538.
16. ibid., p. 559.
17. The records of the Punjab Boundary Commission were made available in full for the first time to the author for research for her PhD thesis at Cambridge, 'The Transfer of Power to Pakistan and its Consequences'. The records were subsequently published in 1983 in four volumes by the National Documentation Centre Lahore: *The Partition of the Punjab 1947: A Compilation of Official Documents*.
18. See especially Police Abstracts of Intelligence, Government of the Punjab, Lahore, for 1946–7. Also ToP, Vols. XI and XII.
19. Papers of Maj-Gen Thomas Wynford Rees (hereafter Rees Papers), India Office Records, hereafter IOR: Mss Eur F274/12 and 17.

20. IOR, Mss Eur F274/48, ibid.
21. This account is based on Major General T.W. Rees, 'Report on The Punjab Boundary Force (The PBF), 1 August-Midnight 1/2 September 1947', 15 November, 1947, IOR, Mss Eur F274/70, ibid.
22. Col. J.N. Mackay, 'Report on the Situation in Dalhousie', 4 September 1947, IOR, Mss Eur F274/50, ibid.
23. 'Report on the Punjab Boundary Force', 15 November, 1947, IOR, Mss Eur F274/70, ibid.
24. Later Field Marshal Ayub Khan, president of Pakistan.
25. 'Report dated 11th October 1947 made by Brigadier M. Ayub Khan, Liaison Officer, Punjab Boundary Force' in *Disturbances in East Punjab and Contiguous Areas During and After August 1947: Selected official statements and reports, Part II* (Karachi: Governor-General's Press, 1948), p. 17.
26. 'Extract from the situation report on the Muslim evacuees in the East Punjab as on 7th September 1947 by Mr E. de V. Moss, Pakistan Commissioner for Refugees and Evacuees', ibid., p. 45.
27. IOR, Mss Eur F274/77, Rees Papers.
28. Ambala Meeting, 17th August 1947, IOR, Mss Eur F274/52, ibid.
29. Jullundur Conference, 22nd August 1947, IOR, Mss Eur F274/66, ibid.
30. 'Copy of a note prepared by the Chief Liaison Officer, West Punjab' in *Disturbances in East Punjab and Contiguous Areas During and After August 1947, Part II*, pp. 5–13.
31. 'Extract from the situation report on the Muslim evacuees in the East Punjab as on 7th September, 1947 by Mr E. de V. Moss, Pakistan Commissioner for Refugees and Evacuees', ibid., p. 44.
32. Rees to Auchinleck, 21 August 1947, IOR, Mss Eur F274/56, Rees Papers.
33. 'Notes on situation', IOR, Mss Eur F274/66, ibid.
34. 'Copy of a note prepared by the Chief Liaison Officer, West Punjab', in *Disturbances in East Punjab and Contiguous Areas During and After August 1947, Part II*, p. 13.
35. *Hindustan Times* (New Delhi), 5 December 1947.
36. Note in IOR, Mss Eur F274/62, Rees Papers.
37. Maulana Abul Kalam Azad, *India Wins Freedom* (the complete version) (New Delhi: Orient BlackSwan, 2009), pp. 198, 225.
38. In a speech to the diplomatic corps, 12 September 1947, IOR, Mss Eur F274/62, Rees Papers. For the exchange of population between Turkey and Greece, see Bruce Clark, *Twice a Stranger:The Mass Expulsions that Forged Modern Greece and Turkey* (Cambridge Mass: Harvard University Press, 2006).
39. 'Letters and a report on the series of communal disturbances in India between 1946–47', IOR, Mss Eur F274/48, Rees Papers.
40. Details in *Disturbances in East Punjab and Contiguous Areas During and After August 1947: Selected statements of non-officials, Part III* (Karachi, Governor-General's Press, 1948).
41. See G.D. Khosla, *Stern Reckoning: A survey of the events leading up to and following the partition of India* (Delhi: Oxford University Press, 1989) and M.S. Randhawa, *Out of the Ashes: An account of the rehabilitation of refugees from West Pakistan in rural areas of East Punjab* (Chandigarh: Public Relations Dept., Punjab, 1954).

42. *Disturbances in East Punjab and Contiguous Areas, Part III*, p. 66.
43. *Tuzak-i-Timuri: The Autobiography of Timur*, edited by Sir H.M. Elliot and John Dowson (Reprint, Lahore: Sang-e-Meel Publications, 2004), p. 64.
44. Nehru-Liaquat Appeal: 'To the People of East and West Punjab', Mountbatten Papers: IOR, Neg 15552, File 128.
45. All references to my grandfather's narrative are drawn from 'Statement of Khwaja Akhtar Hussain (sic: should be Akhtar Hasan), Retired Tehsildar, Panipat, Distt. Karnal', *Disturbances in East Punjab and Contiguous Areas, Part III*, pp. 3–12.
46. See statements of officials and non-officials in ibid., Parts II and III.
47. *Disturbances in East Punjab and Contiguous Areas During and After August 1947: Chronological summary of recorded events, Part I* (Karachi: Governor-General's Press, 1948), p. 85.
48. 'Information on Jathas', IOR, Mss Eur F274/54, Rees Papers.
49. Mehdi Hasan, note to the author. Mehdi Hasan travelled in this convoy to Lahore.
50. *Disturbances in East Punjab and Contiguous Areas During and After August 1947, Part I*, p. 89.
51. Rajmohan Gandhi, *Mohandas: A True Story of a Man, his People and an Empire* (Delhi: Penguin Viking, 2006), p. 659.
52. ibid., p. 660.
53. ibid.
54. Khwaja Rafat Ali, interviews, 23–26 May 1999, 25 July 1999.
55. Khwaja Wasiq Hasan, interviews, 5 and 23 March 1999.

Chapter 5: Fatehyab and the Anti-Ayub Movement

1. The narrative about Fatehyab's family and their migration to Pakistan is based on an interview of his elder sister, Sughra Bano, on 18 April 2005 and of Fatehyab on 7 April 2005.
2. Fatehyab Ali Khan, interview, 4 June 2004.
3. ibid.
4. Ahmad Zaheer Khan, *Merey aziz tareen dost Fatehyab Ali Khan ki yad mein*.
5. Adibul Hasan Rizvi is the legendary founder of the Sindh Institute of Urology and Transplantation (SIUT). Haroon Ahmad is one of the pioneers of psychiatry in Pakistan.
6. See Hasan Zaheer, *The Times and Trial of the Rawalpindi Conspiracy 1951* (Karachi: Oxford University Press, 1998).
7. For Z.H. Hashmi's version, see *Dawn*, 9 January 1953.
8. *Dawn*, 12 and 13 January 1953.
9. Imam Ali Nazish Amrohi gave me several interviews in 1990. Unfortunately, these interviews were called off abruptly at Fatehyab's insistence because Amrohi's colleagues suspected that I was gathering information for the establishment. However, his recorded narrative was a rare moment of trust in an 'outsider' and much to my amusement, he occasionally addressed me as 'comrade'. He gave these interviews when the Soviet Union had already started unravelling, and although he defended the strategies his party had followed, he narrated his story with some degree of introspection.

10. *Dawn*, 11 January 1953.
11. ibid., 9 January 1953.
12. ibid., and editorial, 'Yesterday's Tragedy', ibid.
13. Fatehyab Ali Khan, interview, 21 October 2006.
14. ibid.
15. ibid.
16. Mohammad H.R. Talukdar (ed.), *Memoirs of Huseyn Shaheed Suhrawardy* (Karachi: Oxford University Press, 1989), p. 189.
17. Fatehyab Ali Khan, interview, 21 October 2006.
18. ibid.
19. Ahmad Zaheer Khan, *Merey aziz tareen dost Fatehyab Ali Khan ki yad mein*.
20. Fatehyab Ali Khan, interview, 21 October 2006.
21. ibid.
22. The material on coffee houses, their culture and the eateries in Karachi is drawn from Fatehyab's interview, 21 October 2006 and B.M. Kutty's interviews, 14 and 23 February, and 2 March 2005.
23. Fatehyab Ali Khan, interview, 21 October 2006.
24. It was a reaction also to Prime Minister Suhrawardy's support to Britain and France during the Suez crisis. See S. Akhtar Ehtisham, *Across Three Continents: A South Asian View*, n.d., p. 106. Ehtisham was a prominent student activist of Dow Medical College who became an orthopaedic surgeon.
25. ibid.
26. Nazish Amrohi, interview, 5 July 1990.
27. S. Akhtar Ehtisham, *Across Three Continents*, p. 109.
28. ibid., and editorial, 'Crime most foul,' *Dawn*, 20 February 1961.
29. *Dawn*, 28 February 1961.
30. S. Akhtar Ehtisham, *Across Three Continents*, p. 111.
31. Husain Naqi, interview, 29 August 2009 and 'Students' struggle in historical perspective', 10 November 2011, pakistanhorizon.wordpress.com. He was being held in the same lock-up.
32. *Dawn*, 8 March 1961.
33. ibid., 10 March 1961.
34. The bailed out students were Akhtar Ehtisham, Husain Naqi, Hasan Raza Rizvi, Masood Jafri, Anwar Saleem, Mukhtar Ahmad Shaikh.
35. *Dawn*, 17 March 1961.
36. ibid., 23 March 1961.
37. ibid., 25 March 1961.
38. Processions were taken out in Peshawar, Rawalpindi, Sialkot, Multan, Sukkur, Lahore and Thatta.
39. *Dawn*, 26 March 1961.
40. ibid., 12 March 1961.
41. ibid., 31 March 1961.
42. The material on their incarceration in Bahawalpur prison is drawn from Mairaj Mohammad Khan, interview, 13 April 2012.
43. *Dawn*, 3 September 1962.
44. ibid., 5 September 1962.
45. Mairaj Mohammad Khan, interview, 21 July 2012.

46. Apart from Fatehyab they were Mairaj Mohammad Khan, Khurram Mirza, Husain Naqi, Jauhar Hussain, Nafees Siddiqi, Amir Haider Kazmi, Nawaz Butt, Abdul Wahid Bashir, Ali Mukhtar Rizvi, Agha Jafar and Syed Saeed Hasan.

47. *Dawn*, 15, 16 September 1962.

48. ibid., 23 September 1962.

49. ibid., 24 September 1962.

50. ibid., 27 September 1962.

51. ibid., 28 September 1962. Besides the University of Karachi, the colleges affected by the strike were D.J. Science College, S.M. Arts College, NED College, Karachi College for Women, Islamia College, Government College, Sir Syed Girls College, Raza Ali College and Nabi Bagh College.

52. ibid., 30 September 1962.

53. ibid., 5 October 1962. The events of October 1962 were reported daily in all newspapers, but I have consulted *Jang* and referred only to *Dawn* for the month of October 1962.

54. For the government's press note on the clash, see ibid.

55. For the list of these twenty-five unions, see *Dawn*, 8 October 1962.

56. ibid., 9 October 1962.

57. See the government's press note, ibid., 16 October 1962.

58. Husain Naqi, 'Students' struggle in historical perspective', 10 November 2011, pakistanhorizon.wordpress.com. Also I.A. Rehman's tribute, 'In Memory of Fatehyab Ali Khan: The Politics of Dissent', *Dawn* and *News International*, 25 January 2015 and pakistanhorizon.wordpress.com.

59. The run up to Bangladesh was marked by students' participation on a massive scale, but it was limited to East Pakistan.

Chapter 6: Education and Employment

1. From 1941 to 1951, Karachi's population grew from 435,887 to 1,137,667. In 1961, it was 2,044,044. Arif Hasan, *Understanding Karachi: Planning and Reform for the Future* (Karachi: Citi Press, 2002, 2nd ed.), p. 39.

2. Ecochard made master plans for Beirut and its suburbs (1963), Damascus (1964–8), Tabriz (1969), regional master plan for Corsica (1969), the city centre of Tehran (1978), redevelopment of the city centre of Meshed (1971) and for the new capital of the Sultanate of Oman (1973).

3. See Architect Arif Hasan's views on Interface. Also Mariam Karrar and Shabbir Kazmi, 'Architecture: Ecochard in Karachi', *Dawn*, 26 November 2017.

4. Taj Abidi passed away in 1989.

5. Mahmud Husain Khan (1907–75) was vice chancellor of Dacca University 1960–3, and the University of Karachi 1971–5. Earlier he had served as minister for education 1952–3. He was the younger brother of Zakir Husain, third president of India.

6. Testimonial, 3 December 1962, Fatehyab's Papers, hereafter FP.

7. For the debate on women's education, see T.E.B. Howarth, *Cambridge Between Two Wars* (London: Collins, 1978).

8. Leila Ahmed became professor of women's studies and religion at the Harvard Divinity School. See her latest work, *A Quiet Revolution: The Veil's Resurgence, from the Middle East to America* (New Haven: Yale University Press, 2011).

9. Graham Castor, fellow of Gonville and Caius College; Gar Alperovitz, American political economist and historian, fellow of many institutions and policy adviser; Irfanul Haque, economist, worked for the World Bank; Kaniz Sharif studied English at New Hall, taught at Kinnaird College Lahore; Camellia Panjabi, economist, the diva of Indian cuisine; Ted Margadant, historian, professor of history at the University of California Davis, now professor emeritus; Amit Bhaduri, unconventional Indian economist, advocate of alternative development strategies; Simon Schama, celebrated British historian, now professor of history and art history at Columbia University, New York; Anil Seal, fellow of Trinity College and with John Gallagher one of the founders of the Cambridge School of Indian History, founder director of the Cambridge Commonwealth Trust and director of many other educational trusts.

10. David Harkness, 'Nicholas Mansergh (1910–91), Historian of Modern Ireland', *Etudes Irlandaises*, 1994, Vol. 19, No. 1, p. 94.

11. ibid., p. 93. See W.K. Hancock's tribute, 'Nicholas Mansergh: Some Recollections and Reflections' in Norman Hiller and Philip Wigley (eds.), *The First British Commonwealth: Essays in Honour of Nicholas Mansergh* (London: Frank Cass, 1980). Also the obituary in *The Eagle* (Cambridge: St John's College, 1991), pp. 35–9.

12. See Chapter 4, note 12.

13. Philip Abrams, *Historical Sociology* (Ithaca: Cornell University Press, 1982).

14. Ronald Robinson and John Gallagher, *Africa and the Victorians: The Official Mind of Imperialism* (New York: St Martin's, 1961).

15. John Maynard Keynes 1883–1946; Joan Robinson 1903–83; Piero Sraffa 1898–1983; Nicholas Kaldor 1908–86; Richard Kahn 1905–89; Austin Robinson 1897–1993.

16. Nazir Ahmad Chaudhry, *Anarkali, Archives and Tomb of Sahib Jamal: A Study in Perspective* (Lahore: Sang-e-Meel Publications, 2002).

17. *The Partition of the Punjab 1947: A Compilation of Official Documents*. See my review of this publication, 'Punjab Boundary Commission and the Radcliffe Award', in *Dawn*, 12 and 15 May 1984.

18. Masuma Hasan (ed.), *Pakistan in a Changing World: Essays in Honour of K. Sarwar Hasan* (Karachi: Pakistan Institute of International Affairs, 1978).

19. Sushila Sham Nath wrote a touching response to my father's letter of condolence on her husband's passing away.

20. Before our family left Delhi for Karachi in August 1947, my father sent some of his teak furniture for storage to Ravi Brothers, a furniture store in Kashmere Gate. The list is available in his papers, the shop still exists.

21. Norman Harper from The Australian Institute of International Affairs, co-author of *Australia and the United Nations* (New York: Manhattan Publishing Company, 1959).

22. George Masterman's letter to the author, 16 January 1965. Later he became Ombudsman of New South Wales and Queen's Counsel.

23. Dr Kamal Hossain, later member of the Awami League, minister of law 1972–3, and foreign minister of Bangladesh 1973–5.

24. A.B.A. Haleem, chairman of The Pakistan Institute of International Affairs, was the leader of our delegation to the conference.

25. Susan Haque, wife of the economist Irfanul Haque.
26. Percival Spear (1901–82), historian, fellow of Selwyn College and author of the tenderly written, *The Twilight of the Mughals: Studies in Late Mughal Delhi* (Cambridge: Cambridge University Press, 1951). Hugh Tinker (1921–2000), was professor at the School of Oriental and African Studies, London.
27. Hassan Habib, *Babus, Brahmins and Bureaucrats* (Lahore: 1972).
28. Apart from his landmark judgements, see his memoir, *Testament of a Liberal* (Karachi: Oxford University Press, 2000).

Chapter 7: The Bhutto Years
1. Abul Hashem was elected general secretary of the Bengal Provincial Muslim League in 1941 and believed in a united and independent Bengal. He moved from West Bengal to Dacca in 1950 and later became Director of the Islamic Academy.
2. The memorial meeting was held in the library of the Institute on 26 February 1973.
3. Mairaj Mohammad Khan joined the PPP when it was founded. Bhutto appointed him minister of state for political affairs. He resigned in October 1972 and was arrested by Bhutto. Subsequently, he formed his own political party, Qaumi Mahaz-i-Azadi. To the disappointment of his followers, he joined Tehreek-i-Insaf, only to leave it after becoming disenchanted with Imran Khan. He held Bhutto responsible for the loss of East Pakistan, *Dawn*, 26 October 1977. He passed away in 2016.
4. M. Asghar Khan, *My Political Struggle* (Karachi: Oxford University Press, 2008), p. 17.
5. ibid., p. 15.
6. ibid., p. 20. For Bhutto's version of the events leading to the division of Pakistan, see *The Great Tragedy* (Karachi: Pakistan Peoples Party, 1971).
7. Related to me by Ibrahim in our meeting in Karachi, March 1982.
8. M. Asghar Khan, *We've Learnt Nothing from History – Pakistan: Politics and Military Power* (Karachi: Oxford University Press, 2005), pp. 54, 62. It appears, however, that Yahya Khan was also in the loop. See Mubashir Hasan, *The Mirage of Power: An Inquiry into the Bhutto Years 1971–1977* (Karachi: Oxford University Press, 2000), Chapter 1.
9. *Memoirs of Lt. Gen. Gul Hassan Khan* (Karachi: Oxford University Press, 1993), p. 347 ff.
10. ibid., p. 373.
11. ibid., p. 364.
12. Gul Hassan's version, ibid., pp. 367–75; Mubashir Hasan's version, *The Mirage of Power*, pp. 82–5.
13. *Memoirs of Lt. Gen. Gul Hassan Khan*, p. 378.
14. ibid., p. 380.
15. ibid., p. 407.
16. ibid., p. 416.
17. ibid., pp. 428–9.
18. Sherbaz Khan Mazari, *A Journey to Disillusionment* (Karachi: Oxford University Press, 1999), details in Chapter 7.

19. ibid., p. 146.
20. ibid., pp. 172, 212, 363, 396, 399, 524.
21. M. Asghar Khan, *We've Learnt Nothing from History*, p. 22.
22. ibid., pp. 35–6. He said the same to Asghar Khan in 1969: Asghar Khan, *My Political Struggle*, p. 16.
23. M. Asghar Khan, *We've Learnt Nothing from History*, p.60.
24. ibid., p. 38.
25. ibid., p. 43.
26. ibid., p. 50.
27. ibid., p. 57.
28. ibid.
29. ibid., p. 59.
30. ibid., p. 122.
31. ibid., p. 159.
32. Mubashir Hasan, *The Mirage of Power*, pp. 242–3.
33. Bhutto's relationship with Ghulam Mustafa Khar, ibid., pp. 238–44. Bhutto feared assassination from Khar, Mumtaz Bhutto, Hayat Sherpao among others.
34. Such as Mukhtar Rana and Hanif Ramay.
35. See Mubashir Hasan, *The Mirage of Power*, about how Bhutto humiliated Hanif Ramay, p. 242 and Kausar Niazi, p. 272.
36. The J.A. Rahim episode has been well recorded in numerous works. Mubashir Hasan writes that even after the event was over, 'true to feudal tradition, Bhutto made Rahim's life miserable and humiliated him and his son Sikander no end', *The Mirage of Power*, p. 256.
37. ibid., p. 279.
38. Those who left Bhutto or were pushed out were Mahmud Ali Kasuri, Rafi Raza, (later returned as minister for production), Mumtaz Bhutto, Hanif Ramay, Khursheed Hasan Mir, Mairaj Mohammad Khan, Mubashir Hasan, J.A. Rahim, Ghulam Mustafa Khar.
39. Rafi Raza, *Zulfikar Ali Bhutto and Pakistan* (Karachi: Oxford University Press, 1997), p. 381.
40. The parties in the alliance, also called *nau sitaray* (nine stars), were Tehrik-i-Istiqlal, Jamiat Ulema-i-Islam, Jamiat Ulema-i-Pakistan, Jamaat-i-Islami, Pakistan Democratic Party, Muslim League, National Democratic Party, Khaksar Tehrik and Muslim Conference.
41. For figures of the number of casualties, processions and assets destroyed or damaged, see M. Asghar Khan, *We've Learnt Nothing from History*, pp. 139–40. As Bhutto's attorney general, Yahya Bakhtiar also gave figures for casualties and damage to public and private property on 6 June 1977, referred to by the Supreme Court of Pakistan in its judgement on Nusrat Bhutto's petition, R I of 1977, PLD 77 SC 657.
42. For the slender sovereignty available to Third World countries, see Z.A. Bhutto, *The Myth of Independence* (Karachi: Oxford University Press, 1969).
43. The PWP was formed under the leadership of Mirza Ibrahim, president of the Railway Workers' Union.
44. Bhutto's rejoinder, 26 October 1977, www.bhutto.org.
45. Supreme Court of Pakistan's judgement, 10 November 1977, PLD 77 SC 657.

46. Constitution Petition R II of 1977, 22 October 1977, is available in FP.
47. All these petitions are available in FP.
48. Misc. Petition No. 1 R of 79: Legal Objections to the Assistance of Mr Sharifuddin Pirzada Before This Honourable Court, FP.
49. *The News* (Karachi), 22 November 1998.
50. For example, Lal Mai was flogged in Khanpur in the presence of thousands of people for taking a paramour.
51. Copy of telegram, 4 January 1979, FP. The programme was subsequently challenged also by Bhutto and Kausar Niazi.
52. Contempt of court application under Article 204 of the Constitution of Pakistan 1973, FP.
53. Copy of telegram, 8 February 1979, ibid.
54. Copy of telegram, 11 February 1979, ibid.
55. Copy of telegram to CMLA, 11 February 1979, ibid.
56. Colonel Rafiuddin, *Bhutto Ke Akhri 323 Din (Last 323 Days of Bhutto)* (Lahore: Ahmad Publications, 2012, 2nd edition).
57. ibid., p. 180.
58. ibid., pp. 53–4.
59. ibid., p. 54.
60. ibid., p. 16.
61. Saleem Cheema's recollections are based on this interview, 20 November 2009, Lahore.
62. *Dawn*, 2 March 1979.
63. Colonel Rafiuddin, *Bhutto Ke Akhri 323 Din*, pp. 97, 189, 194.
64. ibid., p. 131.
65. *Dawn*, 30 March 1979.
66. ibid.
67. ibid., 1 April 1979. Abdul Hafeez Pirzada filed a clemency appeal under Article 45 of the Constitution of Pakistan 1973.
68. ibid.
69. ibid., 5 April 1979.
70. Quoted in J.C. Batra, 'Trial and Execution of Zulfikar Ali Bhutto', www.bhutto.org.
71. Colonel Rafiuddin, *Bhutto Ke Akhri 323 Din*, pp. 94–5.
72. ibid., p.136.
73. For example, Abdul Hafeez Pirzada and Mubashir Hasan.

Chapter 8: Movement for Restoration of Democracy

1. Sherbaz Khan Mazari, *A Journey to Disillusionment*, p. 509.
2. ibid., p. 504.
3. See ibid., p. 411, for an expression of Asghar Khan's ambition.
4. Such as Mahmud Ali Kasuri, J.A. Rahim, Nawaz Sharif, Musheer Pesh Imam, Khurshid Kasuri, Aitzaz Ahsan, Zia Ispahani, Nafees Siddiqi, Nisar Khuhro, Shahida Jamil, Mahfoozyar Khan, to name a few.
5. M. Asghar Khan, *My Political Struggle*, p. 121.
6. ibid., p. 230.

7. *Repression in Pakistan* (New York: Pakistan Democratic Forum, 1983). Monographs in this series were written by Feroz Ahmad.
8. Asghar Khan, *My Political Struggle*, p. 224.
9. ibid., p. 201.
10. Sherbaz Khan Mazari, *A Journey to Disillusionment*, p. 535.
11. ibid., p. 537.
12. ibid.
13. ibid., p. 538.
14. Raja Anwar, *The Terrorist Prince: The Life and Death of Murtaza Bhutto* (London: Verso, 1997), pp. 25–40.
15. Sherbaz Khan Mazari, *A Journey to Disillusionment*, pp. 162–3.
16. ibid., p. 308.
17. Asghar Khan, *My Political Struggle*, p. 230.
18. ibid.
19. ibid., p. 248.
20. Benazir Bhutto, *Daughter of the East: An Autobiography* (London: Mandarin, 1989), p. 164.
21. ibid., p. 83.
22. Raja Anwar, *The Terrorist Prince*, p. 22.
23. Benazir Bhutto, *Daughter of the East*, pp. 166–7.
24. For the history of the MKP, I have drawn upon my conversations with Fatehyab and *Pakistan Mazdoor Kisan (Worker-Peasant) Party (MKP)* (New York: Pakistan Democratic Forum, 1984).
25. Khawaja Humayun Akhtar was a member of Tehrik-i-Istiqlal and courted arrest on 4 September 1983.
26. For B.M. Kutty's account of this interrogation, see his *Sixty Years in Self-Exile: No Regrets: A Political Autobiography* (Karachi: Pakistan Study Centre, 2011), pp. 448–9. According to Kutty, the interrogation was held in the Frontier Corps camp in Baldia Town.
27. Shahida Kazmi has written a poem about our friendship. She lives in Washington DC.
28. Sherbaz Khan Mazari, *A Journey to Disillusionment*, p. 542; Benazir Bhutto, *Daughter of the East*, pp. 225–30.
29. *Dawn*, 20 November 1982.
30. Masuma Hasan, 'Bizenjo: A warrior all his life', ibid., 21 August 1989.
31. B.M. Kutty (ed.), *In Search of Solutions: An Autobiography of Mir Ghaus Bakhsh Bizenjo* (Karachi: Pakistan Study Centre, 2009), pp. 205–16.
32. Sherbaz Khan Mazari, *A Journey to Disillusionment*, pp. 104, 135, 243.
33. ibid., p. 301.
34. ibid., pp. 452, 486, 517.
35. B.M. Kutty, *Sixty Years in Self-Exile: No Regrets*, pp. 449–50 and pp. 467–8.
36. ibid., p. 444.
37. ibid., pp. 444–5.
38. *Dawn*, 3 September 1983.
39. ibid., 16 August 1983.
40. For Qari Sher Afzal's account of the arrests see his memoir, *Yadon Ki Saughat* (Karachi: 2014).

41. Fatehyab Ali Khan, 'Federalism and Democracy: Objectives of the Pakistan Movement', *The Muslim* (Islamabad), 4 May 1984.
42. Documents related to Nasir Baloch's trial, FP. The death sentences of Nasir Baloch's three co-accused, Ayub Malik, Muhammad Essa and Saif Ullah Khalid were commuted by Ziaul Haq. They were awarded life sentences, fines and lashes.
43. *Dawn*, 5 and 6 March 1985.
44. There are scores of letters from these young prisoners in the private papers of Rao Sulaiman.
45. Documents related to Ayaz Samoo's trial, FP. See also Benazir Bhutto, *Daughter of the East*, pp. 274–8. Ayaz Samoo was a trade union activist in Naya Daur Motors, charged with the murder of the regime's supporter, Zahoor ul-Hasan Bhopali.
46. Sherbaz Khan Mazari, *A Journey to Disillusionment*, pp. 572–3.
47. *Dawn*, 27 July 1986.
48. ibid., 31 October 1986.
49. ibid., 22 and 31 July 1986.
50. Interview, Nazish Amrohi, 3 August 1990.
51. Fatehyab's statement: 'PMKP emerges stronger', *Dawn*, 31 July 1986.
52. ibid., 1 August 1986.
53. ibid., 4 August 1986. Also B.M. Kutty, *Sixty Years in Self-Exile: No Regrets*, pp. 458–9.
54. See the coverage in *Dawn* and *Jang*, 4 May 1986.
55. *Dawn*, 14 August 1986.
56. Statement of Shah Mohammad Amroti, *Dawn*, 20 August 1986.
57. 'SHC orders Fatehyab's release', *Dawn*, 4 September 1986.
58. For full coverage of the meetings, see *Dawn* and *Jang*, 19–22 June 1987.
59. Muhammad Khan Junejo (1932–93) was prime minister 1985–88, and was dismissed by Ziaul Haq. He contested the elections held in 1985 from the platform of the Pakistan Muslim League. The round table conference was held on 5 and 6 March 1988. See *Dawn*, 6 and 7 March 1988 for details of its sessions.
60. A list of those who were hanged or tortured to death by 1985 appeared in *Victory*, June/July 1985, published from Frankfurt and New York.
61. Sherbaz Khan Mazari, *A Journey to Disillusionment*, p. 546.
62. Asghar Khan's statement, *Dawn*, 8 October 1986, and 'Benazir Bhutto defines Bhuttoism', ibid., 21 October 1986.
63. ibid., 31 October 1986.
64. Because of other instances of negligence, David Dandy has been described as the 'butcher' of Cambridge.

Chapter 9: Vienna
1. Later Pakistan's permanent representative to the United Nations in Geneva and New York.
2. Later Pakistan's ambassador to Egypt.
3. Vienna is called the 'city of dreams' because of Sigmund Freud's association with it.
4. Hans Blix was Sweden's minister for foreign affairs 1978–9, and director general of the IAEA 1981–97.

5. The regional groupings are: North America, Latin America, Western Europe, Eastern Europe, Africa, Middle East and South Asia, South-East Asia and the Pacific and the Far East.

6. In 1997, they became the United Nations Office on Drugs and Crime (UNODC) by combining the United Nations International Drugs Control Program (UNDCP) and the Crime Prevention and Criminal Justice Division.

7. In 2010, the Turkish ambassador in Vienna, Kadri Ecvet Tezcan, created a diplomatic furore when he accused Austria of treating the Turks 'like a virus'. He said 250,000 people of Turkish origin were forced to live in ghettos among a hostile population.

8. These countries are the Czech Republic, Germany, Hungary, Italy, Liechtenstein, Slovakia, Slovenia and Switzerland.

9. Farzana Rahman passed away on 25 June 2017.

10. Filiz Dinçmen became Turkey's first woman ambassador in 1982.

11. Moeenuddin Qureshi held high positions in the IMF and World Bank and was Pakistan's interim prime minister for three months in 1993. Mahbub ul Haq was Ziaul Haq's finance minister 1985–8.

12. Hundertwasser has designed many irregular buildings in other parts of Austria.

13. Letter, 30 May 1995.

14. Akram Zaki (1931–2017) was a career diplomat and Pakistan's ambassador to China and the United States. Later he joined the Pakistan Muslim League, was elected to the Senate of Pakistan and became minister of state for foreign affairs.

Chapter 10: Last Posting

1. See the text of Parvez Musharraf's speech in *Dawn*, 13 October 1999.

2. ibid., 12 October 1999.

3. ibid., 15 October 1999.

4. ibid., 14 October 1999, in an interview to BBC Television.

5. See the text of Parvez Musharraf's speech, ibid., 18 October 1999.

6. ibid., 21 October 1999.

7. ibid., 16 October 1999.

8. ibid., 19 October 1999.

9. Parvez Musharraf, *In the Line of Fire: A Memoir* (New York: Free Press, 2006), p. 144.

10. Attiya Inayatullah's letter, 15 May 2001.

11. All developments and decisions about the code plate are available in the publications of Atash Durrani who worked on Urdu informatics in the NLA.

12. Shaukat Aziz, *From Banking to the Thorny World of Politics* (London: Quartet, 2016), pp. 16–18.

13. *Dawn*, 20 December 2000.

14. The Report of the Commission of Inquiry – 1971 War, Volume 1–Main Report, p. 1.

15. ibid., p. 4.

16. Commission of Inquiry 1971 – War, Volume 1, Supplementary Report, p. 3.

17. ibid., p. 2.

18. Main Report, p. 434.

19. ibid., p. 437.

20. ibid., p. 441.
21. ibid., p. 444.
22. ibid., p. 445.
23. Supplementary Report, p. 7.
24. ibid., p. 13.
25. ibid., p. 20.
26. ibid., p. 33.
27. ibid., p. 34.
28. ibid., p. 35.
29. ibid., p. 38.
30. ibid., p. 66.
31. ibid., p. 186.
32. ibid., p. 122.
33. ibid., pp. 139, 141–2.
34. ibid., pp. 143–4. Major General Rao Farman Ali was the adviser to Governor Malik. His memoir about the tragedy is published in *How Pakistan Got Divided* (Karachi: Oxford University Press, 2017).
35. Supplementary Report, pp. 151–3.
36. ibid., p. 158.
37. ibid., p. 162.
38. The list of exhaustive recommendations can be seen in Part V, Chapter V of the Supplementary Report.
39. Lieutenant General Niazi was known for his valour and called 'Tiger Niazi'. He has given his own version of what befell East Pakistan in *The Betrayal of East Pakistan* (Karachi: Oxford University Press, 1998).
40. Supplementary Report, p. 77.
41. D.K. Palit, *The Lightning Campaign: The Indo-Pakistan War 1971* (New Delhi: Lancer Publishers, 1998), pp. 16, 110. Palit was a major general in the Indian army.
42. Field Marshal Sam Manekshaw's interview to Karan Thapar in Face to Face, YouTube, 1999.
43. Abdul Salam Zaeef, *My Life with the Taliban* (London: C. Hurst and Co, 2012), translated from Pashto.
44. John Nixon, *Debriefing the President: The Interrogation of Saddam Hussein* (New York: Penguin Random House, 2016), p. 128.
45. Associated Press, 30 December 2006.
46. John Nixon, *Debriefing the President*, p. 126.

Chapter 11: For Fatehyab

1. *Dawn*, 27 March 1948.
2. Ehsan Rashid was vice chancellor of the University of Karachi 1976–9 and ambassador to Jordan from 1981. His last appointment was as rector of the Islamic University in Islamabad.
3. Justice Noorul Arfeen was a judge of the High Court of Sindh. Later, he joined the PPP and was elected to parliament.
4. Pakistan Institute of International Affairs (Administration) Ordinance 1980 or Ordinance VII of 1980.

5. Maulana Zafar Ahmad Ansari was joint secretary of the All India Muslim League, a politician and expert in constitutional and Islamic law. Colonel Hashim was a close friend of Ziaul Haq. He belonged to Fatehyab's Qaimkhani clan.

6. The provisional constitutional order was promulgated by Ziaul Haq for the first time in the history of Pakistan on 24 March 1981. It was an extra-constitutional order that suspended the Constitution of Pakistan.

7. Yahya Bakhtiar (1921–2003), was attorney general in Zulfikar Ali Bhutto's government, and also defended him in the murder trial against him. He was appointed attorney general again when Benazir Bhutto became prime minister in 1988.

8. *Pakistan Times* (Lahore), editorial, 21 April 1989.

9. Shahryar Khan (born 1934), a career diplomat, was foreign secretary, 1990–94.

10. Mehboob Ali Khan and Aneesuddin Ahmed were foreign service officers dealing with the Institute's case in the foreign office at that time. Later they both held ambassadorial positions.

11. Civil Appeal No. 770-K of 1990. Rasheed Razvi and Mazharul Jameel were lawyers practising in Karachi. Rasheed Razvi became a judge of the High Court of Sindh for a short term and president of the Supreme Court Bar Association.

12. The bench comprised Chief Justice Nasim Hasan Shah, Justice Muhammad Rafiq Tarar (later president of Pakistan, 1998–2001) and Justice Manzoor Hussain Sial.

13. Kaleemullah Lashari was formerly Secretary, Department of Antiquities, Government of Sindh.

14. Related to me by Shaista Ikramullah's daughter, Princess Sarvath of Jordan.

15. Bharat Ratna is the highest civil award of India, followed by the Padma Bhushan series.

16. For coverage of public protests see *Dawn* for December 1971 and January 1972.

17. S.M. Altaf, a lawyer and trusted colleague of Fatehyab, became president of the PMKP after Fatehyab passed away.

18. Mudassir Mirza is news editor of *Jang*, the largest circulated Urdu daily in Pakistan.

19. Niaz Siddiki, my former colleague at NIPA Karachi, was additional inspector general of police, Sindh.

20. In 1988, Nasrullah Khan contested the presidential election against Ghulam Ishaq Khan, who had the support of Benazir Bhutto and the establishment.

21. Foreign fighters attacked Karachi airport on 8 June 2014 and the airport was closed for a few hours. Thirty-six people lost their lives in the counter operation. The TTP claimed responsibility for the attack launched jointly with the Islamic Movement of Uzbekistan.

22. Nigar Ahmad, an economist who studied at Cambridge, was the founder and moving spirit of Aurat Foundation. She passed away in 2017 after a heroic battle against Parkinson's disease. Shahla Zia was a lawyer who was closely associated with the drafting of pro-women laws. She passed away in 2005.

23. The United Nations had declared 1975–85 as the decade for women in which three women's conferences were held in Mexico City (1975), Copenhagen (1980), and Nairobi (1985). The fourth conference was held in 1995 in Beijing and resulted in the landmark 'platform for action' which is considered as the women's charter.

24. I attended the festivals celebrated in Rumbur and Bumburet. The Kalash are indigenous people with a unique culture, residing in Chitral. Some anthropologists believe they are descendants of Alexander the Great's forces.
25. Work on the Lowari tunnel, which traverses the Lowari Pass and now connects Dir and Chitral in Khyber-Pakhtunkhwa province had long been held up, causing great hardship to the people of the area.
26. Samina Baig from Gilgit-Baltistan scaled Mount Everest in 2013 at age 21 and all the Seven Summits by 2014. The Seven Summits are located in the seven continents: Mount Everest in Asia, Aconcagua in South America, Denali in North America, Kilimanjaro in Africa, Mount Elbrus in Europe, Mount Vinson in Antarctica, and Puncak Jaya in Australasia.

Index